Pearson New International Edition

Strategic Management
in the Hospitality Industry
Olsen   West   Tse
Third Edition

PEARSON®

Pearson Education Limited
Edinburgh Gate
Harlow
Essex CM20 2JE
England and Associated Companies throughout the world

Visit us on the World Wide Web at: www.pearsoned.co.uk

 ISBN 10: 1-292-02741-X
ISBN 13: 978-1-292-02741-8

British Library Cataloguing-in-Publication Data
A catalogue record for this book is available from the British Library

Printed in the United States of America

Table of Contents

Strategic Management in the Hospitality Industry

Strategic Management in the Hospitality Industry

Learning Objectives

Upon completion of this chapter you will:

1. Understand the concept of strategic management as applied to the service and hospitality industry.
2. Be able to describe the coalignment model and its application to the hospitality industry.
3. Appreciate that strategic management is a way of thinking, not a process to be performed annually and then forgotten for a year.
4. Understand the supply-and-demand and technology relationships that exist in the service industry and how they affect strategy.
5. Understand the unique elements, especially quality and value, of the service industry and how they affect strategy making.
6. Develop an appreciation of the forces driving change in the hospitality industry and what impact they will have on the manager of the future.
7. Understand the importance of leadership to the strategic management process.

Key Concepts

Strategic management

Coalignment model

Leadership and strategy

Strategy in the service industry

Supply-and-demand relationships in the service industry

From Chapter 1 of *Strategic Management in the Hospitality Industry*, Third Edition, Michael D. Olsen, Joseph J. West, Eliza Ching Yick Tse. Copyright © 2008 by Pearson Education, Inc. Published by Pearson Prentice Hall. All rights reserved.

Technology in the service industry

Managing quality service

Forces driving change in the hospitality industry

The value-adding manager

Chapter Purpose

This chapter will prepare you to understand our position that hospitality leaders of the future must be proactive in adapting their firm to the forces driving change in the environment to achieve sustainable competitive advantage over their competition. This chapter provides you with the theoretical underpinnings and the practical knowledge to compete successfully in a complex and dynamic environment. We begin the chapter with the concept of strategic management and the manner in which it has evolved in modern times. It must be recognized that in developing a strategy and a set of competitive initiatives, managers attempt to respond to the external forces of the environment. This principle is introduced by the coalignment model, which describes and explains how successful hospitality managers respond to the external environment and make strategic choices to attain sustainable competitive advantage. The importance of leadership in strategic management is discussed in the chapter to emphasize that strategy is all about leadership. In addition, you are introduced to the unique characteristics that differentiate the service sector from the manufacturing sector and require special strategic focus. We then explain the importance of strategic management in the hospitality industry as the chapter evolves from a discussion of general strategic principles to focus on the distinctive characteristics of the hospitality industry. Finally, the chapter concludes with a discussion of the challenges facing the hospitality manager of tomorrow.

Overview of the Concept of Strategic Management

The Concept of Strategy[1]

The concept of "strategy" was first presented formally to the world by the Prussian general Carl von Clausewitz[2] while he was serving as the officer in charge of the Prussian Military Academy in the 1840s. He defined strategy as "The use of engagements for the object of the war." However, his writings were not applied to the business environment of the time, for he lived and wrote at the end of the First Industrial Revolution, which covered Europe and America from 1750 until 1850. This period marked the end of cottage industries where products were made by craftsmen who mainly serviced the area in which they were located and the beginning of the introduction of machines and large-scale manufacturing that served markets beyond the local area. This period was characterized by intense competition among the industrial firms with international trade focused on a few commodities such as cotton. Most of the firms were small by today's standards, and the markets were chaotic with no government oversight or regulation. It was during this period that Adam Smith published his thesis on the nature of market forces, which he conceived were guided by an "invisible hand" and did not allow individual firms to exert control on the market. As one would suppose if the leading economic thinker of the period espoused the idea of market forces being guided by an invisible hand, managers would not worry about formal planning and strategy during the course of their battle for market share.

The Second Industrial Revolution, which began in the 1850s, endured until the early 1990s. It was born when the expansion of railroads enabled manufacturing firms to develop mass markets for their products. Items that were made in the garment district of New York City could be shipped by rail to markets in California much quicker and less expensively by rail than by ships, which had to sail around South America (before the construction of the Panama Canal in the early 1900s). Suddenly firms in the eastern United States had markets in the West and Midwest. Firms in England had markets all over Europe, and large quantities could be inexpensively shipped to distant markets. This prompted large-scale investments in production and distribution systems that forced managers to consider concepts such as economies of scale, vertical integration, and multidivisional organizations. The concept of strategy to shape competitive environments gained favor along with the idea of the "visible hand" of professional managers.

It was during this period that managers realized the need for a formal approach to corporate strategy. Two highly successful corporate leaders of this period—Alfred Sloan of General Motors and Chester Barnard of Atlantic Telephone and Telegraph (AT&T)—successfully built their firms to preeminence in the early 20th century, even though this was one of the most turbulent periods in U.S. business. Sloan was able to overcome Henry Ford's dominance in the auto industry when he developed a strategy of offering the automobile buying public a variety of choices. Whereas Ford developed the low-cost strategy of mass producing one model and one color (black), Sloan differentiated his products with different brands, models, and colors. Ford's famous quote of "People can have any color they want as long as it is black" did not ring true to a car-buying public whose choice of car turned from basic transportation to status.

Barnard,[3] as CEO of AT&T in the 1930s, wrote that managers must pay close attention to "strategic factors" that depend on personal or organizational action. This was one of the first instances of the term *strategy* being introduced into the literature of business.

During World War II, businesses had to compete in an economy of scarce resources because most goods were manufactured to advance the massive war effort. During this period the emphasis was on attaining enough materials to remain in business if the firm was not supporting the military. There were some significant strategic insights gained by managers during the massive economic explosion of World War II. Formal strategic thinking was introduced to guide managerial decisions. The concept of the learning curve where production costs decrease by a constant percentage as quantity doubles was introduced during the mass production of aircraft in the years leading up to World War II and refined during the war. Solving the problems of "zero-sum games" (where there are insufficient resources and there must be a winner and a loser) and "non-zero-sum games" (where there are sufficient resources and there can be multiple winners) were confronted by industrial managers. It was during this time that Peter Drucker[4] espoused that management is not passive and that managers must take actions to bring about desired results. Thus was introduced the rationale for business strategy: *By consciously using formal planning, a company can exert some positive control over market forces.*

At the conclusion of World War II, the military-industrial complex was fully developed and in position to rebuild the world, which had been ravaged by global conflict. In such a scenario, demand exceeded supply, which created an environment in which there was no need for strategy because everything a firm manufactured it could sell somewhere at a profit. This was true for civilians but not so for the military. After the war the government had no need for such a powerful military and began to dismantle the massive war machine. This downsizing created an interservice competition for scarce resources and led to the U.S. Navy developing the concept of "distinctive competence." Under this concept, the U.S. Army became manpower-centered with large divisions of soldiers while the U.S. Navy became machine-centered, engineering-based, with sophisticated weapons platforms able to reach any theater of operations. The concept of distinctive competence soon found its way into business strategy as firms fought for sustainable competitive advantage.

Academic Underpinnings

The Harvard Business School was founded in 1908 and was one of the first schools to suggest that managers should have more than just a functional focus. In 1912 the faculty introduced a course on business policy. This course integrated the functional areas for a broader perspective of strategic problems faced by corporate managers of the time. In the 1950s they began examining the basis on which one company can compete with another in a specific industry. During this period they also examined the benefit of the firm having a defined set of goals to guide the decisions of top management.

In the 1960s Harvard's Business School faculty member Kenneth Andrews,[5] in his book *Strategy Framework,* introduced business managers to SWOT analysis. This concept examined the firm's strengths and weakness versus the opportunities and threats (risks) it faced in the marketplace. One problem with this framework was that the SWOT analysis did not define a firm's distinctive competence.

Following the U.S. Navy's introduction of distinctive competence, business scholars began to explore the concept's applicability for use in the development of business strategy. They found that distinctive competence was important but could present significant problems because some strategic decisions are long term and may outlast some distinctive competencies, thereby enhancing risk. It became important to recognize which distinctive competencies were enduring and unchanging over the long term and which responded to changes in the marketplace and other environmental pressures. Ansoff[6] wrote that managers of the firm should ask whether new products have a common thread with existing products. This common thread could be either an existing market or the mission of the company. He warned that a specific type of customer was not a common thread because customer needs changed over time.

Strategy Consultants

The 1960s and 1970s ushered in the rise of strategy consultants. These consulting firms attempted to discover why one competitor is able to outperform others in their market. The early pioneer among these consultants was the Boston Consulting Group (BCG), which posited that good strategy must be based on logic. They also held that the experience curve explained price and competitive behavior in extremely fast-growing industry segments, where total costs could decline 20% to 30% due to economies of scale, organizational learning, and technology. Other researchers then began to question what happens to a competitor when another competitor enters the segment late and benefits from the experience curve.

To answer these and other questions, BCG introduced the concept of portfolio analysis. Under this analysis after experience curves are drawn, diversified units are analyzed for potential investment and divestment. Strategic managers were expected to balance "cash cows" with "stars" and allocate more resources to "question marks" while divesting "dogs." By the end of the 1970s, every major consulting firm used some type of portfolio analysis.

Also in the 1970s, McKinsey and Company introduced the idea of "strategic business units." These were natural business units that were unique in the diversified firm. It allowed a firm such as General Electric (GE) to compete in many unrelated industries from turbines to home appliances to medical equipment. With GE, McKinsey introduced the concept of "industry attractiveness." The top management of GE did not want to take action based on two performance measures as characterized by portfolio analysis. They worked with McKinsey to develop a matrix that used 12 measures to screen an industry for attractiveness and 12 more for competitive positioning.

Unfortunately, each of these concepts and strategic tools was found to possess significant weaknesses. In their pursuit of strategic dominance through the experience curve, managers found that their focus on a cost reduction strategy reduced their ability for innovative change and response to competitors. This was readily seen by the success of Sloan's (GM) innovation over Ford's low-cost focus. Portfolio analysis was found to leave businesses vulnerable to unexpected moves by new competitors entering the market. Also its focus was on minimizing risk versus investing in new opportunities requiring long-term commitment. A strength of portfolio analysis is that it did focus management's attention on industry attractiveness and competitive advantage. Bain,[7] in a study of the return on equity of various industries, found that some industries seemed to be inherently much more profitable or attractive than others. Porter[8] introduced his "five forces" in an attempt to understand the attractiveness of an industry.

In the mid-1990s Brandenburger and Nalebuff[9] introduced the concept of "value creation" as a strategic tool. Value creation was a process for creating value in the marketplace that would provide the firm with a competitive advantage over its competition. The idea was that there were four constituents in the marketplace: customers; suppliers; competitors; and complementors. The idea was for the managers of the firm to discover these complementors—firms from which the firm's customers buy complementary products and services—and form strategic alliances and partnerships with them. The idea of Disney partnering with rental car companies and airlines to market the destination is an example of value creation through complementors.

As we proceed into the globalization era of the 21st century, one thing is certain: Successful strategies and sustainable competitive advantage are moving targets. Managers and researchers must be constantly alert to changing market decisions and competitor initiatives. We present this text as a guide for hospitality managers as they fight for competitive advantage on a global stage. In the rest of this chapter we introduce the coalignment model for strategic analysis and implementation in the hospitality industry. We examine the impact of leadership on strategy, strategy and value creation, strategy in the service industry, and finally, the forces driving change in the global hospitality industry.

The Coalignment Model

The authors and their colleagues have conducted extensive research on firms in the hospitality industry and their attempt to gain sustainable competitive advantage. As a result of our studies, we posit that the concept of strategic management refers to the ability of the management of the firm to properly align the firm with the forces driving change in the environment in which the firm competes. This alignment requires that management invests in competitive methods that yield the greatest overall financial value to the firm. To accomplish this, managers must create a business structure that consistently allocates resources to those competitive methods that provide the best value over time. If the firm is able to identify opportunities that exist in the forces driving change, identify competitive methods that enable the firm to gain competitive advantage through these opportunities, and allocate sufficient financial resources to the competitive methods that will create the greatest value, the financial results desired by the owners and investors have a much greater chance of being achieved. This relationship is referred to as the *coalignment model.* Exhibit 1 is a simplified model of this relationship.

As the directions of the arrows indicate in Exhibit 1, the business environment of the firm is where the concept of strategic management begins. The business environment is defined as the domain in which the customers, competitors, suppliers, and regulators of a firm exist in a context of rapid change and increasing complexity in the broad global environment. In this context, opportunities and threats exist that are both immediate and long term. Management's challenge is to identify the forces that will drive change, and, within those forces, to seek opportunities that will add value to the firm in both the short and long term. Exhibit 2 illustrates the basic elements of the concept of the environment in relationship to the coalignment model.

Once management determines what it considers to be the best opportunities for the future, it must then invest in competitive methods that will match those opportunities. Competitive methods in the hospitality industry are made of portfolios of products and services designed to bring the unique resources and capabilities of the firm together to achieve advantage in the marketplace. A firm's overall strategy is the reflection of all of the competitive methods in which management has invested. Each competitive method must be viewed by the firm as an important value-adding dimension of the enterprise's overall strategy. Management must be constantly aware of the fact that each competitive method, with its portfolio of products and services, has an increasingly shorter effective lifespan in the context of today's dynamic business environment. Thus, if the firm's management is to be successful long term, it must regularly scan the

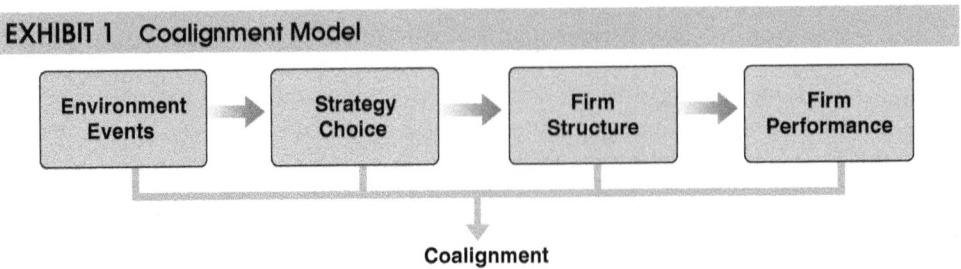

EXHIBIT 1   Coalignment Model

Environment Events → Strategy Choice → Firm Structure → Firm Performance

Coalignment

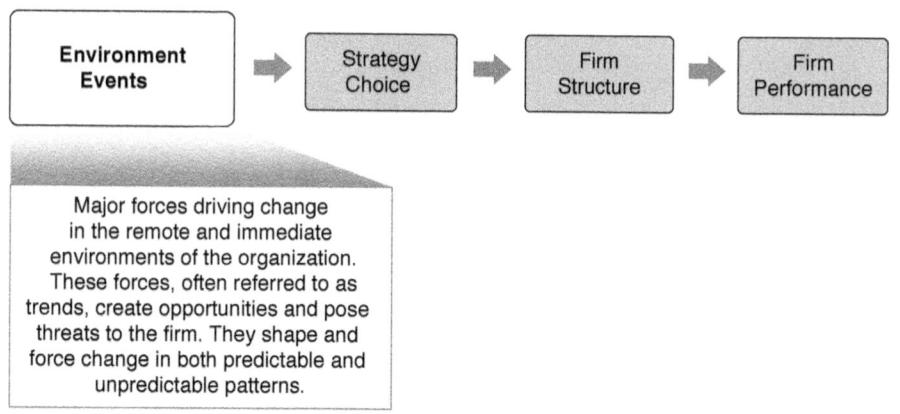

EXHIBIT 2   Coalignment Model—Environment Events

business environment to ensure that they are able to identify and adapt to the changes that are constantly occurring. Exhibit 3 provides a closer look at this important element of the coalignment model: strategy choice.

Subsequent to management's identification of opportunities and investment in what they consider to be the best value-adding competitive methods, they consistently allocate sufficient resources to ensure their successful implementation. This activity is referred to in the model as *firm structure*. Structure is defined as the methods by which the managers of the organization choose to group tasks and activities together to accomplish their objectives. It refers to how organizations are governed and responsibilities defined by the resource allocation process.

The resource allocation process requires managers to identify the core resources and capabilities that are essential to the successful implementation and execution of each competitive method. In addition to this important activity, management must create an internal environment that supports these core resources and capabilities. This

EXHIBIT 3   Coalignment Model—Strategy Choice

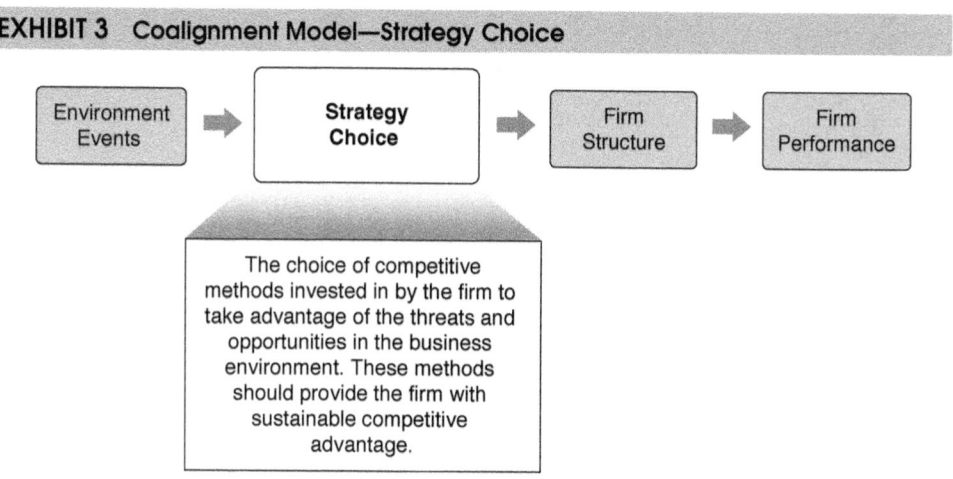

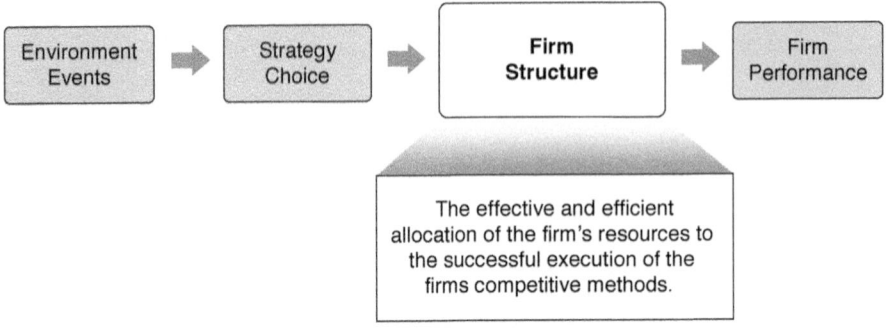

EXHIBIT 4 Coalignment Model—Firm Structure

internal environment consists of the appropriate structure, processes, and culture. The internal environment must be in alignment if it is to support the correct allocation of resources to the best value-producing competitive methods. Exhibit 4 provides a more detailed examination of this component of the model.

As the coalignment model suggests in Exhibit 1, if management is able to identify the correct opportunities in its competitive environment, invest in the best value-adding competitive methods, and create a structure that supports effective implementation and execution of these methods, they will achieve the desired level of financial performance expected by investors. The measure of financial performance most commonly utilized today is cash flow per share of owner's/investor's equity. It must be recognized that this is a future-oriented measure of cash flow. Therefore management must seek to maximize future value. To do this, they must estimate the cash flows to be generated by each competitive method over its expected useful life.

Although other measures of financial performance have been used for decades, they have been only able to report on past performance. They have no ability to reflect future performance and are therefore of no use to managers who must make resource allocation decisions based on their judgment of which competitive methods will yield the best value in the future. This is why it is so important for managers to concentrate on scanning the business environment for future opportunities. This future-based orientation is the basis of the coalignment model. Exhibit 5 provides

EXHIBIT 5 Coalignment Model—Firm Performance

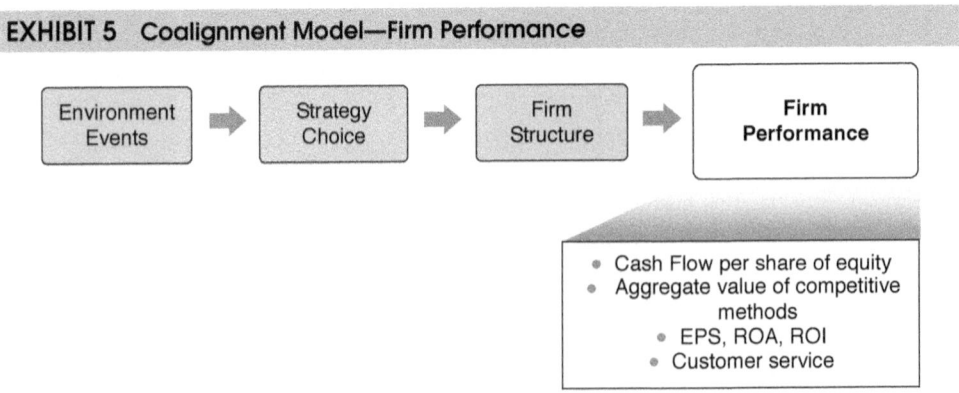

8

an illustration of the firm performance component of the model and includes both the historical measures of performance and the future-oriented measure of cash flow per share.

Note that in today's business environment there are many different measures of firm performance other than financial. It is our assumption that no matter what other arguments are presented for other performance measures, the long-term survival of any business organization will depend on management's ability to generate value for ownership. If they cannot successfully accomplish this, the organization will cease to exist. Moreover, the value generated must exceed the cost of capital invested to create the value. If it does not, the owners will place their funds in more attractive investments. This is a simple, basic rule of business today.

Our second assumption in this regard is that a firm will only be able to accomplish this value-adding objective if it is meeting the demands of its customers both today and in the future. Thus performance measures such as customer satisfaction can be of great value in evaluating performance; however, the firm could not be adding value unless the customer was satisfied. Therefore these other measures are useful in assessing how well a strategy is being implemented through proper resource allocation and are good diagnostic tools. However, the ultimate test remains how value is being added today and into the future.

Strategy Is a Way of Thinking

Achieving coalignment does not result from a single onetime strategic planning activity. Management must view strategic management as a way of thinking and not an annual process. It must be imbedded in every decision, every activity, and every service encounter with the customer. It must be the fabric woven into every management decision regarding the acquisition and transformation of all resources used by the firm to achieve its objectives. Strategy making must be future oriented, dynamic, and interactive at all levels of the firm. This is because planning is the easiest component of strategic management. It is the implementation and the realization of the strategy that demands the time, energy, and commitment from all members of the firm if strategic objectives are to be achieved.

Leadership and Strategy: Inseparable Concepts

In dynamic and uncertain times, people need leaders not only to guide them in their day-to-day life but to help them see what they can become in the future.[10] There have been many failings in leadership in the early 21st century. Simply ask the employees of Tyco or Enron or any other of the disgraced multinational firms whose tomorrows were ruined when the top management team neglected or failed to recognize their duty of leadership.

Peter Drucker, in his book *Leader of the Future*,[11] holds that good leadership must be learned and that effective leaders understand four very important truths:

1. *Leaders have followers:* Without followers there is no leader. Effective leaders must communicate a message that resonates with people; in other words they have a vision that people understand and accept as theirs. Leadership is about attaining goals. If no one clearly understands the goals, there is no need for leadership.

Ritz-Carlton is very clear about their mission: "*Ladies and Gentlemen Serving Ladies and Gentlemen.*" This vision is simple and communicated daily through gatherings that all employees must attend prior to commencing their tasks. How effective are the leaders of Ritz-Carlton in communicating their vision? In a survey conducted by J.D. Powers and Associates, 96% of employees surveyed were able to identify the mission of the company successfully. Once the vision is clarified and shared, the leader can focus on serving and being responsive to the needs of the people. The greatest leaders have motivated others by energizing those around them with their vision.

2. *Popularity is not leadership:* **Results** are what define effective leaders. Their followers do the right thing. This is essential in the hospitality industry where customers purchase goods and services on promise. If hospitality employees don't do the "*right thing*" in the countless daily service interactions with the firm's customers, the organization will not be able to compete successfully regardless of the strategy implemented. Effective leaders may not be loved, but they will motivate their followers to succeed.

3. *Leaders are highly visible:* They set the example. Jonathan Tisch, chairman and CEO of Loew's Hotels and Resorts, requires that he and his top management spend time each year working in all of the hourly positions in the company. This sets the example to the employees that all jobs and the people who hold them are important and that management understands the hardships and rewards of each position. Tisch is very involved in leading what he considers to be the family business. Growing up he held most of the positions in the company, and he thoroughly understands its values. He is the public exhibit. Appearing on popular television shows and being interviewed by the press, he defines the values and goals of Loew's Hotels and Resorts for not only the general public but also his employees.

4. *Leadership is responsibility:* In the end the leader is judged by the success or failure of the organization. When leaders stop realizing that they are responsible for all of the actions of the organization, it is the beginning of the end. As Ken Blanchard and Jesse Stoner note,[12] when leaders forget their responsibility, the organization soon evolves into a self-serving bureaucracy where all of the money, status, recognition, and power move up the hierarchy away from the people serving the customer. Leadership soon begins to cease serving the employees and the customers and begins serving the leaders with the ensuing degradation of the organization's purpose and goals.

Leadership Defined in a Strategic Context

Bardwick,[13] in his essay "Peacetime Management and Wartime Leadership," discusses the conflict between those who want to lead others through major changes as though it was wartime and those who refuse to become followers because they are convinced it is peacetime. That is the challenge of today's strategic manager. If one is to define peacetime as a state of constancy, then managers in the hospitality industry are in a state of war. To harken back to the origin of strategy, hospitality leaders must lead their organizations in an environmental state of constant change with intense competition from well-organized competitors (wartime leadership). Among other drivers of change, globalization has destroyed any peacetime illusions. Unfortunately, peacetime managers are comfortable in a stable environment that is highly predictable, an environment in which few hospitality firms exist. Therefore, to be successful, strategic leaders must convince peacetime managers in the hospitality industry to become wartime leaders.

What are wartime leaders? They are leaders who embrace major change because they are able to see the opportunities presented in a dynamic environment. Strategic leaders understand that to be successful they must:

1. *Define the business of the business:* They decide where and how the firm will compete. Strategic leaders define the firm's competitive domain;
2. *Create a winning strategy:* They accurately designate what the firm will do better than any other firm in order to achieve competitive advantage. In order to accomplish this they determine and develop the distinctive competencies and competitive methods necessary to successfully implement their strategy in the industry segment in which the firm competes. These are the most important components of successful strategy creation;
3. *Communicate effectively:* Strategic leaders limit the number of their communications and they simplify the message. They determine what people need to know and then they state it simply and repetitiously. This is reflected in the previously mentioned Ritz-Carlton Hotel company's simple yet effective message: "Ladies and Gentlemen serving Ladies and Gentlemen" and the daily transmission of it to their employees;
4. *Behave with integrity:* The best leaders are transparent and live what they espouse. They do not manipulate people. They are also honest with themselves; they understand their strengths and weaknesses and work within their capability. Strategic leaders are predictable in their behavior and personal life because they follow their own publicly held truths.
5. *Respect others:* Strategic leaders are comfortable receiving input from those around them. They encourage debate among the leadership team and remember that hearing others' views is a sign of respect. Most importantly, they understand when to make a decision and understand the importance of the environment when making decisions;
6. *Act:* When conditions are ambiguous and decisions are difficult, they decide and act. In today's dynamic, complex, and uncertain environment, strategic leaders must be decisive and action oriented. The environment offers opportunities to those who understand the forces driving change and the distinctive competencies necessary to implement the strategies to take advantage of the opportunities available. As we stated earlier, leadership is based on action and achieving goals. Today's strategic leader must clearly understand this.

Strategic leaders understand that leadership is, above all else, emotional. It falls to them to create a passionate commitment in other people. It is up to them to develop the *"want-to"* attitude in their followers. They remember that their grand strategy must be implemented by people who believe in them and their message. Strategic leaders know that without the commitment of their followers, no matter how good their strategy, they will fail.

The Leader of Tomorrow

Many authors and researchers hold the idea that the question of what the leader of the future should know and understand is not new. It is one of the oldest questions of history. People have been striving to understand the critical aspects of leadership since the days of Alexander the Great, arguably the world's greatest leader. Alexander[14] changed the history of civilization and shaped the present world. He accomplished greater deeds than any other leader in history. Today, over two thousand years after his death, business leaders are still using his ideas as a guide.

We must remember that leadership is about people—it is personal. Although people respond to different stimuli over the years, the secret of the effective leader is to understand what Alexander did:

1. *Have a compelling vision that speaks to the collective imagination*—followers respond to a leader who possesses a vision, is totally focused on it, and is able to clearly communicate it to them.
2. *Develop a creative strategy that is responsive to enemy strengths*—business strategy requires that effective leaders understand themselves, their organization, the environment, and the competition. With this knowledge, the leader is capable of responding innovatively to the competition to achieve competitive advantage.
3. *Create a well-rounded executive team*—strategy must be implemented and supported by the top management team. Leadership is a team function. The best team with the best leader wins.
4. *Model excellence*—it is not necessary to reinvent everything about the organization. Effective leaders recognize excellence in others and work to develop it in themselves and their organization.
5. *Encourage innovation*—the future will not be the same as today or yesterday. Effective leaders recognize that innovation is a requirement for success and it can come from anywhere in the organization.
6. *Manage symbols to foster group identification*—people like to belong to groups, especially groups that reflect their personal values. Awards, benefits, actions of the leadership demonstrate the values of the organization to the followers and either help in developing a group identity or destroying it.
7. *Encourage and support followers*—effective leaders realize that without dedicated followers they are doomed to fail. They take time to recognize the accomplishments of others positively, and they pay attention to the needs of their followers.
8. *Invest in training and development*—without a well-trained organization, no leader will be able to compete in tomorrow's dynamic environment.
9. *Consolidate gains*—understand when it is time to stop and strengthen the organization. Too many leaders continue to expand the organization at a time when they possess insufficient support services. The failure to consolidate gains has been the demise of many organizations as well as armies.
10. *Plan for succession*—the effective leader recognizes that the organization will outlast them. They groom followers to succeed them.
11. *Create mechanisms for effective organizational governance*—leaders have the responsibility to put proper mechanisms of organizational governance in place. There must be a system of checks and balances.

The leadership demands of the future will not change that dramatically from today or the past. The history of the world has always been dynamic in the time of great leaders. If we examine the past we will find it is the environment that defines the leader regardless of the time and place. We can safely say that leadership depends on the particular situation. Effective leaders of tomorrow will be required to supply energy, vision, and a strong personal conviction to their organization. They will be the role model for their followers, building an organization with similar-minded people. Effective leaders will be capable of changing the organization to meet the requirements of the environment. The leaders of the future must prepare themselves to lead effectively. Leadership is a learned art that requires dedication and intelligence. In the end it all comes down to vision—that is the difference between the ordinary and the extraordinary.

Strategy in the Service Industry

Manufacturing Industry versus Service Industry

The service industry continues to overwhelmingly dominate the U.S. gross product and has the largest percentage of the labor force. Increasingly, manufacturing companies are cutting costs by shipping jobs to low-wage countries such as China, Russia, and India. India is becoming increasingly important because its universities graduate more English-speaking scientists, engineers, and technicians than the rest of the world combined.[15] There are few industries where outsourcing will not be felt, but hospitality is an industry that appears to be safe from this trend. It is difficult to outsource a beach-front hotel or a golf course. Hundreds of thousands of businesses throughout the world are part of the vast service industry sector. Organizations, both for profit and nonprofit, that operate in such diverse settings as financial services, health care, and hospitality have different needs, markets, and competitive situations they must address daily. All of these organizations are in need of models to help them compete and maintain effectiveness. However, until recently, they have had to rely solely on models developed in the manufacturing sector to guide their competitive decisions.

What is presently considered to be the body of literature in strategic management has resulted from considerable research and writing of managers and scholars who have examined the concept in the context of manufacturing firms. It has become obvious that using these industrial models to manage service firms makes as little sense as using agricultural models to run multinational corporations. Similarly, it must be recognized that although these research efforts have contributed considerably to the understanding of the concept of strategy, it must be accepted that this knowledge cannot be applied directly to an industry such as hospitality whose attributes are notably different. Nonetheless, they should not be ignored. Whenever possible, elements of the body of knowledge in strategic management, although developed in a manufacturing context, should be explored and understood. A growing contingent of managers and scholars agree and are encouraging, or have developed, management models that reflect the unique attributes of the service industry but that have been built on the body of knowledge developed from the manufacturing sector.

What are the attributes that distinguish the service industry from manufacturing? They have become well known to scholars and practitioners as intangibility, simultaneity of production and consumption, customer participation in the production and delivery of the service, heterogeneity, and perishability. Each is described next.

Intangibility refers to the immaterial nature of service—that is, it is difficult to describe, measure, or standardize. Services are experienced and customers have difficulty readily appraising their value and nature. They are judged by the standards of the receiver, and these standards are subject to their perceptions. Management's efforts to make the service product tangible often revolve around the culture of the organization. For example, Outback Steakhouse, a leading casual restaurant chain, emphasizes "No Rules, Just Right"; Swissotel describes their hotels as the "Swiss Experience." Hyatt Hotels in earlier advertising campaigns referred to the "Hyatt Touch." In each case, these firms attempted to create a tangible concept of their service product to their customers. They also communicated a common set of service values for management and staff to facilitate the creation of a "culture" that will provide some tangibility of the overall experience to their customers.

The concept of simultaneous production and consumption suggests that the service experience is produced and consumed at the same time. Continuing with the example in the preceding paragraph, when you check into a hotel operated by Hyatt, you are experiencing the first in a series of events that constitute the total "Hyatt Touch" service experience. This experience is not produced ahead of time and stored waiting for your arrival; only the physical assets of the property are. Customers are unable to investigate the experience ahead of time. They receive and experience it as it is produced. Errors in service are readily apparent and require immediate recovery. This is not the same with a manufactured product whose manufacturing defects were repaired prior to delivery and are unknown to the customer.

The customer is a part of the service delivery process. He or she participates in the experience. In other words, the *customer is involved as a coproducer* in most service experiences in the hospitality industry and must be present to receive it. This participation of the customer in the service delivery process makes it difficult for the service provider to exert maximum control over the quality of the service experience. To limit the uncertainty associated with the customer's involvement; many organizations have tried to "engineer" out as much as possible the variability created by the customer's participation. For example, quick-service restaurant firms have developed menu-ordering devices with a touch-screen item selection to prevent a customer's possible indecisiveness—in choosing menu items—from slowing down the order-transaction process. Similarly, hotel firms know that installing "in-room" checkout facilities has helped improve the speed and level of service of this aspect of the service experience. In these examples, the customer is being relied on to help produce the service while aiding the service provider to assure a more consistent and smooth flow to the entire service delivery process.

Service is said to be heterogeneous because the quality of the service experience is measured in the perception of the customer. It is also complex because it is usually included in a portfolio of products and services that come together in different bundles for each customer. Thus it can almost never be the same for two different individuals. Nor is it often the same for the same person twice. It is too dependent on the emotional ups and downs of both the customer and the service employee. Consequently, it is very difficult to standardize. This problem creates a considerable challenge for service firms that have many units throughout the organization, each trying to provide consistent quality service. To illustrate, with Marriott International approaching 3,000 hotels and McDonald's over 30,000 units worldwide, it is easy to see how extremely difficult it is for both firms to guarantee equal levels of service quality continually in each and every unit every day. Although they may be able to standardize the physical assets, it is very difficult to match that level of standardization for each customer transaction.

The service product is perishable. It is impossible to inventory services because they are produced and consumed simultaneously. It is difficult even to recover from a lost service opportunity. A guest who waited too long for a food or drink order to be taken or the guest needing assistance with luggage handling and not finding a bellman in sight are lost service opportunities. They will never become available again. Lost opportunities can accumulate quickly in service businesses.

As you can see from these attribute descriptions, the problems associated with producing a service can be quite different than those of manufacturing a product. These differences suggest that strategy in service businesses require models relevant to the industry. Creation of these models will require a thorough analysis and understanding of the relationships already existing within the industry.

Demand, Supply, and Technology Relationships in the Service Industry

To further support the concept that manufacturing models cannot be directly applied to the service industries, it is important to understand the basic differences in the supply-and-demand relationships as well as the technology dissimilarities that exist between manufacturing and service enterprises. The attributes of service firms identified earlier create the underpinning needed to explain the supply-and-demand relationship and the technology used to produce services and to help differentiate them from manufacturing enterprises.

In the manufacturing industry, the demand for durable consumer products such as housing, appliances, and personal items is reasonably constant and partially determined by the demographics existing in the market at the time. Thus, for manufacturers of these consumer products, it is a reasonable task to estimate how many units of a product will be sold. This is done by looking at previous demand, changing demographics, competing products, and other variables and then deciding how many units to manufacture in the coming planning period. It is also the case that these products will be produced in one of a few manufacturing facilities strategically located to take advantage of access to raw materials, transportation systems, and nearness to market. These products are likely to be produced in economical quantities to ensure there will be sufficient numbers to meet the total demand. Items produced in excess of current demand are usually inventoried to buffer against unexpected changes in the demand curve and/or sold later. Seldom are these inventory items considered highly perishable.

These features of the demand curve for manufacturing industries are seldom present in the service industry. There are several reasons for this. First, it is difficult to aggregate total demand to predict how many products will be sold by a service provider over a specific planning period. The nature of the demand curve in the service industry is local. For a quick-service restaurant chain such as McDonald's, with over 30,000 units, there are over 30,000 separate demand curves. Second, the products produced by McDonald's do not come from a few manufacturing plants strategically located to take advantage of raw materials sources and transportation systems. Instead, McDonald's has over 30,000 separate manufacturing units that must be located near their markets. And they cannot store finished products for much longer than 15 minutes before they become unacceptable to the customer. The supply of individual products produced in each unit must be sold almost immediately. Thus the demand curve can be said to be very temporal, fluctuating from hour to hour, day to day, week to week, and month to month. It is not influenced as much by macro features such as demographics but more by local economic conditions, local competition, and even weather. As can be seen here, the demand curve for service businesses contains characteristics not similarly found in the large-scale consumer durable goods businesses.

The supply of manufactured goods can be somewhat homogeneous and produced in large quantities in relatively few locations and inventoried for later sale. Thus supply can be produced to meet total aggregate demand. This is not the case in the service industry where the supply of services can be very heterogeneous and originates from a few—to potentially thousands of—physical units. This is because, as stated earlier, services are produced and consumed at the same time. Therefore, the supply of all services must be produced at the point of customer contact. This must be done by service personnel who face, in some instances, a fair amount of task complexity in delivering exactly the level of service the customer wants.

Another point of difference between manufacturing and service has to do with the management of inventory. As stated earlier, the total supply of products produced by manufacturers can be inventoried if it is not sold immediately. Inventory is also created to buffer firms from wide swings in the demand curve of the business. If finished products remain too long in inventory, management can alter their prices to reduce inventory. As pointed out, the products and services produced by service firms such as those in the hospitality industry have little to no inventory life. If a restaurant does not fill its supply of seats on any given day it can never sell them again. The same can be said for hotel rooms, airline seats, and other forms of service industry inventory.

In other words, this inventory is highly perishable with almost no shelf life. The same can be true of the physical products sold by hospitality enterprises. Fresh products have only a limited life, with some products like french fries and hamburgers having a life of relatively few minutes. Thus service firms have unique challenges in determining how much of any product or service to produce. This problem is not easily tackled in a consumer marketplace where consumer demands are changing all the time.

Another way of recognizing the need for different strategy models of service businesses is to consider the nature of the goods and services provided by an organization and the technology used to produce them. In some cases, service firms provide only information as their output; in other cases, a mixture of goods and services is provided. In the hospitality industry, there is substantial variation from firm to firm in the degree of goods and services offered. The quick-service restaurant firm can be said to provide a greater proportion of physical product to service product, whereas the full-service elegant restaurant may have a more nearly complete balance between goods and services. Similar mixtures exist in the lodging industry as well. The specific nature of this goods-to-service mix creates a need for technologies that reflect services as well as goods. This relationship is illustrated in Exhibit 6.

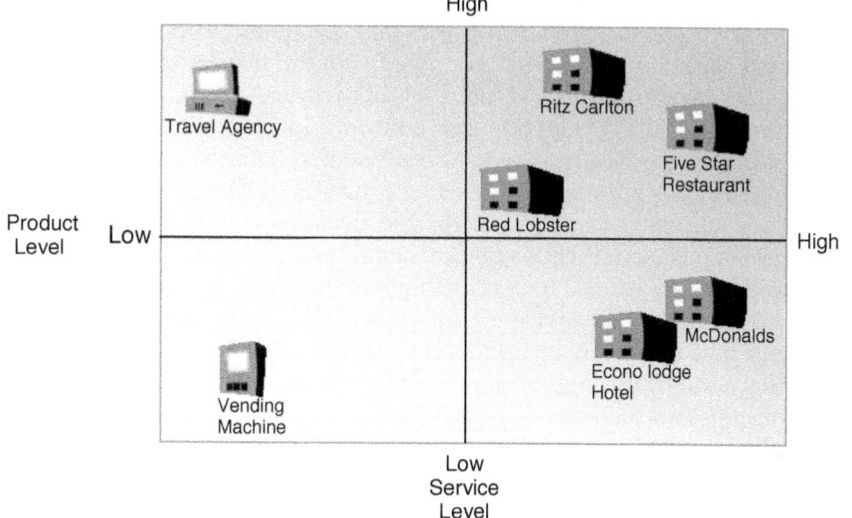

EXHIBIT 6   The Product Service Continuum

As indicated by the various shapes in the exhibit, some firms offer low levels of both products and services. A typical vending machine occurring in the lower left quadrant is an example of such a case. It offers only a limited number of products such as beverages or snacks and no personal service. In contrast, a full-service restaurant or hotel would offer high levels of products and services as indicated by the symbols in the upper-right-hand quadrant. A travel agent offers almost no product but does provide only services, whereas quick-service restaurants and limited service hotels are heavy on product but limited on services provided. What this graphic suggests is that a firm will require both manufacturing and service technologies with a number of different types of processes to meet customer demands for products and services. The firms that offer high levels of both are very capital and labor intensive and require an extensive array of competencies and resources to meet these demands. Creating strategies and implementing them for these firms is a very complex and demanding job. For firms appearing in other quadrants, this need changes depending on the levels of products and services provided. Regardless of level of services, the firm must invest in technologies to produce the desired output. Although it is less problematic to invest in processes and machines to produce goods, it is more challenging to invest in processes and machines to produce quality service, for all the reasons provided thus far.

As you can see from the forgoing discussion, the service industry has some unique strategy issues that require a different approach to strategy than that outlined in the classic literature on the subject. The uniqueness centers on the fact that each service encounter the employee has with a customer represents a complete manufacturing process where the product is intangible, heterogeneous, and the results difficult to measure. The outcome is based on the perceptual feeling of both the producer and the consumer of the final outcome. The nature of this encounter is more a craft, based on know-how, feelings, and emotions. This being the case, it requires the employee to exercise a great deal of self-management to ensure that the level and quality of service is appropriate for the need. It suggests that this quality control is in the hands of the employee and thus not subject to a quality control inspector who, in a manufacturing setting, can review products before they are delivered to the customer. Because of the simultaneity of the production and consumption process, the only quality control inspector is the service employee in combination with the customer. If the product is substandard, it cannot be held back or returned. It can only be remembered by the customer and used as the basis for the decision in the future regarding another purchase of this service. Thus service technology is highly dependent on employees and how well they are trained to provide high-quality service in a variety of settings.

The nature of the service enterprise and the hospitality enterprise, in particular, suggests that each unit in each location is a small manufacturing operation that provides a varying range of goods and services. As such, the demand-and-supply relationships and the need to create service technologies, as well as goods producing technologies, bring about the requirement for a specific understanding of the strategic management process in the hospitality industry.

The Importance of Strategy in the Hospitality Industry

The hospitality industry is a significant and distinctive economic force in the service economies of most Western nations and is growing fast in the developing world. It is distinctive for several reasons. First, it is both capital and labor intensive. Second, it is considered to be a fragmented industry with more than 900,000 food service establishments and 50,000 hotels in the United States alone. Third, the ownership of the assets deployed in this industry often does not belong to those who are managing them. Instead, real estate investment groups, private equity firms, hedge funds, insurance companies, and pension funds, along with international business venturists, have expended considerable amounts of capital to acquire assets of the industry and have employed specialized hospitality companies to manage them. Fourth, a considerable amount of real estate across the globe is devoted to supporting all types of hospitality organizations. Fifth, innovative ideas for hotels and restaurants have little protection from being immediately copied by competition and thus are subject to competitive forces that create an environmental dynamism and uncertainty unique to this industry. Sixth, the industry has been a fertile field for those pursuing the American dream of owning your own business and exercising the entrepreneurial spirit. Seventh, it is part of the service industry phenomenon with unique demand, supply, and technology relationships. It is these principal attributes that have made the study of strategic management an important subject for hospitality managers and readers alike.

Is there a need for the study of strategy in the hospitality industry today? This question can, in part, be answered affirmatively by considering the industry characteristics just described. Support for this suggestion also arises from the patterns of industry growth. Although the industry has existed in one form or another for centuries, its present structure has developed over the past three decades. Well-known lodging chains and foodservice companies emerged in the 1960s as a result of the changing demographics of the United States. The maturation and economic power of a workforce seeking new opportunities for travel, food, and entertainment drove these changes. Well-known chains such as Holiday

Inn and McDonald's resulted from needs in the marketplace for their types of products. These firms were founded by visionary entrepreneurs who were propelled by one principal goal—growth—which meant numbers of new units and subsequent profits. Not only did these entrepreneurs build huge enterprises during the 1960s and early 1970s; they inspired others to do the same.

The early success of such entrepreneurs brought about the inevitable interest of investors participating in the capital markets. Throughout the 1970s there was considerable activity by investors as they acquired ownership or control of these growing and profitable businesses. This activity was especially true in the foodservice segment where cash-rich firms from related industries sought to acquire growing hospitality organizations and use that acquisition to satisfy the demands of stockholders for more growth and higher returns. Today, this era is over. These once cash-rich firms divested themselves of their once proud acquisitions. General Mills Corporation spun off its restaurants into a separate company—Darden. PepsiCo, the parent of such chains as Pizza Hut, KFC, and Taco Bell did the same, creating Tricon Global, which morphed into Yum! The reasons are many, but the most significant one is the inability of these chains to produce the value necessary for these parent companies. This strategy seems to have benefited the shareholders of both firms because both Darden and Yum! are competing successfully in a mature, highly competitive market. Today, the cycle of investing in hospitality companies has now been taken over by private equity firms and hedge funds with recent acquisitions of Hilton Hotels and resort developer operator Intrawest. Outback Steakhouses and other restaurant chains are now targets by this group of investors. While the investment landscape has changed, the demands for value maximization have not.

The challenge continues to be to develop strategies that will interest both customers and investors in their future value. Over the next five to ten years, some of the key drivers of the restaurant industry will include the increased time demand on the American family, improving domestic economy, and increasing capital investment on the part of franchisers and franchisees.[16] Today, approximately 46% of the consumer's food dollar is spent on food away from home. The National Restaurant Association estimates that this trend will reach 53% by 2010—a 14% increase in sales—or $40 billion over 2005.[17] As more and more of the food dollar in the United States is spent outside of the home, it becomes important to define the typical restaurant customer because the profile is that of a resident of the country. Therefore, if managers are to be successful they must understand the forces driving change in the marketplace because these for the most part impact all members of society.

Although lodging firms did not experience the same degree of acquisition interest as did foodservice enterprises, the top management of these organizations used capital generated through public offerings to grow their chains at a considerable pace. A favorable investment climate, facilitating tax laws, a baby boom generation flexing its buying power, and a good transportation system continued to fuel growth in this sector. For the decades of the 1960s, 1970s, and early 1980s, one could almost do no wrong in this industry. Little strategy was necessary: Just find a good location and build. With increasing interest from investors in the capital markets, it was inevitable that the management of these firms would have to respond to the demands of the investment community—which almost always translated into the need for more growth. This is the primary challenge facing lodging executives today.

The 1980s represented a period of major change for the industry. The demand curve, although still increasing in the early half of the decade, began to level off. The rapid growth in the 1960s and 1970s resulted in the saturation of most primary markets by the close of the 1980s. Tax-law changes in 1986 removed incentives for investing in the lodging industry, which was probably good because supply was outpacing demand. Otherwise, the overbuilding that went on throughout the 1980s might have continued. The investment climate changed as the high-flying hospitality firms of the 1970s turned into the poor performers of the 1980s.

When the industry looked at the challenges of the 1990s, it did so with the least optimistic forecasts for the start of any decade. In the United States alone, there are over 600,000 foodservice operations that at the start of the decade were generating an estimated total of $248 billion in sales. These sales were mostly generated from small businesses, where, for example, in 2004 the average sales of a restaurant was $730,000, and seven out of ten were single-unit independent operations (Foodservice Industry Pocket Factbook 2004). There are approximately 50,000 hotels with approximately 4.4 million hotel rooms generating estimated sales of $105 billion in sales. As is the case in the foodservice industry, the majority of the hotels and motels in the country are individually owned and operated but affiliated with national chains.

The revenue growth that generated all the expansion in industry capacity over the past three decades while dipping in the early 1990s experienced new growth in the latter half of the 1990s. The reason is that the earlier growth in demand resulted from the cresting of the maturation wave of the population segment known as the baby boom generation. This demographic group constitutes the largest proportion of the total U.S. population, a phenomenon replicated in many European nations. This cresting suggested to us at the time that the demand curve would no longer rise in response to the increase in numbers of people entering the market. Although slight increases may occur, due to increased travel by individuals from other countries, demand can be expected to remain stable with growth being experienced in selective markets and nations. The early 2000s saw the burst of the expansion bubble with the double hit of both the economic recession of 2000–2001 and the terrorist attacks of September 11, 2001, at the World Trade Centers in New York. The domestic market is now rebounding, although unevenly, with growth in the luxury segment outstripping the overall growth. This suggests that firms will have to think through how they will maintain market share and tap new markets if they are to add value. This will require managers who think and act strategically.

Several other signs indicate that the competitive environment is heating up. Price discounting has become common practice along with—in some cases—permanent price reductions. Quick-service chains have led the way in the foodservice industry, and budget hotels have promoted it in the lodging industry. There has been a greater emphasis on service, with firms in both segments trying to implement improved service programs. There has been a proliferation of brands, especially in lodging. As marketing expenditures have increased, there have been significant efforts to create strategic marketing alliances where firms become linked together under varying forms of arrangements. For example, in the travel industry, car-rental firms, hotels, and airlines have blended their reservations and marketing programs to try to gain or protect market share.

Although competition has been heating up, the suppliers to the industry have either been cooling down or gaining power to affect business transactions. Obtaining financing for new hospitality projects was almost impossible as the decade began. Suppliers of capital such as banks, lending institutions, and investors in the capital markets became shy of any opportunities. Labor supply created additional problems because slow birthrates at the end of the baby boom of the 1940s and 1950s have resulted in fewer young people entering the workplace. Travel agencies, tour operators, and corporate travel managers have been concentrating purchasing power through consolidation and more sophisticated technology as they strive to create value for their clients. Interestingly, a recent study by American Express revealed that less than half of the luxury consumers questioned thought that their travel agent, personal assistant, or personal concierge added value to their trip. According to the National Leisure Travel Monitor, households with annual incomes of greater than $100,000 are more likely to make reservations online. In fact, in 2003, 61% of travelers in this income bracket made reservations online.[18] It is becoming evident that travelers are frequently using the Internet as a value-adding option, feeling it is a more convenient and cost-efficient method of booking lodging rooms. These efforts are forcing the lodging industry into a situation where it has less control over its capacity and thus must compete less on its own terms and more on the terms of these increasingly technology-driven, value-conscious customers.

Challenges Facing Tomorrow's Hospitality Manager

Throughout this chapter we have laid the groundwork necessary to understand the role of strategic management in the hospitality industry. The most important concept to achieve this understanding successfully is the coalignment model. We have suggested that this model is dynamic and future oriented. This implies that managers should be anticipatory and must think strategically about the future. They must be preemptive and anticipatory in their decisions about what competitive methods to invest in. Thinking and acting strategically also means viewing the role of the manager differently. It begins by attempting to identify what changes lie ahead to aid in this endeavor. In the following section we outline the major forces driving change in the hospitality industry and how they will shape the role of tomorrow's value-adding manager as he or she seeks to develop strategies for the future.

The forces to be outlined have been identified in research that has been conducted globally through the support of the International Hotel and Restaurant Association.[19] Researchers conducted a series of "Visioning the Future" workshops across the globe to determine what industry leaders considered to be the major changes occurring in the hospitality industry. This research is currently still continuing and has now involved over 4,000 industry practitioners who have helped validate the forces driving change in this industry and their impact on the hospitality manager and organization of the future. A summary of these forces is provided in the following paragraphs. We have become convinced that these forces will have significant and long-term impact and will change the way hospitality organizations are managed and the strategies they will select to compete with in the future. In many cases, change is already occurring. The challenge is to stay ahead of that change.

Forces Driving Change

The participants in the "Visioning the Future" workshops identified seven major forces driving change. Space here does not permit a complete and thorough review of each. The forces and a brief explanation are presented in this list:

- *Marketing, Distribution, and Capacity Management:* As the information superhighway increasingly exerts its influence on the sale of the inventories of hotel rooms (as well as airline seats, car rentals, tickets to attractions, and seats in restaurants), the hospitality industry will lose control of the sale of that inventory. What this force suggests is that the industry will be marketed differently in the future. Technology will begin to determine how this inventory is advertised and promoted. It will influence pricing. The customer can be expected to gain more control over all decisions regarding the selection and booking of the travel experience. As previously stated, the majority of travelers consider that the use of the Internet provides them with a convenient and cost-efficient method of booking hotel rooms, restaurant reservations, and other services of the hospitality industry. There is a continuing move away from brand-based marketing to destination marketing as consumers first decide where they want to travel and then make their decisions on travel and lodging. As technology enables destinations to consolidate portfolios of hotels, restaurants, and attractions into a single distribution center (i.e., convention and visitor's bureau website), brand will become secondary.

- *Safety and Security:* With today's traveler being increasingly confronted with potential risks to personal safety and health, the industry must assess the impact of such major issues as: terrorism, the AIDS epidemic, the spread of new and old diseases such as so-called mad cow disease, avian influenza (bird flu), and *E. coli* as well as a growing gap between the haves and the have-nots of wealth and information across the globe. These risks have now become the number-one concern of travelers as well as domestic residents. This problem is compounded by the fact that governments all across the globe are struggling to obtain sufficient funds to protect their own citizens and travelers in this post 9/11 world. This is putting increasing burdens on hospitality enterprises to meet the challenges of this force.

- *Assets and Capital:* The global shift to market economies has resulted in tremendous competition for available capital for investment in productive assets, especially from China and India. This competition has resulted in the flow of funds to those investments that provide the highest level of return for the funds invested. This puts pressure on all firms to focus on *value-adding* strategies that will be sustainable over time. This does not bode well for the hospitality industry where in mature markets the returns on capital have been recognized by many investors as insufficient. Thus attracting capital to support industry growth in the future will be a significant challenge for managers, putting greater pressure on effective strategic management practices. Managers must focus on competitive methods that generate the best future cash flows for the organization.

- *Technology:* It is no secret that technology is influencing almost every part of life today. The convergence of telecommunications, the computer, and information is making it possible for firms to compete in new ways. Whether it is in marketing the industry, managing resources, or investigating the future, one thing is clear: Technology will be the most important competitive method that hospitality firms will employ in the future. As long as advances in information technology continue at a rapid pace, it will continue to drive change and have significant impact on the hospitality industry.

- *New Management:* The study made one thing very clear. No matter where in the world the researchers worked, the old way of learning the business is out. Managers are expected to be masters of the business world more so than masters of the craft of hospitality. There will always be a need for those with the necessary skills to provide the customer with the desired products and services, but tomorrow's manager must be a strategist. The skills necessary to succeed will demand that the manager know how to use technology, be capable of analyzing and synthesizing large amounts of information from a variety of sources, and capable of functioning in an uncertain environment. These and other challenges will require the manager to think in an interdisciplinary manner. This thinking will have to be future oriented. In addition, leadership will be based on performance not seniority. This change in the leadership paradigm will be driven by the increasingly complex relationships among the customer, employee, and manager. Customer expectation of value and quality and employee need for enlightened leadership will continue to drive change in hospitality management.
- *Sustainable Development:* As the world continues to grow closer economically and populations continue to accelerate in growth rate, sustainable growth becomes a significant requirement. It is becoming apparent that emphasis on sustainable development is becoming increasingly important for public and private economic activity. Governments are already developing policies that favor sustainable economic development. Various tax incentives for green projects is a ready example. The challenge for hospitality leaders is to recognize the full range of issues that must be addressed to execute environmentally sound activities and ensure the highest standards in operations and development.
- *Social Issues:* In view of its impact on development especially in job creation, we anticipate that industry leaders will be called on to address the gap between the haves and the have-nots of the areas in which they conduct business. This will require that managers effectively develop and utilize the local labor force as well as the physical environment in which their employees live. The private sector will be expected to bear an increasingly larger share of the social costs related to their role in the community.

What these forces suggest is that there is no more business as usual in the hospitality industry. It is a more competitive, dynamic, and complex industry subject to global forces. Even the smallest most rural of enterprises is now subject to competitive forces from across the world. To meet these challenges, Exhibit 7 outlines the skills necessary for tomorrow's managers if they hope to be successful in this changing environment. These skills were identified in the research project previously described and have been presented to the international sample of managers indicated earlier. Although there were some differences from one region to another globally, they were mostly differences of timing as opposed to skills. In other words, there was general agreement that these were the required skills, but when they would become important in different parts of the world would depend on the level of economic development in that region. To validate this list, we encourage you to read the industry trade literature over the last several years and take note of how each of these issues has become more a part of the fabric of the industry like never before.

- A strategist—less craft skills, more business skills
- A multifunctional manager
- A change agent/boundary spanner
- Visionary
- Technologist
- A Knowledge worker—information manager
- Marketing on the information highway
- How to buy and sell your way into the information highway
- Evaluating and maintaining the best strategic alliances
- Recognize, interact with, and utilize the resources of those who will own the information systems (information highway)
- Capable of receiving, analyzing, synthesizing incredible amounts of information regarding: guest, internal operations, external data from capacity controllers
- Utilize information to adjust to the speed of change
- Monitor changes in an increasingly diverse/complex demand curve
- Provide information to guest to satisfy their needs for safety and security
- New leadership skills to motivate a more diverse workforce consisting of more knowledge workers

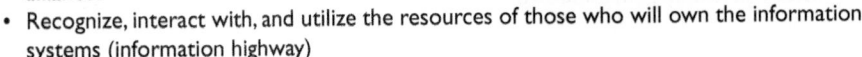

EXHIBIT 7 Tomorrow's Hospitality Manager

A close look at the skills identified in Exhibit 7 suggests several important differences in the skill and capability inventory of tomorrow's hospitality manager compared to what has been viewed as important in the past. Historically, the skill training that was done focused on topics like food production, cost control, layout and design, front-office management, food and beverage management, catering, sales, merchandising, and accounting. This body of knowledge reflected the importance of internal operations and pleasing the guest. Without a doubt, these skills are still very important to the success of today's hospitality firm. However, although they may have been sufficient for decades, they no longer meet the needs of today's competitive environment. The emphasis must now be on the making of the hospitality enterprise a viable long-term investment. It means addressing the need for managers to know and understand how to add value strategically in a complex, dynamic business environment.

The Value-Adding Manager

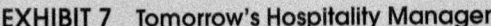

A value-adding manager recognizes that every product and service combined into a portfolio to create a competitive method must be thought of as a value-adding investment, one that will yield value over and above the firm's cost of capital for as long a time as is possible. This view of management recognizes that each competitive method has a distinctive lifespan that is becoming increasingly shorter in the context of heightened competition. This view also supports the notion that any investment will create risk and this risk must be considered and managed. For the investor, the value-adding manager is expected to provide the owner with a return on capital equal to, or in excess of, alternative investments. This return must also compensate the investor for the risk taken and the inflation over the life of that investment. Considering these requirements reinforces the idea that managers must be future oriented and think strategically about what to invest in to be able to add future value.

Becoming a value-adding manager means being a change agent, constantly spanning the boundaries between the firm and the business environment, seeking new opportunities to invest in. This spanning activity becomes a very important role in bridging the gap between the internal craft orientation required to deliver products and services and looking externally for opportunities and threats. It requires managers to monitor their environment regularly looking for changes in a demand curve that is becoming increasingly diverse and complex. This will require from every decision maker the need to receive, analyze, and synthesize incredible amounts of information that is being generated today about the guest, internal operations, and those who are increasingly gaining control over the inventory of the industry's total capacity. Tomorrow's manager will be an information manager who uses information to adjust to the speed of change.

The future will require a *multidisciplinary* approach to decisions. Thus the manager must become multifunctional. What this implies is that managers will have to be able to combine their knowledge in several disciplines as they approach investment decisions. This will also require managers to become leaders in situations where they will have to rely on the advice of internal and external experts more than ever. This is because the body of knowledge associated with the disciplines essential to hospitality management is expanding exponentially as the knowledge revolution continues to sweep across the globe. Put another way, tomorrow's manager is not expected to have all the answers. She or he will have to rely on others who possess greater knowledge and then synthesize this input into the decision-making process.

The *multifunctional manager* role means that the education and learning associated with careers in this field will also have to change. At present, learners and managers are both given education and training in narrowly defined capsules of knowledge. These can be specific courses in a hospitality curriculum or specific training programs. What often happens in that the learner digests the information to earn the appropriate reward for going through this experience (usually a grade or certificate). Unfortunately, this knowledge is not always transferred and/or combined with other capsules of knowledge when it comes to putting it to work in a real-world setting. This is not the fault of the learner; it is most likely the fault of the learning process being used. Educators and trainers reward individuals for mastering a unit of knowledge but do not reward them as effectively for demonstrating the successful transfer of that knowledge to a new setting. This must change because adding value requires that the manager understand operations, finance, marketing, the business environment, and leadership and can bring these functional areas together to make the most effective investment decisions. In other words, we need to change our thinking by teaching people to be multifunctional managers where the learning process begins with the decision to be made and then adds the necessary functional expertise. Presently, it is done the other way around, which is insufficient in creating tomorrow's multifunctional, *value-adding* manager.

The information highway metaphor is now well known to many. It suggests that an information society is developing. Many believe this change is similar to that brought on by the Industrial Revolution. As signs continue to point to this becoming a reality, it suggests that tomorrow's manager will have to develop significant capabilities in this regard. This we have already pointed out in the preceding paragraphs. This is important because hundreds of new businesses are developing that were unheard of just five years ago. Data warehousing and data-mining companies did not really exist a few years ago. Yet today, they promise to revolutionize how we obtain and use information to make better decisions in marketing, finance, human resources, and for many other purposes. To meet the challenges brought about by these changes, the manager not only needs to know how to be an effective knowledge worker but also how to interact with those who will be owning and managing that knowledge. Thus they will need to know how to buy and sell their way into this information revolution if they are to be the most effective value-adding manager.

The information revolution is partially brought about by technology. In particular, the convergence of the computer, telecommunications, and knowledge industries has brought about the realization that to compete in tomorrow's world, the managers of the future will have to be able to understand how this convergence will impact their jobs and firms. Therefore tomorrow's managers will find it necessary to become technologists, in the most generic sense of the word. Technology is not just machines. It is information, processes, and ways of doing business. The managers of the future must know how to use it to best gain a competitive advantage and value-adding capability.

Tomorrow's value-adding manager will also experience the need to change leadership styles. It will no longer be possible to give lip service to human resources management or to adopt a "my way or the highway" approach to managing the workforce of the future. The changing workforce, brought on by the knowledge revolution and free flow of information, no longer is willing to tolerate the old-fashioned control-oriented style of the industry's former leadership.

The industry has and will continue to experience labor shortages that will demand from them a more behavioralistic approach to human resources management if it expects to attract qualified labor. The labor shortage will also require them to employ individuals from diverse backgrounds demanding a much greater understanding of what motivates individuals who are uniquely different but must still function as a team. Not only will tomorrow's labor force be diverse based on personal physical and behavioral characteristics, they will also be diverse in level of education and knowledge level. Additionally, they will also be different regarding their ability to access information. This growing level of diversity in the workforce as well as in the marketplace will create many challenges for tomorrow's manager as he or she seeks to become a value-adding one.

Perhaps the most interesting challenge facing tomorrow's manager will be the need to be a *visionary* and possess the *creativity* to see opportunity where others will see threats and to invest in competitive methods that will lead the firm into advantage over its present and future competition. Many argue that one is born with vision and creativity and that it cannot be learned. Although the answer to this argument must still be determined, the need to possess these capabilities is no longer in doubt. In a fast-paced changing world, to stay ahead of competition the manager of tomorrow must think ahead of the competition. She or he must look for opportunity and develop the ability to see how the forces driving change will ensure that that opportunity will provide long-lasting *value-adding* investments for the firm. Strategy tomorrow will demand more vision and creativity in this context. Coalignment will not occur without it.

SUMMARY

Strategy has been defined here in the context of the coalignment model. This model suggests that hospitality enterprises of the future will only succeed if their managers are able to see opportunities in the environment of the business, invest in *value-adding* competitive methods, and allocate resources to those methods that add the greatest value to the firm. The underpinning of success begins with the business environment, which is filled with change and complexity. Thus the manager of tomorrow must know how to use information, human, physical, and capital resources to take advantage of the opportunities presented by this turbulent environment.

To achieve successful coalignment the manager must recognize that strategy in the service industry is different than in manufacturing. It is different for several important reasons. These include the supply-and-demand relationships, the nature of services, and the technologies used to convert inputs into desired outputs. In many cases these differences present far greater challenges for the hospitality manager because the products and services are so immediate, transparent, and perishable. Additionally, it is probably easier to copy or duplicate products and services in this industry than in any other, adding additional challenges to the hospitality manager. These differences suggest that strategy making and implementing in this industry is different than in others, and that it is important that managers know this if they are to compete successfully in the future.

Change is the way life today. Knowing what forces are driving change is essential to achieving coalignment. The major forces driving change in the hospitality industry are capacity control, technology, assets and capital, new management and safety and security, social responsibility, and sustainability. These forces are creating ripples throughout the globe and changing the way the industry competes. These changes are also changing the job of the hospitality manager. Although craft skills are important, they no longer are sufficient for success. Tomorrow's manager must possess a whole new conceptual toolbox. The most important tool in that box is knowing how to be a *value-adding* manager. Using that tool requires creativity and vision. This in turn results in the investment in future-oriented *value-adding* competitive methods that meet the customers' and owners' needs. This new role for the hospitality manager means thinking strategically about all decisions. The job is becoming more complex.

DISCUSSION QUESTIONS

1. Why is it important to consider the management of a hospitality enterprise in the context of the coalignment model?
2. How does the service industry differ from the manufacturing industry?
3. Why is strategy viewed as a way of thinking and not a process?
4. What is meant by the concept of adding value and how is it applied within the coalignment model?
5. Describe the key concepts within the coalignment model.
6. How is leadership different in the hospitality industry vs. the manufacturing industry?
7. What is unique about the hospitality industry within the context of the overall service industry?
8. What have the forces driving change done to the requirements for today's hospitality manager.

NOTES

1. P. Ghemawat, *Competition and Business Strategy in Historical Perspective* (Harvard Case Study #9–798–010, revised April 2000).
2. C. von Clausewitz, *On War* (1848).
3. C. I. Barnard, *The Functions of the Executive* (Harvard University Press, 1938).
4. P. Drucker, *The Practice of Management* (Harper & Row, 1954).
5. K. R. Andrews, *The Concept of Corporate Strategy* (Dow Jones-Irwin, 1971).
6. I. Ansoff, *Corporate Strategy* (McGraw-Hill, 1965).
7. J. S. Bain, "The Relation of Profit Rate to Industry Concentration: American Manufacturing 1936–1940," *Quarterly Journal of Economics* (August 1951).
8. M. Porter, *Competitive Advantage* (Free Press, 1985).
9. A. M. Brandenburger and B. J. Nalebuff, *Co-opetition* (Currency/Doubleday, 1996).
10. R. Leider, "Is Leading Your Calling?" *Leader to Leader*, 21 (Winter 2004).
11. P. Drucker, "Leader of the Future," in *Leader of the Future*, ed. F. Hesselbein, M. Goldsmith, and R. Beckhard (Jossey-Bass, 1997).
12. K. Blanchard and J. Stoner, "The Vision Thing: Without It You'll Never Be a World-Class Organization," *Leader to Leader*, 31 (Winter 2004).
13. M. Bardwick, "Peacetime Management and Wartime Leadership," in *Leader of the Future*, ed. F. Hesselbein, M. Goldsmith, and R. Beckhard (Jossey-Bass, 1997).
14. M. Kets de Vries, "Doing an Alexander": Lessons on Leadership by a Master Conqueror," INSEAD Working Paper Series (2003).
15. M. Cetron, "Coming Global Growth Is Hospitable for Hospitality" (CHRIE Conference, 2005).
16. R. Rothman, *Restaurant Industry—In-Depth Report* (Merrill Lynch, October 2004).
17. Ibid.
18. D. Anders and A. Bryant, *In-Depth Look at the Luxury Lodging Segment* (Merrill Lynch, December 2004).
19. M. D. Olsen, "Into the New Millennium," a White Paper on the International Hospitality Industry (International Hotel & Restaurant Association, 1995).

C A S E S T U D Y

Turnaround at McDonald's

MCDONALD'S AROUND THE WORLD

Founded by Ray Kroc in 1955, McDonald's has built its success not so much on the taste of its food as on its solid standards of consistency of product, cleanliness of operations, and good service. Today, McDonald's has more than 30,000 restaurants in 121 countries, serving 46 million customers daily (Rogers 2002). It generates revenue from 9,000 company-owned restaurants and franchisees and license holders (*The Economist* 2004). McDonald's possesses a 43% market share of the quick-service hamburger market. With earnings of over $1 billion in international profit, the chain is considered the largest restaurant operator in the world, thus the primary competitor internationally. Not only is it the best known American icon, it is also one of the most recognized brand icons around the world. Measured by sales, McDonald's is about twice as large as its next global competitor, Yum! Brands, operator of Kentucky Fried Chicken (KFC), Pizza Hut, and Taco Bell (*The Economist* 2004).

Outside of its domestic market in the United States, McDonald's has more than 16,000 units internationally. Approximately 85% of its restaurants are located in 11 major markets: Australia, Brazil, Canada, the United Kingdom, France, Germany, Hong Kong, Japan, The Netherlands, Taiwan, and the United States. McDonald's first outlet in Japan opened in 1971. Since then, more than 2,400 restaurants have opened in Japan (Rogers 2002). McDonald's opened its first restaurant in London in 1974. Today the chain has 1,200 UK outlets in almost every town and city across the United Kingdom employing 68,000 people (Rogers 2002). After building on its American heritage using U.S.-originated advertising, McDonald's has in recent years adopted a localized marketing strategy for the United Kingdom (Rogers 2002). It has developed menus for British tastes such as Anglo-Indian food and has produced commercials featuring icons of British culture (Rogers 2002). In 1990 it opened its first McDonald's restaurant in Russia on Pushkin Square, which continues to be the world's busiest McDonald's. The company opened 79 other restaurants across Russia (Rogers 2002). In 2000, 35% to 40% of McDonald's operating income came from Europe. In China, McDonald's entered the market in 1990, after Yum! Brands. Yum has 1,500 restaurants and enjoys a broader geographical coverage in China than McDonald's.

DISAPPOINTING FINANCIAL PERFORMANCE AT MCDONALD'S

The U.S. market, although mature, provides half the revenues of McDonald's corporation. Approximately 18% of the U.S. population are McDonald's customers, and it is focused on changing consumer tastes (Rogers 2002).

For decades, McDonald's has been one of the blue chip stocks, and it has been a component of the Dow Jones industrial average since 1985. For many years, McDonald's was the representative growth stock guaranteed to deliver 12% to 15% earnings. However, this growth phenomenon began to change in the 1990s. Beginning in the late 1990s, McDonald's earnings per share grew just 4% (Stires 2002). The tipping point came in 1996 when McDonald's had four consecutive quarters of declining same-store sales and lost significant market share to Burger King and Wendy's (Stires 2002).

It appeared that the mass market for quick-service restaurants was gradually losing its public appeal. As a result, McDonald's sales growth diminished to 2% annually instead of the norm of 15%. It faced a dilemma—its needs to open a certain number of stores to continue to generate 10% to 15% profit growth, demanded by shareholders, while the mature markets domestically and internationally could not support more unit growth indefinitely. Even though McDonald's opened more stores, profit margins were declining. Some critics thought that McDonald's should slow down its growth rate and close some stores to boost corporate returns and share price, avoiding cannibalization. In 1998 McDonald's posted its first-ever decline in annual earnings (Pallavi and Arndt 2003).

From 1998 to 2002, McDonald's spent $10 billion in capital expenditures and opened many new units. Consequently, McDonald's outlets have grown from 27,500 to almost 30,000. McDonald's expanded so fast it ran out of room to grow (Stires 2004); sales had not increased since 1999 while costs kept rising. In 2002 the company slowed its expansion by opening 300 new restaurants in the United States, a fraction of the 1,130 restaurants it added in 1995 (Stires 2004). However, McDonald's did not address the issue of slowing international growth. The chain continues expanding at a faster pace internationally. However even internationally, where growth rates tend to be more pronounced (Stires 2004), it is not a consistent profitable operation. Sales in Europe rose only 1%, and the chain plans to add only 200 units to the existing 6,070 (Pallavi and Arndt 2003). The company had 30% fewer openings in 2003 than the year before. It closed 176 of its 2,800 stores in Japan due to slow economic growth. McDonald's planned to add only 250 new outlets in the United States in 2003 (Pallavi and Arndt 2003), 40% fewer than in 2002.

McDonald's same-store sales were flat in 2001, and according to the consulting firm, Interbrand, the value of the name "McDonald's" dropped by $2.5 billion that year (Stires 2004) while the S&P Restaurant Index was up 18%. Meanwhile, Wendy's and Yum! both experienced increases in stock price. In 2002 McDonald's same-store sales for the United States dropped 2%, and sales in the United Kingdom and Germany, McDonald's two biggest European markets, were also weaker than forecasted (Rogers 2002). The company recorded disappointing profits for the sixth consecutive quarter. Investors were selling the stock while analysts downgraded it. Some analysts stopped covering the stock because their clients were not interested while analysts at Salomon Smith Barney downgraded its forecasts for McDonald's stock to "underperform" (Rogers 2002). Its 2002 share price of $17.90 stood at a seven-year low. Profit margins were no more than half of what they were 30 years ago. In 2003 McDonald's reported its first quarterly loss since 1954. By June 2003 McDonald's same-store sales had fallen for each of the previous 12 months (Enz 2005). Both external and internal factors led to McDonald's decline in sales after 40 years of growth.

EXTERNAL FACTORS IN THE BUSINESS ENVIRONMENT

Within the past decade, fierce competition has led large restaurant firms to aggressively engage in tactics to retain market share resulting in discounting. Recently, in an attempt to regain profitability, firms have begun to move away from price discounting and are now focusing on site locations, upgraded menus and decor, investment in staff training programs, and customer-loyalty programs (Enz 2005). Mass market is no longer the formula for success. Management knows there is a need to make McDonald's more relevant to today's consumers.

McDonald's early expansion in the 1950s was linked with the golden years of U.S. society (Rogers 2002). The restaurant industry progressed through its growth stage in the 1970s and the 1980s and is now entering the maturity phase of its life cycle. The U.S. marketplace is saturated and extremely competitive. Slow same-store sales and a sluggish economy have negatively impacted quick-service restaurant chains in recent years.

Demographic Shift

The first Americans to grow up with fast food, the baby boom generation, have matured and are seeking alternative dining options of fresher and more nutritious food. Customers who used to prefer meat and potatoes only have become increasingly sophisticated. Today, they are more willing to try once-exotic foods such as sushi and burritos, as well as quick meals from supermarkets, convenience stores, and vending machines (Pallavi and Arndt 2003). It is a necessity for any brand to evolve according to the customers' needs (Rogers 2002). The emergence and rapid growth of the "quick casual" segment is evidence of this trend. Quick casual restaurants that provide limited or self-service concepts, such as

Panera Bread Co., and Corner Bakery Co., are capturing the lunchtime meal period. These restaurants offer slightly more expensive menu choices, but customers find the food healthier and better tasting. Most fast-food chains such as Burger King and Wendy's have responded by altering their menu items, adding salads, and changing ingredients of existing items. McDonald's market share is unchanging as its customers turn to coffee shops and delicatessens as alternatives to their menu.

McDonald's had lost more than direction. Chains such as McDonald's are facing a rapidly fragmenting market. Not only does McDonald's have to compete with a revitalized Burger King and Wendy's, it faces many new niche entrants in an overcrowded fast-food arena (Rogers 2002). Arby's has introduced Market Fresh sandwiches. In addition, McDonald's also competes with coffee shops, sandwich bars, casual dining, pub-restaurants and even supermarkets, all of which are feeding the grab-and-go demand from office workers, students, shoppers, and travelers. McDonald's seems to have lost favor with its core market. The company has finished last among fast-food restaurants every year since 1992, according to a survey administered by the Michigan's American Customer Satisfaction index (Stires 2004). Critics wondered whether McDonald's has evolved quickly enough to keep up with consumers' changing tastes in the increasingly health-conscious and quality experience–driven society (Rogers 2002).

Unhealthy Image

Worldwide, a wave of anti-American feeling turned the famous McDonald's golden arches from an asset into a liability (*The Economist* 2004). McDonald's has been hit by fears of mad cow disease in Europe, damaged by the McLibel trial, negatively portrayed by the bestselling book *Fast Food Nation*, sued by vegetarians who ate its beef-based cooking oil (Rogers 2002), and attacked by the documentary *Super Size Me*. There is also growing concern about obesity and junk food and their impact on health and disease.

INTERNAL CONDITIONS

Unsatisfied Franchisees

Ray Kroc's idea of franchising has allowed the company to become the industry's giant. However, the concept works best when the market is expanding and owners can be rewarded for meeting incentives. A study by Citigroup Smith Barney reported that the average McDonald's franchisee expected annual sales of approximately $1.7 million and an operating profit of $150,000 from their restaurant (*The Economist* 2004). The slowdown in McDonald's expansion has caused problems with its franchisees. For decades, there have always been a number of entrepreneurs lining up to become McDonald's franchisees. However, in 2002 a record number of franchisees either opted to leave the system for faster growing competitors or were forced out due to poor performance. McDonald's was forced to take a pretax charge of $292 million in 2002 to close down over 700 restaurants and buy back franchises that could not be sold.

Quality Standards are Compromised

McDonald's was also confronted by the problems of poor unit-level execution and a menu lagging behind changing consumer tastes. The key philosophy of emphasizing QSC&V (quality, service, cleanliness, and value) that had set McDonald's apart was no longer working (*The Economist* 2004). Sales for McDonald's has been flat, with an increasing number of customers complaining about slow service, rude employees, dirty restaurants, and cardboard-tasting food. In the past, McDonald's sent out "mystery shoppers" to evaluate the service, cleanliness, and food quality of its restaurants (Stires

2004). During its expansion period of 1990s, the company stopped grading franchises for cleanliness, speed, and service. In fact, slow service is the biggest complaint from U.S. customers. McDonald's finished third in average service time (163 seconds), behind Wendy's (127 seconds) and Chick-fil-A Inc. (151 seconds). CEO Greenberg stated that saving 6 seconds at drive-through windows brings a 1% increase in sales (Pallavi and Arndt 2003). Training for McDonald's employees declined when there was a labor shortage in the industry, leading to a decrease in their skills.

TURNAROUND STRATEGY

Diversification through Acquisition

McDonald's has expanded its menu while diversifying within the operations of the restaurant industry. The company has been steadily buying chains that operate under different brands. As part of its strategy, McDonald's has diversified by investing in a variety of fast casual restaurants, including the acquisition of Boston Market in 1999, Chipotle Mexican Grill, Donatos Pizza, and a 33% stake in the British quality-sandwich chain Pret A Manger. These U.S. chains cater to the middle ground between limited service fast-food and full table service, or fast casual dining. The purchase of Boston Market, a quick casual concept in 2000, signaled that the days of mass media marketing are over. Later, the company decided to focus on its core brand and divested its interest in Donatos Pizza in 2003 and Chipotle in 2006.

Change of Leadership

By the late 1990s, the McDonald's system was exhibiting signs of poor planning. New menu items to attract new markets failed to increase sales. As a result, Michael Quinlan was replaced by Jack Greenberg, a McDonald's veteran of 16 years, as CEO in 1998 (Pallavi and Arndt 2003). Greenberg attempted to reverse the decline in sales by making operational changes in McDonald's management. He initiated a corporate restructuring in 2001 that cut the number of regional divisions in America and added a new layer of management to monitor quality and impose tougher standards on franchisees. Greenberg also started to trim back the U.S. expansion. His management style of decentralization was believed to have hurt the image of the McDonald's brand of service, quality, and cleanliness (*The Economist* 2001).

CEO Greenberg began testing a costly new "Made-For-You" food assembly system designed to improve quality, supported by a high-tech kitchen retrofitted across McDonald's outlets. However, the new system did not deliver and failed to boost sales. At the same time, it crippled service time and eventually backfired. The franchisees had to pay for the expensive system, which strained their relationship with the corporation. Some analysts suggested that the company should kill the "Dollar Menu," a promotion introduced to reverse traffic declines. They thought that it slowed down operations of new units and cut McDonald's store base by at least 10%. Greenberg's four-year tenure was marked by declining U.S. sales growth and mad cow disease concerns that crippled its European business. He was blamed for letting the burger business deteriorate, by running McDonald's more as an amalgamation of local businesses operated by local entrepreneurs from Indonesia to France than as one worldwide company (*The Economist* 2001). Greenberg also planned an aggressive expansion of 1,400 stores in 2002. However, investors wanted McDonald's to concentrate on the profitability of existing stores with a tighter, more centralized McDonald's. McDonald's stock slid by 60% in three years, and its shares were trading at a seven-year low of $15.75 in 2002, which was half of its share price in 1996. Eventually, the board removed Greenberg as CEO.

In 2003 Jim Cantalupo, a McDonald's veteran who headed the successful international expansion in the 1980s and 1990s, was brought back from retirement to launch a turnaround and recovery strategy. Although some analysts would have preferred to see McDonald's tap an executive from outside the company (Zuber 2003), the board chose Cantalupo. They thought that he was familiar with the company culture and system and could adapt much quicker than an outsider. Cantalupo, chairman and chief executive officer, sharpened his focus and took the actions necessary to optimize business. He realized his management team had to rebuild the foundation. He expected to achieve a turnaround in 18 months. He chose to work with his chief operating officer Charles Bell, and Mats Lederhausen, who was in charge of global strategy. Bell was formally president of McDonald's Europe. He became a store manager in Australia at age 19 and rose through the ranks. Under Bell's leadership, McDonald's Australia became the model market. He was responsible for the launching of McCafe globally. He also individualized McDonald's outlets from the cookie-cutter orange and yellow stores to offer local fare. Cantalupo cancelled an expensive revamp of the company's technology that would have cost $1 billion due to the mature state of the market. This action returned some of McDonald's cash flow to shareholders.

In 2004, 90% of McDonald's growth was predicted to come from incremental sales at its existing restaurants, compared to 50% in 2003. Unfortunately, Cantaloupe died while attending a McDonald's convention in Florida. Succession occurred swiftly according to the company's existing mechanism, and Charlie Bell became the first non-American to head the company.

McDonald's present strategy is to develop its brands separately so that the company could capitalize on cobranding in the future.

Improve the Basics

According to the formula for success, there are three stages of turnaround: (1) fix what is wrong internally—McDonald's has inconsistently hit the mark on delivering on the critical aspects of its brand promise to customers: consistent, fast and friendly service, safe, family fun; and all-around enjoyable experience (Davis 2003). (2) Reestablish relevant quality product offerings. McDonald's took steps in the right direction with its gourmet salads and its newer, healthier all-white meat Chicken McNuggets (Davis 2003). Such menu enhancements help McDonald's reconnect with adults, especially those with children who only come to McDonald's for Happy Meals. Family is one of the most critical components of McDonald's brand asset base for long-term success. (3) Messaging: informing the market through advertising or other communications channels that all the problems have been fixed and the company is ready to deliver on its brand promise again (Davis 2003).

With the recent revitalization plan, McDonald's turnaround efforts began in 2003 and included remodeling stores with automated machines in the kitchen, upgrading service, improving employee training, remodeling and streamlining the menu, overhauling cooking procedures, and enhancing the taste and consistency of its food. McDonald's hoped to attract new customers while encouraging existing customers to visit more often, and to create brand loyalty particularly among young adults, kids, and moms. Using mystery shoppers and unannounced inspections, McDonald's attempts to ensure that its outlets adhere to the required standard of service, quality, and cleanliness.

McDonald's best hope of recapturing its sliding market share is to turn to its most innovative franchisees and to rejuvenate its marketing. Typical of any mature product, McDonald's has reached a critical juncture of its life cycle: What it does today will determine whether it will continue to decline or rejuvenate and start its growth cycle again. To formulate the right basis for its service and quality, McDonald's launched the *"I'm lovin' it"* campaign. This new brand positioning is bringing a new attitude and energy to customers and crew alike. Instead of opening many new restaurants, McDonald's has focused on generating more sales from its existing ones. Physically, McDonald's has begun refurbishing restaurants and experimenting with more modern redesign, although some critics consider better manager training to be more important than refurbishments. It also is reviving cooking techniques and sauces used decades ago on some of the most popular sandwiches. Analysts attributed McDonald's new line of premium salads as a major factor contributing to its mid-2003 rebound. The salads are sending a message to customers that it is now acceptable to eat at McDonald's again because the menu is healthier, although the fact that the vast majority still order a burger and fries is reality. This is the second time that McDonald's has experimented with salads (*Business Week* 2004). The first time was in 1987. With the market pushing for a more healthful menu, the company is more serious this time about cleaning up the negative image that the film documentary *Super Size Me* has portrayed.

Every McDonald's store has a "travel path" along which a member of staff must walk to ensure that all is well with its operation to reinforce standardized operating procedures (*The Economist* 2004). The company is now testing small handheld devices that can be used like electronic clipboards by those making the rounds to enhance monitoring. McDonald's detailed plans to drive sales at existing restaurants are by keeping more U.S. stores open longer, including some for 24 hours a day. This policy reflects an attempt to respond to competitors such as Wendy's and Taco Bell, which offer late night drive-through service. The company is also planning for selected stores to accept credit cards and other forms of cashless payment, again a response to similar programs launched by Jack in the Box and Wendy's (Garber 2004). The company is developing a "Flexible Operating Platform" kitchen system to offer breakfast all day long and enable additional menu variety and efficiencies (Anonymous 2006).

Innovate or Perish

Franchisees own 85% of all U.S. McDonald's restaurants. Therefore it is critical for McDonald's to ally with franchisees. For any major renovation or change in its business model, the company must ensure that its franchisees support its plan. Moreover, companies such as McDonald's rely on franchisees to be creative with menu items or service to foster the entrepreneurial spirit in the company's culture. It was the franchisees who had created the winning Big Mac and Egg McMuffin, although the last successful item from McDonald's own test kitchens was Chicken McNuggets in 1983 (Pallavi and Arndt 2003).

At McDonald's Innovation Center, various items are being developed that may change the future of fast food. One experimental item is "Oven Selects," new sandwiches that are being tested for acceptance at 400 restaurants in the United States. If successful, McDonald's will compete more directly with chains such as Subway and other independent operators. This is important because sandwiches outsell hamburgers ten to one in Europe (*The Economist* 2004).

To grow the business in some of its mature markets, McDonald's must take market share from competitors. McDonald's has pioneered gourmet coffee for its customers in the Australian market and later introduced it successfully into the U.S. market (*The Economist* 2004). This concept, called McCafe, now provides coffee lounges inside 500 existing McDonald's restaurants. There is a trade-off for these initiatives. It will be a challenge for the company to manage a multiformat operation under one brand. Having a larger variety of items on the menu means more potential problems and higher costs. It also means McDonald's has to appeal to one group of customers without alienating another (*The Economist* 2004).

KFC was the first Western fast-food chain to open a drive-through in China in 2002. McDonald's followed by opening its first drive-through in China two years later. This is important because an average of 65% of sales at McDonald's in the United States .is generated by drive-through orders (Grant 2006).

In recent years, McDonald's performance in the United Kingdom has been disappointing. Besides closing of poor performers, as the UK market has become more sophisticated, McDonald's is testing five new-look restaurants in a bid to improve its high-street image. This is part of McDonald's strategy of reinventing itself under a program called the "Plan to Win." McDonald's must compete for market share with companies such as Subway to attract new customers. On a global scale, McDonald's is already seeing positive results in 2006 (*Caterer and Hotelkeeper* 2006).

WHAT DOES THE FUTURE HOLD?

The maturing of the fast-food industry has forced key players to rethink their strategies and reinvent their operations. Management reorganization, new product development, aggressive marketing, and strategic redirection helped the industry giants rebound in

late 2003 (Enz 2005). McDonald's new brand direction must be creative, relevant, and connecting to today's culture in new and exciting ways. However, not many people are optimistic about a successful turnaround occurring in a company of McDonald's size unless there are favorable market conditions.

What should McDonald's do now? It is trying to reestablish its dominance by designing a 17,500-square-foot restaurant in New York City. It has outlined a bold turnaround strategy that recommits the chain to several programs widely blamed for the brand's current problems. McDonald's is pursuing modifications rather than dramatic changes in its business plan (*Restaurant Business* 2003). The results have been excellent so far.

The world's biggest fast-food company has pulled off a remarkable comeback. In October 2003 the corporation posted its strongest monthly U.S. sales gain in five years, with a 15% increase after an extensive global reorganization of senior management (Enz 2005). The top 400 largest chains reported a total sales gain of 5.6% in 2002 for a total of $207.6 billion. McDonald's was at the top of the list with around $40.5 billion in sales, followed by Burger King with $11.3 billion.

In the fist half of 2004, sales were up by 13% to $9.1 billion, and net profits rose by 38% to $1.1 billion, compared to the same period a year earlier. In October McDonald's announced stunning third-quarter preliminary results. Its earnings per share jumped by 42%, and sales again grew strongly. However, much of McDonald's growth has come from America. In 2006 the company reported estimated third-quarter earnings per share up 17.2% from a year ago, a global systemwide sales increase of 6.9% in constant currencies, and same-store sales gains in all markets. Domestic McDonald's restaurants posted third-quarter same-store sales gain of 4.1% over the year earlier (*Nation's Restaurant News* 2006).

McDonald's recorded a nearly $50 million first-quarter pretax gain from the initial public stock offering of Chipotle Mexican Grill in January 2006. Chipotle grew from 18 units in 1998 to more than 500 in 2006. The company plans to divest the remaining 69% stake by year-end. The divestiture would enable the company to focus on its burger brand (*Nation's Restaurant News* 2006). Same-store sales rose 7.6% in Europe and 6.1% in McDonald's Asia-Pacific, Middle East, and Africa region (*Nation's Restaurant News* 2006).

To boost its Shanghai-based management team, McDonald's brought in three experienced executives from the United States and Australia in 2005. By 2006 McDonald's had more than 750 restaurants in China and expects to have 1,000 restaurants in China by the 2008 Olympics, which it is sponsoring, in Beijing. Because China is the fastest growing regional business, the company even relocated Tim Fenton, the executive in charge of its Asian operations to Hong Kong. The Asia geographical portfolio, which also includes Middle East and Africa, contributes 8% of McDonald's consolidated operating income and encompasses 15 times zones and 800 languages and dialects (Grant 2006).

DISCUSSION QUESTIONS

Briefly discuss the impact of globalization competition in the quick-service restaurant industry.

1. Using McDonald's as an example, discuss the efficacy of using the coalignment model to assist the firm in responding to changes in the external environment and adapting its internal operations.
2. McDonald's advocates promotion from within when it comes to succession of executive positions. Briefly discuss the importance of leadership in turning around McDonald's from declining sales and profits.
3. Identify the key decisions that have resulted in the most recent successful turnaround for McDonald's.
4. Based on your analysis, explain how the company's implementation of changes in strategy reflected conditions in its environment.

REFERENCES

Bowman, J. 2006. "Can McDonald's Steal Yum's China Crown?" *Media*. January 13, 15.

Business Week. 2004. "McDonald's: Fries with That Salad?" July 5, 72–73.

Caterer & Hotelkeeper. 2006. "Makeover for McDonald's." August 17–23, 8.

Davis, S. 2003. "McDonald's Strategy Doesn't Deliver." *Brandweek* 44, no. 41: 20.

Enz, Cathy A. 2005. "Multibranding Strategy: The Case of Yum! Brands." *Cornell HRA Quarterly*, February.

Garber, A. Z. 2003a. "McD Food: Everything Old Now New Again." *Nation's Restaurant News* 37, no. 15: 1, 80.

———. 2003b. "McD Cooks Up New Strategy to Turn Around Chain." *Nation's Restaurant News* 37, no. 16: 8, 92.

———. 2004. "McD Adds Credit Payment, Extends Hours to Continue Sales Boost." *Nation's Restaurant News* 38, no. 12: 4, 97.

Grant, J. 2006. "McDonald's Drive Towards Big City Sales Expansion Strategy." *Financial Times*. February 22, 12.

Lazo, Shirley A. 2003. "There's Sizzle on That Griddle: McDonald's Plumps Payout Again." *Barron's*. September 22, 29–30

Leung, S., and K. Helliker. 2003. "As McDonald's Braces for Loss, CEO Has a Plan." *Wall Street Journal*. January 20, B1.

Lockyer, S. E. 2006. "McD to Double Payouts to Shareholders over Next 2 Years." *Nation's Restaurant News* 40, no. 42: 9.

MacArthur, K. 2003. "McDonald's Challenge: Winning the Love Back." *Advertising Age* 74, no. 24: 3.

Mullen, R. 2006. "Is McDonald's Still Lovin' It?" *Caterer & Hotelkeeper.* June 1–7, 11.

Nation's Restaurant News. 2006a. "McDonald's Plans Full Chipotle Divestiture by Year-End." May 15, 32.

———. 2006b. "McD CEO Skinner: All-Day Breakfast, More Variety, 'Transparency' Envisioned Via Modular-Kitchen Plan." May 15, 32.

———. 2006c. "McDonald's Says Strong Sales Helped Boost 3rd-Q EPS 17.2%." October 23, 10.

Pallavi, G., and M. Arndt. 2003. "Hamburger Hell." *Business Week.* March 3, 104.

Racanelli, V. J. 2000. "Recipe for Growth." *Barron's* 80, no. 50: 19–20.

Restaurant Business. 2003. "McD's Plan: Back to the Future." February 15, 19.

———. 2002. "Growing Pains." *Barron's* 82, no. 51: 13.

Rogers, D. 2002. "Can Mac Fight Back?" *Marketing.* October 17, 22–23.

SinoCast China Business Daily News. 2006. "McDonald's Seeing China Business Growing Fast." November 10, 1.

Stires, D. 2002 "Fallen Arches." *Fortune* 145, no. 9: 74–76.

The Economist. 2001. "Business: Where's the Beef?; Face Value." November 3, 84+.

———. 2004. "Big Mac's Makeover—McDonald's Turned Around." October 16, 88.

Walkup, C. 2006. "2006 Golden Chain: Jim Skinner." *Nation's Restaurant News* 40, no. 43: 88–89.

Zuber, A. 2003. "McD Plots Turnaround." *Nation's Restaurant News* 37, no. 1: 1–3.

Thinking Strategically

From Chapter 2 of *Strategic Management in the Hospitality Industry*, Third Edition, Michael D. Olsen, Joseph J. West, Eliza Ching Yick Tse. Copyright © 2008 by Pearson Education, Inc. Published by Pearson Prentice Hall. All rights reserved.

Thinking Strategically
A Working Model

Thinking Strategically

Upon completion of this chapter, you will:

1. Understand that strategic management is a way of thinking about the future.
2. Describe the differences among corporate, business, and functional strategies.
3. Comprehend the key concepts of strategy and their role in organizational success.
4. Utilize the strategic management model to develop effective strategies for the future success of the hospitality enterprise.

Key Concepts

Thinking strategically

Corporate, business, and functional strategies

Concepts of strategy

- Environmental assessment
- Strategy formulation
- Strategy choice
- Strategy implementation

The strategy model

Chapter Purpose

The purpose of this chapter is to more completely examine the major components in the underpinning of the coalignment model. It begins with a definition of strategy and strategic management and continues with a discussion of the three levels of strategy in business organizations in general. To further develop and illustrate the concept of the coalignment model, each of the major components—environmental scanning, strategy choice, and firm structure—are discussed and how alignment among the three affect firm performance. An overview of the strategy formulation process is also presented that is consistent with the more detailed version of the coalignment model presented later in the chapter.

Introduction

The coalignment model is further explored in this chapter. Exhibit 1 suggests that firms must achieve an alignment with their environment (labeled environmental events) to make the right strategic investment choices (referred to as strategy choice). They must develop competitive methods that will produce value for the firm (firm performance). These competitive methods should reflect a management philosophy that calls for anticipatory action in the face of rapid change. Once that decision is made, managers allocate the necessary resources to implement and execute them successfully (firm structure). Thus the environment provides the opportunities, and then management decides what investments in competitive methods it will make to take advantage of them, and at that point it consistently allocates resources to those methods that add the greatest value to the firm. This alignment should lead to sustainable competitive advantage and superior returns to the investor. This is the essence of the coalignment model.

To understand this model more completely, we develop a framework that provides concepts that can assist management in accomplishing the objective of coalignment. These concepts include the different levels of strategy, such as corporate, business, and functional. Additional concepts, including environmental scanning, strategy choice, firm structure, and firm performance, are explored. Finally we develop the model in Exhibit 1 into more detail and illustrate how the model can assist managers in formulating strategy.

Thinking Strategically

Before looking at each of the concepts, it is important first to recognize that strategy is not a process, *it is a way of thinking*. It includes many activities that must come together synergistically to produce the results expected by the stakeholders in the firm. To

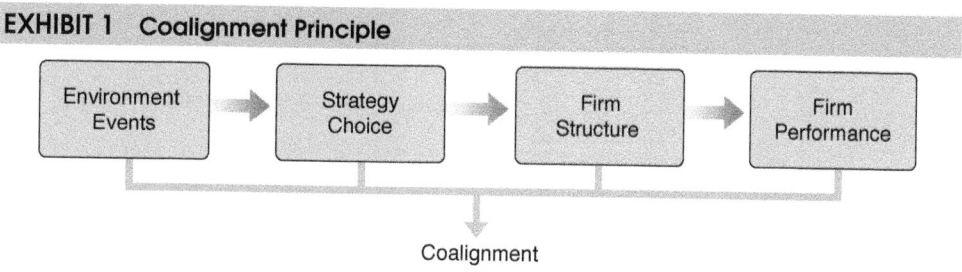

EXHIBIT 1 Coalignment Principle

Environment Events → Strategy Choice → Firm Structure → Firm Performance

Coalignment

achieve this synergy, strategy must be a way of life in the firm, not something that is done once a year. *Strategy* is defined as a consistent pattern of resource allocation directed to those competitive methods that add significant value to the equity base of the firm's owners. It demands high levels of energy and an orientation to the future. It is the activity by which organizational members determine the long-run direction and performance expectations of the organization through ensuring that careful formulation, proper implementation, and continuous evaluation of the strategy take place. In addition, employees at all levels must be involved. Until management and employees are committed, allocate necessary resources, and provide a supportive culture and environment, a successful strategy will probably never be realized.

Corporate, Business, and Functional Strategies

In essence, an organization's strategy provides a basic understanding of how the organization will compete. Strategies can occur at all levels of an organization: corporate, business, and functional. These strategies differ in focus, as well as in responsibility for decision making, time frame for implementation, and specificity (Exhibit 2). Corporate strategy is concerned with the decision regarding what business should the firm be in and is directed toward the achievement of the firm's overall objectives and scope of operation. Business strategy is designed to help each division or business unit of the firm contribute as effectively as possible to the overall company while achieving a competitive advantage in its market. Functional strategies direct the efficient allocation of the organization's resources to each of the various functional areas. These three levels of strategy should be in alignment if the firm is to achieve maximum levels of cash flow per share.

Corporate Strategy

Corporate strategy is the grand design for managing the entire organization. It determines what business in which the firm will be engaged (industries, segments, products, and services). It is a process that establishes what strategic objectives should be pursued and how individual businesses should be managed to achieve those objectives. The CEO

EXHIBIT 2 The Relationship Among Corporate, Business, and Functional Strategies

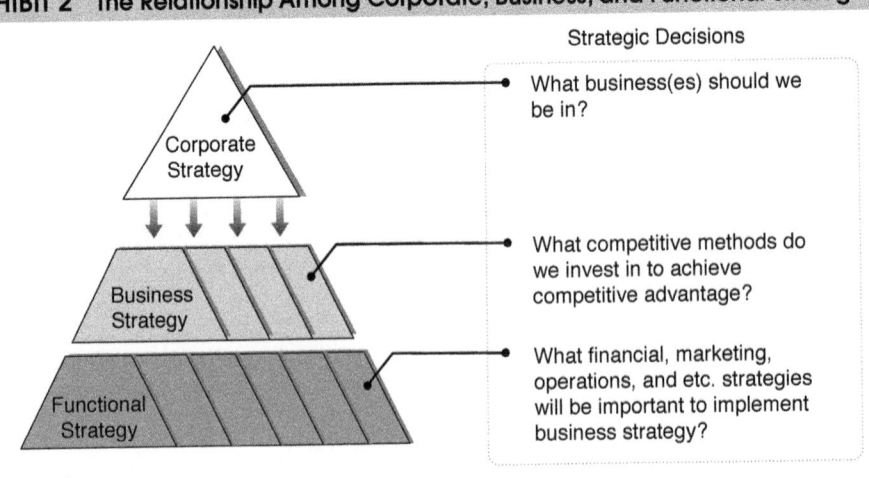

Strategic Decisions

Corporate Strategy

What business(es) should we be in?

Business Strategy

What competitive methods do we invest in to achieve competitive advantage?

Functional Strategy

What financial, marketing, operations, and etc. strategies will be important to implement business strategy?

and/or the top management team is generally responsible for designing the strategic plan that guides the enterprise into a profitable future. The fundamental question for the corporate strategist is to decide whether the firm is going to concentrate on a single business, as in the case of Wendy's, the quick-service hamburger chain, or diversify into different businesses, such as the Cendant Corporation, which includes hotels, car rentals, real estate firms, and time-share businesses under its corporate umbrella.

Once the business or businesses the firm will engage in have been decided on, decisions must then be made on the allocation of resources to be allocated among those businesses. Consequently, the portfolio or mix of businesses, the problems of generating and allocating resources to these businesses, and how different businesses may be integrated to create the maximum return for the investment (synergistic effect) are issues that confront the corporate strategist.

Corporate strategies usually reflect a time frame of from one to ten years. Whether a firm is acquiring another or building a new business from scratch, there are many decisions that must be evaluated and made that require large blocks of time for study and analysis. For example, the process referred to as *due diligence* must be performed by firms who seek to acquire another. This process is designed to evaluate the firm to be acquired by assessing the assets of that firm to determine their long-run viability and quality. Also, it is a thorough review of the firm's past and future performance. This type of study and analysis cannot be done overnight. It often takes months to accumulate the necessary information and then more time to study and analyze it. It is easy to see how one hotel company seeking to acquire another would have to look carefully at all the hotels in the portfolio of the firm to be acquired. If there are hundreds of hotels, this is time consuming and expensive. In another example of this time frame, it may take a firm several years to create a new business.

This was the case when the top management team of Darden Restaurants worked for over two years to launch their Bahama Breeze restaurant concept. They had to engage in product development and testing, site location analysis, and financial feasibility studies before they decided that they had a new business ready to add value to the firm's owners. Their hard work paid dividends because the concept launch was a success. Bahama Breeze continues to grow and evolve and as of September 2005 had 32 restaurants in operation, adding positive cash flow to Darden (according to the Darden Fiscal 2005 midyear report). To continue to maintain its position as the largest casual theme company in the world by investing in new competitive methods, Darden is developing a new restaurant concept: "Seasons 52" in Orlando, Florida.

Ultimately, the corporate decisions such as those just illustrated are the responsibility of the firm's board of directors to make. It is this group of individuals who have to answer to the shareholders of the firm. Increasingly, these decisions are also being influenced by others. Institutional investors who hold a significant number of shares in the firm are becoming more vocal regarding the board's decisions. Environmental groups, employee groups, and regulatory bodies are also having influence on corporate strategic decisions.

Business Strategy

Once the corporate strategy is determined, the next strategy level is business strategy. Business-level strategy is concerned with the question of "how do we compete within this particular industry?" to obtain a strategic advantage over the competition. This level of strategy considers how to use the firm's competitive methods and distinctive competencies to compete in a specific business within a defined industry domain.

Business strategy is directed at determining the competitive methods that companies develop to compete in a specific domain or industry sector. For a company that competes only in one sector, the corporate strategy and business strategy are essentially the same, as in the case of Wendy's, a quick-service hamburger chain. For companies with diversified portfolios such as Cendant Inc., there is usually a difference between the corporate- and business-level strategies. Business-level strategy making is more specific than at the corporate level regarding the methods to use to counter the competition. It focuses on how to compete in a particular industry or product/market segment—that is, what sustainable competitive advantage should be developed or maintained to compete successfully. Thus the distinctive competencies of the firm and its competitive methods are usually the most important components of strategy at this level. We focus primarily on this level of strategic management throughout this text.

The time frames that strategies at the business level cover are very similar to corporate strategies and usually range from one to five years, although firms are experiencing a shortening of this time frame as the business environment becomes more competitive. Normally, the president, executive officers, and heads of functional positions are the ones responsible for formulation at this level of strategy making. Increasingly, this circle of planners is being enlarged to include many more individuals at all levels of the organization. Business strategies must be derived from and supportive of corporate strategies.

As we have mentioned elsewhere in this text, the hospitality firm is really a small- and medium-size enterprise where strategy is local. Thus, although there are many corporate names and brands, the individual hospitality enterprise is really competing locally for business volume. This implies that all the levels of strategy we are discussing here could and often are at work in one single unit, and the individual responsible for the leadership of that firm must wear all the strategy hats we have been discussing.

Functional Strategies

The third level of strategy making is within the business unit at the functional level. Functional strategies are narrower in scope than business strategies. They encompass those activities associated with the running of the day-to-day activities of the business. These activities are detailed in Exhibit 3. They constitute the functions of finance, marketing, human resources, operations, administration, and research and development. Strategy making at this level focuses on implementing the strategic plan so as to achieve the greatest efficiency and effectiveness possible within the resource constraints of the firm.

Whereas business strategy identifies the means to combat one's competitors, functional strategies detail the courses of action in each functional area to achieve successful implementation of the firm's most value adding competitive methods. Not only should strategies in one functional area be consistent with those in all the other functional areas, but they should mesh with and mutually support these competitive methods. This level of strategy is most specific and detailed and covers a time frame of no longer than one year.

Compared to the other levels of strategy, functional strategies change quite frequently, often influenced by competitors' daily movements. Normally, the vice president of each functional area, along with key staff, formulates the strategy, and this level of strategy impacts the operating staff in the greatest degree during their

Functional Area	Elements in which strategy is developed
Finance	Asset management, capital budgeting, capital structure, financing, risk management, financial planning, dividend decisions, forecasting, mergers and acquisitions, control systems, asset valuation
Human Resources	Personnel management, organizational behavior, labor-management relations, leadership, high performance work practice systems
Marketing	Distribution, advertising and promotion, pricing, product and services offered, customer segments, research
Administration	Insurance coverage, accounting systems, management information systems, strategic planning, legal issues, decision making systems
Operations	Production management, quality control, resource acquisition and storage, safety and security, process management
Research and Development	Product development, customer development, new business development, mergers and acquisitions

EXHIBIT 3   Functional Strategies

daily work experiences. The principal focus of functional strategies is on the maximization of resource productivity.

In considering functional level strategies in today's contemporary business environment, management must consider the fact that this environment requires managers who are able to perform as multifunctional decision makers. In the context of traditional management thinking, these functions were often considered separate activities to be performed by specialists who had acquired specific qualifications in the functional area, with little or no interaction with other functional managers. Functional managers responsible for the marketing and finance functions would only come together when required to create strategy at this level. Otherwise, they frequently considered themselves as mutually exclusive of each other and acted like rivals or held conflicting postures. In the present environment, this idealogy is becoming increasingly unacceptable as firms demand that their management team synthesize and integrate the knowledge they possess in each functional area to achieve the best strategic decisions possible. Today's manager is expected to think strategically and multifunctionally. Only in this thinking mode can we expect to achieve the highest value-adding strategies for the firm's stakeholders.

It should be stated here that although the preceding discussion reflects the normative literature in strategy and appears oriented to large corporate organizations, for the small-and medium-size firm, these levels of strategy may all blur together. In other words, these levels of strategy are not mutually exclusive. Managers of these types of firms may not have the resources to organize their firms this way and often face the challenges of doing all the strategic thinking while trying to operate the business successfully on a daily basis. This is one of the reasons that the coalignment model is offered in this text because it can be applied to any level or size of organization. Note that the model itself emerged from over 20 years of research in the hospitality industry.

Major Concepts of Strategy Making and the Coalignment Model

Developing strategy is not a onetime activity; it is something that is done continuously. It is a way of thinking about competing in the future. Strategy is incorporated in the day-to-day activities of all levels of personnel within the firm including frontline customer employees through to top-level management. It focuses on how the firm should compete by anticipating what competitive methods will lead the firm to financial success. Financial success is defined throughout this text as the maximization of cash flow per unit of equity ownership of the firm. Throughout, strategy requires the firm to match the choice of competitive methods with the opportunities in the environment and to allocate its resources to those methods that generate the highest level of cash flow per share of equity.

To help us to understand this dynamic ongoing relationship, there are four constructs that we need to explore: (1) environmental scanning and assessment, (2) strategy choice, (3) firm structure and (4) firm performance. A summary discussion of each construct is presented in the sections to follow. You can use the more detailed version of the coalignment model presented in Exhibit 4 to visualize these discussions.

Environmental Scanning and Assessment

Environmental scanning and assessment has become an increasingly important function of the firm. Today, change is occurring throughout all elements of the business environment making scanning one of the most important responsibilities for all those with management responsibilities. The environment creates uncertainty. It is discontinuous, presenting new challenges to management almost daily. It is increasingly complex and unforgiving. Management's primary responsibility here is to identify the forces driving change within the environmental domain in which the business unit operates. Management must be able to understand what variables comprise the major forces that will provide management with the opportunities to seek competitive advantage. These variables come together to form patterns that will likely influence how customers and businesses relate to each other in the future. Successful identification of these variables is contingent on the perceptual, cognitive, and experiential skills of management.

Once management has identified the patterns, variables, and forces emanating from the environment, it must learn to understand how these forces are evolving. The history of the evolution, the speed of this evolution, and its emerging intensity are of great interest to management as it seeks to identify the opportunities that are available to it. This ability takes time, often years to develop, and requires of the manager the ability to analyze and synthesize large quantities of information to be able to understand how forces will impact the firm. Once this understanding is achieved, managers will then possess an important skill to be used in identifying and selecting the most important opportunities to pursue to achieve competitive advantage in the marketplace.

The environment presents opportunities and threats to every business. Opportunities are situations that offer an organization the chance to accomplish its value-adding objectives and/or to excel, whereas threats are those situations that prevent the firm from achieving its goals and perhaps even threaten its existence. To succeed in this context, the firm has to monitor the remote, task, functional, and firm categories of the environment

EXHIBIT 4 Strategic Management Model

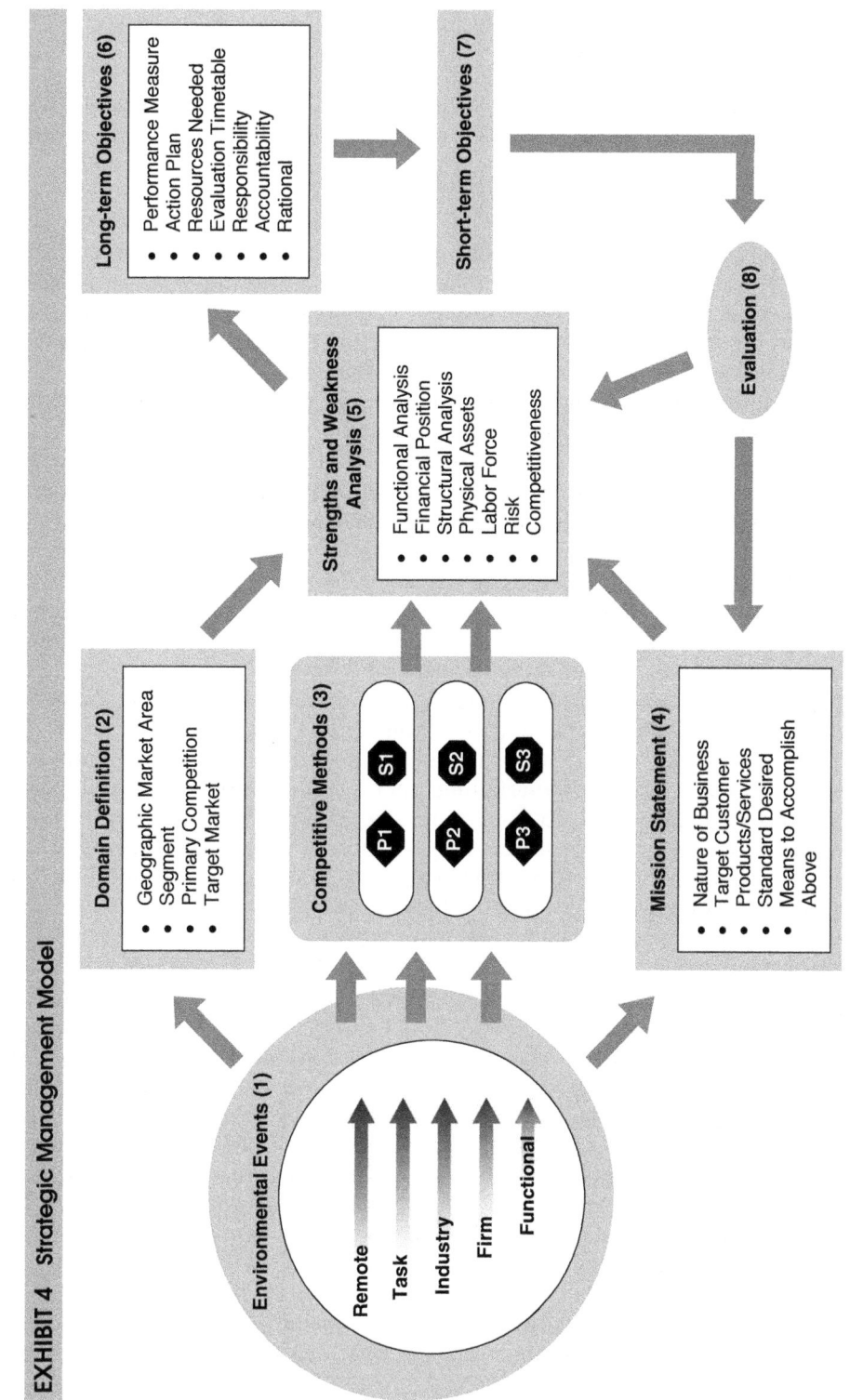

of the business so those forces that can cause the greatest threats and/or generate the greatest opportunities in the future can be accurately identified.

In looking at the model in Exhibit 4, the environment is in the first symbol (#1). It is a symbol containing arrows designed to reflect forces driving change. Within the symbol are references to the remote, task, and firm environments that constitute the major categories of the environment that executives should scan regularly. We have provided a brief review here of the subcategories of each and detail these more completely in the section of this text on the environment.

The remote environment consists of forces that originate external to the firm and, as a rule, cannot be altered or controlled by actions of the organization. Nonetheless, a firm must constantly and systematically scan the environment to anticipate the potential impact that forces emerging in the remote environment will have on the firm's ultimate financial performance. Examples of remote environmental categories that should be monitored to identify these forces are sociocultural, technological, political/legal, ecological, and economic factors.

The task environment includes categories that have more direct impact and usually with more immediate consequence to a firm than the remote environment. Examples of task environment categories include market and consumer behavior, industry structure, competitors, government agencies, and suppliers. Often, the patterns of change developing in these categories originate in the remote environment and then create impact in the task environment. For example, an improved economy (remote environment category) can result in greater disposal income for the customer (task environment category) and more business for hospitality enterprises. Strategic actions by a firm can also influence the forces of change in this category of environment resulting in a more competitive situation for firms.

The functional environment consists of forces driving change in areas such as finance, human resources, marketing, operations, research and development, and administration. Changes occur here usually as a result of advances in the body of knowledge in each functional area. They also occur from changes in generally accepted best practices taking place in each. As firms continue to seek the best methods and processes to compete successfully, they often discover better ways of achieving improved performance in each area. Unfortunately, these are quickly copied by firms throughout an industry. Therefore, it is essential that managers scan the functional environment to be sure that they stay current with, or even ahead of, their competition in the industry.

The firm environment is especially important to the hospitality enterprise. We stated earlier in the discussion of the task environment that managers should monitor their competitors. For the hospitality firm that competition comes from international and national as well as local firms. The hospitality enterprise often competes at all the levels. They feel the pressure from international, national, or regional chains and the strength of their marketing and advertising programs, but they also feel this competition from local firms. The hospitality firm is unique in this way. Conditions locally may not always mirror things nationally or regionally. Therefore, the firm must be sure to understand what forces are driving changes at both levels.

The concept of the environment and environmental scanning is important to the overall understanding of strategic management, especially in today's dynamic world.

Anticipating change and leading competitors in taking advantage of the opportunities resulting from this change is what management is all about today. This concept is complex. It requires managers to possess the ability to think and act differently. They must be future oriented and able to move swiftly, sometimes at considerable risk, if they are to be able to add value to the firms they manage.

Strategy Choice

The concept of choice focuses on the competitive methods (CMs) that firms invest in to achieve their objectives. The term *choice* is crucial to understanding this concept. It suggests that management is constantly engaged in making choices about how to compete. These choices should be the result of the *environmental scanning* activity of the coalignment model. This effort requires that only those competitive methods that generate the highest levels of cash flow should be chosen by the firm to meet the opportunities provided by the environment.

Competitive methods (CMs) are defined as the portfolio of products and services that the firm chooses to compete within its environment as illustrated in symbol 3 of Exhibit 4. The ovals in the symbol represent the CMs, and within each are products and services of the firm making up this portfolio. The choice of each product and service and how they are combined into a portfolio is the responsibility of the firm's management. This leadership group will make its decision about what products and services to invest in by considering the opportunities presented by the environment, the forecasts of cash flow from each product and/or service, and how this investment will impact the value of the firm. In this process, careful scrutiny will be given to the viable economic life of each competitive method. This scrutiny will include a comparison of how each competitive method stands relative to the competition not only now but also in the future.

A CM must be considered the primary reason why customers are willing to purchase the products and services of the firm. They drive revenue and must be managed with passion if the firm is to meet customer expectations. They also require resources of all types to be able to properly meet the expectations of customers, employees, and owners. Their role is to produce value. They must be considered as investments and valued as such. This requires the use of financial management skills related to the valuation of the business and what creates value for that business. In creating value the CM must meet the return on capital expectations of the owner as well as compensating for inflation or risk. These three imperatives are critical if the manager expects to grow the business.

The value creation capability of the CM is determined by discounted cash flow analysis and techniques. The net present value (NPV) is often the most preferred technique. Simply put, the total value of the firm is the sum total of all the NPVs of the CMs the firm has invested in. Therefore, from a strategic perspective the manager must direct resources and capabilities to those CMs that create the greatest value for the firm.

Meeting the investor's demands relative to these imperatives is not a simple task in the service industries. Unlike manufactured products such as airplanes and consumer products like Coca-Cola, services are very intangible and subject to very short life-spans. Therefore, strategy choice in the service business is very complex compared to more tangible products. Seeking to obtain a constant cash flow stream from a customer over the longest chronological period as possible in the life of that customer requires strategic thinking that is much more agile and future oriented. It requires strategy choices that challenge the very foundations of the coalignment model. Put another way, the alignment is far more tenuous in the hospitality industry than in most. The portfolio of products and services making up each competitive method must be viewed as constantly changing within the context of future-oriented decisions regarding what to invest in. These conditions clearly validate the statement made earlier: *Strategy is a way of thinking*, not a process one does once a year.

Firm Structure and Core Competencies

In Exhibit 1, the third construct in the coalignment process is referred to as firm structure. This construct of the model relates to how the firm ensures the consistent allocation of resources to the competitive methods that are viewed as creating the greatest value. This is a rather complex construct because it has so many dimensions to consider, as indicated in the symbols 5 through 8 in Exhibit 4. The manager must be able to develop a framework for analyzing the competencies that are necessary to execute the CM properly and then assess the current strengths and weaknesses relative to those competencies. Once the manager knows and understands this assessment, it then becomes essential that the CMs and CCs are in alignment. If not, the CMs chosen to add value in the future may not reach performance expectations. Additionally this match is essential if the firm expects to achieve sustainable advantage within the competitive set of firms it competes with daily.

Implementation refers to this resource allocation process. Resources are defined as capital, human, and materials. Implementation means bringing all competencies into alignment so there is no compromise in achieving the mission of the firm. Generally, these competencies are believed to provide the firm with competitive advantage. The alignment between core competencies and competitive methods is perhaps the most important internal match-up that can be achieved. If a firm is to realize its intended strategy, it is at this juncture that management must focus all its alignment energies.

Strategy implementation can be most directly defined as a number of variables that come together most effectively to achieve greater value for the firm. These variables refer to the *processes* used by the organization to achieve successful implementation. The *processes* used in this setting refer to how the firm has set up its systems for planning and control, resource allocation, management information, and rewards and incentives. Also included here is how the enterprise approaches its training and education efforts as well as the strategic thinking process itself. This should be achieved through the financial strength of the firm, and thus this can then be considered a key competency as well.

If the firm is to achieve coalignment, then, it must not only consider the alignment between competitive methods and the environment. It must also be sure that it achieves alignment within the process variables that constitute the enterprise. This alignment can only be achieved if management recognizes that it is the choice of competitive methods that must drive resources allocation and not the opposite. That is, the process variables should not be allowed to overly influence the decision on what competitive methods to invest in. They should only be considered after this choice is made. These variables must be evaluated in terms of their strengths and weaknesses as they relate to the firm's competitive methods.

Once the firm has assessed its core competencies and considered carefully the process variables that constitute the alignment, it must conduct a thorough review of the strengths and weaknesses of the alignment relationships. Therefore every ingredient making up the alignment must be evaluated in this way. To the extent that they constitute strengths, management must determine why and how they are strengths so they may allocate resources to preserve this strength. To the extent that they are weaknesses, management must concentrate on allocating resources to strengthen those that are central to the competitive methods that generate the highest levels of cash flow per share.

Once the strengths and weaknesses analysis has been completed, management engages in establishing the firm's short- and long-term objectives (symbols 6 and 7). One criterion that is most important in the implementation process is the need to be sure that a majority of the firm's objectives are tied to the alignment between core competencies and competitive methods. In other words, management must review each objective and ask this key question: How does it relate to our competitive methods and the core competencies needed to execute the methods? How this question is answered is a good test as to how well alignment is going in a firm. If the objectives developed cannot be easily and completely tied to the firm's most valuable competitive methods, it is highly unlikely that management is guiding the firm toward strategy realization.

There are some objectives that must be set that do not directly relate to each competitive method. These usually relate to goals mandated by laws and regulations. Laws mandating environmental practices, or adjusting facilities for those customers with disabilities, are examples of such objectives if a firm is not in compliance. Other examples of objectives not related to specific competitive methods relate to such basic administrative needs as new computers, software, or investments in insurance programs for risk reduction purposes. What management must keep in mind is that if it is to add value to the firm, these objectives must be in proper balance with those directed at competitive methods. In other words, effort must be continuously made to be sure that attention is directed at the value producers.

Objectives fall into two major categories: routine and exception. The routine objectives are designed to target performance for each of the firm's competitive methods. In other words, each competitive method has a targeted level of value-adding performance. Setting routine objectives has been very much a part of management literature for quite some time. In most cases these objectives have focused on such key result areas such as sales targets, cost reduction, performance process improvement, and so on. Although these are important objectives, they are seldom linked to specific competitive methods. They are generic objectives. Setting objectives in this fashion creates performance pressure and often does result in improvement. However, unless objectives are linked specifically to the most important value-producing methods, there is much less likelihood that the firm will achieve the realization of its strategy.

The second category of objectives are those that focus on exceptions and often reflect the efforts of the firm to create new products and services. Put another way, they represent out-of-the-ordinary goals. For example, if a firm has decided to move forward and invest in a new competitive method, it may want to engage in research and development activities where the objectives would focus on determining the feasibility of such an investment. Exceptions are also possible where a firm may have to work to come up to standard regarding legislative or regulatory environments. Here again, the rationale used by management must be that the objective is focused on a competitive method that has the potential for producing positive value-adding results.

The objectives in both categories must meet certain criteria. First, they must be measurable. As indicated throughout this text so far, the one measure related to strategy we recommend is cash flow per share of equity ownership. Second, the objective must be time oriented. Short-term objectives are generally accepted to be one year or less; long term are considered to be over a period of one or more years. Third, the objectives must be obtainable. Implied in this last criterion is the fact that objectives must be realizable given the circumstances, resources, and capabilities of the firm. This is perhaps the most challenging of the three criteria in this world of fast change. With new products and services being introduced at a more constant rate, managers must accept the fact that their investments must now reach full potential in a much shorter period or be abandoned, thus making objectives ever more challenging.

Objectives are the blueprint of implementation. They are the prescriptions for resource allocation. They define the priorities and become the primary yardstick for performance. They are the thread that weaves the cloth of strategy. No objective should exist that does not support the competitive methods chosen by the firm. As you will see later in the chapters on structure, the first thing that must be done to be sure this fabric is strong is to require each objective to be compared with the environmental event driving change and to be tied to a competitive method that is taking advantage of the opportunities presented by these events. The second thing is the comparison with the mission and domain of the firm. Here the manager must be sure that the objective is consistent with these two important elements of strategy. Third, regarding the relationship of the objective to the competitive method, does it meet the goals of no objectives being written that do not relate to a competitive method? Lastly, does the objective accurately reflect the core competencies of the firm and take full advantage of them? If the manager is able to meet these criteria, she or he can confidently say that coalignment has been achieved. All that is left is to manage the execution and follow-through to achieve the value-adding potential.

Evaluation is essential to be sure that execution and follow-through occur (symbol 8). Evaluation can occur at several levels of the organization, from overall strategy to individual performance review. Our focus here is on the overall strategic plan. In this case, management and employees are charged with the responsibility of assessing whether or not the firm is actually following the correct course. This decision is made based on the thorough analysis of the environment and the changes occurring in that environment. If significant patterns of change are developing, it may then become time to evaluate thoroughly the total mix of competitive methods deployed by the firm or only just a few. If a significant number are out of alignment, the firm must also evaluate its domain and mission statement. This strategic evaluation must be done frequently, such as once each calendar quarter, and more completely every year.

On a more regular basis, the firm's competitive methods must be evaluated. The first question asked is how well the method is meeting its cash flow per share projections. Second, the focus should turn to the potential for this to continue. In other words, what is the life cycle of the products and services making up the method? This requires input that is based on effective environmental scanning. The best way to accomplish this type of evaluation is to put it on the agenda of the regular meetings of management so the economic life of each product and service can be assessed. It is so important it should be the first item on the agenda.

The next step in evaluation is to look at whether or not objectives are being met at realistic levels and times. Here, the focus is on how well resources are being deployed to execute the competitive methods. Attention is applied in two ways. First, are the processes used to implement competitive methods working as planned? If not, management must determine why. This leads to the second question: Are the necessary resources being applied in the desired manner to the correct methods? This level of evaluation is more operational and tactical. It is most closely tied to implementation.

Evaluation is assisted by effective management information systems that provide management needed data on how each competitive method is performing. What is important here is that the management information system reflects the activity of the competitive method. Activity-based systems allow management to manage and control the performance of each method and become one of its most important allies in the implementation process.

At the start of this chapter we said that strategy is not a process, it is a way of thinking about the future and how the firm will compete in the future. We also suggested that the process was ongoing, not a onetime thing. The essential element in the implementation process that helps ensure that the process is continuous is the evaluation effort. Evaluation is the element that focuses on the performance of each competitive method. It must measure the value-adding capability of each competitive method against objectives.

Firm Performance

We have stated thus far that this chapter on strategy is designed to link strategy and performance. The focus is on value. Strategy and strategic thinking leads to value creation. There are many ways to measure value, but we prefer to do so using the metric of cash flow per share of ownership equity. Because the service industry as exemplified by the hospitality industry is very labor and capital intense and the transaction between the customer and the firm is so immediate, we argue throughout that cash flow from operations is the most realistic measure of performance. Our argument is that if cash flow from the strategic decisions made relative to CMs is maximized, cash flow to the investor is most likely also going to be maximized. Thus our judgment on the value-adding capability of the manager will be based on how well CMs meet the three investor imperatives stated earlier.

Strategy Formulation

Although strategic management is *a way of thinking*, strategy formulation is a process. It is the activity that management engages in to establish the direction of the firm's future. As a concept, the formulation process is most closely represented by Exhibit 4. The coalignment model is a reflection of the normal flow of activities that take place in the strategy formulation process. Although it implies that formulation begins with scanning the environment and ends with the evaluation process, it should not convey to the future strategist that this is a onetime thing. It simply represents an orderly process that must occur if a firm initially is to develop its strategic direction. Once the process is completed for the first time, it then becomes a part of the manager's daily activities. It becomes a way of thinking in which each element of the model is in constant evolution. The paragraphs and subsections to follow will provide a brief overview of each step in the formulation process.

As the model suggests, firms begin to formulate strategy by *scanning the environment* (the arrow symbols labeled 1) in which they plan to compete. We have made this symbol the largest in the model to convey the importance of this activity to the entire strategic management process. Within the symbol is a list of the possible categories of the environment (as outlined earlier) that management must scan for opportunities that lead to competitive advantage. After scanning this environment, the next activity is to define the business *domain* that will constitute the boundaries in which the firm will compete. This is necessary so management will be able to understand, analyze, and monitor changes in the environment to achieve a competitive leadership position within the boundaries of this domain (symbol 2).

Once the domain has been established, the firm's leaders then identify the competitive methods they will invest in to take advantage of the opportunities presented (symbol 3). These competitive methods (as indicated in the model by the ovals in the symbol) consist of the products and services (as indicated by the six- and eight-sided symbols inside the oval) that are combined together into portfolios in ways that will allow firms to achieve sustainable competitive advantage and the highest level of cash flow generation per share of ownership. Once these decisions have been made, it is then time to establish the firm's *mission statement* (symbol 4).

The mission statement guides the firm as it seeks to achieve its long-term objectives. There are no universally recognized guidelines for writing mission statements. In general, they should be short so they can be easily communicated to customers, employees, investors, and/or owners. They should reflect the intentions of the firm as it seeks to implement its strategy. The mission statement becomes the guide to action for all members of the organization. The key components generally present in mission statements are listed in symbol 4 and reviewed in the paragraphs to follow.[1]

As the model indicates, the mission statement describes the nature of the business and should reflect the corporate-, business-, and functional-level strategies of the firm. This refers to whether the firm is a service business, like restaurants and hotels, or a production business, such as an equipment manufacturer. This sets the general direction and defines the boundaries of the business so resources can be allocated to the most value-adding competitive methods.

Once the nature of the business is defined, then the target customers are identified. Today, the definition of the target customer is changing. In the early stages of the field of marketing, one of the most important concepts to emerge was the target market. Marketing executives, consultants, and scholars stressed the importance of knowing your targeted customer. To accomplish this, managers were encouraged to segment their customers into demographic or psychographic groups. From this thinking, segment labels, such as business travelers, leisure travelers, budget travelers, and others, have served to guide the strategic thinking of many firms. Firms were encouraged to position themselves within a segment so they could target new customers within a segment. This has led to a variety of brands and products in the hospitality industry.

Today, with the increasing role of technology in marketing, a new perspective is emerging on the target customer. It is referred to as *the segment of one*. What this implies is that customers are becoming defined more individualistically. They are demanding more customized products and services to meet their needs and will make their purchase decisions by selecting the products and services that most directly meet these needs. If hospitality enterprises know what these are and can consistently provide them, they will likely get this business. Thus, although the traditional mission statement has been heavily influenced by the marketing thinking of large segments, it is now becoming more defined by the products and services offered.

The products and services offered by the hospitality firm today are expected to meet the needs of these more individualistic, discriminating, and demanding customers. The hospitality enterprise must include a sufficient number of competitive methods to be able to attract those customers falling into the *segment of one* category.

The mission statement should also contain the guiding values of the firm. These values include how the firm plans to treat the customer, employee, and owner. The idea of core values is important so all members of the organization work in concert with each other as they guide the firm toward achieving its objectives. Without a declaration of these values, firms have difficulty in building an essential culture that will serve as an enabling force for achieving their intended strategy.

The last element normally found in a mission statement is a pronouncement of what means will be used to achieve strategy. This often contains such terms as *efficiency, thoroughness,* and *reliability.* It also suggests how resources will be used to achieve goals. So comments such as "respectful of the environment" or "achieving diversity" are often used. Although these are similar to statements that could also be included in the statement of core values, they are mentioned separately here because many firms prefer to identify and highlight them separately.

It must be reemphasized here that the activities represented by symbols 1 through 4 in the model occur routinely. They are iterative, constantly in a state of change and evolution. As the environment changes, so too does the firm's choice of competitive methods. Even the domain and mission statement may change. The interaction of these activities should not be thought of as based on linear thinking. A change in any one can result in a change in all of them. Management must be prepared to live in this uncertain world where change is the state of nature.

SUMMARY

Strategic thinking is the most important skill a manager can have. This skill is developed over time as managers experience success associated with their strategy efforts. It demands a thorough understanding of the concepts of environmental scanning and analysis, strategy choice, and firm structure. The primary underpinning of this understanding is the coalignment model. Only if managers have a deep understanding of each construct can they use this knowledge to realize their intended strategies.

DISCUSSION QUESTIONS

1. Explain the similarities among corporate, business, and functional strategies.
2. Discuss why strategy is a way of thinking as opposed to simply a process.
3. Explain the key relationships among the constructs of the coalignment model.
4. Discuss how the mission statement reflects the strategy of the firm.
5. How does strategic thinking add value to the firm?

C A S E   S T U D Y

Strategy for Mature Life Cycle: Yum! Brands

COMPETITIVE STRATEGIES FOR SURVIVAL AND PROSPERING IN THE MATURING INDUSTRY

The food service industry in the United States, a $440 billion market, is maturing. It has showed signs of maturity with intensive competition and slow same-store sales growth. The leading chains of the fast-food segment of the foodservice industry, McDonald's, Burger King, and Wendy's, are chasing the same customer base. To survive and prosper in the maturing industry, operators are forced to rethink their strategies to satisfy the changing demands of the customers; that is, strategy is a major determinant of success. The need for the operators to develop new, differentiated, and effective strategies is greater than ever before (Cunneen 2004).

Facing strong competition, chains, regardless of the size, have to be creative. Among the key players in the industry, there are differences in the strategies that they espouse. The quick-service restaurant industry has traditionally expanded by multiunit franchising with operators concentrating on a single concept. For example, McDonald's has grown to its current size and market share by focusing on a core brand. In the late 1990s, as part of its strategy to cater to the trend toward the middle ground between limited service fast food and full table service, or fast casual dining, McDonald's had diversified through a variety of investments in fast casual concepts, including the acquisition of Boston Market, Chipotle

Mexican Grill, and Donatos Pizza, and an initial 33% stake in the British quality sandwich chain Pret A Manger. However, the turn of the century saw McDonald's reformulating its strategy once again to ensure greater corporate focus on its namesake brand. The company divested some partner brands such as Donatos Pizza. Other brands like Boston Market will continue to develop independently, without significant resource investment by McDonald's. This way, the company grows substantially in sales simply by focusing on the basics of quality, service, cleanliness, and value, as it was before (Cunneen 2004).

On the other hand, other operators in the industry have responded to environmental forces through multibranding. In fact, it has become a major trend in the industry, which some even believe is changing the face of the industry. Multibranding is seen as portfolio management similar to stock portfolio management (Enz 2005). The philosophy is that two brands are better than one. Achieving higher unit volumes is at the heart of the corporate multibranding strategy. The goal of adopting this strategy is to attract customers in new towns without big advertising dollars by offering a wider selection of food and without opening new locations, which is expensive. Big brands share real estate in prime locations to save costs and facilitate expansion. Some brands even share the kitchen with a competitor to facilitate nationwide growth, such in the case of Good Time Burgers teaming up with Taco John's

(Muller 2005). If they operated separately in the same market, they would be major competitors. This way they share customers. In addition to Yum! Brands, other examples includes Starbucks and Bruegger's Bagels, Taco Bell in Target stores, Dunkin' Donuts in Wal-Mart (*Denver Post* 2004). In the case of HMS Host Corp., it is a multiconcept with over 100 brands. This company commented that one brand would not make it given the mature stage of the industry life cycle. It has built an infrastructure with a portfolio of national and international brands covering a variety of day parts (Bernstein 2003).

MULTIBRANDING AND YUM! BRANDS

Yum! Brands has taken the lead role in co-locating its various brands. Yum! Brands Inc., the parent company of KFC, Pizza Hut, and Taco Bell, is the world biggest food management group. Thus it is one of the major players in the highly competitive quick-service segment. Each of its restaurant concepts is a leader in its respective segment: chicken, pizza, and Mexican food. Since the pairing of Taco Bell and KFC in the mid-1990s, the concept of multibranding has firmly taken hold in the quick-service restaurant industry (Waldner 2005). Multibranding was a key growth strategy by PepsiCo until 1997 when the company spun off KFC, Pizza Hut, and Taco Bell to form Tricon Global Restaurants (Currin 2003). PepsiCo's very fast-moving, individually focused, consumer packaged goods and entrepreneurial culture proved not to be a great fit for the relatively mature, slow-moving, team-oriented, and quick-service restaurant business. In other words, a performance-based, consumer-packaged-goods company like PespiCo was not a natural fit with the restaurant business. The company began to change its business and corporate culture, transforming itself into a successful restaurant-focused company.

Yum! Brands also owns A&W All-American Food and Long John Silver's. Although a smaller player in the large hamburger segment, A&W is the longest-running quick-service restaurant in America. It has long adopted a multibranding strategy. In fact, A&W's first cobranding deal was with a KFC franchisee before it was acquired by Yum! Brands. The cobranding strategy developed over the years and proved a successful way to grow the brand. Later when the company Yorkshire Global Restaurants bought Long John Silver's, it put Long John Silver's and A&W together as cobranded partners. The cobranding strategy enabled the two well-known but troubled franchise systems, A&W and Long John Silver's, to capitalize on their brand equity and bring new life to them, which resulted in a successful turnaround. This strategy ultimately led to their acquisition in 2002 by Yum! Brands (Larson 2003). To reflect the expansion of its company portfolio, Tricon changed its name to Yum! Brands.

According to the company, multibranding is a result of years of research and the development of its customer base. An extensive marketplace planning process is undertaken to decide which two restaurant brands should be housed under one roof; it takes all aspects into consideration, including demographics, real estate costs, traffic, and competition, among others. The company's decision to implement its multibranding strategy was an attempt to offer its consumers more choice, convenience, and value in one restaurant location from a combination of its various brands (Currin 2003). The company claimed that customers preferred branded choices six to one over a single brand restaurant. Yum! Brands has seen increased sales in locations that house more than one brand over its traditional locations. With multibranding, the company's sales increased at least 20% on average with the second brand, and unit cash flow increased on average

30% (Currin 2003). The idea behind the cobranding was to build and improve profits in the restaurants.

The multibranding concept has proven successful for Yum! Brands partially due to the high percentage of patrons who use drive-through window service. In fact, one of Yum! Brands' major strategies is to drive global growth by leading the way in multibranding innovation. Yum uses this strategy to leverage its major brands and build penetration for its smaller Long John Silver's, A&W, and Pasta Bravo brands (Currin 2003).

In 2003 this publicly traded company operated over 33,000 units in 100 countries. In the United States, Yum! Brands operates over 2,600 multibrand restaurants representing about 10% of its total traditional domestic units (Currin 2003). The company's U.S. operation has only average sales and is under pressure to improve the sales performance of restaurants through improvement in marketing and operations. Domestically, the cobranding strategy of pairing at least two concepts under one roof remains a top priority. For the future, the company plans to grow Taco Bell (with 3% sales increase in first quarter 2004) and Pizza Hut (10% increase for the same period) but believes that KFC's growth has leveled off (4% decrease in sales). The company has stopped KFC from further U.S. cobranding; that is, cobranding will be left for the other four brands. It also has heightened its emphasis to grow Long John Silver's into a national brand.

As the multibranding leader, Yum! Brands has created a structure to drive that strategy. Recently, the company launched a "One Best Way" strategy for technology at all five chains. The project will provide all brands with a common point of sale (POS) system because some of the exiting systems were aging and outdated. These old systems made support and maintenance costs very costly. The prototype technology launched features of an open platform that can be integrated easily with back-office systems.

Yum! Brands Inc. was among the four restaurant chains that are on *Fortune* magazine's list of the "50 Best Companies for Minorities" in 2004. The other three restaurant companies on the list included McDonald's Corp. (rank number 1), Denny's Inc. (number 5), and Darden Restaurants Inc. (number 33). Yum moved up 20 positions points from its debut spot at number 35 in 2003 to number 15 in 2004. The company considers diversity an important way of doing business, and its diversity practices gives it a competitive edge. Its diversity strategy includes a mentoring program, leadership development, and franchise and community involvement (Berta 2004).

YUM! BRANDS IN CHINA

With a higher increase in international sales as compared to domestic sales, Yum is increasingly looking abroad for expansion. In fact, overseas expansion will remain Yum's primary earnings per share (EPS) driver for years to come. For its international market, Yum is adding single-brand restaurants overseas, primarily through KFC and Pizza Hut expansion (Garber 2003). Internationally, China is the company's number-one market, but the United Kingdom is also very strong with 600 each of Pizza Hut and KFC restaurants. For the moment, Yum dominates the quick-service and casual dining sectors in China. Yum! Brands, Inc. has over 1,600 KFC units and 220 Pizza Huts in China. KFC is in 280 cities, and Pizza Huts operate in 43 cities. Yum opened its first KFC in China in 1987 and its first Pizza Hut in 1990 (*SinoCast China Business Daily News* 2004a).

To the company, the only competition outside of the United States is McDonald's. The number of outlets of KFC in China is almost double the market penetration of the McDonald's 600 units.

The China market has grown so large that the company will establish the China region as a third reporting segment in 2005, along with the United States and the rest of the international markets. All three report quarterly. In 1998 the United States generated 80% of Yum's operating profit, and China contributed only 2%; all other foreign countries accounted for 18% (Spielberg 2004). The company expects half of its operating profit by 2007 to come from international operations and half of that to come from its China division, with $1.1 billion annual sales by 2007 (Spielberg 2004). The company even predicts that at one point in the future the market in China will be so significant that operations there will surpass those in the United States (Spielberg 2004). Yum also is developing some new concepts in China, including one called "East Dawning." The strategy in China is to build dominant restaurant brands in every significant category.

The company supports its Chinese operations with a countrywide distribution system that has 21 warehouses and more than 450 employees. The system has helped the company penetrate across the country. It has just completed construction of the largest logistic distribution center in Asia in the Beijing Economic Techno-logical Development Area. The distribution center provides services to the 250 KFCs and Pizza Huts in Beijing, Hebei Province, Inner Mongolia Autonomous Region, and Shanxi Province, with an annual distributing capacity of 5 million boxes (*SinoCast China Business Daily News* 2004b).

IS THE MULTIBRAND CONCEPT FOR EVERYONE?

The foodservice industry is not the only industry that has adopted a multibranding concept. There are successful applications of a cobranding or multibranding concept in the marketing of prepared food products. The advantages of cobranding include borrowing expertise from sibling brands, leveraging combined brand equity, reducing production costs, reducing marketing costs, expanding brand meaning, increasing consumer access points, and increasing unit revenues.

However, those concepts do not guarantee success if executed ineffectively. Even with a company's large size and support network, such a strategy must be conducted very carefully. Restaurant cobranding raises some potential problems. Not every franchisee has the infrastructure to deal with different brands. There are documented cases of failure. Combining operations can become complex; franchisees must adhere to two separate contracts in one store. Operationally, two different sets of menu items and operating procedures can cause confusion among managers and employees. It may potentially slow down the time for production and service. There is a need for very specific skills in multiunit franchising because requirements vary in each chain. With more items to handle, there is a need for increasing costs in training employees in two systems. There are also more items to stock from the inventory perspective. From a marketing perspective, companies also risk diminishing their brands. It may dilute the image of one brand and hurt sales with the addition of another brand in the same restaurant space. They may compromise their signage and their restaurant ambiance. Customers may be confused in terms of the focus of what the restaurant is offering, especially for new brands. For brands that do not fit, potential customers may be driven away instead.

DISCUSSION QUESTIONS

Refer to Exhibit 1, the coalignment model, and Exhibit 2, the strategic management model (especially environmental events, domain definition, and competitive methods). Discuss these concepts in reference to multibranding and Yum! Brands as illustrated here, specifically addressing these questions:

1. How has the role of the life cycle changed for the restaurant industry from the 1970s to the present time?
2. Why is multibranding a strategy to pursue in the mature quick-service industry? What are the claimed benefits? What are the challenges? What are the pros and cons for cobranding or multibranding in the foodservice industry? Discuss the issues from the perspective of operations, marketing, and customers.
3. What environmental events led to Yum! Brands' decision to adopt the multibranding strategy?
4. Besides cobranding, what are other viable strategies that would allow for survival and prosperity in a maturing industry?

REFERENCES

Bernstein, C. 2003. "Multiconcept Confusion?" *Chain Leader* 8, no. 5: 12.

Berta, D. 2004. "Movin' on Up: Yum! Climbs to No. 15 on '50 Best Companies for Minorities List." *Nation's Restaurant News* 38, no. 27: 16

Cunneen, C. 2004. "Recipe for Success: Fast-Food Bigwigs Vary Strategies, Menus to Make It in 2004 Market." *Nation's Restaurant News* 38, no. 2: 30.

Currin, D. 2003. "Louisville, Ky.-Based Yum! Brands Introduces Multibranding Concept in OKC Area Restaurants." *Journal Record.* September 8, 1.

Denver Post. 2004. "Golden, Colo.-Based Restaurant Chain Teams with Taco Maker for Shared Eatery." May 24, D3.

Enz, C. A. 2005. "Multibranding Strategy: The Case of Yum! Brands." *Cornell Hotel and Restaurant Administration Quarterly* 46, no. 1: 85–91.

Garber, A. 2003. "Yum! Tastes Int'l. Success; Plans Long John's Growth." *Nation's Restaurant News* 37, no. 51: 5.

Muller, C. 2005. "The Case for Cobranding in Restaurant Segments." *Cornell Hotel and Restaurant Administration Quarterly* 46, no. 1: 91–95.

SinoCast China Business Daily News. 2004a. "Yum! Brands Expands Chinese Market." October 13, 1.

SinoCast China Business Daily News. 2004b. "Yum! Brands China Puts Its Distribution Center into Service." October 15, 1.

Spielberg, S. 2004. "Yum Halts Co-Branding of KFC Chain in U.S." *Nation's Restaurant News* 38, no. 51: 5–6.

Waldner, E. 2005. "Yum! Tries Multi-Branding with Fast-Food Chains in Bakersfield, Calif." *Knight Ridder Tribune Business News.* January 14, 1.

Environmental Assessment

From Chapter 3 of *Strategic Management in the Hospitality Industry*, Third Edition, Michael D. Olsen, Joseph J. West, Eliza Ching Yick Tse. Copyright © 2008 by Pearson Education, Inc. Published by Pearson Prentice Hall. All rights reserved.

Environmental Assessment
Conceptual Tools

Upon completing this chapter, you will:

1. Understand the importance of the environment in making strategic decisions that are future oriented.
2. Describe the major concepts underpinning the environmental assessment process.
3. Understand the dynamic and complex nature of the business environment.
4. Have an appreciation for the challenges and uncertainties associated with the business environment.

Competing in tomorrow's world

The parable of the *boiling frog*

Concepts of the environment

- Perception
- Dimensions of the environment
- Classifying the environment
- The power and rules dimension

Environmental volatility and how scanning can reduce risk and uncertainty

Challenges in assessing the environment

Chapter Purpose

This chapter is devoted to the role of scanning the business environment, the heavily shaded symbol in the complete strategy model illustrated in Exhibit 1 labeled *environmental events*. The symbol is used to represent change or the forces driving change that will impact a business. *This chapter is designed to introduce the basic concepts necessary to understand the role the environment plays in thinking strategically.* These concepts serve as necessary underpinnings for managers to learn to anticipate the future and seize opportunities to invest in.

Competing for the Future

In their classic bestselling book, *Competing for the Future* (1994), contemporary strategists Hamel and Prahalad suggest that companies must stop thinking about the past and compete for the future. To do this, they must reinvent industries and strategies. This is no small task and demands that managers take seriously their responsibility to vision the future of their business environment. Although it is easy to make this recommendation, it is not so easy to implement it in the complex and dynamic nature of today's hospitality industry environment. To achieve implementation, the manager must possess the creative thinking ability to scan the environment and identify those forces that are driving change and likely to lead to preemptive competitive opportunities. This chapter provides the basic underpinning to the environmental scanning concepts necessary to assist managers in achieving this elusive goal.

Visioning the future is the ability to understand how the business environment provides opportunities and threats. It requires a comprehensive knowledge of all the elements in that environment that are likely to drive change. This ability begins by asking, and answering, the questions outlined in Exhibit 2. These questions are all about the future.

To answer these questions, managers must have the ability to think about the future by expanding their perceptual frameworks beyond the immediate world around them. In addition to expanding their perceptual skills, managers must also focus on both short-term and long-term horizons. Too often managers focus too much attention on the immediate business environment without thinking long term. This focus is understandable, of course; however, failure to think out of this context can be hazardous to business growth and survival. The focus must be on the future not just on the present.

The focus on the future also assumes that the manager works toward creating an organization that is able to gather, transform, and interpret information for strategic purposes. In other words, the manager must see to it that the organization can receive signals from the world in which it exists, interpret these signals within the context of the structure and personality of the organization, and from there draw conclusions that will enhance strategic decision making.

EXHIBIT 1 Strategic Management Model

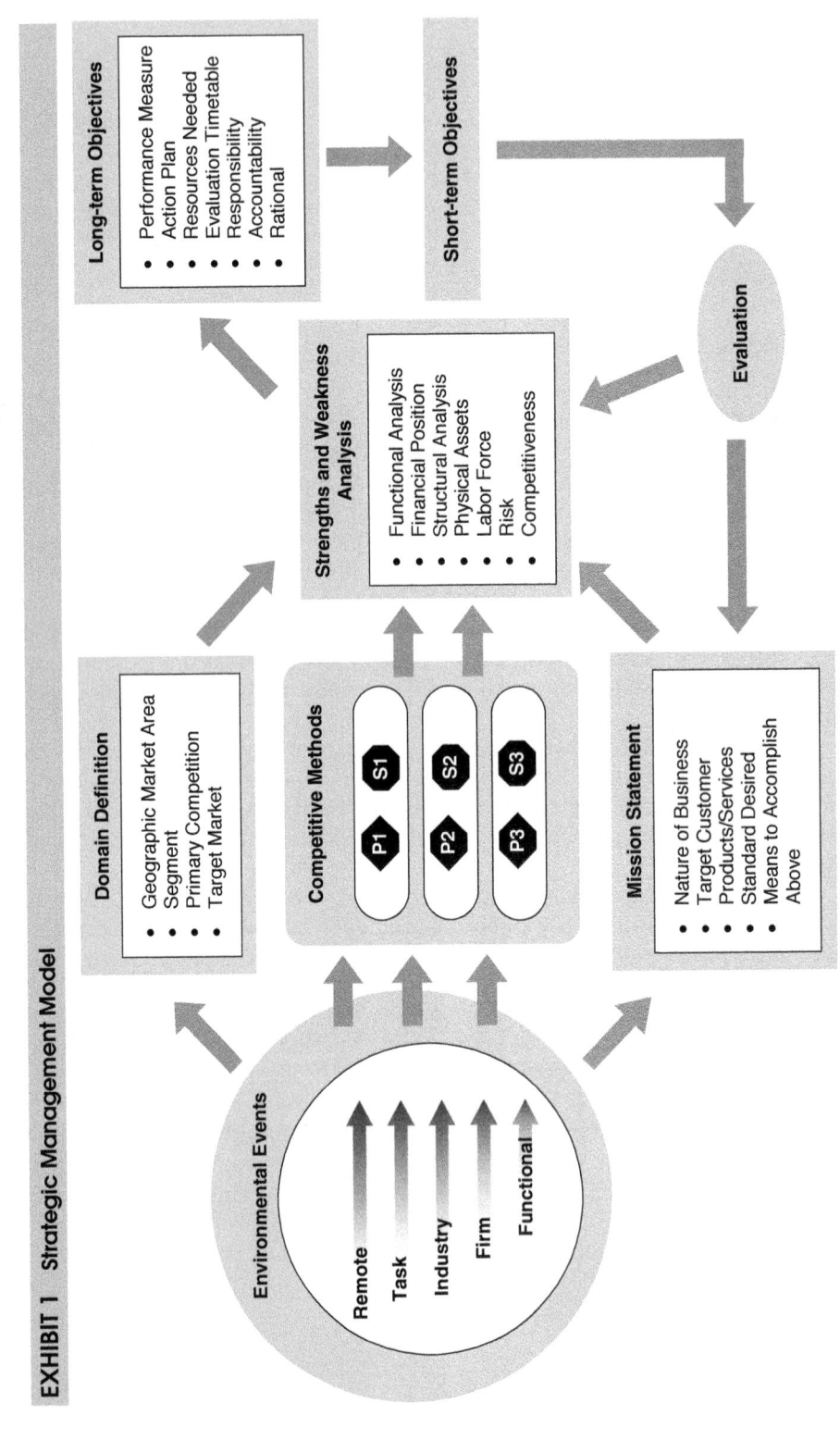

- How will the guest be traveling in the future?
- How will the guest be communicating in the future?
- How will the firm's products and services be distributed to the guest in the future?
- What new customer benefits will be needed to meet future demand?
- What competencies will be needed to serve the guest in the future?
- What standards will be accepted in the future?
- What will the successful hospitality firm look like in the future?
- What new competitive methods will demand the majority of your resources in the future?

EXHIBIT 2   Questions About the Future

The Parable of the Boiling Frog

The parable of the boiling frog can serve as a good metaphor to describe the need for anticipating the future and monitoring change. As this well-known parable suggests, if you remove a frog from its present domicile and put it into a pot of boiling water, its immediate response will be to take appropriate action and jump out. When it jumps, one can only hope that it leaps to safe ground and not another boiling pot. Luckily, most frogs do not find themselves in this dilemma, nor do most managers or businesses. Instead, they often experience environments that change over time. This change often occurs in small increments that in many cases are not even noticed, given little consideration, or perhaps even ignored.

This would be similar to taking the frog and putting it into a pot of water that is at a temperature it has been used to. Its response might be to look around, decide this was a pleasant new environment, and assume little has changed. It will probably do little more than adjust to its new surroundings. If the frog was not a scanner it would fail to see that trouble may be ahead in this new place. That trouble may be a foreboding trend that can best be likened to adding some flame to heat the water, as our example in the textbook illustration indicates. Normally, if the frog was like most people, it will begin to adjust to this subtly changing environment. It will probably conclude that this is just a slight and maybe temporary change. This same type of incremental analysis will continue until the water begins to boil, and then it is usually too late to jump out.

What the frog did in this parable was to adjust incrementally to the changes in its immediate environment. As the parable illustrates, this action can be fatal for the frog and most businesses. Examples of this kind of thinking exist throughout the history of the hospitality industry. The small roadside motels that flourished during the 1950s and early 1960s have disappeared because their owners thought the chain hotel companies that emerged during that period, like Holiday Inns, Howard Johnsons, and Quality Inns, would not affect their individual businesses. These owners ignored the signs of a warming competitive environment, and, like the frog, they failed to see the need to think about the forces driving change (which in the case of the frog was one too many matches heating the water).

This failure to recognize important forces driving change hurt many companies like Hotel Corporation of America and Victoria Station Restaurants, both once leaders in their industries, but now it is doubtful that few in the industry remember them. In this instance these firms failed to recognize changing consumer patterns and shifts in capital market requirements, even though it was possible to identify them and do something about them. Today, terrorism, e-commerce, and food- and health-related dangers that affect the hospitality industry further point out how important it is to look around you and try to anticipate change before it is too late. The message in the metaphor of the frog and these few examples should be very clear: In today's increasingly complex business environment, firms must be at the cutting edge of change if they are to survive. To be at this cutting edge, managers must develop the ability to identify the forces driving change, understand the variables making up these forces, and assess how they will impact the organization. In doing so they must be able to also create ways and means internally in the organization for these activities to be carried out so all stakeholders in that organization learn to develop a scanning capability.

Perhaps another metaphor can help address the urgency with which managers must change their thinking to be future oriented. This metaphor suggests that most of us look at the future from a *rearview mirror* perspective. That is, we try to interpret the future by looking at the past. Think of the danger today of driving down a crowded superhighway looking mostly in the rearview mirror. Unfortunately, the distractions that are behind can often limit the ability to develop a clear vision of the future, especially if the driver needs to anticipate fast-moving changes ahead. Most drivers know better and look as far down the road as they can to anticipate these, yet many managers today ignore the need to foresee the immediate and long-term future and rely too heavily on experiences that have served them well in the past but are not relevant in today's and/or tomorrow's business environment. Although many of yesterday's experiences do help strengthen the manager's perceptual window on the business world, and may even help in thinking about the future, today's manager must not be weighted down by them at the risk of not seeing the opportunities brought about by forces driving change.

Some managers in the hospitality industry may still argue that using the past to anticipate the future is still the best way to manage. Indeed, this was quite possible in the hospitality industry's golden years of the 1950s through the 1970s and the early 1980s. With the baby boom generation coming of age and creating a huge population bubble during this period, it was not very difficult to be successful in this industry. Demand was growing because the boomers were entering into their most productive earning years, and they wanted to travel and eat out more often. Unfortunately, this great boom era has reached its peak, creating a more balanced demand curve ahead and thus a heightened level of competition in all segments of the hospitality industry. Therefore the successful competitive methods used in the past have less effectiveness today because consumers have more choices and are more discriminating in those choices. Moreover, managers cannot count on this population bubble driving their unlimited growth plans. In other words, looking to the future through the lenses of the past will not suffice.

Another example of the metaphor of looking through the rearview mirror to predict the future is how managers attempt to forecast sales. Traditionally, managers have usually relied on basic forecasting models to project future cash flows. These models simply extrapolated prior revenue data from previous periods. This was fine during the golden era just described. But this is not the case today because these simple linear extensions of the past do not point the way to competing in the future. In the context of tomorrow's competitive environment, looking to the past will offer little in terms of real clues as to investment opportunities. Not only must managers think differently about the future today, but they are also increasingly being asked to forget these old tools of yesterday if they are to succeed in a growing competitive environment.

What these metaphors suggest is that to be effective in tomorrow's competitive and complex environment, managers must develop a forward-thinking philosophy. To do this will require new skills that will demand a growing investment in their own intellectual capital and that of their organizations. This investment should lead to an expansion of their perceptions of their business environment. It will require the acceptance of the fact that change is increasingly complex and discontinuous, that old patterns of change can no longer be counted on as guides to the future. In accepting this viewpoint, managers are asked to realize that they "don't know what they don't know because they don't know what they don't know." This implies that many aspects of competition today extend beyond their experiential, conceptual, and cognitive skills. Thus effectiveness in the management role of the future will depend partially on how quickly the manager can fill this void.

This notion is amply supported in the quote in the nearby box by Jack M. Greenberg, former chairman of McDonald's Corp. His message implied that to exist in today's environment managers must possess the skills to assess signals coming from the increasingly complex and dynamic business environment and to interpret them in such a way as to take advantage of the opportunities that present themselves. Put another way, managers must develop the ability to scan the environment and to determine emerging patterns taking shape that will ultimately drive change, and thus impact their businesses. Yet despite this pronouncement by its newly appointed chairman in 1996, McDonald's struggled in the late 1990s and early into the new century due to perhaps unforeseen developments back then. Mad cow disease, growing anti-Americanism demonstrations internationally against well-known brands, cholera outbreaks affecting the beef supply, and labor shortages were all events that had negative impacts on the company. These negative forces affected earnings, stock prices, and jobs, forcing McDonald's to make important strategic decisions to meet these challenges.[1]

> *The fast food business today is much more complicated and requires more sophisticated efforts than in the past.*
> *Wall Street Journal 10/9/96*

From these examples we see four important challenges facing the manager of the future: (1) The need to identify forces that drive change through robust scanning efforts, (2) the ability to understand and estimate their timing, (3) the capability to estimate the impact they will have on the firm, and (4) the ability to make wise investment decisions that reflect the successful meeting of the first three challenges in this list. These challenges are never ending and require the manager to develop a different way of thinking about how businesses are to be managed in the future.

Some Basic Concepts About the Environment

To avoid a fate similar to that of the boiling frog, managers today must enhance their conceptual toolbox (i.e., the ability to use key concepts in a variety of ways to achieve the best decisions possible) to understand the complex and dynamic nature of the business environment. In a day and time when business problems are more complex requiring high levels of thinking skills and creative problem solving, the more tools and

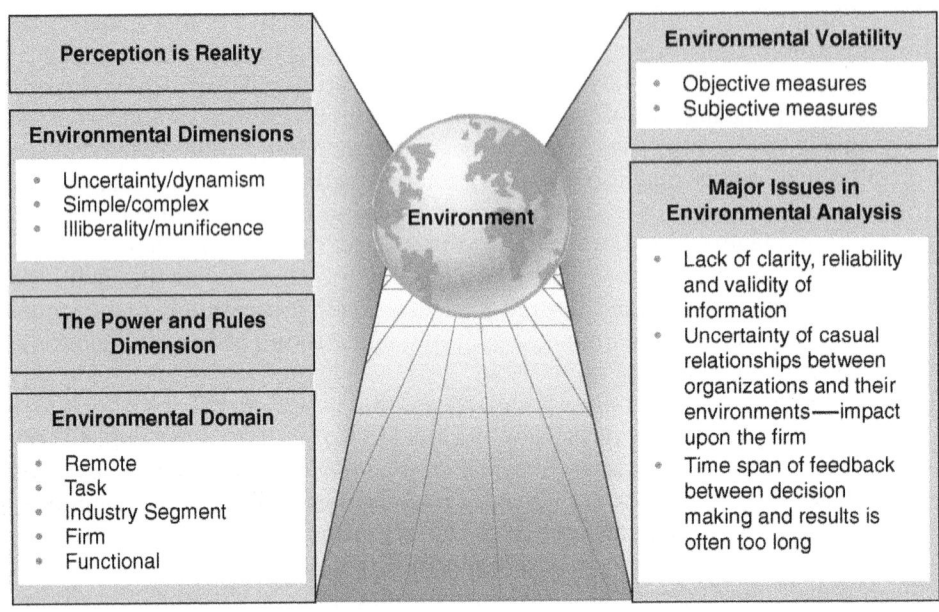

EXHIBIT 3   Concepts of the Environment

frameworks that managers possess, the greater the likelihood that they will come up with better solutions. In essence, managers are being asked to formulate their own theories about what the future will hold and how it will affect their businesses. This requires a different type of thinking than just relying on past experiences to make decisions about the future. It requires the ability to observe cause-and-effect relationships about the many variables that exist in the environment surrounding the business. It necessitates estimating the timing of change relative to these relationships and when they will affect the business and for how long. Exhibit 3 contains a list of these key concepts essential to understanding how to manage change in an increasingly complex environment. These concepts are further developed in the following sections of this chapter and applied in the following three chapters in this section on the environment.

Perception Is Reality

The first concept essential to understanding the environment is the notion of perception. Perception is the mental image we develop regarding our world. This image is based on past experiences accumulated throughout life. These experiences generally occur in a narrow band of activity that begins with the family, neighborhood, schools, and initial job experiences. They are often enhanced by new experiences and opportunities, but it is safe to say that in most cases, the band of activity tends to be closely tied to the frame of reference we develop in the early years of life resulting from those sources of influence most important to us.

As a consequence of this rather narrow band of life activity, we tend to interpret the world from this vantage point. In other words, our threshold of awareness to new ideas, cultures, and so on, is rather limited. We possess a short list of cues about the environment. Consequently, many opportunities or threats are missed because we are viewing the world from a perceptual window that is too small. The downside of this narrow view is that perception is what usually drives decisions. Therefore, if either opportunities or threats are present and likely to impact the individual or firm, but if they are not perceived as such, they will be ignored. This can and usually does result in the same fate as the previously mentioned frog.

Perception is also a function of emotion. Often, it is emotion rather than objectivity that controls how the environment is viewed and the subsequent decisions made as a result of this view. This influence of emotion in decision making can affect rational and objective thinking, which is probably why so many professional athletes and actors have agents to negotiate their salaries and contracts for them. It is often best to have a third party approach this emotional decision-making process to achieve rational results. In many cases, a manager is in the same setting, relying on emotion shaped by past experiences to make important decisions. To avoid this problem, it is often recommended that when assessing the forces driving change a team of individuals, with many different perceptual windows, those who can complement each other and can ensure emotion is limited in the decision-making process should be assembled. They can also provide balance and rational challenges to the influence of past experiences (the rearview mirror metaphor) used in the decision-making process by all individuals.

The strength of the cognitive skills (awareness, judgment, and reasoning) of each individual involved in scanning the business environment can improve the perceptual abilities of the manager. That is, the greater the number of concepts understood, and the ability to apply them to a wide range of situations, implies a broader perceptual window. The wider the window, the less likely the manager is to be confused by the uncertainty of the business environment. Exhibit 4 illustrates this relationship. As the relationships in the exhibit suggest, the managers are able to enhance their perceptual window through (1) utilizing a wide range of information that is of high quality, (2) expanding their cognitive skills, and (3) building on a wide range of previous experiences. If this

EXHIBIT 4 The Relationships Among Uncertainty, Information, Perception, and Cognitive Processes

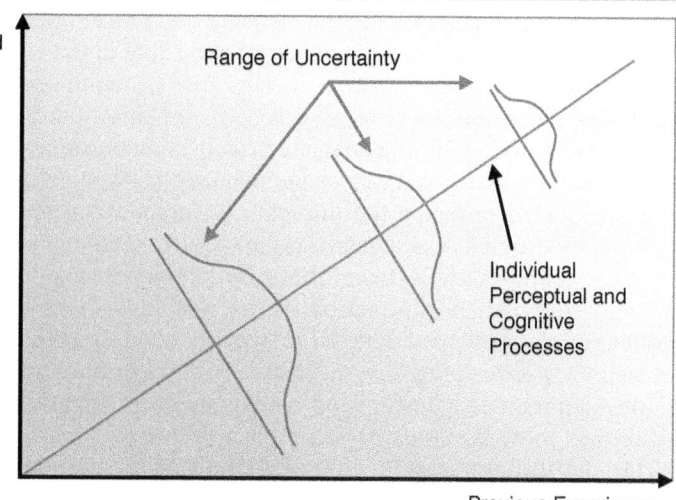

combination of activity is developed and managed well, then the manager is able to use this wealth of perceptual skill to remove some of the uncertainty associated with making decisions about the future. As the exhibit suggests, as the manager moves up the diagonal line and outward on each axis, the range of uncertainty (as depicted by the smaller bell curves as you move up the diagonal) associated with any decision can be reduced if the perceptual window has been widened by more information, experience, and cognitive skills.

It is essential to point out here that it is uncertainty about the future that makes stakeholders cautious when investing in a business. They want to feel comfort that the manager is able to anticipate the challenges of the business properly. In other words, they don't like the risk that every business must face. In this context, they want leadership that will grow value while minimizing that risk. Some, however, are viewed as less risky than others. For example, in a recent Harvard University study of successful leaders in the 20th century, the author looked at those leaders whose companies had generated outstanding and continuous shareholder value over a 15-year period. Also looked at were the new products or services that opened up new industries or markets and new business or management practices that were broadly adopted.[2] The author of the study, Nitin Nohria, a Harvard professor, suggested that "contextual intelligence" was key to all the successful leaders. He indicated that they all seemed to have an excellent understanding of where they were in terms of an evolving business environment. This supports the notion that if a manager can combine experience, cognitive skills, and quality information successfully, this manager becomes a leader who is recognized for keeping uncertainty from bringing risk to the organization.

An example can help illustrate this relationship. If a manager is contemplating the investment in a new marketing database to focus marketing efforts on each and every individual customer, several steps must be taken. First, quality information about the latest trends in marketing must be gathered. Gathering the most appropriate information will be a challenge if the manager's cognitive processes surrounding database marketing, technology utilization, and *direct to consumer marketing* are limited (the manager doesn't know what she or he doesn't know), resulting in the likelihood that the decision is likely to be less than optimal. If, however, the manager seeks more *information* from a wide variety of sources, learns the important concepts regarding direct to consumer marketing, and talks with others whose *experience* level is greater, the uncertainty about the impact on financial performance this decision has on the organization is reduced. The manager has been able to move up the diagonal line from the first uncertainty curve to perhaps the second or third. By taking these steps the manager has opened the perceptual window to a wider state, thus reducing the uncertainty surrounding the decision-making process regarding investments in leading edge competitive methods.

As a second example, the authors are familiar with an upscale international hotel company whose chief information officer was unaware of the latest advancements in application service providers. In a strategy session, one of the hotel managers in the chain was explaining how difficult it was to get the hotel owner to finally finance the development of a customized management information system in the hotel. The system was to be designed to accomplish the direct to consumer marketing concept. During the strategy session when the manager learned that instead of investing the $250,000 to develop the system he could obtain the same product from an application service provider for approximately $1,000 per month, he was extremely angry at the chief information officer for two reasons. The first was that he was not current on developing trends, and second, this manager felt he would lose the confidence of this owner once he discovered the much less expensive alternative. It is these types of situations that support the notion that all members of the firm should engage in scanning so these potentially damaging situations do not occur.

The challenge to improving the "Visioning the Future" process is to expand the perceptual framework that most individuals use to view their environment. Although space limits a thorough discussion of the topic of perception and how to enhance it, it must be pointed out that effective future oriented decision making demands that managers expand their perceptual windows through improved cognitive processes, information sources, education, and experiences that allow them to escape from the limited band of life activities that normally shape their views.

Environmental Dimensions

Three dimensions are generally used to try to describe and understand the environment. The first is *uncertainty.* It is defined as the degree of change occurring in the environment and the rate of that change. The old phrase "nothing is more certain today than change" clearly states it all. It seems like no day goes by without some new change reported, whether it be in science, health care, transportation, banking, or whatever. Change is generally a function of key variables in the environment that affect all aspects of life. These variables we call *value drivers,* and in subsequent chapters we indicate the importance they play in affecting the firm and its overall performance.

The role of the value driver is often one of creating uncertainty or variability in the firm's performance or, as we have stated earlier, risk. Some of these performance measures include such items as cash flow per share of stock, return on invested capital, or just plain profit. In highly volatile business environments, the variability of the firm's cash flows is subject to many forces and the value drivers that make them up. The objective of any manager in this context is to try to identify and understand what forces and their value drivers contribute to this variability. Once this is accomplished, the manager can concentrate on monitoring them and determining their impact on the firm's cash flow. This in turn can lead to investment decisions directed at reducing the variability or risk and give stakeholders more confidence in the decisions of management.

Many variables contribute to *uncertainty.* These are identified in Exhibit 5. As can easily be seen in the exhibit, *uncertainty* results from a wide range of activities emanating from the actions of competitors, suppliers, customers, and regulators. The *uncertainty* dimension can be viewed on a continuum from stable to very volatile. Stable environments suggest that change is continuous, which makes it easier for the manager to anticipate and plan for it, usually by relying on experience and past information. If it is volatile, change is considered discontinuous, one cannot count on old patterns holding true and thus, the old theories held by the manager about how things work have difficulty holding up. In these contemporary times, few businesses have the luxury of a stable environment. It continues to grow more uncertain as the world moves toward greater globalization. In this case, the more the manager is able to enhance the necessary perceptual skills to understand the role of the variables that are driving change and making up the *uncertainty* dimension, the better the decision making that will result.

Uncertainty Dimensions	Complexity Dimensions
• Prices charged by suppliers/competitors • Labor force supply and cost • Demand curve for products and services • Cost of Capital—Capital availability • Financing opportunities • Competitive methods used by competitors • Regulatory activity in the market area • New product introductions • New entrants in the market • Taxation • Product quality expectations • Technology • Cost of raw materials • Overall economic conditions • Real estate values • Safety and security • Changing profile of labor force	• Number and variety of suppliers • Geographic concentration of suppliers • Dispersion of the labor force • Number of brands in competition • Number of political bodies affecting market • Economic variables creating risk • Concentration of customers • Number of potential target markets • Degree of social/cultural diversity • Variety and volume of businesses in market • Potential substitutes for products/services • Number of steps in the service delivery process • Interdependencies among firms

Environment

EXHIBIT 5 Variables Making Up the Dimensions of Uncertainty and Complexity

Complexity is the second dimension of the environment that creates challenges for the manager. *Complexity* is defined as the number of different variables impacting the business. The larger the number of variables, the more *complex* is the environment. As can be seen in Exhibit 5, many potential variables can be an active part of a business environment. This number can be compounded for hospitality firms that operate in several market areas and/or internationally. Each market area has its own set of these variables. This demands from each manager a much more complete view of his or her business environment.

Exhibit 6 demonstrates the relationships between *uncertainty* and *complexity*. The y-axis in this exhibit demonstrates the continuum of uncertainty. It suggests that environments can range from being very volatile to very stable. The x-axis represents the complexity dimension. It suggests that environments can vary from being very simple to complex.

If a manager could wish for the best of all worlds, it would probably be to operate in the lower left quadrant where the environment is simple and stable. This would mean that there would be few variables to monitor and they would be stable as indicated by the few symbols of the same shape and similar size in the lower left quadrant. The symbols suggest little diversity and possible variability from elements in the environment. In this quadrant, old theories about how the business environment interaction plays out can be relied on for the most part in anticipating the future. Continuous or predictable change would be the order of the day.

The opposite high-pressure environment would be in the upper right hand quadrant, illustrated here by the wide array of different symbols, shapes, and sizes. In this case there are many variables to monitor, and they change often and in unpredictable ways. The hospitality industry certainly falls to the right of the y-axis, and depending on

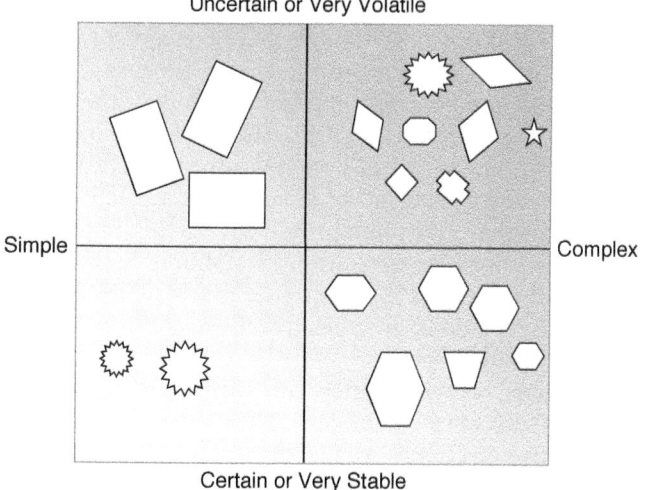

EXHIBIT 6   The Relationship Between Complexity and Uncertainty

which segment a manager is operating in, it can be very dynamic. What can be certain in these contemporary times is that stability and continuous change, so much a part of the golden days of this industry, have long since departed.

The third dimension of the environment, *munificence*, refers to the amount of potential capacity for growth that exists in an industry environment. In considering today's mature hospitality environment, few would suggest there is much excess capacity. For example, in the North American marketplace, the restaurant industry is generally believed to be saturated across most subsegments, with an approximate ratio of one restaurant for every 330 people in the United States. The less munificence in the environment, the more unforgiving it becomes. The term often used to describe this intolerance is *illiberality*. It implies there is little room for significant growth or for mistakes. In the case of the restaurant industry, which consists of many choices for the customer, we see how quickly customers can easily abandon their brand loyalty to a restaurant if they experience bad service or feel there is a poor price-to-value relationship.

Understanding the relationships among *uncertainty, complexity, munificence,* and *illiberality* requires a high level of cognitive skill. It requires the manager to use thought processes that enhance the understanding of the cause-and-effect relationships that exist among all the variables likely to make up each dimension. It requires the expansion of perceptual skills. To anticipate the future, managers will be required to increase their understanding of all the variables affecting each dimension and the relationships that exist among them. Thus not only will they be required to know the operational basics of their industry, but also they must now grow individually in their thought processes and creativity.

The Subjective versus the Objective Environment

The discussion so far has centered on the concepts of the environment, which for the most part are theoretical. Managers use these concepts to help them further understand how their organizations relate to their environment in a qualitative way. Often these conceptual tools just help the manager describe what is going on and how it relates to their businesses. In other words, they formulate their own individual theories of how the world works. Although these conceptual tools help managers understand their environment, not all of them lend themselves to precise measurement, which is frequently demanded by the stakeholders of the firm when investments are required in new competitive methods. Stakeholders such as investors and lenders generally are more interested in how investment decisions will influence return on invested capital and will demand of managers an objective assessment of how forces driving change in the environment will affect this important financial yardstick. Managers and investors are used to understanding their environment by looking at economic data or past sales histories (the rearview mirror concept). Thus they are often reluctant to include their subjective assessments of the environment in a world where objectivity is the norm.

Using the phrase "subjective measure" seems like a contradiction in terms. How can something that is subjective be measured? What is meant here is that a manager can say that my competitive position is weakening due to the number of new competitors that have entered my market. In some ways this can be measured. However, that manager cannot say with the same degree of assurance that the competition is heating up because the customer is expecting better service. This is more of a subjective assessment based on the observations of the manager and the cause-and-effect relationships she or he feels create this situation. The customer can be surveyed, of course, but it is very difficult to measure this expectation because service quality is so personal. Thus the manager is in a dilemma. Some measures prove a point and have good metrics to support them; at other times only subjective ideas are put forward reflecting what the manager believes. In this latter case, managers must then attempt to try to gather as much evidence and support for their theory and, if not, expect that theory to be challenged by investors who are risk averse and don't want to deal with a manager's guesswork.

To meet this challenge, managers are in constant search of ways to try to determine how an environment, made complex and uncertain by many forces driving change, can be measured. Such tools as expected value analysis, simulation modeling, and various statistical and econometric models are often used to accomplish this objective. Other examples of objective measures are industry business cycles, supply-and-demand measures, and market feasibility studies. The expectation of both the stakeholders and managers in this case is to achieve a high degree of correlation between objective and subjective measures. Unfortunately it is often difficult to achieve this correlation because there are a great many variables in any business environment making it almost impossible to assure that opportunities viewed through a subjective window can be validated by objective measures.

Although these measures help tangibilize thinking about the business environment and partially meet the needs of stakeholders, they seldom capture all the cause-and-effect relationships, which exist in any complex and dynamic business environment. Yet in many cases, it is these dimensions and the variables making them up that will affect long-term business success. Thus managers must recognize the paradox that exists in assessing the environment. On the one hand, stakeholders expect quantitative (often reflecting the rearview mirror metaphor referred to earlier), objective assessments, but these often fail to capture the true forces that drive change and affect future business success. Thus managers must work hard to synthesize the quantitative and qualitative views of the environment. This synthesis reinforces the need for the manager to constantly work on improving the cognitive, experiential, and perceptual skills that are so important in a complex and dynamic environment.

Classifications of the Environment

The concept of environmental refers to the context in which a business functions. It defines the boundaries of the organization's effective operating environment. Such terms as *industry segment, strategic group, competitive set, target market,* and *competitive arena* are often used to express the business domain. In essence, the context is a reflection of the pattern of interrelationships that exist between the organization and the forces that drive change within that environment. To understand the interrelationships and assess their impact on the organization, managers must utilize appropriate conceptual frameworks to define that environment. These frameworks help managers in reducing the complexity of the environment. They assist with the process of developing appropriate methods to study and monitor change. They help managers more effectively direct their environmental scanning efforts. These frameworks also assist in determining the appropriate information to review and use in providing valid insights into what forces drive change and how to measure them objectively.

Once defined, the operating environment can be thought of in terms of several frameworks or classification schemes. These schemes are hierarchical and consist of the *remote, task, industry, firm,* and *functional* categories. In general, forces that drive change have their beginnings in the remote category and filter down through each category until they affect the firm itself and the functions that managers perform within it. Exhibit 7 represents the relationships that exist among the various ways the business

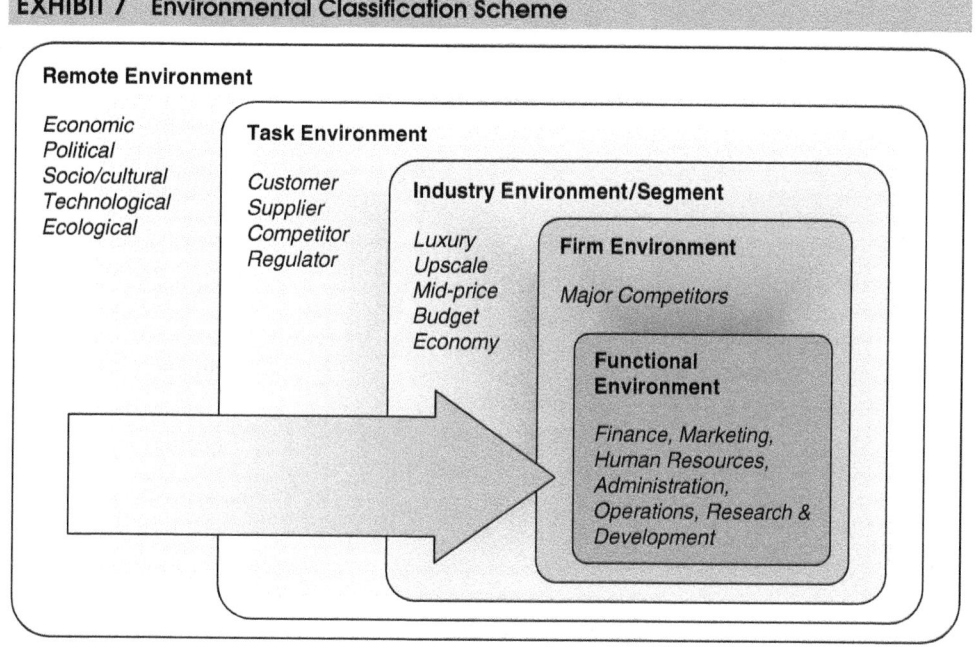

EXHIBIT 7 Environmental Classification Scheme

environment can be classified. Although the exhibit suggests there are borders around each category, implying that they are mutually exclusive, this is not really the case. In reality there are a considerable number of cause-and-effect relationships that occur between and among the categories. These relationships are illustrated by the two arrows pointing inward and illustrate that change usually begins in the remote environment and then cascades through the several layers of environmental classifications before having final impact on the firm and the functional environment within the firm.

The first category of environment making up the operating environment of the firm is referred to as *remote*. It is called remote because it is far removed from the day-to-day lives of people and managers in general. The remote classification consists of five subcategories: ecological, economic, political, sociocultural, and technological. Within each of these five subcategories are a number of variables (value drivers) that ultimately drive change and lead to opportunities or threats for the firm. Exhibit 8 lists the major variables within each subcategory. As can be seen by examining each heading, the number of variables in each column suggests there can be a considerable amount of complexity and potential uncertainty in each category.

The variables listed under each of the five subcategories help establish a framework to enable managers expand their perceptual window and identify the possible opportunities and threats that could potentially affect the organization. If managers develop a thorough knowledge and comprehension of each variable and how these variables interact with each other within and among the categories, it becomes easier to see emerging patterns of change that can impact the organization.

EXHIBIT 8   Key Variables in the Subcategories of the Remote Environment

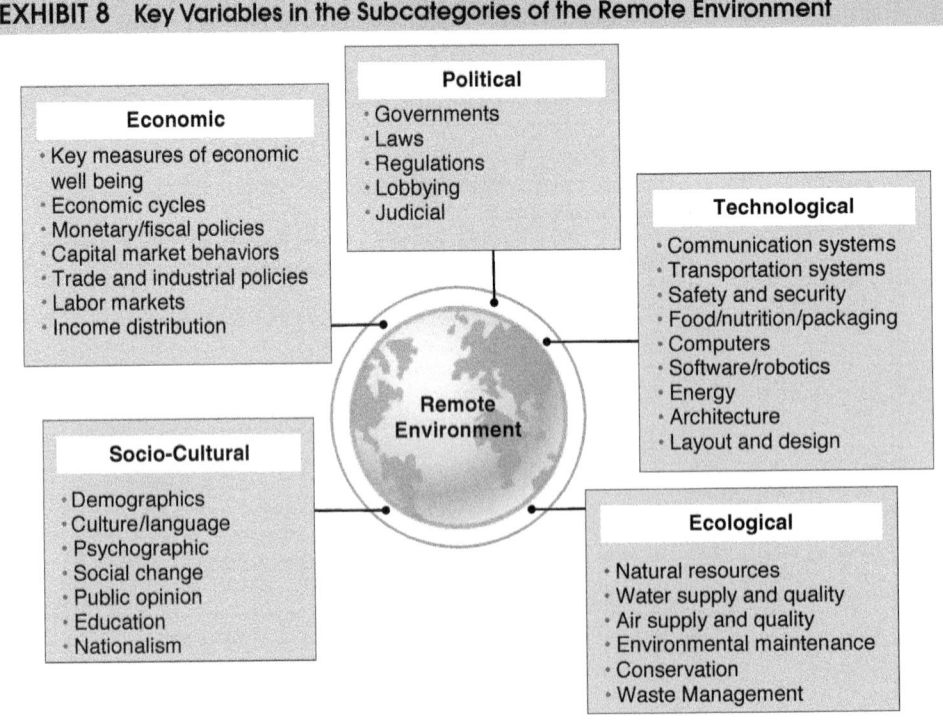

What is important to recognize here is that activities occurring in each variable reflect the potential for change. Monitoring change within each variable is already a challenge for most managers, but when you combine these changes with those taking place in other variables and subcategories and the relationships that exist among them, it is easy to see how important it is for managers to enhance their cognitive and perceptual skills if they hope to be effective in identifying change. For it is usually the relationships occurring within and among the variables that serve to shape trends or events that ultimately drive change and impact the firm.

The challenge for managers is to try to determine how activities taking place in this remote environment will affect the firm, over what time frame, and at what level of intensity. Although this is the most difficult of all responsibilities for the manager to accomplish because of the abstract nature of activities occurring so seemingly removed from the day-to-day activities of the firm, it is the most important task the strategic manager can perform. It is from this environmental classification where most events emerge.

An example may help to illustrate. Since the 1960s, there has been a growing concern for protecting the environment. This trend is a reflection of activities taking place in several of the subcategories of the remote environment. First, people of all ages have been influenced by *sociocultural* changes that have focused attention on the need to protect the environment. The laws (*political*) of many states and nations have reflected this concern, and businesses have been active in accepting their responsibility for a clean environment (*ecological*). The interrelationships occurring among activities taking place in each of these three subcategories have resulted in the identification of strategic opportunities for some hospitality firms. This is also illustrated by the example of the International Hotels Environmental Initiative (IHEI). As the illustration of the home page of IHEI in the text box indicates, the international body was formed in part due to the convergence of the issues just outlined for the purpose of encouraging the continuous improvement of environmental performance by the hotel industry worldwide. This program is part of the Prince of Wales Business Leader's Forum and the International Tourism Partnership (www. ihei. org). The IHEI promotes this effort by giving annual awards to the hotel that best exemplifies the environmental practices promoted by the organization as well as sharing best practice and case study findings with the industry. This represents one of the best examples of how an industry can respond to emerging forces driving change emanating from the remote environment.

INTERNATIONAL
HOTELS
ENVIRONMENT INITIATIVE

Mission Statement:
To encourage the continuous improvement of environmental performance by the hotel industry worldwide

One step below the remote environment is the task environment. This is the more familiar environment for most managers. Here, the environmental context is easier to see and understand. It consists of categories such as the customer, supplier, regulator, and competitor segments (including potential competitors). These subcategories usually dominate the attention of a manager daily. Although the focus of most managers is directed at these categories, the manager must not forget that many of the changes taking place in these categories are a direct result of activities developing in the remote categories. In the IHEI example, the strong forces driving environmental-friendly development in the remote environment translated into factors influencing the selection decision process for many customers, and it was felt that this must be reflected by hotels worldwide. In addition, it was hypothesized that if hotels had this focus it offered them a competitive advantage over their competitors that did not. It was also deemed to be useful in the event that probable legislation or regulatory activity in the future would be enacted by local governments. In other words, if hotels followed IHEI guidelines, the advantages of doing so would outweigh the possible threats emerging from the environment.

The relationships interacting in and among the remote and task environmental categories ultimately impact the industry segment the firm is in. The segment environment further defines the business domain. This environment category appears less abstract to the manager's thinking because he or she focuses in on the segment in which the business competes. Generally, the manager is most comfortable in assessing activities taking place in the segment and more completely understands the relationships at work in this environmental category.

The actual local environment of the firm is the next classification of the environment and reflects the immediate competitive situation in which it exists. In the hospitality industry, this most often means the local environment. Because the demand curve is, in part, localized, the manager must recognize the forces that drive change locally as well. Here, the focus on the customer, supplier, regulator, and competitor is more defined to the immediate competitive environment rather than the entire industry segment. The difference between this environment and the task environment is the immediate and direct impact an activity in this category has on the firm.

The functional environment reflects the key responsibilities generally performed in most organizations and includes Finance, Marketing, Human Resources, Operations, Administration, and Research and Development. Although these responsibilities are normally performed by management within the organization, they represent collectively an important environmental category for the manager to assess. This is because developments in any of the areas can often provide competitive advantage to the firms that are leaders in each category. For example, a firm that develops a leadership position in new marketing technology will have the competitive advantage over those that do not. Thus it is important for managers to recognize the importance of monitoring activities in this important part of their contextual business environment.

The contextual task environment is not a concept that is absolute. The borders of the domain are not firm. They are constantly changing. The range and scope of the environment is a function of how developed the manager's cognitive, experiential, and perceptual skills are. If the manager looks at the business environment from a narrow window, some opportunities and threats will not be seen, whereas the opposite will be true if the view is wide. The classification scheme just discussed should be viewed not only as a way of viewing the environment but also as a way for the manager to understand how activities and relationships taking place in each of the classifications will result in relationships that are likely to impact the organization.

The Power and Rules Dimension

The final concept useful in understanding the environment reflects who has control over the environment. The power and rules dimension suggests that the firm has a choice between trying to control its environment or reacting to it. This implies that there is a continuum on which the organization falls. The continuum reflects on one end, being totally dependent with no control at all, to the other where the organization actually achieves control over its environment. It is unlikely that in a free market system an organization will be at either end. However, where the firm is must be assessed, and management can make decisions about where it wants to be on this continuum.

The power dimension suggests that a firm can influence its environment. Firms attempt to do this by forming strategic alliances and coalitions among themselves or even with their competitors. For example, Cendant Corporation has built a company that includes e-commerce travel companies, hotels, car rental agencies, mortgage lenders, and real estate firms. Cendant felt that through gaining control over many of the customer's transactions they could serve that customer's needs better and buffer its own earnings stream by having a portfolio of travel- and leisure-related companies. Unlike Cendant, which actually acquired these companies, United Airlines has forged partnerships with other airlines to gain market dominance on international routes. The Star Alliance now contains over 14 international airlines, all cooperating in terms of code sharing of flights, some customer information, and the earning of frequent flyer miles.

Similarly, Pan Pacific Hotels and Resorts (Singapore), Kempinski Hotels and Resorts (Geneva, Switzerland), Wyndham Hotels and Resorts (United States), and Rydges Hotels and Resorts (Australia) have formed a strategic marketing alliance referred to as the Global Hotel Alliance (GHA) to enhance their ability to compete on key industrywide critical success factors. They provide a worldwide portfolio of properties and a reservation system as well as website. Travelers who book through the GHA receive better rates and future awards.

Power is also achieved by trying to influence regulation that is either favorable or unfavorable to an industry. Trade associations, such as the American Hotel and Lodging Association, National Restaurant Association, the World Travel and Tourism Council and International Hotel and Restaurant Association, are groups that represent the interests of their members on many matters but generally focus their attention on monitoring governmental activities that could impact their industries. In addition to monitoring, they also actively lobby governments and regulators to gain influence over important decisions that could affect the hospitality organizations. These organizations help to bring about a balance in the environment between businesses and regulators. This balance can be thought of as a power match between two players, each trying to achieve a satisfactory level of control over the business environment.

Similar to the power dimension is the rules dimension. In this case, it is less far reaching as compared to the concept of power and suggests that firms must be in the process of constantly monitoring those forces that promulgate rules that can impact them. Local regulatory bodies such as health departments, business license departments, insurance companies, or consumer protection and advocacy groups are likely to be at work creating rules or regulations designed to impact organizations within their domains. Management must keep a constant vigilance on their activities so as not to be surprised by their actions.

Firms can also be proactive in this regard. They can work to establish rules that give them competitive advantage. For example, in the continuing debate over the extent of health care coverage in the United States, there are several hospitality firms that opposed their trade association's position on this issue, which is generally against the establishment of rules that will require employers to provide coverage to all employees. They opposed it because they were already providing it and thus experience a higher cost per employee than those firms that do not. To provide a more competitive situation, they felt that those who do not presently pay should be required to do so. Thus they worked to establish rules that are equal for all employers, and they level out the competitive playing field.

The need to be able to assess how their organizations are affected by either the power or rules dimensions within their environment is a fundamental responsibility of all managers. They should not be in a position where they are only reacting to the power and rules of others. Thus they must develop an outward-looking perspective. In an increasingly turbulent and complex environment, this need will grow in importance.

Major Issues in Understanding the Environment

The concepts just discussed in this chapter imply there is a need for managers to understand the forces that drive change in their business environment. These concepts help improve the manager's ability to do so. To be effective in that assessment of the environment, managers face many challenges. Being aware of these challenges can help in improving effectiveness.

The first challenge that the manager must deal with is the quality of information. As illustrated in Exhibit 9, the manager has a wide variety of sources of information to consider in scanning the environment. These sources are both personal and impersonal. The frequency with which they are consulted is a decision of the manager. Some managers are very formal and regular in this consultation process. Others are less directed and are serendipitous in their processes of scanning the business environment. Because the scanning process is a function of the perceptual, experiential, and cognitive skills of the manager, the extent of information reviewing, the range of individuals consulted, and the formality of the scanning process tend to be very individual.

In relying on these sources of information, the manager needs to be aware of the fact that forces driving change seldom jump off the page or out in conversation. The forces represent a pattern of events that have emerged from several categories of the environment and are reported in a wide range of sources of information relevant to the business environment. Moreover, there is generally a lack of clarity about each force driving change, no matter what source the manager relies on. Thus, through strong cognitive, experiential, and perceptual skills, the manager is often expected to see the patterns emerging and then take action before others see them. This was the basic premise at the start of this chapter. Managers must anticipate change if they are to lead their organization into the future. As can be seen thus far in this chapter, this is no easy task.

In addition to the problem of clarity of the information in providing accurate assessments of emerging forces driving change, managers must also deal with the challenges of the validity and reliability of the information used. Validity addresses the issue of consistency of information across a variety of settings. It implies that if managers are beginning to see the same pattern of activity emerging from a wide variety of

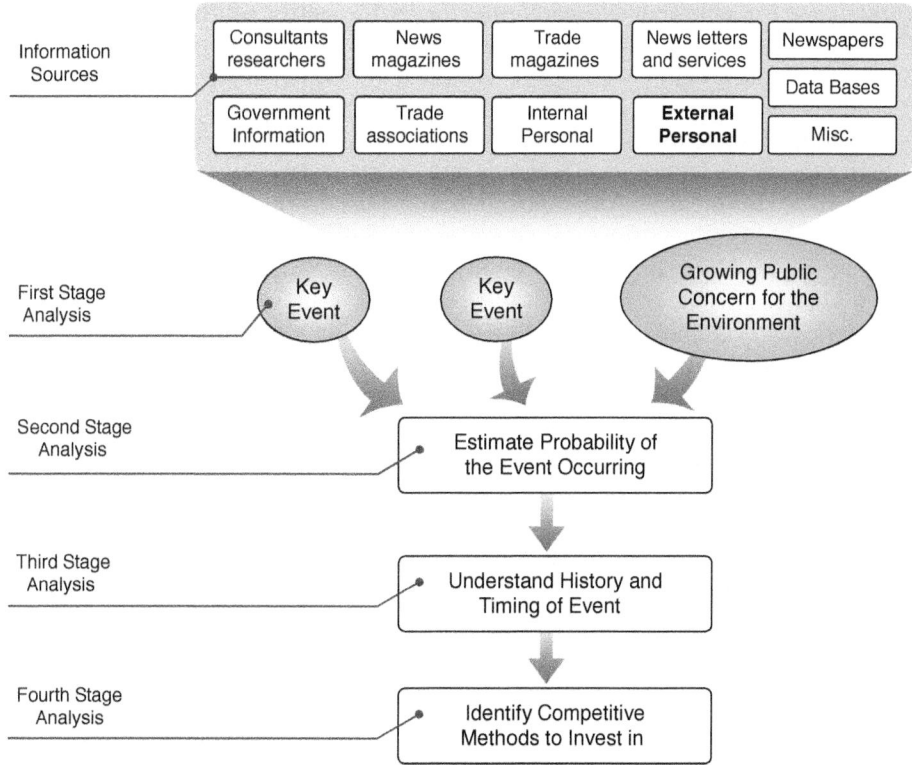

Information Sources

Consultants researchers	News magazines	Trade magazines	News letters and services	Newspapers
Government Information	Trade associations	Internal Personal	**External Personal**	Data Bases
				Misc.

First Stage Analysis — Key Event · Key Event · Growing Public Concern for the Environment

Second Stage Analysis — Estimate Probability of the Event Occurring

Third Stage Analysis — Understand History and Timing of Event

Fourth Stage Analysis — Identify Competitive Methods to Invest in

EXHIBIT 9   Key Relationship of Information Sources and Environmental Analysis

sources of information, it becomes more comfortable for that manager to conclude that a trend is developing.

For example, in the case of the IHEI, if in scanning the environment a wide range of sources suggested that a large and growing number of individuals across a variety of walks of life were expressing the need for more attention to be paid by businesses to the environment, the IHEI would serve an important role in helping managers meet customer needs related to this growing trend. The fact that this trend was being expressed in a number of settings and information sources supports the validity that this was becoming a major and important force driving change and thus should be factored into the strategic decisions of all hotels.

In addressing the validity concern, management must also pay attention to the reliability of the sources of information they are consulting. The important standard here is whether or not these sources of information have been correct over time. Have they demonstrated consistency in gathering and providing information? Do they use valid measures repeatedly to reach their conclusions? Decisions are only as good as the validity and reliability of the information. Managers should expect only the highest levels of performance in these two important measures of information quality.

The second major challenge the manager faces is the uncertainty of the cause-and-effect relationships that exist. As suggested earlier, the stronger the manager's cognitive, experiential, and perceptual skills, the better will be the assessment of the relationships that exist among the classifications of the environment. The IHEI example and Exhibit 9 can be used again to illustrate this point. In viewing the public's growing concern about the environment as a key event driving change, as indicated in the exhibit by the lowest level oval under *first stage analysis*, the IHEI had a choice to ignore it or factor it into their information-sharing activities. In this case they viewed the cause-and-effect relationship positively. That is, the attention being paid to the environment (the cause) would have a positive effect on the hotel business if hotels made this an important part of their development strategies.

This leads to the *second stage* of the analysis, which is the need for the manager to try to understand the history and timing of the event. In many cases events or trends begin almost unnoticed within the environment and take some time to develop. For example, the public's concern over the quality of the environment has been developing for almost 50 years, but it is only recently that the international hotel industry has decided it should respond, with the IHEI being just one case in point. This is not atypical because many managers want to wait to be sure that they do not make a mistake in making strategic decisions on something that is a fad as opposed to a real event. In this case they make probabilistic assumptions about whether or not something like the customer's concern about the environment would be substantive and not just a passing fancy. We can now be sure that there is almost a 100% probability that the customer will be considering a hotel's position on the environment as part of their decision package. This is the *third stage* analysis in Exhibit 9. The *fourth stage analysis* is the decision to invest in competitive methods that meet this growing trend. We will cover both stage's 3 and 4 in later chapters in the text and at that time will link back to this exhibit primarily because this information will be needed for more in-depth decision analysis by managers as they execute the coalignment model (specifically it will be useful in helping managers estimate future cash flow streams for investments in competitive methods).

Of course, managers of hotels could have guessed differently about this emerging pattern and ignored the efforts of the IHEI. This is the chance managers take everyday in trying to determine how to compete in the future. The chance that the cause-and-effect relationship was wrong can be greatly reduced by improving the relationships illustrated in Exhibit 4. The more valid and reliable the information used, the greater the cognitive, experiential, and perceptual skills employed in the cause-and-effect analysis, the greater the likelihood that the manager will be making decisions within a range of certainty that offers less risk to the organization. Put another way, what the manager is doing is building theories about how the firm interacts with the environment. These theories will ultimately lead to investments in the future success of the firm.

These challenges represent important issues to managing for the future. They point out how difficult it is to see patterns of change emerging and then for managers to make strategic decisions about them such as setting corporate objectives and making investments that add value. They suggest that managers of tomorrow must invest in their own intellectual capital to expand their perceptual window. In a day and age when information is abundant and easily accessible, the manager must possess the skills to retrieve it, analyze it, and make inferences about the future. This requires greater use of thought processes and cognitive skills. It demands a greater use of concepts and frameworks to aid in understanding the complexities of this modern competitive world. This is a challenge each manager has little choice but to accept.

The Importance of Concepts

The environment is a rather abstract concept. Yet it is the primary determinant in the success of hospitality firms. The environment generates the forces that drive change. These forces emerge from the interactions of a large number of variables working in discontinuous patterns. Managers must attempt to understand how these interactions will ultimately result in forces driving change and the impact they will have on their firms. In trying to understand these relationships they are in need of ways to view their environments so they can make some sense of the patterns that are developing. To do this they require frameworks to assist them in this most challenging task. This chapter provided several frameworks and concepts that strategic managers can utilize to determine the forces driving change, understand how these forces will impact their firms, and what new competitive methods will be necessary to compete in the future.

SUMMARY

This chapter provides an introduction to the concepts of the environment. These concepts provide an underpinning for understanding the environment, the first element of the coalignment principle. The most important concept is *perception*. It suggests that adding value depends on how management perceives its environment and the events which will drive change in that environment. If the manager has a very narrow perception, it is likely to ignore important forces that could either provide opportunity or pose a serious threat. Managers can enhance their perception by improving their knowledge, experience, and sources of information.

Once managers have been successful in enhancing their perceptual skills, it becomes much easier to address the uncertainties in the environment. This uncertainty is also reduced by understanding that the environment can be defined by such concepts as uncertainty, complexity, and illiberality. Using these concepts will assist managers in analyzing forces that can occur in the various categories of the environment, such as the remote, task, functional, and firm. Additionally, understanding how rules and power relationships interact in these categories further helps reduce the uncertainties surrounding investments in competitive methods.

DISCUSSION QUESTIONS:

1. What is meant by expanding ones perceptual window?
2. Discuss the classification scheme for the environment provided in this chapter and explain how a force emerges in the remote environment and works its way into the decision making investment opportunities for the manager.
3. Discuss why it is essential that the manager seek to combine cognitive, perceptual and experiential skills for the purpose of improving the risk return relationship in making strategic investment decisions.
4. Discuss which of the dimensions of the environment brings about the greatest challenge for management.
5. Describe the major issues the manager must face when trying to scan the business environment.
6. Identify any recent environment events which you feel have occurred and the firms in the hospitality industry failed to recognize (the boiling frog). Likewise, identify and discuss events that the industry has seemed to be ahead on.

NOTE

1. R. Weisman, "Key to Business Genius? Spotting the Trends," *International Herald Tribune,* March 31, 2004, 16.

C A S E   S T U D Y

The Industry and Environment Issues: The Case of Orchid Hotel

The greening of the hospitality and tourism industry that began in the late 1980s is an issue of increasing importance to customers and firms. The hospitality and tourism industry has a responsibility to reduce its impact on the environment as it is expected to respond to pressures from its various stakeholders. For example, the green tourist will demand green accommodation, legislation regarding the disposal of waste has implications for the hospitality industry, and the continued increase in energy costs will necessitate reductions in energy usage.[1] It is believed that the industry has a great stake in safeguarding environmental and cultural resources.[2] The Environmental Concerns Task Force of the White House Conference on Travel and Tourism used a three-part definition for environmental issues (1995):[3]

- Physical environment—ecological systems necessary to sustain life including air, water, other natural resources, and human-made environments;
- Sociocultural environment— human aspects of the environment, including a diversity of cultures and a wealth of historic resources; and

- Economic environment—the primary basis for travel and tourism development including employment, revenue, and taxes attributable to the industry.

The Economist Intelligence Unit (EIU) provides a narrower definition of the environment. It includes six target areas: waste management, energy and water conservation, air and water quality, noise, and attention to various potential environmental contaminants (fuel, pesticides and herbicides, and other hazardous materials).[4]

Environmental issues have long been of concern to the lodging industry.[5] Some industry examples on steps taken to reduce the impact of their business on the environment date back to the 1920s. There are more hotels taking the initiative to educate staff and guests to become more environmentally friendly. Increasingly, they are using environmental strategies as a competitive method to create advantage in the market. In a study of the best practices in the U.S. lodging industry, four hotels were selected as champions, all of which have developed excellent recycling programs: the Colony Hotel, Hotel Bel Air, Hyatt Regency Chicago, and Hyatt Regency Scottsdale.[6] The four properties have made major commitments to environmental conservation by focusing on natural resource conservation, education, and community involvement.[7] The study suggested that adopting environment-friendly practices will become essential for all hotel properties, both in terms of customer preferences and government mandates.[8] There is also a study of the environmental strategies adopted in Spanish hotels based on their environmental protection activities and their impact on a firm's performance.[9] As a part of a global charter, Accor Paris announced a long-term commitment for hotels across the world to implement an environmental charter of 15 initiatives per hotel.[10] Bass Hotels & Resorts is a founding member of Asia Pacific Hotel Environment Initiative (APHEI). In Hong Kong, The Grand Stanford InterContinental is so committed to the environment that it established its own environmental management system. One of the goals for these hotels is to receive ISO 14001 certification from Quality Assurance Services (QAS). In general, hoteliers appear to recognize that the hospitality industry has an impact on the environment.[11] They consider the results of these practices not just in environmental terms but also in terms of real business benefits, such as reduced costs and liabilities, greater service quality, and customer satisfaction.[12]

However, many hoteliers will only adopt environmental improvement strategies in the hotel if a cost-saving or another tangible benefit is identified.[13] Their concern for the impact of environmental initiatives often relate to the perceived quality and service of the hotel as affected by these changes and whether green factor alternatives are perceived as less or more efficient and customer appealing than the normally used products.[14] Environmental concern has resulted in a number of hotel companies adopting an environmental policy.[15] To ensure the successful implementation of the policy, it is essential for hotels to recognize environmental issues at all levels of the organization, as well as incorporating environmental reporting in their control system.[16] There is a need for the hotel sector to take a

proactive approach to recognize environmental concern as a strategic issue and part of the control and reward system.[17]

Environment-friendly hotel operations may be the wave of the future.[18] Being green will be a highly effective promotional tool and a competitive advantage. Some operators consider operating in an environment-friendly manner as the right thing to do.[19] Experts say energy, waste, and water consumption can account for up to 10% of total operating costs for a hotel. Going green appears to be a smart way for hotels to improve their profitability.

Increasingly, governmental regulations and hotel guests are demanding green operations. An increasing number of planners are taking their business to meeting facilities that are environmentally conscious. In addition, environmental efforts make sense financially because the benefits include cost reductions and enhanced customer and employee satisfaction.[20] As to whether and how the development of hotel accommodation and tourism infrastructure can be more environmentally and socially sustainable, the International Tourism Partnership (ITP) is establishing guidelines for sustainable location, design, and construction that are compiled specifically for the hotel industry and are intended for use both in new accommodation developments and during major renovations and refurbishments (http://www.greenhotelier.com.)[21]

In 2004 a "Greening the Hospitality Industry Conference," organized by the Virginia Housing and Environmental Network, attracted planners, hoteliers, state tourism executives, federal government and municipal government employees, and consultants. National groups concerned with environmental issues as they relate to the industry include Green Seal, Coalition for Environmentally Responsible economy (CERES), and U.S. Green Building Council (USGBC). The meeting was held in Airlie Conference Center, Virginia's first facility (and one of only 40 nationwide) to receive certification by environmental advocate Green Seal.

Green Seal is a private, not-for-profit organization that distinguishes products and services that demonstrate a commitment to the environment and adhere to the organization's guideline for water management, water conservation, and energy efficiency.[22] The state of Virginia is making sustainable tourism a priority, and a green lodging program is a statewide focus. In the same year, the Convention Industry Council (CIC) released the Green Meetings Report, a series of guidelines for event organizers and suppliers on how to run environmentally friendly events.[23]

THE IH&RA ENVIRONMENTAL AWARD

The International Hotel & Restaurant Association's annual Green Hotelier & Restaurateur Environmental Award recognizes hospitality industry efforts that go beyond in-house environmental programs to promote sustainable tourism.[24] The award is presented to hospitality professionals who provide outstanding examples of leadership in planning and implementing environmental actions, and a personal commitment to ongoing improvements in environmental performance and staff awareness.[25] Hotel and restaurant operators are invited to demonstrate how they are promoting sustainable development while safeguarding local culture and protecting the environment.[26] The award is a way to signify and reinforce human determination to maintain a peaceful coexistence with the environment and nature.[27] The IH&RA chose this theme to coincide with the focus of the United Nations Commission on Sustainable Development meeting in 1999, which addressed the efforts of the travel and tourism sector in implementing Agenda 21.[28] Agenda 21 is the blueprint for environmental action adopted by 182 governments at the Rio Earth Summit in 1992.[29]

Applicants are judged by representatives of the International Hotels Environment Initiative (IHEI).[30] The IHEI was created in 1992 as a nonprofit organization when a group of chief executives of twelve multinational hotel companies joined forces to promote continuous improvement in environmental performance by the hotel industry worldwide.[31] IHEI focuses exclusively on hotels and how to improve their environmental management.[32] It aims to promote the advantages of environment management as a fundamental part of running a successful and efficient hotel operation.[33] The IHEI[1] has published an environmental manual, *Environmental Management for Hotels: The Industry Guide to Best Practice*,[34] as well as an action pack.

Applicants are judged by the following criteria:[35]

- An active interest in environmental issues and a leadership role in planning and implementing environmental actions, particularly in the area of sustainable development
- Initiatives for environmental improvement in the hotel
- Promotion of environmental awareness among staff
- Communication of their environmental performance to guests, staff, and the wider hospitality industry

INDUSTRY EXAMPLE: THE ORCHID HOTEL

The Orchid Hotel in Mumbai, India, is a certified Ecotel hotel. To the Orchid, Ecotel is the hallmark of environmentally sensitive hotels.[36] It was the recipient of the International Hotel & Restaurant Association (IH&RA) former IHEI environmental award twice, in 1999 and 2001. The Orchid belongs to Kamats' group, which is one of India's most successful and best known hotel and restaurant chains.[37] Kamats is a diversified hospitality group with interests in both

---

[1]The IHEI is now part of the International Tourism Partnership as referenced in the text earlier.

luxury and budget hotels, restaurants, family leisure and sports clubs, travel business, catering and educational institutions, and department stores.[38]

Kamats had a humble and modest beginning.[39] It started with a small restaurant in Mumbai in 1958, which laid the foundation of a successful restaurant chain in India.[40] In 1986 the company Kamat Hotels (India) Limited was incorporated.[41] Continued growth resulted in The Group going public for the first time.[42] In 1997 the management of Kamats Plaza opened the Orchid Hotel, an ecotel hotel, as an eco-friendly five-star property, which it claimed to be the first of its kind in Asia.[43] The hotel has 221 rooms and 12 suites, and every room is a "green" room. It enjoyed over 80% occupancy in 2000–2001.

Kamats recognized that over 80% of international travelers do patronize green hotels. Therefore, it hired HVS Eco Services of HVS International in New York to undertake environmental programs designed to lower operating costs, increase revenues, and evaluate the hotel's environmental performance in various areas.[44] The Orchid was awarded the Ecotel Certification by HVS Eco Services USA, which is the hallmark of environmentally sensitive hotels.[45] It is the first hotel in Asia to obtain such certification. The HVS has also designated the Orchid Hotel as an Industry Pioneer.[46] The Hotel has been awarded the Green Globe Award in 1998 at the World Travel Mart in London.[47] Since then, the hotel continues to receive many national and international awards, including the Green Globe Achievement Award in 2000.

The Environmental Program.

As Asia's five-star ECOTEL Hotel, the environmental program at the Orchid Hotel in Mumbai aims to enhance guest experience and set a new standard of environmental responsibility by conserving natural resources, educating consumers, enlightening and motivating staff, and cultivating community relationships.[48] Specific environmental actions were developed in response to three major challenges facing the city: air pollution, solid waste management, and water management.[49] The Orchid incorporates its environmental-friendly commitment in all aspects of its construction and operation, ranging from civil engineering and architecture, to its use of water and energy. For instance, the cement used in the construction of the Orchid is environmentally friendly;[50] and the hotel's facade has been deliberately designed with depressions and protrusions to reduce the surface radiation. At the Orchid, energy-efficient PL lamps are used;[51] even the mini-bars in the guest rooms save up to 40% in typical energy costs because they are equipped with so-called fuzzy logic, which senses the load inside the refrigerator and cools it accordingly.[52]

The Orchid reduces air pollution by installing air scrubbers in the boiler outlet connected to the chimney. The hotel believes in the three "R" theory of reduce, reuse, and recycle.[53] They conserve water by employing a number of techniques including recycling of wastewater. The hotel also makes use of materials like wood from rubber trees and cotton stalks, which normally have no other uses, for its interiors: window frames, master control panels in guest rooms and walls.

In addition, an environmental purchasing program ensures the purchase of locally manufactured products.[54] Many of the innovative items in guest rooms are made from recycled materials and sourced from local suppliers.[55] These include coat hangers made from sawdust, tissue boxes, and reed slippers.[56] The state-of-the-art, ozone technology is adopted in the hotel for its drinking water treatment, wastewater, swimming water treatment, and cooling-tower water. Other actions include ensuring that hotel vehicles and cars rented out at the travel desk run on lead-free fuel, reducing the use of plastic bags, and optimizing water consumption.[57] To monitor progress, a detailed environmental report is drawn up monthly.[58]

To ensure full participation of the staff, a "green team" is formed and headed by an environment officer who is responsible for training, conducting refresher courses, and solving "green" problems. The Orchid's staff is also involved in numerous community works and has formed partnerships with local schools and colleges to introduce them to the hotel and convey its environmental message.[59] The Orchid also spearheaded the Municipal Corporation of Greater Mumbai's Advanced Locality management program, which encourages residents to be responsible for cleaning and maintaining the area in which they live.[60] For instance, 45,000 schoolchildren were involved in a unique campaign to rid Mumbai of plastic bags. The Orchid collaborates with C.L.E.A.N—Air Island, Dignity Foundation and Transport Commissionerate—Maharashtra for a campaign to catch motor vehicles violating the pollution control standards.[61]

The Orchid works closely with nongovernmental organizations (NGOs) toward improvement of the environment.[62] There is the Orchid Evergreen Loyalty Program where guests earn eco points. Other examples include the establishment of an interactive television that lists on its environment page the names of the various NGOs. Guests can support the causes of the NGOs by calling the telephone number to make contributions.

DISCUSSION QUESTIONS

1. Briefly discuss the challenges and barriers to developing and managing of eco-friendly hotels. How can hotels integrate environmental responsibility into their practices while ensuring customer satisfaction at the same time?
2. Using Orchid Hotel as an example, discuss the importance of the environment in making strategic decisions that are future oriented.
3. Do you foresee all hotels in the future being built and operated in an eco-friendly manner like the Orchid? Why or why not?
4. Think through how the Orchid may have gathered information, statistics, and other ideas to formulate the importance of the environment in the future. Discuss how this process may be established within a hospitality firm. Who should be involved and how should it be managed to achieve the excellent results obtained by the Orchid?
5. Discuss how the timing of the decisions leading up to the investments in the hotel may have affected the types of environmental programs initiated.
6. Identify the most valid and reliable sources of information about the environment that may be utilized in arriving at the same conclusions as the management of the Orchid Hotel.

NOTES

1. M. Brown, "Environmental Policy in the Hotel Sector: "Green" Strategy or Stratagem?" *International Journal of Contemporary Hospitality Management* 8, no. 3 (1996): 18+.
2. Anonymous, "Hoteliers in Fiji and India lauded for commitment to sustainable development." *International Hotel & Restaurant Association (IH&RA)* (1999), Retrieved from http://www. hospitlaitynet. org/news.
3. D. M. Stipanuk, "The U.S. Lodging Industry and the Environment: An Historical View," *Cornell Hotel and Restaurant Administration Quarterly* 37, no. 5 (1996): 39–45.
4. Ibid.
5. Ibid.

6. C. A. Enz and J. A. Siquaw, "Best Hotel Environmental Practices," *Cornell Hotel and Restaurant Administration Quarterly* 40, no. 5 (1999): 72–77.

7. Ibid.

8. Ibid.

9. E. Camona-Moreno, J. Cespedes-Lorente, and J. D. Burgos-Jimenez, "Environmental Strategies in Spanish Hotels: Contextual Factors and Performance," *The Service Industries Journal* 24, no. 3 (2004): 101.

10. Anonymous, "Environmental Survey Shows Growing Importance of Environment for Hotel Guests," Press Release of Accor Hotels (2000). Retrieved from http://accorhotels. com. au/ corporate/press.aspx.

11. Op. cit., no. 1.

12. Anonymous, "Environmental Action Pack for Hotels: Practical Steps to Benefit your Business and the Environment," *The International Hotel Association. UNEP Industry and Environment Technical Report, 1995.*

13. Op. cit., no. 1.

14. Ibid.

15. Ibid.

16. Ibid.

17. Ibid.

18. Op. cit., no. 6.

19. Ibid.

20. Ibid.

21. Anonymous, "Sustainable Hotels and Resorts—an Achievable Goal?" *Greenhotelier Magazine* (2005). Retrieved from http://www.greenhotelier.com.

22. K. Carter, "Airline Earns Highest 'Green' Honors for Its Environmental Initiatives," *Press Release of Airline Center* (2004). Retrieved from http://www.airlie.com/ pressroom.

23. Convention Industry Council, "Convention Industry Council's Green Meetings Report" (2004). Retrieved from www. conventionindustry.org/projects/.

24. Anonymous, "IH&RA Environmental Award Lauds Efforts to Promote Sustainable Tourism," Press Release of International Hotel & Restaurant Association (1999). Retrieved from http://www.ih-ra.com.

25. Anonymous, "Winners Announced for the IH&RA Environmental Award 2002— Hoteliers in Sweden and India Lauded for Commitment to Energy and Air Quality Management," press release of International Hotel & Restaurant Association (2002). Retrieved from http://www.ih-ra.com.

26. Anonymous, "The Green Hotelier & Restauranteur Environmental Award—1999 (n.d.). Retrieved from http://www.orchidhotel.com/ bombay/ihra.htm.

27. "Company Profile, The Orchid: An Ecotel Hotel." Retrieved from http://www.orchidhotel.com/mumbai_hotels /hotels_profile.htm.

28. Op. cit., no. 26.

29. Ibid.

30. Ibid.

31. Anonymous, "What Is IHEI? (n.d.). Retrieved from http://www.ihei.org/ history.htm.

32. Ibid.

33. Anonymous, "Hoteliers in Germany and Tanzania Lauded for Commitment to Energy Conservation" (2001). Retrieved from http://www.ihrestaurantsforsale.com/.

34. Op. cit., no. 1.

35. Anonymous, "IH&RA Environmental Award Lauds Effort to Promote Sustainable Tourism" (1999). Retrieved from http://www.hospitlaitynet.org/news.

36. Op. cit., no. 28.

37. Op. cit., no. 27.

38. Ibid.

39. Ibid.

40. Ibid.

41. Ibid.

42. Ibid.

43. Ibid.

44. Ibid.

45. "Company Profile, Kamat Hotels India Limited." Retrieved from http://www.khil.com/about_us.htm.

46. Op. cit., no. 27.

47. Ibid.

48. Ibid.

49. Ibid.

50. Ibid.

51. Ibid.

52. Ibid.
53. Ibid.
54. Op. cit., no. 2.
55. Ibid.
56. Ibid.
57. Ibid.

58. Ibid.
59. Ibid.
60. Ibid.
61. Op. cit., no. 27.
62. Ibid.

ADDITIONAL REFERENCES

Aitken, A. 2000. "Green Means." *Asian Hotel & Catering Times*, 15–16.

Asian Hotel & Catering Times. 2000a. " 'Green Games' Inspire Hotel Clean Up," 21–22.

Asian Hotel & Catering Times. 2000b. "Green Keepers," 18–19.

Hill, R. A. 2004/2005. "The Greening of the Hospitality Industry" *HSMAI Marketing Review*, 25–29.

Jones, P. 2002. "The Orchid Hotel." *Tourism and Hospitality Research* 3, no. 3: 277–80.

Kalwani, R. 2000. "Switching Gears to Green." *Asian Hotel & Catering Times*, 28–29.

McCarthy, C. 2004/2005. "Going 'Green' Gets Serious with Certification." *HSMAI Marketing Review*, 30–32.

Environmental Scanning

Identifying Forces Driving Change

EXHIBIT 1 Strategic Management Model

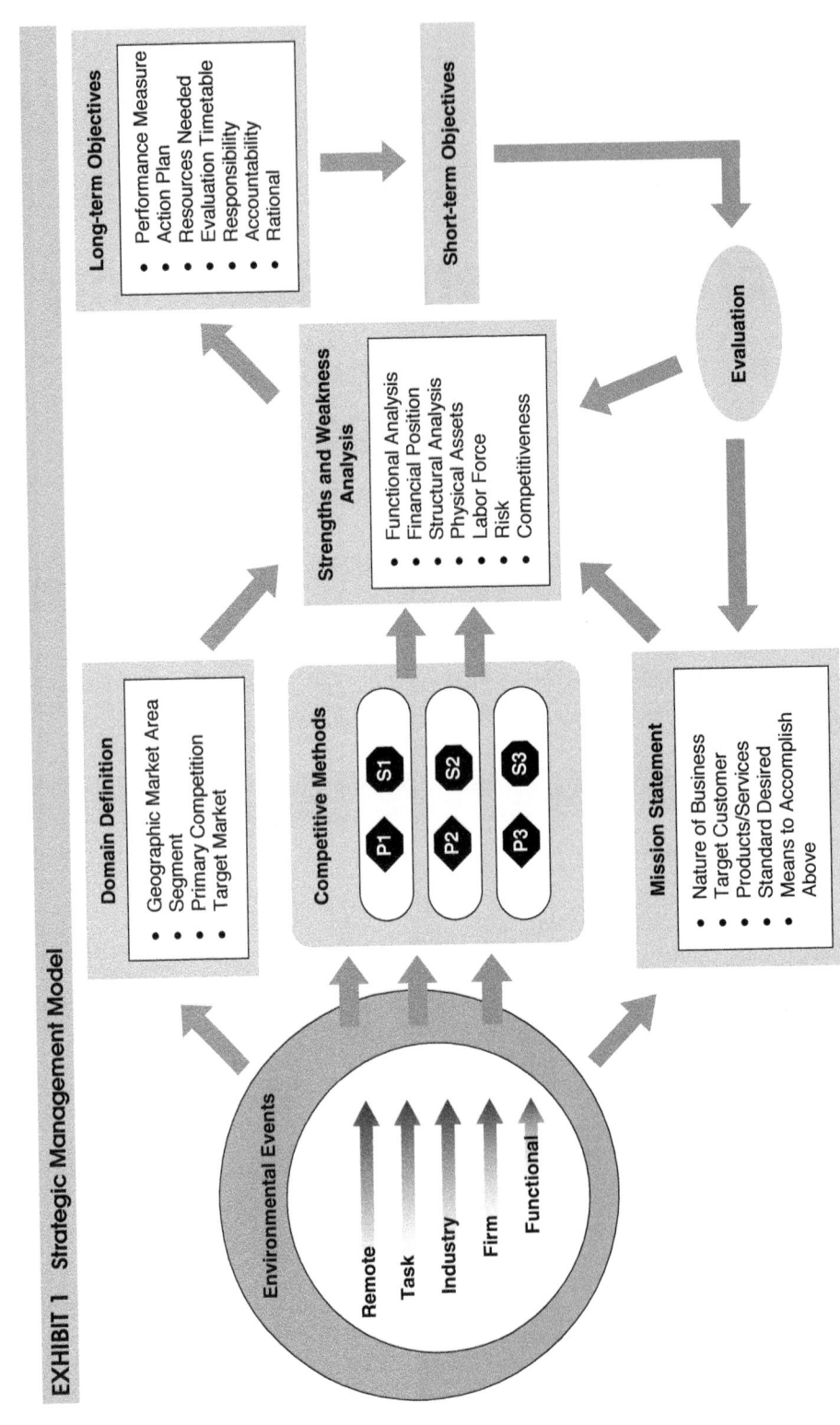

Chapter Purpose

In this chapter the environmental scanning process is explained. The importance of developing an effective scanning process is essential to achieving coalignment among forces driving change, strategy choice, and organization structure as detailed in Exhibit 1. The first step in effective strategic management is to identify emerging forces driving change and choose competitive methods that will allow the organization to compete in the future.

Scanning the Business Environment

Identifying the Forces Driving Change

The goal of any environmental scanning process is to successfully identify the key forces driving change within the contextual environment of the organization. To do this, managers must set up personal and organizational scanning systems to be sure that the widest perceptual view of the environment is achieved. This scanning system should (1) identify each force, the variables (value drivers) making it up, and their interdependencies with other variables, (2) suggest cause-and-effect relationships, (3) determine the history and timing associated with the development of the forces, and (4) assist the manager in estimating the impact of forces driving change on the firm.

Identifying the forces driving change requires the manager to synthesize information that comes from a variety of sources. In assessing each source's contributions, the manager will likely begin to see similarities among the information coming from each source. These similarities when synthesized should begin to suggest that a pattern is emerging; one that needs to be further analyzed and monitored. Exhibit 2 demonstrates an example of how these emerging patterns are developed.

EXHIBIT 2   Identifying Events in the Environment

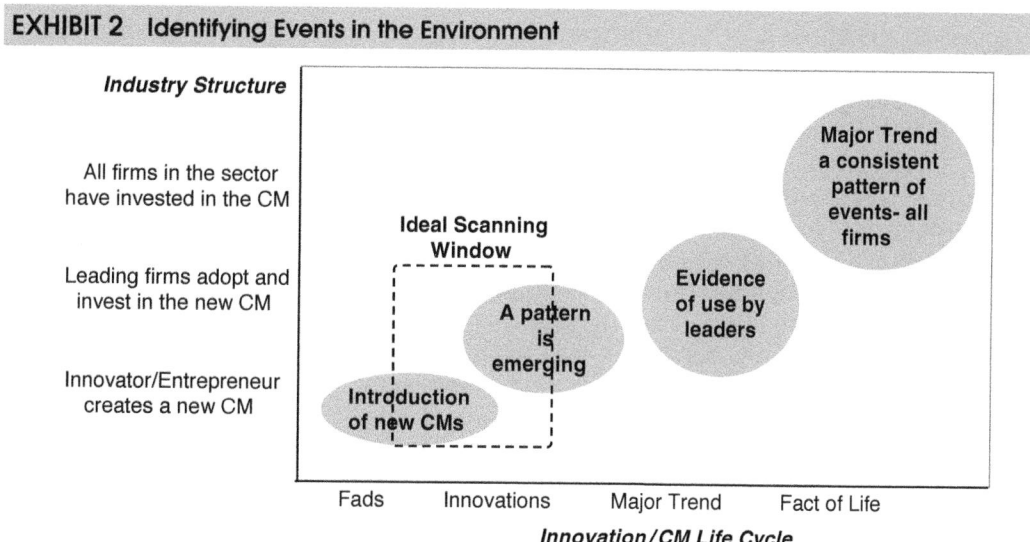

A careful look at Exhibit 2 suggests that change often falls on a continuum. The x-axis in the exhibit represents this continuum. Moving from left to right along this axis you can see that many competitive methods (CMs) in the business environment begin as fads and then move from there to innovations, major trends, and finally, facts of life when they turn into industrywide critical success factors (CSFs). The y-axis offers a similar continuum where it suggests that change in the overall structure of an industry segment begins with the creative spirits of the entrepreneurs who often are the champions of ideas that drive change and introduce new competitive methods that will ultimately lead to industry change. As the ideas catch on, the evolution of the CM moves from the limited introduction by entrepreneurs to those more established firms that like to wait and see how the new ideas play out in this environment before investing in them. Eventually some of these creative ideas find their way into common practice in all firms within an industry.

The size of the ovals in Exhibit 2 suggest the number of firms that adopt new ideas and/or competitive methods that can often emerge from the entrepreneur group. Many of these ideas are often just fads. However, if conditions are right (i.e., market demand is present), these fads gain momentum and emerge as innovations, and other firms begin to copy what appears to be a competitive method that will add future value to the firm. At this point these innovations begin to establish themselves as important new competitive methods that industry leaders embrace as they compete for the future. If the innovation continues to gather momentum because it has proven to be successful, then it usually transcends into a major trend and ultimately a fact of life, in which case all firms by then have adopted the competitive method. Once the leading firms have adopted a competitive method, it usually then becomes an industry wide-critical success factor. In other words, all firms must now invest in it if they are to compete in an industry sector. The relative increasing size of the ovals in the Exhibit 2 demonstrates this relationship.

The shaded area encompassing the oval, referred to as *introduction of new competitive methods* and *a pattern is emerging* in Exhibit 2, offers what many forward-thinking managers believe is the best window for scanning, for it is here that many opportunities arise to lead in the industry. It is here that future demand is usually first developed based on forces emerging in the remote environment. Although it is not the only window, it is one of value for creative managers seeking to always be a step ahead of the competition.

An example will help illustrate this idea. The managers in the hotel industry have rather slowly embraced over the past two decades the use of technology to assist them to compete. Holiday Inn Corporation (the forerunner to the current InterContinental Hotels and Resorts) was one of the first entrepreneurial hotel companies to develop its own reservation system, which in their view was an innovative industry-leading competitive method. Others were quick to follow, and today, it is almost impossible to compete without one because it has become an industrywide critical success factor. After leading the industry for many years, managers in Holiday Inn Worldwide (then a subsidiary of Bass, the British Brewer) realized in the late 1980s that they needed to reinvent their reservation system to take advantage of recent developments in technology. They invested heavily in merging their yield/revenue management systems, property management systems, data warehousing and mining systems, and their reservation systems. Once again Holiday Inn Worldwide took the lead in the use of technology with the approximately $100 million investment and was followed by their leading competitors. However, this time it outsourced this development to both aggressive entrepreneurial and established firms that had the necessary expertise and could help them lead the industry forward. Using the entrepreneurial thinking of these technology companies, HIWW built a new management system using the latest technology from the ground up.

What is clear in this case is that many years ago, Holiday Inn Corporation could easily have been identified as the entrepreneurial firm whose bold ideas about reservations ultimately reshaped how the industry handled its reservations process. Other firms were quick to follow in adopting this innovation. The same is true in the more recent example, but in this case HIWW was adopting the thinking and products of other entrepreneurial firms. In this most recent example, HIWW recognized that the effective utilization of technology would become one of the most important competitive methods of the 1990s. They also recognized that they could not use technology to its fullest without integrating all the various dedicated software products that they had purchased over the years. If they could achieve a seamless integration of all their management information and reservations needs ahead of their competitors, they could lead the industry forward and enjoy a competitive advantage until others caught up. In accomplishing this they recognized there were many variables in the domain of their business environment affecting the timing of their success in this potential value-adding investment. This recognition did indeed give them competitive advantage over other chains.

Despite this leadership role over several decades, InterContinental Hotels and Resorts (morphed today from Holiday Inn Worldwide) was like all other chains when another development in technology emerged in the form of e-commerce in the late 1990s. What was changing was how the Internet shifted the sale of rooms from the hotel companies to new intermediaries such as Expedia, Travelocity, Orbitz, and so on. These new intermediaries changed the industry, and now hotel companies are fighting back to try to regain some of the control they had. Here again, InterContinental led, but in this case it was in a defensive way, trying to protect its control over pricing and inventory. This emphasizes an important fact in business: You can be leading in a proactive way one minute and then find yourself reacting and defending in the next. The moral of this story is that managers must be on their constant guard and scanning continually if leadership is to be maintained.

The previous example clearly illustrates the value of identifying forces that drive change such as technology, then seeking to find opportunities in which to invest that will lead an industry forward, providing significant value to the firm. There are risks associated with this type of strategic thinking, but business is about taking risks. Our position is that these actions needn't be serendipitous; they can be calculated based on rational approaches to the investment decision. Exhibit 2 represents this rational approach and will be used later in this and the next two chapters to illustrate how risk in investing in the future can be addressed.

Environmental Scanning

To accomplish the level of success throughout the strategic management process as the InterContinental Hotels and Resorts example suggests, managers must establish an environmental scanning system. The type of system will depend on the organization but regardless, there are key elements to any scanning system. Exhibit 3 indicates the elements necessary to establish such a system. Each of these elements is discussed in the following sections of this chapter.

- Establish domain definition
- Organizational structure issues
- Determine information needs—quantitative and qualitative
- Determine information mediums
- Assess timing of information
- Identify sources
- Choose scanning activities—regular and irregular
- Determine analysis and synthesis processes
- Determine information sharing
- Establish information feedback and evaluation systems

EXHIBIT 3   Establishing an Environmental Scanning System

Domain Definition

The task of domain definition is the first step in establishing an effective environmental scanning system. The domain of an organization refers to the context in which it exists and functions. Within this domain an organization engages in transactions with other organizations, customers, suppliers, competitors, and regulators. These transactions often form patterns of relationships that each member of the domain maintains and monitors for change. In stable domains these patterns remain somewhat continuous, allowing managers to predict with some certainty the future of these relationships. In uncertain environments, these patterns are subject to wide swings and eruptions. The manager's challenge is to define the appropriate domain so as to be sure that all forces driving change can be considered when making strategic decisions.

Elements of the Domain

Exhibit 4 contains the important criteria for the manager to use in establishing the most appropriate domain definition. They are introduced here for the purpose of

EXHIBIT 4   Criteria of the Domain Definition

- Elements of domain
  - Geographic market area
  - Segment defined by competitive methods made up of the mix of product and service attributes
  - Primary competition
  - Major descriptors of target market
- Industry structure
  - Existing competitors, potential competitors, substitutes, suppliers and buyers
- Determine interdependencies
  - Relationships with suppliers, competitors
  - Relationships among different environmental categories
  - Primary and secondary relationships (hierarchical)

informing you that this is the first step or activity that managers must take in setting up a scanning system.

Organizational Structure Issues

Once the domain of the firm has been defined, the manager must turn attention to how the scanning system is established within the firm. This includes determining who participates in the process, what resources are allocated to this endeavor, and how the information is processed and used. Organizations must have a system by which resources are allocated to accomplish their stated objectives. This system is often termed the organization's *structure*.[1] Scanning the environment must fit into that structure because resources must be allocated to this important management activity. When considering this structure, management must determine whether or not the scanning process is done by the chief executive officer, senior management, or other combinations of other personnel. The job announcements contained in Exhibit 5 provides some indication of how the

---

EXHIBIT 5 Corporate Job Descriptions—National Hotel Companies

Example 1: Marriott International, Inc, (MI)
Director, Competitive Intelligence

Position description: The director, competitive intelligence is responsible for developing and managing the tools, documents, processes and "virtual team" necessary to provide MI lodging stakeholders at all levels with proactive, timely and actionable information, analysis and guidance regarding competitors, the lodging industry and Marriott's competitive position.

Responsibilities:
- Provides timely, actionable information and analysis to support and inform MI and brand strategy to improve competitive position
- Manages and motivates a cross-functional alliance of associates to gather international knowledge of competitors; creates framework, tools documents, processes to collect and deliver timely, actionable information; develops scorecard to measure success/value of function; effectively manages projects; assists in directing the work of and developing an administrative program specialist; looks for opportunities to streamline and eliminate work that is not value added.
- Provides direction to and informal management of an admin/program specialist.
- Proactively identifies industry and competitor activities that are relevant to MI and brand strategies and analyzes them for their implications-both current and future for the business.
- Manages communication to and interaction with associates at all levels, both within and outside the Brand Management and with MI's senior management team; leverages the broader organization through managing and motivating a cross-functional alliance of associates to gather internal knowledge of competitors; builds strong networks within the industry and outside of MI.
- Strong understanding of the lodging industry and MI's brands (e.g. key competitors, business models, operations); effectively communicates orally and in writing to all levels of management; looks outside Marriott for opportunities to improve effectiveness

Experience:
- Seven to ten years of business experience, to include competitive intelligence and /or strategic planning.
- Familiarity with economic principles, the hotel industry and hotel organizations.
- College degree required; advanced degree a plus.

(continued)

EXHIBIT 5 *continued*

Skills:
- Able to work independently to manage and further develop the CI function (i.e. processes, tools, deliverables, etc.) based upon a knowledge of stakeholder needs.
- Able to direct and influence the work of management/non management associates at different levels and in different functions—without direct authority
- Highly effective oral and written communicator
- Strategic thinker: able to deliver competitive/industry information to match the strategic needs of the brands/company and assist in evolving strategies.
- Strong customer service/consultant orientation, able to build relationships with associates at all levels.
- Strong analytical capability.
- Strong project management skills
- Significant knowledge of competitive intelligence methods and tools.
- Broad-based knowledge of the hotel industry and its operating model

Example 2: Interstate Hotels and Resorts (NYSE: IHR) Development Analyst

Interstate Hotels and Resorts (NYSE: IHR) is the nation's largest independent hotel management company with over 300 hotels nationwide. We are seeking an experienced Development Analyst to join the Acquisitions and Development team in our Corporate Headquarters in Arlington, VA.

The Development Analyst will play a pivotal role in supporting the growth initiatives of Interstate Hotels and Resorts through management contracts, acquisitions, and new developments. The Development Analyst will work with the Director of Feasibility and Investment Analysis to provide overall support to the deal executives in all aspects of underwriting and transaction structuring. This high profile, entry level position requires a high degree of accuracy as the information provided by the Development Analyst is the critical support data for the policy decision makers at the senior management level.

Responsibilities:
- Assist in the preparation of project feasibility and investment analysis for new business opportunities
- Assist in the coordination of the due diligence process for new acquisitions
- Assist in the preparation of internal/external investment memorandums and presentations
- Assist development team in working with capital sources
- Assist in maintaining research library and database

Qualifications:
- Bachelor's Degree in hospitality management or accounting/finance
- 1–2 years industry experience, preferably in development, consulting, or finance
- Knowledge of lodging and real estate industries
- Proficiency in Excel modeling as well as other Microsoft Office applications
- Ability to produce high quality reports in a timely manner
- Self-motivated, goal-oriented, and results driven
- Consummate team player with excellent interpersonal skills

scanning process has been handled in two major U.S. corporations, Marriott International and Interstate Hotels and Resorts. What is important to notice about these announcements is that they have a very specific industry emphasis. We address this industry characteristic in the next two chapters in more detail. Also important in these announcements is the emphasis on analytical skills.

Communication skills and self-management capabilities are also an important part of these positions primarily because the task can be unstructured and require significant independent research. It also demands a lot of discussion and listening to other's ideas to formulate inductive theories concerning the relationship between the firm and its environment.

Once individuals who will be doing the scanning have been identified, it becomes essential to decide how formal the structure must be. In many firms the structure is informal with those responsible for the scanning process usually doing it as part of their total job responsibility mix. In other cases, scanning is performed by a formalized department, dedicated to this process as indicated in the two job descriptions earlier. And still in others, it is some type of combined effort. In earlier research reflecting the locus and role of the scanning unit in multinational hotel companies, it was found that 64% of the firms employed some type of combined scanning effort, 23% relied on the efforts of the chief executive officer, with less than 3% utilizing a free-standing unit (Olsen, Murthy and Inagaki 1995).[2] In the 1996 study by the authors, 79% utilized a combined unit and 7% employed a freestanding unit[3]. As can be concluded from this evidence, the trend toward a more formal structure is occurring with greater use being made of a combined process. More recently, observations by the authors suggest that scanning is still minimized in restaurant and foodservice companies and only slightly improved in the hotel industry.

An indication of the growing importance of the role of the scanning function in business in general is the formation of the Society of Competitive Intelligence Professionals (SCIP). As can be seen in the text box, which was taken from the website of the society, the role of environmental scanning has emerged as a professional field. The society has over 3,000 members worldwide. The SCIP's role in business performance analysis is growing and built on a strong ethical and legal foundation. Scanning is also performed by many consulting firms who engage in preparing in-depth studies on key trends affecting a firm or industry such as the Global Securities Research & Economics Group of Merrill Lynch. Trade associations such as the National Restaurant Association and the American Hotel and Lodging Association also perform this type of function. Thus, although individual firms may

---

The society of Competitive Intelligence Professionals (SCIP) a global nonprofit membership organization for everyone involved in creating and managing business knowledge. Our mission is to enhance the skills of knowledge professionals in order to help their companies achieve and maintain a competitive advantage.

Specifically, SCIP provides education and networking opportunities for business professionals working in the rapidly growing field of competitive intelligence (the legal and ethical collection and analysis of information regarding the capabilities, vulnerabilities, and intentions of business competitors). Many SCIP members have backgrounds in market research, strategic analysis, or science and technology.

Established in 1986, today SCIP has over 50 chapters around the world, with individual members in more than 50 nations. In addition, SCIP has alliance partnerships with independent affiliate organizations in many countries.

not actually employ a lot of staff for this purpose, many pay for this service through outsourcing this activity to third parties.

Another important issue for management to decide when creating the structure of the scanning unit is the overall role the unit will have in the strategic decision-making process. Should the role be directed at major *policy* decisions that are usually made by the board of directors of the firm or should it be directed more at *strategic* or *functional* decisions? The policy role focuses on early detection of broad strategic issues that are likely to result in mergers or acquisitions, selling business units, or in public policy impact on the industry and firm. Such issues as environmental protection, government-mandated work standards, and wages are examples of this type of policy activity. The strategic role is defined as looking at the remote and task environments and integrating corporate- and business-level decisions. The functional role refers to assessing events shaping one or all of the management functions. In the two studies referenced earlier, the major role of the scanning unit was in the strategic decision-making process, followed by decisions in the management functions such as finance and marketing. Few firms utilized the scanning process for policy-level decisions.

The final structural issue that management must address is the degree of formality in the scanning process. Formality refers to the degree of codification of rules, procedures, systems, and communication channels that are associated with the scanning. In the two studies cited in this discussion, the results suggested that firms prefer a less formal effort, with fewer than a quarter indicating some degree of formality. Although the results of these two studies should not be generalized to the entire hospitality industry, they do suggest that firms are beginning to make the scanning process a more formal part of the organization structure and allocate resources to this effort. Despite this trend, the process still appears to be loosely defined with no general industry trends emerging to help identify the best of the current industry practices in this area.

Communication of scanning results is essential to effective decision making. How results are communicated throughout the firm is a structural decision. If new exciting opportunities are identified, it is obvious that firms do not want this communicated to a wide group of personnel until decisions about what to do have been made. Beyond this strategic need to be confidential, the results of the scanning process should be incorporated into a communication process that allows a regular sharing with key decision makers. In some firms a scanning update is the first item on the agenda of weekly management meetings. In this case, senior managers report on their own scanning efforts as well as the weekly updates they receive from their subordinates. Firms following this approach feel that this type of communication structure not only helps them to stay ahead of competition but it also helps to create a learning culture throughout the organization. Regardless of the communication process used, the point here is that management must make it a goal to formally structure communications regarding the results of the scanning process so that decision makers at all levels of the organization can enhance their strategic effectiveness.

Like all decisions, the development of an effective environmental scanning unit must meet the needs of the organization. This activity requires resources, which must ultimately add value to the firm. Thus careful evaluation of who is involved in the process, how formal it is, how much time is devoted, and what will be the role of a scanning unit must occur. The decisions made here will determine how successful the firm will be in receiving signals and interpreting their meaning relative to the firm's strategy. This structure will determine how effective scanning will be. It will affect how important interdependencies are to be analyzed. Finally, it will determine the size and relevance of the perceptual window the firm has of its domain.

Determining Information Needs

Determining the information needs of the firm can begin only after the process of defining the domain the firm must compete in is completed. Once established, the information needs will generally fall into four categories: quantitative, qualitative, and personal and nonpersonal. The quantitative information was earlier referred to as objective information, such as the concept of the variables and/or value drivers we have discussed thus far. It includes such items as demographic and census data, econometric statistics, and empirically based information. Exhibit 6 contains examples of the types of quantitative information (value drivers) sought by hotel managers as they seek to estimate the potential demand for their products and services. A close look at the exhibit indicates that in the hotel industry, there are primary and secondary demand generators in a specific market area. Each variable under each type of demand generator is generally measured as part of the U.S. Census Bureau every ten years with estimates updating this information being made by private firms eager to sell it to clients looking for more timely data.

Qualitative information refers to the perceptual information often obtained by scanning a variety of sources of information such as newspapers and magazines, books, scientific articles, or business and trade publications. This type of information is more subjective with less solid data available. Both qualitative and quantitative information can be obtained from personal and nonpersonal sources. Personal sources refer to colleagues, suppliers, bankers, investors, and just friends. Nonpersonal sources refer to published information. This information is often referred to as secondary sources.

Information can also be purchased. Consulting firms, industry associations, universities, and others provide information that is customized to the firm's specific needs. In the case of this type of information, the scanner must know what specific information they are looking for and evaluate each source in terms of its ability to provide reliable and valid results in a timely fashion.

EXHIBIT 6 Examples of Quantitative Information: Primary and Secondary Demand Generators

Quantitative Information

Primary Demand Generators	Secondary Demand Generators
• Population	• Business travelers
• Housing	• Conventions and meetings
• Transportation	• Incentive travel
• Industry	• Government
• Health facilities	• Military
• Education facilities	• Fraternal groups
• Recreational facilities	• Pleasure travelers
• Special events	• Airline business
• Attractions	• Sports teams
• Income levels	• Special events

In today's knowledge environment, there is an abundance of information of all types available from a variety of sources. Thus the manager must now develop the ability to know all the possible sources of information that are available, which would include the latest array of electronic databases, not to mention the Internet. The challenge for the manager once this ability is developed is then to learn how to interpret, analyze, and synthesize all the information that is out there. This most often must be done in a working climate of too little time and too much information. The ability to gather and use information effectively will become one of the most important skills a contemporary manager can develop.

One way to assist the manager in achieving the necessary ability to meet the challenges of today's information-rich environment is to make use of the concept often referred to as the *body of knowledge*. This concept is defined as all the information available regarding a topic in the domain of the industry. This would include all the results of scientific research and its application to specific industry problems and issues. This type of information can be obtained through all the available mediums discussed in the following section. The body of knowledge also includes relevant trade and professional journals that report on activities within the business domain. The most important responsibility of the strategic manager is to be sure that all those involved in the process of scanning know the body of knowledge that they must be scanning. Attempts should be made to identify the most important sources of information within that body so that they may be continually scanned. These sources are usually widely read and familiar to industry members.

What must be faced in this era of information proliferation is that the body of knowledge tends to become more complex. This is partially because of the ease with which information can now be shared across all mediums but in particular due to the increased capabilities brought about by the electronic forms of information sharing.

What can be certain is that information will continue to expand the body of knowledge available to assist in strategic decision making. This expansion will force managers to become information managers, capable of receiving, analyzing, and synthesizing a growing body of increasingly complex information. They will be required to use this information to manage in an environment of volatile and complex relationships. Tomorrow's manager will include among all his or her other responsibilities the growing role of an information manager.

Determining the Information Medium

Just as it is important to determine the appropriate structure for the scanning unit and the information needs, so is the decision concerning information mediums chosen to provide vital information. The most common medium is face-to-face personal interaction. Business meetings, conferences, sales calls, lunches, dinners, and sporting activities are all common settings for face-to-face communication. These are often the preferable settings for this medium because all available verbal and nonverbal cues can be observed and assessed.

The written medium, both personal and impersonal, continues to be an important one. As mentioned earlier, with the advent of the Internet and growing use of the intranet (organization-wide communications network), this medium will begin to match the value of the face-to-face encounter. As firms expand their e-mail systems to include company *chat rooms*, and other forms of written communication, the manager will face the challenges of too little time to address the growing level of information coming through this medium.

The telecommunications revolution will no doubt bring about rapid changes in the mediums used. Teleconferencing and net-based meetings are just two examples of how this technology permits a multimedia approach to information sharing. With high-speed information transfer, and the ability to compress and decompress video images, it is now possible to achieve effective verbal and visual transmission to almost any destination. As the technology in this area advances, this form of communication will expand, making virtual reality an everyday part of communications. At the rate of advancement in this area, it is almost impossible to dream what the future holds. We know that it will require managers to be trained in the use of technology and the analysis and interpretation of the robust information it provides.

The electronic medium will dominate the exchange of information far into the foreseeable future. Its primary role of transferring information has been expanded into a growing role in commerce. In the travel and tourism business it is becoming one of the most lucrative means of selling destinations and modes of travel. In its December 2004 analysis of the lodging industry, Merrill Lynch noted that hotel and lodging is the fastest growing online travel segment and accounted for almost 30% of online travel revenues in 2003. Merrill Lynch estimated that online hotel bookings will comprise 20% of total hotel sales in 2005 and 27% by 2006. This medium is likely to have the potential to dominate the marketing of the industry. The electronic medium will also give new prominence to libraries as they become information and data warehouses that can be mined by anyone with access to a modem, computer, wireless connectivity and access to the Internet. Additionally, most information will be able to be accessed electronically, whether it be newspapers, magazines, or videos. This information will be from anywhere in the world at any hour. Information gathering can be customized and tailored for individual needs.

Assessing Timing of Information

The phrase *timing is everything* has a great deal of validity in the world of strategy. History is full of examples of bad timing such as product introductions that were either too early or too late; or acquisitions that failed due to shifts in demand curves; or loss of market share resulting from delayed introductions of products, brands, or innovations.

Bad timing can be avoided most often when firms have effective scanning systems and the organization has structured itself to improve the processing of information and its timing. This begins by first understanding the actual source of the information and what is the timing of the information flow. For example, trade journals generally have a 30-day cycle for news. This means a reporter picks up a lead on a story and it is usually in print within 30 days. In contrast, Internet-based information is processed and broadcast almost immediately through blogger networks. Thus the first thing the organization must determine after identifying its most reliable sources of information is to understand how quickly that information becomes available after the fact.

Of course, the best of all worlds is for the manager to perform in a role similar to an investigative reporter, seeking news before it actually becomes news. This is also similar to those who perform work in the murky world of spying. These individuals are trained to look for emerging developments long before they become serious. By cultivating sources of information, developing their own theories about how things work, and looking for patterns in things around them, they are able ideally to stay one step ahead of trouble or opportunity.

The timing issue also reflects how managers study the emerging forces that are developing. Knowing the timing of the information helps put some perspective on the evolution, but this must also be combined with enhanced perceptual, experiential, and cognitive skill development. This was pointed out early in this chapter when we discussed Exhibit 2 and the evolution of competitive methods. The more the manager improves on these capabilities, the easier it becomes to assess the timing issue.

The timing issue is closely tied to the risk investors face if managers guess wrong with respect to timing. We have stated repeatedly that risk is a concept that is a reflection of the variation in the cash flow streams of the firm. The manager, when making an investment, must estimate the future cash flow streams of the firm and the life of those flows. Although it is impossible to get this estimation process perfect, investors expect managers to reduce the risks associated with this effort by developing their capabilities to improve on the scanning effort. This helps eliminate the potential variance between forecast and reality.

Identifying Sources of Information

The first step in identifying sources of information is to determine the *body of knowledge* the manager is seeking to obtain information from. As stated previously in the section of this chapter on determining information needs, the body of knowledge is defined as the sum total of the knowledge accumulated in a field relative to the firm's domain. This is no small task in the complex world of hospitality where many disciplines contribute to the total body of knowledge. Exhibit 7 lists only a sampling of the disciplines that contain knowledge that ultimately finds its way into the decision-making processes of hospitality managers.

It is impossible for the hospitality manager of today to keep up with the developments of new knowledge in any one of these fields, let alone all of them. Thus the manager must rely on industry sources of information and the people who research and write for

EXHIBIT 7   A Sampling of Disciplines and Fields of Study Contributing to the Body of Knowledge in the Hospitality Industry

• Economics	• Accounting
• Ecology	• Finance
• Food Science	• Management Information Systems
• Nutrition	• Human Resources
• Organizational Behavior	• Linguistics
• Organization Theory	• Marketing
• Political Science	• Management Science
• Psychology	• Operations
• Technology	• Engineering
• Sociology	• Strategic Management
• Statistics	

these sources as well as others in the organization. The challenge for these individuals is also to stay on top of new knowledge in various disciplines and fields and then effectively translate it into useful industry information. This is an enormous undertaking, and it is growing each day as the body of knowledge explodes in quantity as a result of the development of an information society and knowledge workers.

In this information-based world, there is also a growing array of information sources available. In fact, it is not too uncommon to hear people say there is too much information to comprehend it all. In this environment, one of the most challenging problems future hospitality managers will have is what sources to select and what mediums to use. To make this selection easier, Exhibit 8 presents a look at the typical portfolio of information sources available to managers.

The primary concerns of the manager in selecting the sources of information are validity and reliability. *Validity* refers to fact that the information accurately represents and describes the relationships that are necessary to make important strategic decisions. Oftentimes this means checking with several sources to be sure that what information is provided is consistent across sources and situations. *Reliability* refers to the need for accuracy and consistency over time. If information sources cannot measure up in these two important criteria, they should not be used.

The task of assessing validity and reliability is even more difficult in today's electronic age. This is likely to be a growing problem because the scientific peer review process customarily used by respected journalists and scientists before information is published is not always used by those freely offering information in today's information exchange environment. This process usually requires a review of written work by one's peers, who take the responsibility for validity and reliability seriously. Now, however, anyone can establish a *home page* on the Internet and publish information regardless of its reliability and validity. This phenomenon is

EXHIBIT 8   Common Information Sources Available to the Hospitality Manager

Quantitative and Qualitative Information

Personal	Non-personal
• Researchers	• Conferences
• Internal personnel	• Seminars
• Consultants	• Trade Associations
• Suppliers	• Trade Magazines
• External business associates	• Newsletters
• Friends and family	• News services
	• On-line services
	• Newspapers
	• News Magazines
	• Government statistics
	• Government reports
	• Internal research
	• Databases

referred to as *blogging,* and those who exchange information in this medium are known as *bloggers.* The *bloggosphere* has become very popular in spreading news quickly. The result of this growing free flow of information is the challenge to the manager to get to know the established body of knowledge in the field. By knowing the body of knowledge, managers are able to concentrate their scanning on the most respected, valid, and reliable sources. They will also begin to know who are the leading thinkers and writers. This will help them to filter, analyze, and synthesize the growing amounts of information available on this industry, thus improving their decision-making capabilities. It also enables them to do more efficient scanning of the environment because if they are familiar with the body of knowledge, they need only direct their time to scanning for new ideas and not waste it on assessing old ones.

The greatest advantage of the electronic sourcing of information is the ability of various information services and providers to use hypertext and hypermedia methods to gather greater amounts of information from a wider variety of diverse disciplines. Hypertext refers to the process by which information is accumulated via a series of search algorithms that use keywords or concepts to bring information together. Well known search engines like Google have achieved considerable excellence and influence in the knowledge-sharing world as a result of their capabilities in bringing information on a specific topic together based on just a few keywords typed into the search window.

Additionally, such electronic databases as ABI/INFORM, Factiva, Lexus Nexus, and Wharton Data Research Services offer access to literally thousands of articles covering items of strategic interest to scanners.

The beauty of this form of knowledge search is that it is able to combine knowledge from a diverse group of disciplines. Although at first this combination may not appear to be logically related, the astute manager with strong perceptual, conceptual and cognitive skills may be able to see the relationships that exist and bring new thinking to important decisions.

Once sources have been identified, they cannot be left on automatic pilot. Managers must conduct periodic review of all sources to be sure that they provide the appropriate information, are up-to-date, and meet the validity and reliability criteria. Lastly, they must be of value to the strategic thinking of the firm. If not, they should be discarded. Exhibit 9 is an example of a form to be used to conduct

EXHIBIT 9 Evaluating the Quality of Information Sources

Event or Trend	Top Three Sources	Timing	Estimate of Validity & Reliability	Influence on Strategic Thinking
Asset and capital	Wall Street Journal Business Week Economist	Daily Weekly Weekly	Excellent in short term Excellent in short term Excellent in both short and long term	Very strong Strong Very strong

this periodic audit of the information sources used as part of the established scanning system in the firm.

The form encourages managers to review key events that have affected their business and evaluate the three most important sources of information according to the criteria just established. This periodic assessment will ensure that managers at all levels will look carefully at their information sources and constantly evaluate them as to their relevance to the strategic thinking of the firm.

Choosing Scanning Activities

Scanning is an activity that does not lend itself to neatly defined processes or timetables. Like many tasks in management, scanning is a function of priority, timing, ability, reward, and feedback. Scanning is also a refection of the appreciation for the value of the coalignment model. It cannot be done effectively without strong cognitive, experiential, and perceptual skills.

Scanning activities can fall into several general types of modes: null, reactive, nonroutine, routine, and proactive. In the null mode, the scanner is metaphorically a dry sponge waiting to receive information. Obviously this form of scanning is dangerous because receiving the correct information depends on luck and good timing. It depends on information arriving that is usually not solicited. Although in many cases this type of scanning can have value if some important information is presented unexpectedly, it is ineffective, however, in today's dynamic environment.

Most managers would probably fit into the reactive mode. This mode was used by the *boiling frog* when it was thrown into a pot of boiling water. Managers are always responding and reacting to information that comes their way. In this mode, they may actually have to undertake some form of scanning activity, but it is usually unorganized and reflects a narrow body of knowledge. Seldom do you see a manager in this mode spending time assessing events developing in the remote environment.

Managers also frequently use nonroutine scanning. They apply this mode when they are faced with a problem or opportunity analysis. In this case resources of time, personnel, and money are used to research the latest information pertaining to the need at the time. In this mode the common problem is that there is always too little time and too much information. This is especially true if the scanners are not familiar with the body of knowledge.

Routine scanning provides structure to the scanning process. In this mode, personnel are usually assigned to the scanning process as either a part of some other responsibilities or may even have this as a full-time position. In the routine scanning setting, the body of knowledge has been defined as well as the sources of information and mediums to be used. Generally, the degree of formality, frequency, and scope has been defined. The structure of the firm provides for the most effective communication of information and the sharing of it with key personnel.

The proactive mode is one that builds on the routine mode but provides the futuristic look that is necessary in today's environment. In this mode the routine process comes alive in a way that allows managers to make important decisions about investments in future competitive methods. The timing of the events identified in this mode is usually considered to be an important part of activities. Managers are expected to have a substantive understanding of the body of knowledge shaping the event, the history of its development, the speed with which it is developing, and what are the likely scenarios that must be considered.

	Category	Three Most Significant Events
Scanning the Remote Environment Categories	Political Socio-cultural Technology Economic Ecological	Free market systems, increasing pressure from capital markets, emphasis on value adding capabilities

	Category	Three Most Significant Events
Scanning the Task Environment Categories	Customers Suppliers Competitors Regulators	Investors requiring more value out of assets, lenders demanding more accountability, incorporating risk analysis into capital budgeting processes

	Category	Three Most Significant Events
Scanning the Functional Environment Categories	Human Resources Finance Operations Marketing Administration Research and Development	Value adding analysis, risk assessments for all new market investments, impact of investment decisions on share price

EXHIBIT 10   Scanning the Remote, Task, and Functional Environment Categories

The proactive mode is facilitated by developing a routine and structure to the scanning process. The forms illustrated in Exhibit 10 demonstrate how members of a firm can think through and record the events they see emerging from the scanning process. In this example, there are three forms, one each for the remote, task, and functional environmental categories. Managers are asked to identify the three most important forces driving change in each category of the environment. These forces are expected to yield for management opportunities to invest in.

In many cases, the individuals doing the scanning can customize their own forms to accomplish this process. What is important is that some process be established that is followed routinely. As stated earlier, the difference between the routine and proactive modes is simply the thinking framework utilized by the scanning team. Information

Monthly Updates	Major Events Updates
January February : : : : : : : December	Key investor is seeking seat on the Board Lender raises concern over competitive position given new competitors in the market place Interest rate rise Institutional investors show concern over industry performance

EXHIBIT 11   Scanning

can be gathered routinely, but it takes a future-oriented manager to make this information come alive in the planning process.

For fast-moving events that require closer monitoring, the form in Exhibit 11 provides structure to the scanning process by calling for updates every month. This frequent scanning activity can occur in highly volatile environments where competition is strong. Many firms schedule even weekly updates on the movements of competitors. The airlines do hourly updates, especially with regard to pricing activity. What is necessary is for management to make decisions on how it seeks to monitor each environmental category and in what mode, and then allocate resources to accomplish the scanning process.

Scanning modes can also include such well-known activities as scenario building where groups of individuals gather together to consider various alternatives to forces that drive change. Probable outcomes are identified and debated, and then some process of reaching agreement is chosen to decide which of these scenarios is agreed to by most of the participants. The process of agreement is often the result of what is referred to as a nominal group technique. In this case individuals are given the opportunity to vote (usually without influence from others involved) on which scenario or key point is in their view the most important. The success of this effort is that individuals should not feel pressured into voting for anything but their own choices. Once the votes are counted, the group achieves consensus on which scenario will be most important to the future strategy of the group or organization. The nominal group technique is in its own right a scanning mode and was used extensively in identifying the forces driving change.

The Delphi technique is another version of this process where experts are asked to contribute their views on some future item. This process is often done where participants are anonymous and in remote locations. This process has an advantage of no one individual dominating a group discussion on some issue. However, in some instances this is a disadvantage in that the exchange of ideas does not occur, resulting in narrowly defined responses to some key issue driving change. Organizations are encouraged to try a number of these modes to explore what is the best fit for all participants and strategic needs.

The Analysis and Synthesis Process

Up to this point we have been focusing our attention on the processes used to scan the environment to obtain strategic information. That is actually the easy part. The challenge is to analyze, interpret, and synthesize all this information originating from a wide variety of sources once it has been gathered. The proper interpretation of incoming information requires strong comprehension, analysis, synthesis, evaluative, and application skills. Two useful tools to apply those skills are content analysis and concept mapping.

One of the most difficult challenges facing the manager is reducing the tremendous amount of available information into some form for further analysis. One of the most effective ways of accomplishing this data reduction is a process called *content analysis*. It involves looking at information using a searching scheme that uses one of several units of analysis. The units of analysis can be words, combinations of words, concepts, or major themes. The reader seeks to identify the frequency with which the unit of analysis occurs in all the sources. The more often a unit is mentioned, the greater the reliability in the assumption that this unit is growing in importance and thus could become an important event-driving change. For strategic planning purposes, the concept or theme is a useful unit of analysis.

For example, in the early 1990s, it had been suggested that both the hotel and restaurant industry was in relative maturity. Sales were flat and in some cases in decline. In content analyzing the literature in the hospitality industry during that period, a reoccurring theme that would no doubt be identified were the difficulties hospitality firms were having in obtaining investment capital. No matter what source of information was relied on, the astute strategic manager would be able to see this theme mentioned often.

The content analysis can be very rigorous, with the scanner actually counting the number of times this theme is referenced from all sources. In addition to the times mentioned, the amount of editorial space, and discussion sessions included in conference programs and meeting agendas also represent the degree of importance of a theme or pattern. In this example, as the scanner reviewed all available information, this theme would have emerged as a pattern across all sources and be identified as a possible major force driving change.

To assist the scanner in accomplishing this difficult task, the environmental classification scheme becomes an important timesaver. By using this scheme, the scanner can organize the content analysis according to the body of knowledge underpinning each category and variable. Although many may argue that using such a scheme overly structures and can inhibit the free flow of thought and stifles creativity, this notion must be balanced with the efficiency and effectiveness needed to identify important forces driving change in the complex business environment. For those organizations with limited time, capability, and financial resources, a more directed viewing process such as this is reasonably effective in identifying the major trends shaping the future.

Because of the advances being made in technology, software is now available to assist in the content analysis process. Exhibit 12 is an example of output from a content analysis software program called Catpac. It is a graphical representation of the key ideas that have been mentioned in the annual reports of Marriott International for the period 2000 to 2002.

As you can see in this graphic, there are two major high point clusters in terms of most frequently mentioned themes: One is joint venture (on the left) and the

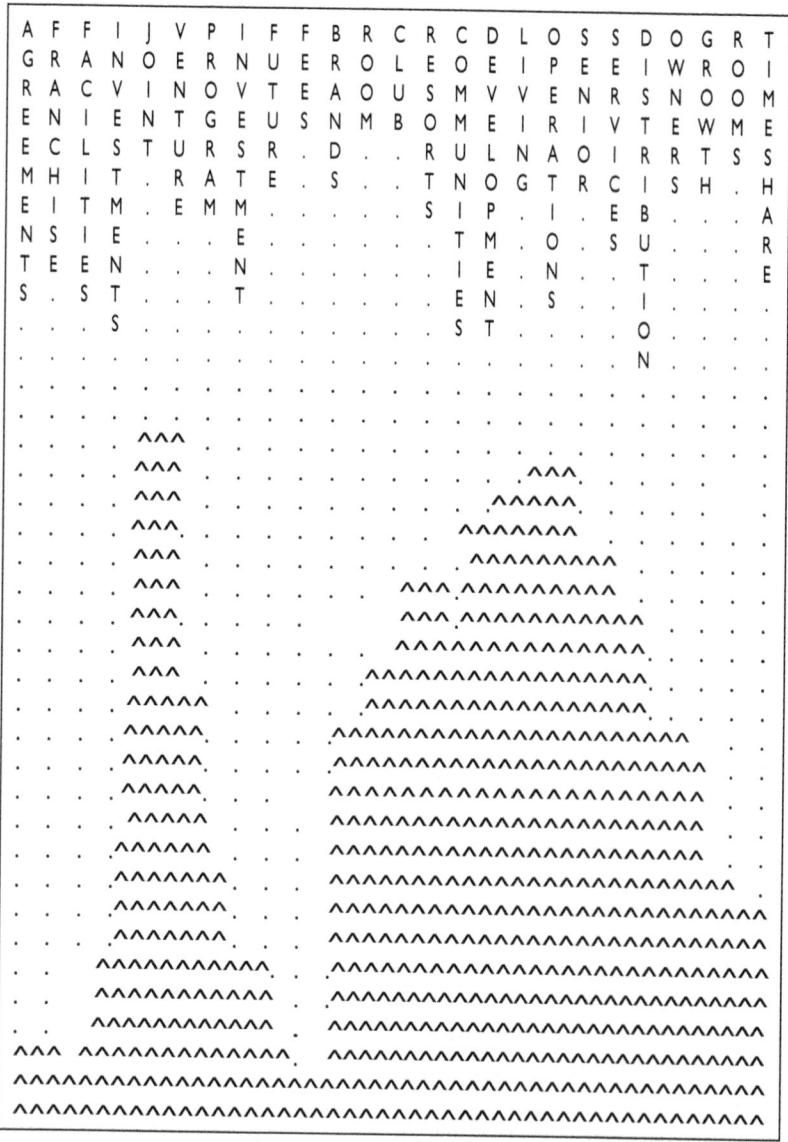

EXHIBIT 12 Catpac Content Analysis Software: Analysis of Marriott International's Annual Reports[1]

[1]The authors wish to thank Nicolas Graf, who at the time this work was performed was on the faculty at the Ecole Hotelier de Lausanne in Switzerland.

other is a combination of operations and senior services. This graphic points out clearly what Marriott International is emphasizing. Content analysis of annual reports is a common practice among competitive intelligence professionals as they look for clues in terms of what a company's competitors are doing to compete. This

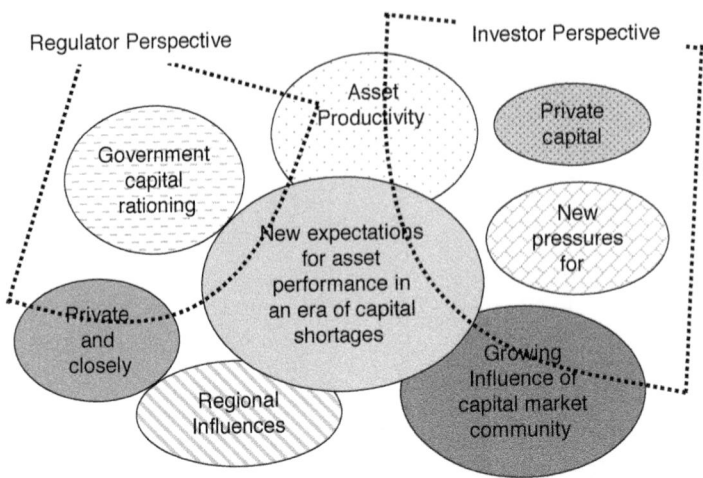

Regulator Perspective

Investor Perspective

Asset Productivity

Private capital

Government capital rationing

New expectations for asset performance in an era of capital shortages

New pressures for

Private and closely

Growing Influence of capital market community

Regional Influences

EXHIBIT 13   Concept Map of Environmental Event

example illustrates the power of new software programs, which can map themes contained in all types of literature, whether it is in the task environment or the remote environment.

Concept mapping is a further extension of the content analysis process. It is illustrated in Exhibit 13. The analysis occurring in this example is of one of the seven forces driving change, *Assets and Capital*. In this case, what the scanner did was group the themes or patterns identified from the content analysis process and map them. In general, the content analysis process simply groups themes on the basis of frequency and degree of importance as usually measured by the amount of space and time given to them in the literature and mediums being analyzed. Once these themed groupings are developed, the next step is to analyze them further to achieve additional data reduction by merging groups with similar contents. Examples of these themes appear in the oval shapes in Exhibit 13. Put differently, each of the ovals represents a consolidation of a number of differing ideas that could still be grouped into a common theme.

Once the themes are identified, they are also assessed in terms of frequency and volume to determine their strength and relative importance. This is indicated by the relative size of the ovals in Exhibit 13. The larger ovals represent the most frequently mentioned themes in the body of knowledge scanned. Also evident in this exhibit are the many interdependencies and relationships among the concepts identified, as indicated by the overlapping of several ovals.

In addition to the overlapping observed, this concept map also groups themes into two broader topics using the V-shaped graphics. These broader themes suggest that this force driving change (*assets and capital*) is being shaped in two ways, first by the investor perspective on the right hand side grouping and the regulatory community on the left. Once the scanner has identified the themes he must set up an appropriate scanning system that will track developments in each. What is critical here is that the scanner understands the synergy (interdependencies) among the various themes so as to appreciate the relationships that are likely to be played out. This should help enable the manager then to be able to anticipate how each force is likely to change and as a consequence, assist in helping him or her invest in competitive methods that will keep the firm ahead of the competition. To achieve this lofty goal, however, the skills identified in the first paragraph of this section must be well developed. These are briefly discussed in the following paragraphs.

Comprehension skills require that managers must first know the body of knowledge in the industry they are scanning. They must possess an awareness and understanding of the key elements of the task environment and how organizations in that environment interact with each other to produce events likely to impact the firm. To accomplish this, managers must develop their *cognitive* and *perceptual* skills to the fullest. This can be developed over time as the manager gains increasing knowledge of the industry. Naturally, the more experience one has in an industry, the greater the comprehension of how forces will interact to impact change and the firm. These capabilities in many cases take years to develop and then only after managers have had the opportunity to understand the various cause-and-effect relationships that are likely to make up the industry environment.

The *analysis* skills come into play when the manager is faced with the volume of information likely to be provided by any scanning process. One thing is certain in this case. There will always be too much information and not enough time to review it all. The information will often be obtuse and usually not always directly related to the issues of concern to most managers. In other words, the information will not be as obvious as we would like it to be. Therefore, managers must engage in the process of examining the information in its raw form, attempting to determine whether or not any patterns or similarities emerge. Here again, knowing the body of knowledge begins to have value for the manager. The greater the knowledge base, the easier it becomes over time to identify these emerging patterns. This is because it becomes easier to determine what information has already been made available in the past and what is new. It is the new information that must be analyzed to determine significant changes in previously identified major forces.

Once the individuals doing the scanning have analyzed the information, it becomes essential that they begin to *synthesize* what has been viewed. In other words, they now must take the key observations or patterns that have been emerging and try to make sense out of them in terms of a larger, more integrated identification of the forces driving change. This step in the process can best be illustrated by looking again at Exhibit 13 and observing the overlapping ovals and the relationship among the V shapes to these and to each other.

To further illustrate this example, we refer to one of the major forces driving change: *Assets and Capital*. When assessing the body of knowledge that was developing with respect to the financing of hospitality industry investments, the literature and discussions by executives involved in the *Visioning the Future* process leading to the identification of this force was rich with themes. Each individual interpreted what they saw differently, yet, when all the information was finally analyzed, certain common themes were recurring. Often they were discussed using different terms or concepts, but as the analysis continued and more comprehension resulted, there were common threads or patterns emerging. These are identified in the ovals in Exhibit 13.

To illustrate further, take the oval containing the concept *growing influence of the capital market community*. In this case, there were literally hundreds of articles or program listings in newspapers, business magazines, newsletters, trade publications, and conference programs that in one way or another presented evidence of a growing pressure from institutional investors on hospitality executives to improve the financial performance of their firms. Similarly, there were many articles that presented arguments suggesting that governments were unable to produce all the revenue necessary to meet the demands for basic security needs of their citizens. This lack of funds was often referred to as capital rationing by governments (see oval).

As you can see in this example thus far, each oval represents the synthesis of what the scanners were seeing from the vast array of information they were analyzing. Information was integrated and combined in such a way because the scanners possessed a strong knowledge base in financial management and could make judgments about how information should be grouped. What is important to acknowledge here is that this is no exact science. If one's knowledge is weak in a particular area, one will naturally see less than someone who is an expert. This fact alone should support the establishment of scanning teams, which are made up of knowledge workers from several disciplines who possess the comprehension skills necessary to achieve maximum levels of analysis and synthesis.

As the information became more easily classified into the ovals in the diagram, two additional observations became clear. These observations are indicated by the two large Vs in the exhibit, one labeled *investor perspective* and the other *regulator perspective*. What these V's imply is that management must view the capital situation from two perspectives, one that reflects the private sector and one the public. In the case of the latter, many governments are trying to promote tourism and thus are encouraging investment in it. However, many others view it as a problem in that it taxes police and fire systems that were originally planned to protect the citizens paying taxes in the community and not the tourist. Thus they are seeking to remedy their capital-rationing problem with higher taxes on the tourist. Compelling arguments on both sides of this issue can be made. It is the manager's job not necessarily to take one argument over another as much as it is to be sure that it is monitored, and when it can be influenced, to be able to produce the right arguments backed with appropriate information.

The second major observation was the overwhelming amount of information regarding the new expectations for asset productivity being demanded by investors of all types. In this case, much of this new pressure was a function of all the competition for capital to be invested into productive assets, which was occurring as a result of the fall of communism and the emergence of free market economies. Suddenly, there were too few dollars chasing the best of investments. This left industries that were marginal producers of the returns on capital with little alternative but to do better. By looking at both perspectives as bounded by the V's in the diagram, it can be seen that the information was further synthesized to reflect these two important change markers in the environment of the hospitality manager.

As the last step in the content analysis and concept mapping process, all the ovals and V's were grouped together to reach the final synthesis, which was the labeling of this major force driving change as the *New expectations for asset performance in an era of capital shortages*. This event emerged because of the patterns that were developing from the information sources used to identify change in the hospitality industry. Others may have seen different outcomes or forces, which is always the risk in environmental scanning. Note that this force remained strong through most of the late 1990s and early into the next century. This has now changed, however, as the U.S. economy has begun to improve midway through the first decade of the 21st century and the hospitality industry has been providing good returns on invested capital. For the environmental scanner, these changes should be no surprise. What is essential is that the firm has a system to allow this observation to be communicated to the appropriate decision makers so the correct strategic decisions can be made going forward.

Exhibit 13 offers further opportunities for analysis. By this effort it may be possible for the manager to better understand the timing of events surrounding activities within each of the ovals. By monitoring what is taking place in each of these activities in each oval, a manager can begin to look back and forward to see how developments in each have resulted in various cause-and-effect relationships with the firm over time. Understanding how these relationships develop takes a lot of the uncertainty and risk out of the scanning process. This has been one of the major concerns managers have always faced, but it is now easier to overcome with the right analysis and synthesis efforts.

From these analysis and synthesis efforts and conclusions and before the manager should go forward with investments, she or he must perform a thorough and challenging *evaluation* of this thinking. At this point in the scanning process, after all the work and effort engaged in to achieve this result, managers are often reluctant to demonstrate the self-discipline to objectively *evaluate* the conclusions they have reached. This, however, must not be the case. As just indicated, what if the manager had not been in a constant mode of evaluation and the changes previously mentioned in the force of assets and capital had not been noticed? The tough questions must be asked: Is this real, do we really think it is significant, have the sources performed as expected? Managers must *evaluate* these conclusions in the context of today's and tomorrow's world.

Matrix Analysis

The content analysis and concept mapping processes are effective ways of identifying the forces driving change. They assist in improving the understanding of the history of the development of each force and how it is evolving. They take some of the uncertainty out of the scanning process. They also assist in helping to identify and understand some of the cause-and-effect relationships that occur between the firm and its environment. In understanding these cause-and-effect relationships, the important ability here is to be able to see relationships and then formulate theories pertaining to those that are important.

For example, it is generally accepted that as personal disposable income rises (cause), all other things remaining equal, the effect will be more money spent on travel and food away from home. However, several variables (value drivers) are involved in this relationship that the strategic planner needs to identify, understand, and monitor. These variables often appear in the concepts, themes, and patterns identified during the content analysis and concept mapping processes. In fact, it is not uncommon to see the more effective scanners concentrating on identifying as many value drivers and relationships as possible.

Relationships are everywhere. The skill needed is to be able to identify the ones that are important to the future strategy of a business. To do this, strategists must first possess the cognitive and analytical skills referred to earlier. The stronger they are in this regard, the more variables they will be able to identify in the vast forests of information. The forest metaphor is useful in understanding this idea further. For example, to the uninitiated (often referred to as a city dweller), a walk in the forest is nothing more than avoiding tripping over or running into trees and animals. They are unable to differentiate among the hundreds of forms of flora and fauna.

In this case, they exhibit a total lack of knowledge of what to see or even look for. Put another way, *they don't know what they don't know because they don't know what they don't know.* They may walk right past rare species or dangerous creatures without noticing. To the knowledgeable woodsman, they will see all the forms (in the business environment we call them variables/value drivers) of life that exist in a wondrous surrounding of trees, plants, and animals. They will also understand the relationships that exist. They will see how tall trees shade the smaller ones but how they both need each other to keep the forest in ecological balance. They will observe hundreds of other relationships, some of which they know about but others that they are only now observing.

To the well-informed, they will always notice the existing relationships that have been documented and recorded. They will also be curious about new observations or changes in the established relationships. It is these observations that suggest change in the old order and bring about emerging ones to create a new order. For the environmental scanner, this is also the goal, except the forest has now turned into the competitive business environment; the trees are now competitors, customers, suppliers, and regulators. Today's manager must be able to understand the present relationships and to see new ones. To do this, the use of matrices to assess relationships becomes extremely useful. It helps to create greater understanding of the present and emerging body of knowledge.

There are several ways to construct matrices, the simplest of which were the ones in Exhibit 10. They simply present information about the events in each of the remote, task, and functional categories. In a sense, they are really summary or descriptive matrices. The ones that assist in understanding relationships are often referred to as *multivariate matrices.* They obtain this name because they are attempting to demonstrate how variables/value drivers relate each other in a multiple of ways. Exhibits 14 to 16 represent examples of such matrices.

In Exhibit 14, the relationships analyzed reflect the firm's position and that of its competitors related to events occurring in the political/regulatory environment. In each of the events occurring in the column titled *list and describe key issues*, the determination is made as to whether the issue is international, national, state, or locally driven as indicated in the cells in the first column labeled *Regulators*. Once the issue is determined on the basis of content analysis and concept mapping and entered into the cell, it is now determined what the firm's position is regarding this relationship, based on whether it views it either as a *threat or opportunity*, the third column. Once this is decided, the next relationship to consider is how the competition is handling this (*Competitor position ...* column 4). As can be seen, a lot is expected here. First, managers must be scanning the political/regulatory environment on the basis of where it falls on the continuum from global to local. Second, they must identify the issue, describe it thoroughly by identifying all the variables making it up, and then evaluate all this as to whether or not it is a threat or opportunity. They must also do the same for their competitor's position.

Regulators	List and Describe Key Issues	Firm Position —Threat or Opportunity	Competitor Position on Each Issue
International	Growing regulation of copyright rules in playing recorded music	Threat creating greater cost and less flexibility	Same as ours
Federal	Regulations on fire and safety issues in hotels	Opportunity because we are ahead of the competition here	In general most are behind on complying
State	State taxation laws supporting local taxes on travelers.	Threat—to be resisted or to obtain better services for tax collected	Same
Local	Local ordinances on food safety increasing	Opportunity to showcase company standards in this area`	In general most are behind in this area

EXHIBIT 14 Environmental Analysis Worksheet: Key Issues Affecting the Firm in the Regulatory Environment

The matrix analysis changes slightly in Exhibit 15 where the relationship now under analysis is that of the remote forces in the environment and how they impact the business customer and the leisure customer in the hotel industry. This type of analysis

EXHIBIT 15 Environmental Analysis Worksheet: Relationship of Remote Environment and Customer Type

Environmental Event	Business Customer	Leisure Customer
Socio-cultural **Political** **Economic** **Technological** The evolution of technology which includes the use of the information highway to access travel and reservations information as well as interactive learning and room environmental control. **Ecological**	Customer expects complete access to information highway through data ports conveniently located in the guestroom. Customer expects to make reservations utilizing the Internet.	Customer expects to be able to make reservations using the Internet. Wants secure surroundings which rely in part upon technology. Customer desires a comfortable room regarding air quality and living environment maintained by the latest technology.

Environmental Category	Customers	Suppliers	Competitors	Regulators
Economic	Rising disposable income results in increases in eating out sales	Greater competition for capital and labor	More disposable income brings about too many competitors	
Political		Increased regulation of packaging and advertising		
Socio-cultural	A customer less tolerant of smoking		Increasing numbers of competitors focusing on cultural values	
Ecological	Greater awareness of a firm's practices	More eco-friendly products available		Limitations on drive thru windows in urban areas
Technological	Growing reliance upon technology in making purchase decisions	Seamless integration and product delivery due to MIS	Growing importance of technology as a competitive advantage	

EXHIBIT 16 Environmental Analysis Relationship Worksheet: Task Environment vs. Remote Environment

is actually a look at the relationships between forces in the remote environment and the task category. In this example, the assessment is made regarding how each type of customer is affected by technological advancements on the information highway, especially as to how they plan to make and book room reservations and the working environment of the hotel room. Here again, secondary information is plentiful so that management can obtain some idea of what the customer is expecting. Of course, in some situations primary information will have to be obtained to see how the firm's customers prefer to have things. Once this is obtained, the manager then must synthesize and make decisions on what investments to make in technology that will give the firm the desired competitive advantage.

In Exhibit 16, the relationships being looked at are between all the remote and task categories. In this example, several relationships have been emerging that are important to watch. The most obvious is the correlation between rising income and eating out. But as the analysis shows, this can lead to too many competitors entering a segment. Rising income is also associated with a solid economy, which generally causes full employment; thus the labor supply becomes more challenging. Also, capital can at times be in short supply as many firms seek to expand. As the statements in the remaining cells suggest, there are many variables likely to contribute to the complex web of relationships that exist in any environment. The challenge as stated often before is for the manager to be able to identify them, understand them, estimate their timing and impact, and then make important investments in competitive methods to take advantage of the opportunities presented.

Information Sharing, Feedback, and Evaluation

The remaining element of the scanning process is the setting up of appropriate systems to share and seek feedback and evaluate the effectiveness of the entire process. Exhibit 17 is a normative model to assist in this important effort. As implied in the model, information should be gathered at all levels, exchanged at all levels, and evaluated at all levels.

As suggested many times in these chapters on the environment, the scanning process is most effective when everyone is involved. Therefore, all organizational units should be given some scanning assignments. By making everyone responsible for looking to the future, the entire organization begins to resemble what today is often referred to as *a learning organization*. This continuous emphasis on scanning helps also to develop *thinking personnel* who will ultimately benefit themselves both personally and professionally as a result of their learning about how to identify and observe important relationships.

One of the most difficult challenges facing the manager today is to have the patience to wait for the feedback as a result of an earlier decision they made to invest in a particular competitive method based on their scanning activities. It can be days, months, or even years before a particular investment in a competitive method begins to pay off. The ability to see a driving force and accurately estimate its timing is only one part of this decision. The next part is to translate what that timing means in terms of cash flows resulting from the investment along with the total life of that investment. Here, the connection between strategy and finance becomes most critical.

In most academic courses in financial management, students are taught to use some form of discounted cash flow technique in the capital budgeting process. Textbooks used in the courses often focus more attention on learning the discounting technique than on the most challenging part, which is the estimation of the cash flows

EXHIBIT 17   Information-Sharing Feedback and Evaluation Systems

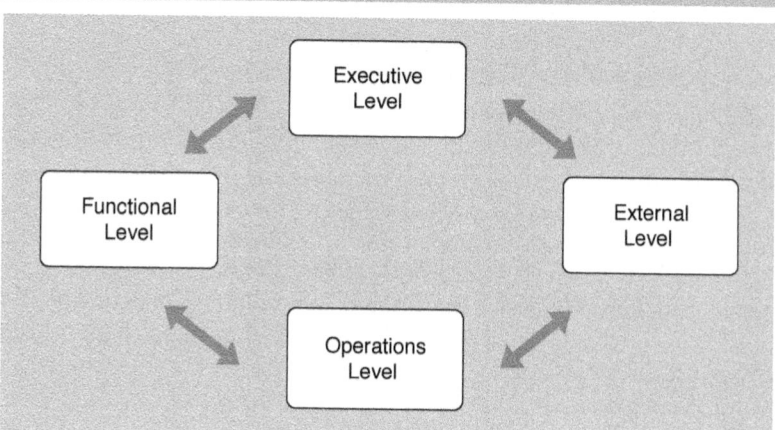

and the expected life of the project. The importance of the capital budgeting process in investing in the most value-creating competitive methods suggests that financial, marketing, and operational managers must pool their scanning capabilities together to provide accurate estimates of the life of the method and its cash flow per share contributions.

In estimating the life of a method, decision makers must thoroughly understand how forces driving change will affect this life. Cash flows will be different over this life as well. These estimates cannot be adequately made unless effective scanning has been done. Because the capital budgeting process is a strategic planning tool, it should not be done without planning for the monitoring and evaluation of the estimates that were made originally. By using management information systems that provide accurate information on the performance of competitive methods, management can assess the wisdom of their analysis and estimates.

A good management information system built into the scanning process will provide important insight into the cause-and-effect relationships that have been so carefully thought out by management. Being able to create models that demonstrate the relationship of forces acting in the environment and how value-adding investments behave in this context helps to further reduce the uncertainties associated with future decisions.

The sharing of information, providing of feedback, and the conducting of evaluations should be systematically performed. These activities should be structured and included on the agendas of management meetings. In fact, it is best to put these tasks at the start of most meetings. This way, personnel will focus their attention on thinking about the future and make judgments about how their current mix of competitive methods is measuring up to tomorrow's challenges. There should be the expectation that at such meetings, key members of management will give reports on how well each competitive method is performing, what is the likelihood of this continuing, and what to do next. This will help to ensure discussion and debate and thus a healthy form of communication about the future of the firm.

This entire scanning process as just outlined here should lead to creative new ideas that astute managers can use to justify investments in value-adding competitive methods. In fact, if managers follow this process diligently, it may not make them creative geniuses, but it should help them to become more creative. Creativity in a fast-moving environment is highly valued by organizations today.

A Continuous Process of Scanning Is Necessary

A good scanning system will never be able to remove all the uncertainty from a decision. It can only help to reduce it. It can also assist in improving the estimation process by providing a greater level of knowledge and understanding about the expected life of the forces driving change. What is essential is that scanning is a long-term process. It cannot be done on a onetime basis to meet a particular need. Scanning should be done on a continuous basis by all levels of executives who contribute substantively to the strategic management process. As this chapter points out, scanning demands strong intellectual skills, ones that can create new opportunities in turbulent environments. These skills only come from a continuous program of scanning that involves a constant evaluation of each event and the cause-and-effect relationships it brings about. It is challenging in a dynamic and complex world, but it is essential.

SUMMARY

This chapter provides an overview of the tools necessary for proper environmental scanning. It begins with the importance of identifying forces that drive change and how to establish a domain for analysis purposes. It then provides insight into the steps in the process necessary to have a comprehensive system of analysis that will ensure the most effective assessment of key forces and opportunities. Exploring the ways in which information is analyzed using such processes as content analysis, concept mapping and multivariate analysis is provided with the chapter concluding with the importance of the evaluation of the process and conclusions resulting from it and the importance of sharing these conclusions throughout the organization.

DISCUSSION QUESTIONS

1. Why is it essential for managers to identify the forces driving change in their environments?
2. Briefly outline the elements in establishing an environmental scanning system.
3. What are the criteria used in defining a business domain?
4. What is the function of organizational structure in regard to environmental scanning?
5. How do you determine information needs, medium, and sources when assessing the environment?
6. Discuss the need for information sharing, feedback, and evaluation.

NOTES

1. In this context, the structure of the scanning process is the focus.
2. A total of 43 top management executives responded to this survey and represented hotel firms across the globe, a 22%
response rate. Respondents represented 570 hotels with 89,793 rooms.
3. A total of 29 responses were received in this survey, a 13.1 % response rate.

CASE STUDY

Technology as a Competitive Method: The Case of InterContinental Hotels*

TECHNOLOGY AS CORE COMPETENCIES

As travelers find it increasingly difficult to leave home without the comfort of information technology (IT), international hotel chains are adding more IT touches to their hotel rooms. Hyatt introduced the position of technology concierge to provide assistance to guests in the area of technology-related needs. Hotels have discovered high-tech services as a

*This case is compiled based on information available up to November 2006.

new competitive method to attract and target business travelers who rely on high-speed Internet connectivity and wireless services to conduct day-to-day business.[1] As a matter of fact, companies like InterContinental Hotels Group, Marriott International, Choice International, and Best Western International are offering free high-speed Internet access as a brand standard in their midscale brands.

It is clear that e-commerce is going to have a big impact on the lodging industry. In 1999 consumers spent $4.2 billion on travel-related purchases through the Internet, which includes airline tickets, rental cars, hotels, and cruises. This number grew to $6.3 billion in 2000 and $16.6 billion in 2003. By 2003 hotels, either through individual sites or third-party sites, were projected to command 25% of all dollars spent online for travel, up from 13% in 1998.

INDUSTRY EXAMPLE: INTERCONTINENTAL HOTELS

Let us take the competencies of Bass Hotels & Resorts (the earlier incarnation of InterContinental Hotels Group as it is known today) with respect to technology as an example. The company went from being the leading hotel chain in the 1960s, to leading once again in the late 1980s and early 1990s, after lagging behind its competitors for over two decades. Much of its success could be attributed to its corporate decisions of how to invest in technology and how much. Proactivity was key to Bass Hotels & Resorts' technology advantage.

Bass PLC was founded in 1777 by William Bass as a brewery in England. By 1860 Bass had expanded to three breweries and was recognized as the largest brewery in England in 1876. About a century later, 1970 marked Bass's entrance into the world of the hospitality industry as it purchased about 50 hotels. Bass won the exclusive rights to the name of Holiday Inn outside the United States, Canada, and Mexico in 1987. As the

English government tried to limit vertical integration within the brewing industry by limiting the number of pubs a brewer could own, Bass responded by continuing to focus on and develop its international hotel business. In 1989 Bass purchased Holiday Corporation's flagship Holiday Inn chain for $2 billion. Included in this purchase were 1,410 franchised Holiday Inns, 177 company-owned/managed Holiday Inns, and Crowne Plaza brands. What remained of the Holiday Corporation, including Embassy Suites, Hampton Inns, Homewood Suites, and Harrah's Casinos of Nevada and New Jersey, was spun off to shareholders as Promus Companies Inc. With the purchase of the Holiday Inn chain, Bass's desire to focus on and develop its hospitality division came full circle.

In 1998 Bass outbid Marriott International, Patriot American Hospitality, and Ladbroke Group to acquire the luxury InterContinental hotel chain from Japan's Saison Group for $2.9 billion. Included in the acquisition were InterContinental's 211 hotels in 77 countries. The company also outlined strategies for profit improvements, which included the brand's reservations and marketing efforts, as well as some management techniques.[2] The company's other established brand, Crowne Plaza, improved its RevPAR by 5.1% to $73.74, raised its ADR by 5.1% to $106.97, and saw its occupancy rate remaining steady at about 69%.[3]

In 1999 Bass's Holiday Inn and Holiday Inn Express brands delivered a strong performance.[4] The two brands were growing in revenue per available room at more than three times the rate of their competitors.[5] The stabilizing of the Holiday Inn brand is considered one of the most important things that the company had achieved.[6] Bass Hotels & Resorts had a good year in 2000 due to strong performances from its midscale brands.[7] It was also reaping the rewards of an acquisition made in 1998 when Bass Hotels & Resorts purchased 161 hotels with more than

40,000 rooms in the Asia-Pacific region for $313 million.[8] Moreover, in 2000 Bass severed its 223-year-old tie to the brewing industry when it entered into an agreement to sell its beer-brewing division to Interbrew for $3 billion. Bass planned to use the proceeds to expand its global hotel business. Financial analysts considered this to be a right strategic move. Along with the brewery sale, Bass also changed its name to Six Continents PLC in 2001.

In 2002 and 2003, Six Continents Hotels & Resorts reached the number-one position in chainwide revenue, followed by Marriott and Accor. In 2003 Six Continents PLC, as a result of demerger from its nonhotel holdings, separated the United Kingdom hotel group's hotel business from its pub businesses. The two businesses were renamed InterContinental Hotels Group PLC and Mitchells & Butlers PLC, respectively. InterContinental Hotels Group (IHG) of the United Kingdom is the world's most global hotel company and the largest by number of rooms. In 2006 IHG Group owned, managed, leased, or franchised close to 36,000 hotels and 539,000 guest rooms across nearly 100 countries around the world. The Group owns a portfolio of well-recognized hotel brands including InterContinental Hotels & Resorts, Crowne Plaza Hotels & Resorts, Holiday Inn Hotels and Resorts, Holiday Inn Express, Staybridge Suites, Candlewood Suites and Hotel Indigo, and it also manages the world's largest hotel loyalty program, Priority Club Rewards, with over 27 million members worldwide.[9]

INVESTMENT IN TECHNOLOGY AS COMPETITIVE METHODS

Building upon the original success of the Holiday Inn's Holidex reservations system, one of the competitive methods developed by Bass Hotels & Resorts was to invest on a global scale in technology and sales and marketing to drive up revenue per available room premiums. There were four prongs in the company's e-commerce strategy, which is a multidimensional process: consumers, customers, franchisees and owners. It contains internal processes as well. The strategy was based on the leadership of its CEO, Brian Langton, who believed in the need to integrate key marketing, reservations, and operating systems into one strong technology based system that would lead the industry as Holiday Inn had during the 1960s. He also foresaw the future of technology in ways that were unique compared to other leaders in the industry. He clearly had a vision for the future with respect to this competitive method.

As e-commerce continued to penetrate deeply into the business community, Bass's system enjoyed a significant leading position on the competition. Holidex, its central reservations system, was the largest transaction processing engine in the industry.[10] The company replaced the property management systems in all of its hotels with state-of-the-art systems.[11] For the company's upscale and midscale brands Inter-Continental, Holiday Inn Crowne Plaza, Holiday Inn Select, and Holiday Inn, licensees were given a choice of three new PMS models, all Windows-based. In Holiday Inn Express-brand properties, the company tested a low-cost, Web-enabled PMS that significantly altered the cost structure of property management (as of 2000).[12]

In the PMS selection process, Bass brought together focus groups of licensees from around the world.[13] A unique satellite network setup enabled Bass to communicate with its many properties and also connects the PMS to Holidex and HIRO, the chain's revenue management arm.[14] The existing satellite network also underwent a systemwide change. Another unusual aspect of Bass Hotels & Resorts' outstanding technological framework was a link between the chain's Internet site and the Holidex system.[15] This setup allowed customers to book hotel rooms with online availability via the Internet.

With representation in numerous countries, Bass's seamless network was extremely adaptable.[16] Bass tested many technology initiatives under consideration at the Holiday Inn Select in Atlanta.[17] The company looked at credit card activated guest room access, which enabled travelers to bypass the traditional lobby check-in.[18] Another innovation was Tech Pack, a completely integrated technology package that Bass provides to operators of its all-new construction Staybridge Suites extended-stay hotels.[19] This kit contains everything necessary to get the hotels up and running, from call accounting software to revenue management programs.[20] Bass marketed all of its brands via its loyalty program, the Priority Club. Televisions and billboards remain key marketing vehicles, particularly for Express and Holiday, but the Internet was a growing marketing channel for Bass.[21]

In 2001 Bass Hotels rolled out services that allowed guests to locate hotels and book rooms from any wireless device by teaming up with wireless "ASP" (application service provider) Air2Web to build a platform capable of spanning a variety of wireless carriers, networks, and devices.[22] Key elements of the Bass strategy were to accommodate many end-user devices and make system access simple.[23] In 2001 Bass tested Bluetooth technology at one of its Holiday Inn locations in New York. Using a Bluetooth-enabled handset device, the system automatically recognizes and checks in guests as they enter the lobby.[24]

Bass Hotels and Resorts also needed to build an international e-commerce site that would efficiently link up with its back-end hosts and reservation databases. The company chose Java for its ease of development and simple methods of tying to back-end databases. The new e-commerce site handled the bulk of the company's reservation traffic. Bass Hotels & Resorts indicated that online bookings had exploded and were expected to reach $150 million in 2003. The company expected Internet bookings to reach $1.5 billion in 2005. For Bass hotels, adopting wireless services made business sense.[25] The company understands that it is not a technology game but an issue of customer service fulfillment.[26]

Bass created an intranet fact book at Bhronline.com (business-to-business portal for its franchise) offering specific sales and marketing information about customers and their buying habits for its franchisees.[27] Bass Hotels & Resorts treated employees using the intranet as consumers of the information. Therefore, its intranet has to be both functional and consumer based.[28] Bhronline.com, Bass Hotels & Resorts' intranet system, provides hotel operators with unlimited operational assistance and data, from quality assurance regulations and scores to chain standards information.[29]

The intranet grew to include quality indicators comparing individual hotels to similar hotels in its region and category, including customer-feedback information.[30] Training material was also added to the intranet, including multimedia and online audio. The intranet portal became an interface to the company's free website, enabling a franchisee to go online to update the information as needed, and learn of special marketing programs.[31] It is an inexpensive way to update data, and ensure that information remains current.

Although the initial purpose of the intranet was to be an information base, allowing employees to access information at any time, it now offers opportunities for adding value to franchisees as well. Essentially, Bhronline.com gives franchisees their own database, empowering them in their own operations[32] while enhancing communication with the corporate headquarters.

The consumer vehicle is Bass's branded websites. The customer vehicle involves a particular subsegment; the new Bass meetings site, www.meetings.basshotel.com.[33] As there was no site dedicated for the meetings and convention segment, at least 1,000 Bass hotels are now on that site which provides information on the destination, the weather, as well as things to do in the area for each hotel.[34] In 2005 InterContinental Hotels Group (IHG) (now doing business under this new name) launched a new global intranet content management system by provider Mediasurface PLC for its employees that are spread across six corporate offices and 614 hotels within the European, Middle Eastern, and African regions.[35] The aim of the project was reportedly to create a dynamic, personalized site to share knowledge and best practices among its different regions, brands, and hotels.[36] The content management system allows integration with all business applications, enabling access to such services as hotel reporting, IHG e-mail, quality audit and guest satisfaction applications, promotions, risk management, guest satisfaction and tracking, and events calendars.[37]

In 2005 IHG completed its first annual pay review using Web and workflow technologies to streamline its human resources process across its worldwide offices[38]. The HRM Software's Connect Pay Review application manages its annual pay review process for more than 4,000 senior staff across 20 global offices,[39] replacing IHG's existing labor-intensive spreadsheet-based application that had been used by over 400 reviewing managers in IHG.[40]

Similar activity is envisioned for devices other than personal computers as IHG sets its sight on interactive TV and mobile phones using wireless application protocol (WAP) technology.[41] Already, it has invested in the spontaneity-geared lastminute.com, which books teamed getaways or spur-of-the-moment corporate retreats. UK-based last minute.com reaches consumers through mobile phones.[42] IHG plans to launch a multibrand website in the UK as well as a UK site for its Express by Holiday Inn

brand. Both sites will include online booking.[43] The new Holiday Inn prototype is also equipped with an electronic menu, called E-menu, which offers diners a wealth of menu information, including photos, calorie counts, complementary wines and foods, and different languages and currencies.[44]

Because only 6% of the world's population speaks English as a first language and due to China's potential for immense growth, IHG launched its first multilingual initiative in Chinese in 2000 in the form of www.china.basshotels.com. A site aiming to strengthen relations with Chinese-speaking consumers, it became the first foreign-language site with online booking capability to be launched by an international hotel company.[45] The company expects 500 to 1,000 weekly online bookings through the Chinese website, mainly from Singapore, Malaysia, Hong Kong, and China.[46]

To cater to the tech-savvy, socialized Generation X customer base, InterContinental Hotels Group implemented a comprehensive virtual concierge service, called eHost, for its Holiday Inn Hotels and Resorts brand in 2006.[47] Guests of Holiday Inn can access via the free high-speed internet access system information normally provided by a traditional concierge, including area dining options, attractions, movies, shopping, transportation, and events.[48] Guests can also play games and send ePostcards as well as participate in online surveys providing immediate feedback to hotel management. eHost provides guests more convenience, choice, and control.[49] Eventually eHost will offer multiple languages and an online menu and room service module. Through eHosts, the company hopes to extend the Holiday Inn heritage of innovation and industry leadership.

In 2006, to further demonstrate commitment to technology advancement, InterContinental Hotels Group appointed Tom Conophy to the newly created position of chief information officer (CIO). This position is part of the Group Executive Committee. Conophy is a 25-year veteran of the IT industry with extensive experience in developing new technology solutions within the travel and hospitality industry.

AN ILLUSTRATION: TWO INTERCONTINENTAL HOTELS ARE CREATING A NICHE WITH TECHNOLOGY

Intercontinental Houston (opened in 2002), and the InterContinental Hotel and Conference Center Cleveland (opened in 2003) are the two examples of technology-centered hotels. They offer guests not only the luxury standard of service and products, but also some of the most advanced technology available. Both center-city properties were built to attract medical and high-tech corporate audiences, and both feature technology as a point of difference from the existing luxury hotels in their market.[50] The hotels make the technology seamless: wireless keyboards, a cyber concierge, and the usual high-speed Internet access (HSIA) make technological functionality a platform at these hotels.[51] To exceed technological expectations, at the InterContinental Houston, TVs are coupled with wireless keyboards allowing fee-based Internet or e-mail connection.[52] The amphitheater in the InterContinental Hotel and Conference Center Cleveland was awarded the grand prize in *Presentations* magazine's "Best Presentation Rooms." The amphitheater hosts a data port for a high-speed Internet connection, a conventional modem, and an audience response system keypad, which can be used to poll the audience.

DISCUSSION QUESTIONS

1. Briefly discuss how the impact of technological advancement in the environment changes our lifestyle and the way that business responds to these changes.
2. Using InterContinental as an illustration, discuss how the company commits to technology as one of its competitive methods to gain industry advantage.
3. Briefly discuss the challenges of using technology in hospitality organizations as competitive methods to differentiate among competitors and gain market share.
4. Identify the key determinants behind technology advancement. Identify and support the three you believe to be most important.
5. Comment on IHG's timing of its investments in technology and compare this to the investments made by its competitors over the same period. How long was the timing advantage for IHG?
6. Are there domain differences between the corporation and the two hotels cited as examples at the end of the case?
7. What information would be helpful in determining the overall demand for the technology investments IHG has made over the years?
8. What information sources do you think would be useful in tracking developments in technology for the travel industry?

NOTES

1. C. Moore, "Hotels Open Doors to Wireless, Broadband," *InfoWorld* 23, no. 13 (2001): 34.
2. J. Higley, "Banner Year Propels Expansion by Bass," *Hotel and Motel Management* 215, no. 3 (2000): 3–4.
3. Ibid.
4. Ibid.
5. Ibid.
6. Ibid.
7. Ibid.
8. Ibid.

9. *M2 Presswire,* "InterContinental Hotels Group Selects HRM Connect to Improve Global Pay Review; IHG Harnesses Web and Workflow Technologies to Streamline HR Processes Across Offices Worldwide and Gain Tighter Control," 2005.
10. G. Wagner, "Staying Ahead of the Curve," *Lodging Hospitality* 56, no. 13 (2000): 45–46.
11. Ibid.
12. Ibid.
13. Ibid.
14. Ibid.
15. Ibid.
16. Ibid.
17. Ibid.
18. Ibid.
19. Ibid.
20. Ibid.
21. C. Wolff, "Bass Plays the Globalization Game," *Lodging Hospitality* 56, no. 13 (2000): 40–42.
22. Op. cit., no. 3.
23. Ibid.
24. Ibid.
25. Ibid.
26. Ibid.
27. B. Adams, "Hoteliers Embrace Intranet to Add Value to Franchisees," *Hotel and Motel Management* 215, no. 5 (2000): 56–57.
28. Ibid.
29. Op. cit., no. 10.
30. Op. cit., no. 27.
31. Ibid.
32. Op. cit., no. 21.
33. Ibid.
34. Op. cit., no. 21.
35. Anonymous, "InterContinental Hotels Launches EMEA Intranet," *Telecomworldwire* 1 (2005).
36. Ibid.
37. Ibid.
38. Op. cit., no. 9.
39. Ibid.
40. Ibid.
41. Op. cit., no. 21.
42. Ibid.
43. *Travel Trade Gazette UK & Ireland,* "Hotel Portals Eye Air Deals," 2001.
44. B. Adams, "Wireless Applications Enable Guest Services," *Hotel and Motel Management* 219, no. 8 (2004): 38–40.
45. Op. cit., no. 21.
46. *Travel Trade Gazette India,* "Bass On-Line in Chinese," 2000.
47. Anonymous, "InterContinental Hotels Group Launches Virtual Concierge Service for Holiday Inn Hotels and Resorts," *Wireless News* 1 (2006).
48. Ibid.
49. Op. cit., no. 9.
50. M. Rowe, "Tech Adds the Sizzle," *Lodging Hospitality* 59, no. 15 (2003): 64–66.
51. Ibid.
52. Ibid.

SOURCES UTILIZED FOR BACKGROUND INFORMATION BUT NOT CITED

Anonymous. 1999. "Technology: Hotels Cater to Tech-Savvy Guests." *Travel Trade Gazette Asia,* 1.

———. 2003. "Six Continents PLC: U.K. Hotel Group Provides Details of Planned Split Up." *Wall Street Journal,* 1.

———. 2005. "Creating Exceptional Events with Style at the InterContinental Hotel Cleveland." *Meeting News,* 1.

———. 2005. "Hotel Group Checks I to Web System." *Computer Weekly,* 22.

———. 2006. "InterContinental Hotels Group Appoints New Chief Information Officer."

Retrieved from http://www.hotelchange.com/news_print.php?sid = 20700.

Adams, B. 2002. "New Six Continents Hotels Chief Outlines Company's Agenda." *Hotel and Motel Management* 217; no. 21: 1–3.

———. 2004. "HSIA Surges into Midscale Hotel Segment." *Hotel and Motel Management* 219, no. 6: 30–31.

Poole, S. M. 2000. "Internet Big Hit for Hoteliers." *The Atlanta Journal-Constitution,* F7.

Environmental Assessment

Scanning the Remote Environment

From Chapter 5 of *Strategic Management in the Hospitality Industry*, Third Edition, Michael D. Olsen,
Joseph J. West, Eliza Ching Yick Tse. Copyright © 2008 by Pearson Education, Inc.
Published by Pearson Prentice Hall. All rights reserved.

Environmental Assessment

Scanning the Remote Environment

Learning Objectives

Upon completing this chapter, you will:

1. Achieve a more practical understanding of how to scan the remote environment.
2. Understand the role of value drivers as determinants of causal relationships between the firm and its environment.
3. Develop an understanding of the timing of value driver movements and how they impact the firm and its future cash flow streams associated with key competitive methods.
4. Achieve a greater understanding of the role of probability theory with respect to creating managerial theories about the firm.

Key Concepts

- Scanning the remote environment
- Value drivers as determinants of causal relationships
- Causal relationships and strategic success
- Estimating timing of relationships using value drivers

Chapter Purpose

In this chapter we introduce ways of applying conceptual tools to the analysis, synthesis, and evaluation of the remote environment. Exhibit 1 emphasizes the environmental scanning construct of the coalignment model and in this chapter we focus primarily on the remote analysis activity.

How Are Opportunities and Threats Recognized by Managers?

Achieving strategic success, many may say, is all about having good luck. Discovering an opportunity is being in the right place at the right time, others might argue. Perhaps there is some truth to these beliefs, but this raises an important question: Do employees, investors, and other stakeholders of your business really want to depend on serendipitous good fortune? We think not. No stakeholder is interested in putting wealth at risk. How then can executives invest in the future without betting the future of the business on an idea that will not succeed no matter how hard people work?

Opportunities do not emerge out of nowhere. They develop over time from patterns occurring in the overall environment in which a business exists. The goal of each manager is to see the opportunities before others do. This sharp eye leads to investments in industry-leading competitive methods that will help the firm achieve significant value over a longer period of time. The ability to achieve this foresight depends on how well developed the manager's ability is to interpret and synthesize information about emerging patterns. This is not much different than when a scientist puts forth a theory based on years of research evidence. Managers must do the same; that is, they must develop theories about how environmental influences will likely affect their businesses and then they make investments based on these theories. These theories result from the manager's experience along with cognitive and perceptual skills, in combination with the analysis (such as content analysis), synthesis (concept mapping, matrices analysis), and evaluation capabilities as presented in the prior chapters.

The quality of a theory is based on how well the manager understands the body of knowledge underpinning the relationships in the theory. For example, technology has influenced how hospitality goods and services are bought and sold. This change in distribution was first observed in 1995,[1] but it was unclear then just exactly how the technological changes that were taking place would actually impact the industry and what was the timing of the impact. In other words, managers had little information to guide their theory building ideas about this force driving change. This was due in part because many of the industry's executives were unfamiliar with all the dimensions and complexity associated with activities taking place in the remote environment category of technology. Today we know the impact has been significant and far reaching, and as pointed out later in the chapter, the industry leaders had difficulty in formulating the correct theories regarding either the timing or the impact.

EXHIBIT 1 Strategic Management Model

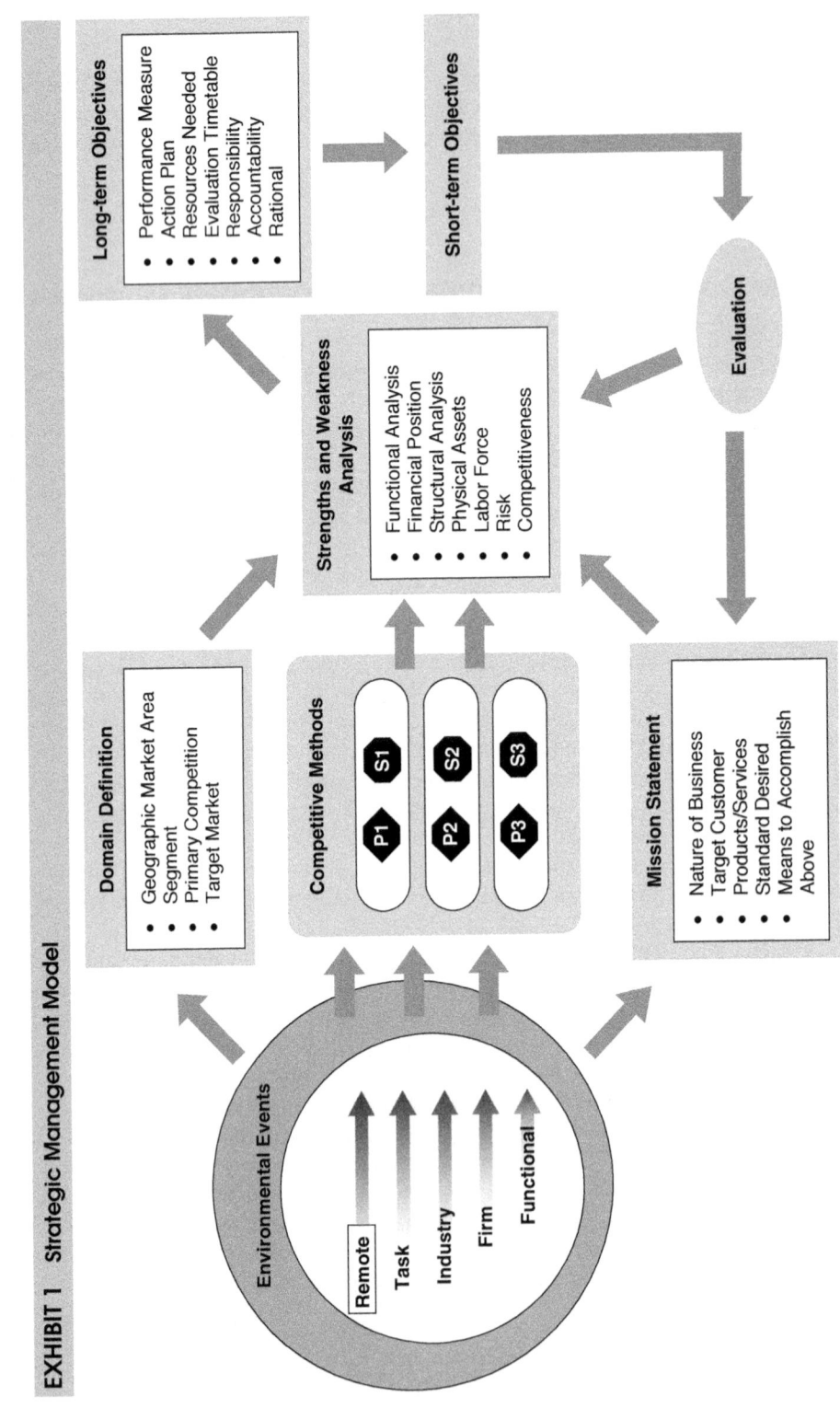

Scanning the Remote Environment

The remote environment is best thought of as the point of origination for most forces driving change and will no doubt affect all activities relative to organizations and people. Ecological, economic, political, sociocultural, and technological change comes from the sprouting of the seeds of change within these general categories. Not all changes occurring here will ultimately impact hospitality enterprises, but there will be many that do. Managers must try to identify and understand the forces and then determine the causal relationships that exist with their firm.

The idea that a force driving change from the remote environment will impact the firm is an abstract thought, primarily because many managers are not used to thinking about the broader issues that are likely to affect them. This is due in part because they are so busy addressing the day-to-day challenges of running a business. Unless they have at some point developed an interest in scanning at the remote level, they will simply assess change in more comfortable surroundings, such as the task environment. However, given the rapid pace of change in today's postmodern society that may be just too late to take advantage of opportunities that are developing across all categories of the remote environment.

Perhaps one reason why managers haven't looked at the remote environment is because it is so abstract and also because they have not been introduced to a conceptual framework that can be used for this purpose. We seek in this chapter to provide such a framework and several concepts to assist in this matter so it can become more manageable and effective. We begin by suggesting that scanning the remote environment requires a different approach to thinking. Most of us tend to be deductive thinkers. That is, we make inferences that lead to conclusions from observing certain facts. This may occur from our observation of a problem, analysis of financial statements, or listening to employee concerns. Once we gather the facts, we make decisions based on our theories of how the outcome should develop. All this is based on our experiences, cognitive skills, and perceptual understandings.

In scanning the remote environment, managers must now engage in inductive thinking. That is, we look at circumstances, information, experiences, and other instances and from these we draw general conclusions. The content analysis, concept mapping processes, and matrices analysis outlined in the previous chapter are examples of ways in which inductive thinking can take place. Exhibit 2 provides a comparative analysis of the differences in the flow of ideas between the inductive and deductive approaches to developing causal theories about the firm and its environment. For example, the forces driving change as outlined in the first chapter resulted from this type of thinking. In the case of their development, experts from across the globe were brought together to share their ideas, observations, and perceptions regarding what they saw happening in the categories of the remote environment. Each idea was explained and recorded. When the analysis of the remote category was completed, all the ideas were reconsidered and grouped into general themes or conclusions that all the experts could agree on.

This inductive process tends to be more conceptual than the deductive approach to thinking. It is less tangible and often challenges one's experience and knowledge backgrounds. It does, however, offer the manager the opportunity to think more creatively because new observations or ideas often result from this type of effort. The

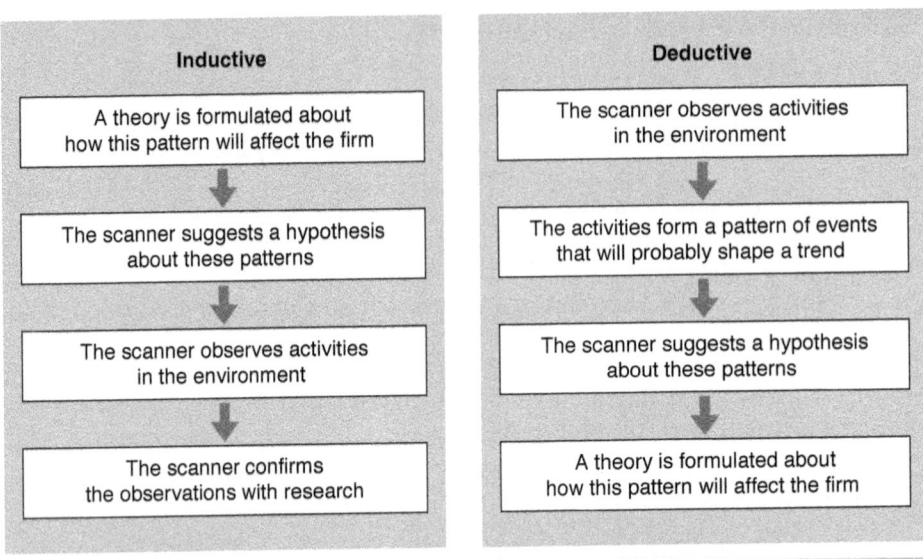

EXHIBIT 2 Comparison of Inductive and Deductive Approaches to Environmental Scanning

ideas emerge because the individual is given the opportunity to bring together diverse facts and interpret this information in a unique way based on past experience, perception, and cognitive skills.

Thus the approach to scanning the remote environment offered here is to begin to develop ways and means of understanding the remote environment by breaking each general category into subcategories. We now further develop the concept of value drivers and how they relate to each force and help the manager understand where change may emanate from. This approach to the scanning process should be helpful to the manager in formulating theories about the causal relationships between the environment and the firm.

Theory Building with Value Drivers

One way of formulating successful theories about the environment and its relationship to the firm is to divide the remote environment into its key categories. As a reminder, they are ecological, economic, political, sociocultural, and technology. There are several subcategories under each dimension that help improve our understanding of each. It is in these categories and subcategories where forces that will influence change emerge. For example, in keeping with our technology illustration, few individuals could envision the full influence the Internet would have on the masses when it emerged primarily from academic and military use in the mid-1990s. There were many pundits, however, who offered aggressive projections and helped drive the frenzy of the so-called dot.com era. Today, in some cases, these projections have proven correct. What was most surprising in this case was the speed with which the influence of the Internet swept across the globe and hospitality industry. In its December 2004 overview of the lodging industry, Merrill Lynch (Anders and Bryant 2004) informed investors: "With value as the most important determinant in travel purchases, consumers are frequently utilizing the Internet to achieve this end, claiming it is a more convenient and cost efficient method of booking" (p. 7).

As this technology example clearly illustrates, managers must be constantly alert for opportunities that emerge from the remote environment. For those who saw the revolution brought about by the Internet, many have been able to achieve first mover advantage. Amazon.com, eBay, and Expedia are examples of companies that saw the opportunities in e-commerce and took advantage of the emerging patterns in the technology category of the remote environment to make investments that today are achieving financial success.

The essential question here is "How and why are some able to see opportunity and others are not?" As stated earlier, the ability to see emerging patterns is a function of the manager's theory-building capability. This capability is a function of how knowledgeable the manager is of the body of knowledge in each of the five categories of the remote environment. This assumes that the manager relies on key sources that provide valid and reliable information. Only by knowing the sources and the state of the art of the body of knowledge and applying strong analytical and synthesis skills can the manager see emerging patterns and take action on them. This means that the manager makes it a priority to remain current in this body of knowledge.

Current conditions require the manager to devote time to this effort. It also requires a longitudinal perspective. Seeing patterns develop can only be accomplished by watching things unfold over time. The question is "What should be watched?" Determining what should be watched is no easy matter because each of the categories of the remote environment is complex in its own right. However, each major category has several subcategories, and each of these subcategories can be further reduced to variables that we call *value drivers*. Value drivers become useful beacons that the manager can monitor. Over time, the manager will begin to develop an understanding of the cause-and-effect relationships between the movement of the value driver and its impact on the firm. This understanding forms the foundation for the theories that managers use to guide future investments for their firms.

Often, it is a combination of movements among several value drivers that bring about strong forces driving change. Going back to our technology example, the convergence of newer and faster computer chips and hardware, software developments, and telecommunications advancements resulted in the emergence of the e-commerce force. If we looked at the developments in each of the three areas and the value drivers for each separately, it is quite possible we would have missed this convergence in its early stages when it would be possible to gain competitive advantage.

It appears then that managers would be best served in their scanning activities if they determined what value drivers should be monitored. This implies that they have sufficient understanding of their industry so they can make selective decisions on which value drivers they should be monitoring. This effort is also a function of the causal theories the manager has developed over time relative to the environment and the firm. This is no uncomplicated endeavor. It requires that the manager gain familiarity with the key components of the body of literature that exists in each of the categories of the remote environment and then selects the key value drivers to be monitored that are relative to their domain. It also assumes that the manager uses valid and reliable sources of information with respect to each value driver. In other words, it takes significant effort to get up to speed on what should be watched. To develop a better understanding of value drivers, the following sections contain definitions and ideas to assist in this challenging process.

Dimensions of Value Drivers

Value drivers are multidimensional and exist in all categories and levels of the environment, from the remote to the functional. A value driver is defined as an independent variable (e.g., the cost of technology) that has a causal impact on a dependent variable (firm profit). It is the relationship between the independent and dependent variables that forms the foundation for a manager's theories about strategic success. To do this successfully, managers must be able to observe these relationships, find out how to obtain data to evaluate the causality between or among variables, in some instances test them, and then analyze and interpret the results.

Value drivers can be both tangible and intangible as well as being internal and external to the organization. External value drivers represent independent variables that exist in all categories of the environment and more often than not will have impact on the firm's cash flow streams. Management generally has little control over these value drivers because they exist in the remote environment and often no one, the individual or the firm, can control their direction. Examples of value drivers that fit this definition include economic items such as the gross domestic product, interest costs on borrowed money, demographics, number of terrorist attacks on soft targets such as hotels, the price of commodities such as beef or dairy products, and insurance costs associated with protecting the firm against terrorism or natural disaster. These are just a few examples of value drivers that the manager has little control over but nonetheless must understand and anticipate the effects they have on the firm.

Internal value drivers can be more narrowly defined and related to the cash flow streams of the firm. They generally are economic success factors and include all the primary revenue and expense factors associated with the cash flow streams of the business. The essential point to consider here is that each must have an impact on the value of the firm in the short or long term. In addition to cash flow items, such metrics as economic value produced, return on invested capital, cost of capital, or growth in income and cost are also important internal value drivers. These internal value drivers are generally impacted by the external drivers just mentioned.

The examples in the preceding paragraphs may be considered tangible in that they can be measured, are normally easily tracked, lend themselves to quantitative assessment, reflect data availability, and are generally well established within the body of knowledge available to the average manager. Intangible value drivers, in contrast, are incapable of being precisely defined with certainty. They tend to be difficult to measure or capture and are more complex than straightforward measures such as the tangible ones given in the preceding examples. They are subject to multiple definitions and interpretations. Examples would include polls assessing consumer confidence, travelers' attitudes toward safety and security, individual perceptions about global warming, and internally such assessments as employee morale and quality of service level. These are difficult to measure reliably, yet they do influence how firms invest in the future.

Success in developing effective theories regarding the causal relationships between the firm and its environment rest on the fact that managers know what value drivers are absolutely essential in terms of understanding where the future value of the business can be found. This means that managers have an in-depth understanding of the industry and business they are in as well as the essential value drivers in each environmental category that must be monitored. This also means that these managers have been observing the behavior of the key value drivers and have developed some sense of how their movements affect the firm over time. Let's use another example to illustrate this.

We assume for the moment that due to activities in several categories of the remote environment, such as the previous wars in Iraq (political), terrorism attacks on soft targets such as nightclubs, hotels, resort destinations, growing levels of fanatical extremists (sociocultural), and the outbreak of new infectious diseases (sociocultural, ecological), the traveling public has developed greater concern over their safety and health. In this case, it would be important for the manager to identify important value drivers to watch to assess where this trend is headed. Tangible drivers such as (1) crime rates in a city or destination, (2) frequency of foodborne outbreaks, (3) instances of disease or infectious outbreaks (the severe acute respiratory syndrome, or SARS, outbreak is a prime example), or (4) number of terrorist attacks within a geographical area may become essential variables on the manager's radar screen in this case. Many of these metrics are maintained by government agencies or organizations and may also be reported in the local/industry press. These can be tracked and analyzed. This makes it possible for managers to correlate the movement of these external value drivers over time with impacts on such internal drivers as revenue and cost streams.

However, the actual shifts underpinning the rise in terrorist attacks are less tangible and more complex, thus making it more challenging to analyze with respect to causes and effects. They result from a confluence of possible drivers such as the growing gap between the so-called societal haves versus have-nots, the geopolitical stresses brought about by extremists in the Islamic world and other groups who seek a means of delivering their message through violence, and the rising instability of many governments in the developing world. It is often up to the individual to correctly perceive and interpret these relationships and their impact on the firm and develop his or her own list of potential value drivers to track these intangible variables. This is no easy task because it is a highly subjective process. It is even more challenging to determine the impact these occurrences will have on various internal value drivers. In the end, it is up to the manager to make the choices of what to monitor, understand the timing of the impact from the external drivers, and make the necessary investments.

Here again we find the manager in a challenging intellectual setting. Success here will depend on the manager's cognitive and experiential skills and abilities to make choices from a wide range of probable internal and external value drivers and to formulate how the firm will have to navigate through this maze of complexity and uncertainty.

Causal Relationships and Strategic Success

For the manager, decisions about future strategic direction must be based on a thorough analysis of the external value drivers and the probable cause-and-effect relationships they have with the internal value drivers of the firm. It must be recognized that these causal relationships suggest the need for serious scanning, analysis, and deliberation by managers if they are to anticipate tomorrow's investment needs. Continuing with the example of the case of terrorism, the ability of all firms to obtain terrorism insurance is nearly impossible in the post-9/11 environment. For those small- and medium-size enterprises of the tourism industry, even if it was available, few could afford it. This interaction between terrorism as an external value driver and value drivers such as rising insurance premiums as the internal effect demonstrate how these causal relationships affect the cash flows of the firm directly. This example further illustrates how important it is for management not only to anticipate the impact associated with these causal activities but also to develop both long- and short-term strategies to deal with them if the value of the firm is to be protected.

Exhibit 3 reflects an example of how value drivers in the remote economic environment of countries within the Organization for Economic Cooperation and Development (OECD) can be tracked and used to accomplish this objective. As the exhibit points out, managers must develop an understanding of the key value drivers related to each category of environment scanned, establish a base of valid and reliable information, and then provide a brief outlook on what they expect to happen to those value drivers. As stated earlier, the outlook is based on the understanding the manager has developed from observing the value drivers over time and assessing their impact on the firm over this period. Based on the quality and strength of this outlook, decision makers should be able to improve their estimation processes regarding what to invest in and the future cash flows of these investments.

Estimating the outlook is a daunting challenge for managers. It implies that they will predict the future. We all know that this is not possible to do with 100% accuracy. Because of this, many managers are reluctant to make an attempt to do so. If this is the case, they are clearly adding risk to the firm because they are simply guessing. We all know that guessing is a game of chance that implies a 50% chance of being correct and a 50% chance of being wrong. We are not sure that investors or owners of a business enjoy playing this game. As the example in Exhibit 3 demonstrates, some forecasts can be purchased from reputable firms who provide this type of information as their core business or from organizations like the OECD.

Providing outlooks or forecasts is a thinking process supported by quantitative and qualitative data. When we say *thinking,* we mean that one cannot simply extrapolate from the data without asking questions about that extrapolation. Are the assumptions going to hold? Has competition changed the competitive landscape? Has government policy changed? In other words, outlooks are built on a set of assumptions that must be backed by either fact or logical inductive reasoning from sets of ideas or facts. Here again the idea of management theory applies. Theory is built on assumptions based on knowledge and observations. There is no substitute for knowing the body of knowledge and scanning for observations that make the theory substantive.

Exhibit 4 illustrates this relationship using another important value driver: labor costs. As the exhibit illustrates, the analysis begins in the economic category of the remote environment and the subcategories therein. In this case, examples of key value

EXHIBIT 3   Tracking Value Drivers

Sub-categories	Identify the primary sources of information	How often do you review this information?	Based upon your information sources used, list and briefly describe the key value drivers you believe are important to monitor in understanding the cause and effect relationship with your firm.
Key measures of economic well being	World Bank OECD Domestic Statistic Offices US Department of Census	Monthly	*KEY value drivers:* • GDP (Gross Domestic Product) • Private consumption *Brief outlook on the key value drivers* Real GDP growth is projected to decline from 3.4% in 2000 to a range from 2.2 to 2.8% in 2001, and to remain in a range from 2.1 to 3.1% in 2002. Domestic demand is expected to decelerate and the contribution of external trade to growth is projected to weaken significantly in 2001 and to be broadly neutral in both 2001 and 2002. Private consumption growth is expected to decline from 2.7% in 2000 to 2.2–2.6% in 2001, and to be 2.0–2.3% in 2002. This reflects continued strong growth of real disposable income, mainly due to the implementation of tax reductions in a number of countries. After a year of particularly strong performance, economic growth in the OECD area has been weakening since the autumn of 2000. The 2001 growth rate is projected to be half that of 2000, at around 2% and the long-running reduction in unemployment is projected to come to a halt. However, the forces dampening economic growth are projected to dissipate in the second half of 2001, leading to a growth rate of 2.5% to 3% over the following twelve months. Inflation is expected to remain low.

EXHIBIT 4   Cause-and-Effect Relationships of Value Drivers from the Remote Environment to the Impact on the Firm

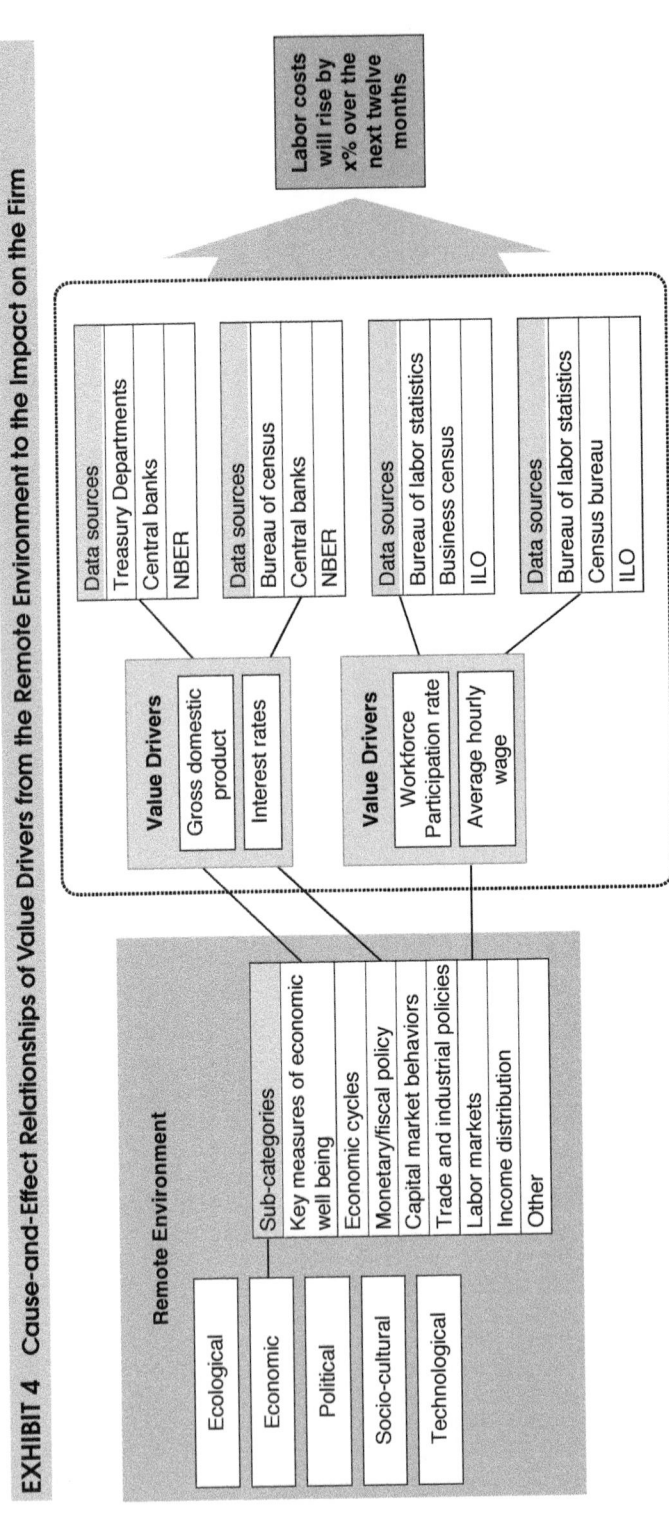

drivers associated with labor cost are identified along with two examples of the metrics used to track their behavior over time (workforce participation rates and average hourly wage). Sources of valid and reliable data are also identified. It should be pointed out here that because the scanning process is complex and time consuming, managers should seek to identify and track only those value drivers that are likely to have the greatest impact on the firm.

Once the most important value drivers have been identified and managers are familiar with their behavior over time, the next step is to identify the primary causal relationships with the internal value drivers of the firm, as in this case, labor cost. In this example, many possible relationships exist between the external and internal value drivers, and the manager is expected to know and understand them and use this knowledge to assist in forecasting the labor costs associated with the future cash flows of the firm. It is also essential that the executive institutionalize the tracking of these drivers as part of an effective environmental scanning system. This is done to encourage all members of the management team to be aware of the causal role they play on firm performance.

Exhibit 5 illustrates another view of how this causal analysis may look. This shows the more direct links between probable scenarios surrounding key value drivers and the cash flow statement of the firm. For now we focus on just the labor cost example to remain consistent with the illustration in Exhibit 4. As indicated in the text block next to the cash flow statement, the expenses of this business are about to be altered due to the potential activity of three value drivers: pending wage settlements with several key unions that will likely raise all wage rates, fewer numbers of potential workers in the labor force who seek industry jobs, and possible new health care insurance premiums. These value drivers, if they proceed as forecasted, will no doubt raise the overall cost of labor for this firm.

EXHIBIT 5 The Relationship of Value Drivers and Possible Outcomes in the Remote and Task Environments of the Hospitality Enterprise

Change in Revenues

less change in operating expenses
equals—change in EBITDA
less change in depreciation and amortization
equals—change in EBIT
less change in interest expenses
equals change in earnings before taxes
less change in taxes
equals change in net income
plus change in depreciation and amortization
equals change in cash flow from operations
less working capital changes
equals changes in operational cash flows to equity
Discount rate for project
Present value of cash flows

Most significant value drivers	3 Key events influencing future of value drivers
Labor cost	Pending wage settlements with unions Insurance requirements legislation Efforts at improving productivity
Food cost	HACCP requirements E-commerce buying groups Rising energy prices
Energy costs	Rising oil prices Production of energy Price controls

What the manager must try to do in this case is reflect back on the prior history of each value driver to determine how it correlates with the actual rise in labor costs. The first question to ask in this case is how long it will take for the firm's labor cost to increase after the value drivers have moved forward. There is no doubt that a lag effect occurs in some cases and the manager should try to understand this. The next question might be to determine what employee groups will be affected. Third, managers will have to decide how they will respond by determining what, if any, action they will need to take to remain competitive. This again takes us back to the notion that managers will be required to develop their own theories about these causal relationships and make whatever decisions are required.

To help the manager in formulating theories, several approaches are available. Scenario analysis is a frequent way of expressing possible outcomes with respect to a value driver. For example, the manager would like to know what will be the average wage increase due to the labor union settlements mentioned earlier. A wide range of possibilities does exist, but the manager knows from tracking prior settlements that the range of increase will be from 1.5% to 4%. If the manager is doing the appropriate job of scanning, she or he will have some sense of how negotiations are going and can begin to suggest the following with respect to wage increases: Wages will go up by 2% under the best case scenario (for management), 2.5% in the most likely, and possibly 3.5% under the worst case (best for the workers, worst for management).

The manager in this case knows that in the past she or he has had to increase wages approximately 0.75% for every 1% increase in the union settlement. This has offered enough of an increase to keep employees happy and yet not match the overall settlement (try to keep in mind that it is management's dual responsibility to add wealth to the owners of the firm and thus they must seek to keep costs down while still demonstrating their appreciation for the value of each and every employee). Now, all that the manager must do is try to determine what the overall increase will be to develop accurately next year's labor cost estimates.

Suppose the following probabilities are selected based again on the manager's experience in tracking the value drivers over time: There is a 30% chance of a 2% increase, a 60% chance of a 2.5% increase, and a 10% chance of a 3.5% increase (note that the probabilities of each chance must total one [1] to equal a 100% overall chance of occurring). The information in Exhibit 6 displays this out in numeric form. As can be seen in this case, the expected increase in wages to be paid in the future will be

EXHIBIT 6 Likelihood of Wage Increase Due to Settlement with the Union

Event (A)	Possible wage increase percentage (B)	Probability of wage increase (C)	Expected value (D) = (B) × (C)
Low increase	2%	30%	.6%
Medium increase	2.5%	60%	1.5%
High increase	3.5%	10%	.35%
Total expected percentage increase in wages due to settlement with union			2.45%

0.0245%. Management would factor this increase in over the period of time that the settlement will be in place. This example is a simple form of what is referred to as *expected value analysis*. It combines what management's theories are regarding the wage increases with their experiences in terms of what will likely be the case.

As can be imagined here, none of this information is definitive. It is all based on assumptions about the behaviors of key value drivers, which are determined by the actions of humans. One might ask, "Is it possible to get more deterministic?" No one can predict the future with precise accuracy, but if future cash flows are to be forecasted the future must be predicted based on sound reasoning and judgment.

Let's explore Exhibit 6 a bit more closely. The first question that would come to your mind is "Where did the numbers or percentages in column C come from?" One could say that they are manufactured out of thin air (which is often the case when someone is guessing). However, this is where experience and effective scanning become really important. A good scanning system has knowledgeable informants who are involved in, or deeply aware of, the negotiations with the unions and can estimate the range of increases (column B) reasonably well. The probabilities are also based on the past experience of the manager or other experts who can be called on for advice. They are judgment calls, estimates, or predictions based on a longitudinal reflection on the past. Of course, by tracking value drivers associated with this type of event, it becomes much easier to estimate these probabilities in the future. This is where experience, cognitive skills, and good quality information really pays off for the manager and the organization.

Put differently, managers make guesses about the future all the time; otherwise they would stand still. The guesses are either based on some belief or passion, rational analysis of available information, or some combination of both. Risk is associated with each guess, and the manager's job is to maximize return and minimize risk. If the manager can improve scanning efforts and track significant value drivers, then the theories that are created become more acceptable to owners and other stakeholders. Managers can improve on these theories as outlined in Exhibit 6 by improving their ability to estimate the probabilities for each possible scenario. They can only do this by gaining knowledge about the forces and value drivers influencing the event and using their experience to draw conclusions about the impact the firm will feel.

Of course the world is not as simple as three scenarios for every forecast that the manager must make. Fortunately, with the help of the computer and management scientists, additional tools are available. Sensitivity analysis allows us hold one of the variables in Exhibit 6 constant while we run an infinite amount of possibilities for the remaining numbers in columns B and C. This allows us to assess the degree of impact the changes in each variable is likely to have on the entire expected value of the exercise.

Thanks to the speed of today's computer, literally thousands of possibilities can be assessed in minutes. Monte Carlo simulation (a process that calculates multiple scenarios of a previously defined model or theory formulated by management) enables us to go even further by suggesting that each variable associated with numbers like those in Exhibit 6 is a random variable with its own probability distribution. Scenarios can then be created by randomly drawing a value from each uncertain variable and plugging it into a model. These scenarios can be recalculated thousands of times, producing a range of possible outcomes that will reduce the risks associated with overly simplistic approaches like that in Exhibit 6. The best part of all this is that it can be done using a spreadsheet program purchased off the shelf.

Estimating the Timing of Value Driver Movements

We have indicated that understanding the causal relationships between and among external, internal, tangible, and intangible value drivers is a longitudinal process. Causal relationships of the type we are discussing generally develop over time. For example, industry sales are said to depend on disposable income, gross domestic product, interest rates, and a general sense of well-being by consumers. This theory has been tested over time and is generally accepted to hold some truth. Thus managers must try to understand the timing of these external value drivers and how they move with the general business environment and subsequently the industry sales curve. Exhibits 7 and 8 illustrate how this may work.

EXHIBIT 7   Hotel Industry Cycle Curve

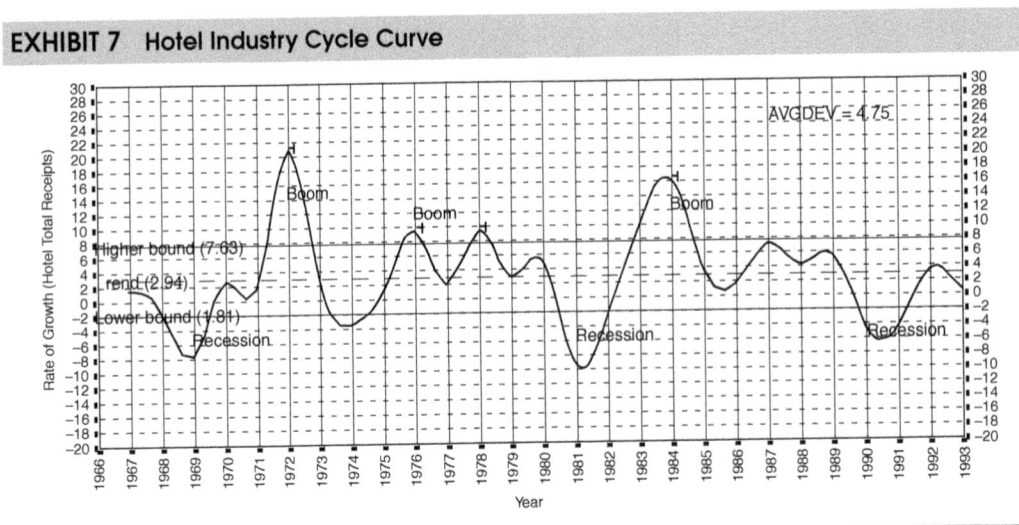

Hotel Industry Cycle Duration (years)					
High	**Low**	**High to High**	**Low to Low**	**Expansion**	**Contraction**
1967	1969				2
1972	1974	5	5	3	2
1976	1977	4	3	2	1
1980	1981	4	4	3	1
1984	1986	4	5	3	2
1989	1991	5	5	3	2
Mean		4.4	4.4	2.8	1.7
Standard Deviation		0.5	0.9	0.4	0.5

Source: Choi, Jeong-Gil. (1996). *The Hotel Industry Cycle: Developing an Economic Indicator System for the U.S. Hotel Industry.* Unpublished Master's Theses, Virginia Polytechnic Institute and State University, Blacksburg, VA.

Performance of Leading Composite Index

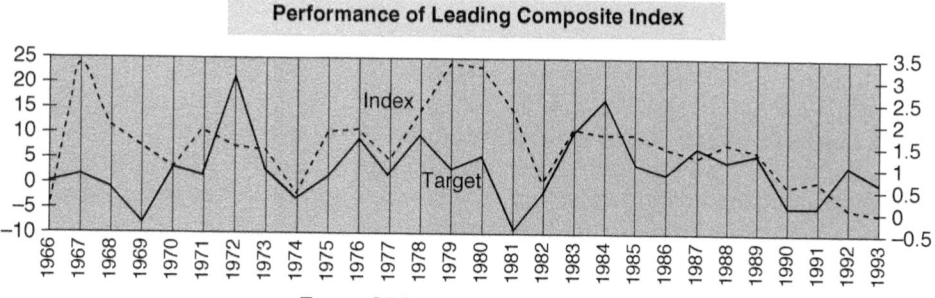

—— Target SPC   ·········· Leading Index SPC

Performance of Coincident Composite Index

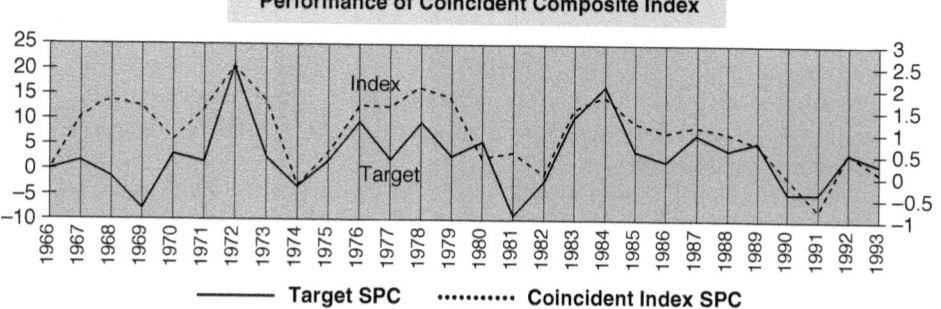

—— Target SPC   ·········· Coincident Index SPC

Performance of Lagging Composite Index

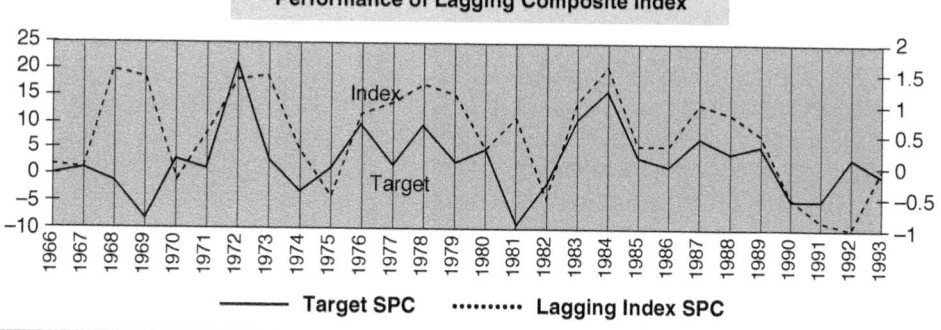

—— Target SPC   ·········· Lagging Index SPC

EXHIBIT 8   Leading and Lagging Indicators for the Hotel Industry

Source: Choi, J. G. 2003. "Developing an Economic Indicator System (a Forecasting Technique) for the Hotel Industry."*International Journal of Hospitality Management* 22, no. 2: 147–60.

Exhibit 7 is the hotel industry revenue cycle as developed by Choi (2003). It is a normalized view of the industry cycle from the years 1966 to 1993. Several observations can be seen in this exhibit. First, take note of the peaks and troughs. This researcher observed that the average number of years from peak to peak and trough to trough is roughly the same, 4.4 years. In looking at the timing of both the upward or recovery periods and the declining periods, they are 2.8 and 1.7, respectively. This is important longitudinal information. For example, if the firm is thinking of expansion, what is the best time in the cycle to do so? If management is thinking of remodeling current foodservice operations, is it better to do this during a recession or during growth? By understanding the industry cycle, management can improve the timing of the investment and the estimate of cash flows associated with it.

Exhibit 8 goes a step further in this type of analysis by identifying leading, coincident, and lagging indicators. The purpose here is to try to improve the understanding of what drives the cycle curve (value drivers) in Exhibit 7. Using basic economic theory, this researcher identified the leading indicators to be the American Stock Exchange Index, the number of business failures, the consumer price index for motor fuels, hotel dividends per share, the gross domestic product for the service sector, the hotel industry stock index, the M2 money supply in constant dollars, the New York Stock Exchange Index, the prime rate, the S&P 500 index, savings as a percentage of disposable income, and aggregate wages and salaries. As can be seen from an analysis of the top graph in the exhibit, the leading indicators lead the actual industry cycle model by about one year, and this carries an accuracy of approximately 67%. This surely improves the chance associated with managerial guesswork.

What we can learn from this research is that it is possible to be able to make reasonable estimates using information about value drivers that have proven to be valid and reliable. This information assists managers in developing theories regarding cause-and-effect relationships that leads to more rational evaluation of future investments. Note that these examples include what we have called tangible external value drivers. We have already recognized that not all value drivers are tangible. Will this inhibit forecasts?

We can try to answer this question with two examples. Exhibit 9 contains two exhibits that reflect headlines with respect to two forces that have been identified by nominal group research techniques (Olsen 1995) as driving change in the hospitality industry: technology and safety and health. In both forces, the value drivers are not as clear and precise as in the industry leading indicator reference just provided—in other words, they are less tangible.

In the case of technology, the hospitality industry was warned of the coming convergence of the computer, computer software, and telecommunications in 1995. Specifically, in an industry report published by the International Hotel and Restaurant Association, it was suggested that if things kept moving in this direction, it was possible that hospitality firms would lose control over the sale of their inventories. Although this message was acknowledged, executives faced the uncertainties surrounding the timing of this force and what it might actually look like. This is because of the lack of clear value drivers as identified from an industry perspective. Put differently, their theories were weak due to limited experience, perceptual view, and cognitive understanding.

The problem of an unclear understanding of the value drivers is more a function of the fact that industry practitioners had little exposure to the body of knowledge in this area and thus suffered from what we referred to earlier as "they didn't know what they didn't know." Of course this is not uncommon in any industry when new forces come into being. And this is why we have stressed the need for managers to

Drive Forces	Headline & Sources		Issues
Safety and security	*Safety:*		
	• "Getting it down cold", by Pacitti & Porter (3/18/01) available: web.lexis-nexis.com	→	$800 billion by 2005 food borne sickness in U.S.
	• "Burger King recalls 2.6 million toys, fearing they could be choking hazard", (7/31/01), available: public.wsj.com	→	Bad toy product
	• "Mad cow threatens to hijack EU summit", (12/3/00), available: www.cnn.com	→	Food borne illness
	• "Foot-and-mouth" virus: a global dilemma", (3/13/01), available: www.cnn.com	→	Food borne illness
	• "Foreign visitors decreased in U.K because of the spread of foot-and month disease", (5/12/01), available" www.chinesenewsnet.com	→	Food borne illness
	• "Contagious stomach virus strikes 100 aboard Disney ship", (11/22/02) available: www.cnn.com	→	Food borne illness
	Security:		
	• "Bali bombing a blow for tourism", by J. Boulden, (10/15/02), available: www.cnn.com	→	Terrorism
	• "Israeli tourists evacuated from Kenya", (11/29/02), available: www.cnn.com	→	Terrorism
Technology	• "Green Suite International's O-Tech cleans up laundry operations waste", (11/2001), available: www.hotel-online.com	→	Laundry system for waste reduction and energy conservation
	• "Twenty-one million Americans "usually" buy travel online, up 75% from 2000", (11/01), available: www.hotel-online.com	→	On-line booking
	• "Biometrics lend a hand to hotel security", T. Ronson, (2/02), available: www.hotel-online.com	→	Hotel security biotechnology
	• "Wireless technology: where we have been, where are we going?" by G. Rinehart, (11/01), available: www.hotel-online.com	→	Wireless technology

EXHIBIT 9   Validation of Forces Driving Change in 1995

open their perceptual windows wide so these forces can be identified. In looking at Exhibit 9 it is easy to see in retrospect that the forecasts of 1995 have for the most part come true. The problem is whether anything can be done to recoup all the losses.

The same example applies with regard to safety and health. Although general drivers of change were identified in this case, little direct action seems to have been taken. It appears that this is one managers have chosen to ignore. In a recent investigation of one multinational hotel chain, hotel general managers have failed to raise this issue on their personal radar screens and even have considered the notion that it could not happen to them. In further inquiry they are not even sure how to value an investment in safety and health because they do not know what to consider in forecasting changes in cash flows due to an investment in this area. The second half of Exhibit 9 suggests that to ignore this force is foolish. No customer wants to gamble with their lives, and no hospitality owner wants to put their businesses at risk due to the failure to make the right investments in safety and health.

The timing of these two forces is difficult to assess, which explains some of the problems faced by managers and their subsequent inaction. Of course, this is no excuse. What had to occur in both cases was an environmental scanning system that provided for the acquisition of the body of knowledge surrounding each force either by hard research performed by the manager or a staff unit or by the purchase of this information from experts. Generally, if the manager is faced with the "don't know what they don't know" situation, obtaining expert advice and counsel is the best. There is no excuse for ignorance in this case. At the speed with which changes occur today, a wait-and-see attitude is not enough.

Tracking change over time can be accomplished relatively easily when the data are quantitative. We saw this in the industry cycle model. Tracking less quantifiable data, although difficult, does not have to be impossible. Exhibit 10 contains a look at investments made by multinational hotel companies over a 10-year period. This type of analysis is often referred to as an event study. In this case, extensive research using a content analysis methodology of 10K reports, annual reports, and searches using popular electronic search engines identified the competitive methods invested in by leading hotel companies. As can be seen, during a period when the broader economy was threatening (1991–1993), firms invested in more competitive methods to stay ahead of the competition. From this analysis the researcher was able to determine what firms were leading and who was following. We use this example to illustrate that even with intangible value drivers, it is possible to seek an improved understanding regarding where forces are headed.

Theories and Strategic Success

In this chapter we have focused on building theories about the firm and its environment. It is in the identification of key relationships between the firm and its environment that managers find the opportunities to lead others in achieving competitive advantage. Because many of the relationships often appear abstract, the concept of value drivers has been introduced as a way of taking the key variables in the environment and bringing some practical meaning to them. Value drivers suggest that managers can track them longitudinally, understand their history, and estimate the timing of future movements. By doing so, the actual impact can be predicted in terms of the causal effect they will have on the firm. As we have stated throughout these chapters on the environment, managers must work hard to identify the forces driving change, understand them (through value driver analysis), and estimate their impact (on such measures as cash flows). We believe that value drivers, whether tangible or intangible, can help the manager accomplish this task.

EXHIBIT 10   Competitive Methods of Multinational Hotel Companies over the 10-Year Period of Analysis

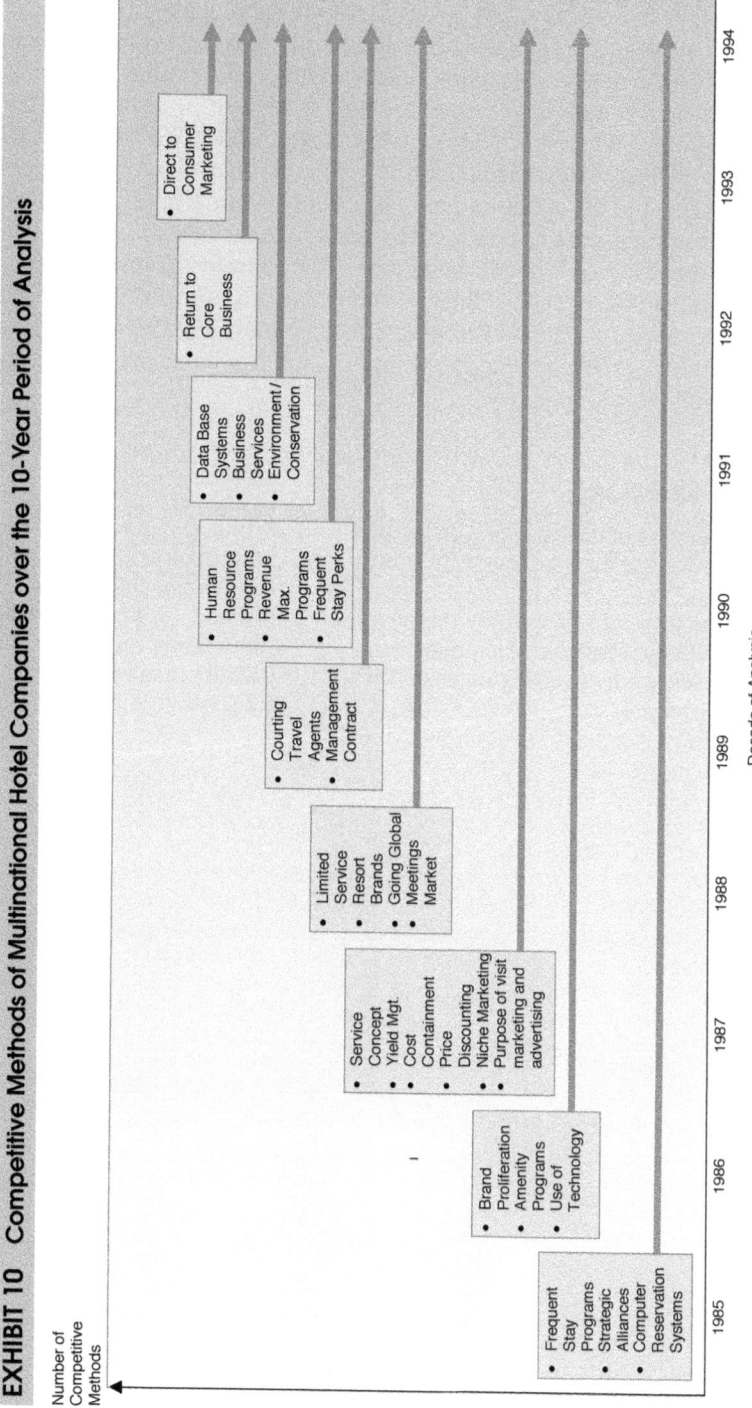

SUMMARY

In this chapter we have taken general concepts and applied them to the scanning of the remote environment. The view presented here is that business opportunities emerge from scanning of the remote categories. Since the causal relationship between the remote forces and the firm is complex, we suggest the use of the concept of value drivers as a way of balancing intuitive thinking with more rational approaches. We also stress the importance of knowing the body of knowledge with respect to the categories of the remote environment in order to enhance the identification of key value drivers. Choosing from a complex array of value drivers and creating managerial theories of how they affect the firm causally is a competency that is increasingly becoming part of the manager's job. We have defined these value drivers as tangible, intangible, internal and external. The goal of the manager is to try to link these to firm performance. In seeking to explain these linkages we used the example of the hotel industry cycle curve and how information can be incorporated into estimating the leading indicators of industry performance.

DISCUSSION QUESTIONS

1. Discuss the roles of inductive and deductive thinking when scanning the remote environment.

2. Discuss the types of value drivers that exist and indicate the challenges that managers will experience when relying on them for forecasting purposes.

3. When using value drivers such as those identified as the hotel industry cycle and the leading indicators associated with it provide your understanding of what the leading indicators can do to assist in helping managers improve their revenue forecasts.

Appendix 1

Remote Environment Category:
Subcategories and Selected Value Drivers
Economic*

Subcategory	Value Drivers	Sources
Key measures of Economic Well-Being	GDP	www.newyorkfed.org; europa.eu.int; www.worldbank.org; www.cia.gov;
	Unemployment rate	www.neatideas.com; www.newyorkfed.org; www.cnn.com; www.bls.gov/home.htm; www.imf.org; www.forecasts.org
	Inflation	www.bls.gov/home.htm; www.neatideas.com
	Consumer prices	www.newyorkfed.org; www.bls.gov/home.htm;
	CPI (Consumer Price Index)	www.newyorkfed.org; www.bls.gov/home.htm; www.economagic.com;
	PPI (Producer Price Index)	www.bls.gov/home.htm; www.economagic.com/
	WWI (West Texas Intermediate) & other commodity prices	www.nymex.com/jsp/index.jsp
	Private consumption	www.newyorkfed.org; www.conference-board.org
	Consumer Confidence Index	www.worldwatch.org; www.conference-board.org
	Structure of output	www.oecd.org
	Household final consumption expenditure	www.census.gov
	Poverty level	www.bls.gov/home.htm; www.census.gov
	GDP per person employed	Please refer to GDP and www.bls.gov/home.htm; www.census.gov
	Income distribution	www.bls.gov/home.htm; www.census.gov
	World trade volume	www.wto.org;
	World real long term interest rates	www.oecd.org
	Real commodity prices	www.bis.org; www.nymex.com/jsp/index.jsp
	Stock market indices	www.neatideas.com; www.finance.yahoo.com; www.ft.com; www.bloomberg.com
	Exchange rates	www.newyorkfed.org; www.bloomberg.com; www.finance.yahoo.com; www.europa.eu.int
	Government debt	www.worldbank.org
	University of Michigan Consumer-	www.newyorkfed.org; www.lib.umich.edu/govdocs/steccpi.html;
	Confidence Index	www.worldwatch.org; www.conference-board.org
	Industrial Production	www.newyorkfed.org;

(continued)

* Prepared by Ines Ghorbal, doctoral candidate, Department of Hospitality and Tourism Management, Pamplin College of Business, Virginia Tech, Blacksburg, 2003.

(*continued*)

Subcategory	Value Drivers	Sources
Economic Cycles	Balance of Payment Account	www.gpoaccess.gov; www.worldbank.org; www.digitaleconomist.com
	Unemployment Rate	www.forecasts.org; www.neatideas.com; www.newyorkfed.org; www.cnn.com; www.bls.gov/home.htm; www.imf.org;
	GDP per Capita	Please refer to GDP and www.census.gov and www.cia.gov; www.whitehouse.gov
	Leading Indicator Index	www.globalindicators.org; www.conference-board.org;
	GDP growth rate	www.newyorkfed.org; europa.eu.int; www.worldbank.org; www.cia.gov;
	Consumer price index	www.newyorkfed.org; www.bls.gov/home.htm; www.economagic.com
	Rate of inflation	www.bls.gov/home.htm; www.neatideas.com
	Oil pricing	www.oil.com; www.eia.doe.gov
	CPI (Consumer Price Index)	www.newyorkfed.org; www.bls.gov/home.htm; www.economagic.com;
	Index of consumer expectations	www.economagic.com; www.globalindicators.org; www.investorsgroup.com
	Index of Industrial Production	www.federalreserve.gov; www.ubos.org; http://forecasts.org;
	Deflation	www.bos.frb.org; www.imf.org; www.economist.com/
Monetary Policy	Unemployment Rate	www.neatideas.com; www.newyorkfed.org; www.cnn.com; www.bls.gov/home.htm; www.imf.org; www.forecasts.org;
	GDP	www.newyorkfed.org; europa.eu.int; www.worldbank.org; www.cia.gov
	Inflation Rate	www.bls.gov/home.htm; www.neatideas.com
	Money supply Growth Rate	www.federalreserve.gov
	CD rates	www.bankrate.com; www.economagic.com
	Treasury Rates	www.newyorkfed.org; www.bloomberg.com; www.finance.yahoo.com; www.economagic.com
	Federal Funds Rates	www.finance.yahoo.com; www.bondsonline.com; www.oecd.org
	Discount Rate	www.newyorkfed.org; www.bls.gov/home.htm; www.neatideas.com; www.economagic.com
	Federal Bank Interest Rates	www.federalreserve.gov; www.economagic.com;
	Currency Exchange Rates	www.newyorkfed.org; www.bloomberg.com; www.finance.yahoo.com
	Interest Rates	www.bankrate.com; money.cnn.com/markets/bondcenter; www.finance.yahoo.com; www.economagic.com;
	Fiscal Policies	www.imf.org; www.cbpp.org/pubs/sfp.htm; www.cato.org; www.cbpp.org
	CPI	www.newyorkfed.org; www.bls.gov/home.htm;
	Lending Rates	http://treasury.worldbank.org; www.afdb.org; www.uobgroup.com;
	Indices of consumer prices	www.bls.gov/home.htm;

Subcategory	Value Drivers	Sources
Fiscal Policy	Repatriation of funds	europa.eu.int; www.unitar.org;
	Foreign Direct Investment	www.unctad.org; www.earthsummit2002.0rg; home.developmentgateway.org; www.oecd.org
	International Tax Rates	www.taxfoundation.org; www.tax-news.com; www.taxsites.com
	International agreements on tax issues	www.taxfoundation.org; www.un.org; www.itpa.org
	Personal Income Tax Rates	www.oecd.org; http://taxes.yahoo.com; www.bankrate.com;www.bea.doc.gov
	Corporate Income Tax Rates	www.taxadmin.org; www.taxfoundation.org; www.cbpp.org
	Total Federal Revenues	www.cbo.gov, www.heritage.org; www.bea.doc.gov; www.cbpp.org
	Federal Outlays	www.taxfoundation.org; www.irs.gov; www.cbpp.org
	Federal Budget	www.house.gov; www.cbpp.org; www.treas.gov
	Long term government bond yields	www.federalreserve.gov
	Inflation rate	www.bls.gov/home.htm; www.neatideas.com
	Taxation of Dividends	www.cato.org; www.is4profit.com; http://taxesandgrowth.ncpa.org
	Taxation	http://taxesandgrowth.ncpa.org; www.cato.org; www.cbpp.org
	Consumption tax	www.ustreas.gov; www.oecd.org; www.ustreas.gov; www.oecd.org/
	Social insurance taxes/payroll taxes	www.cbpp.org
	Individual income taxes	www.oecd.org; http://taxes.yahoo.com; www.bankrate.com; www.bea.doc.gov
	Property taxes	www.window.state.tx.us
	Stock Market Indices	www.ft.com; www.finance.yahoo.com; www.stockcharts.com
	Stock Market capitalization end of month	Factiva Database; www.finance.yahoo.com; www.stockcharts.com
	Long Term Rates	www.finance.yahoo.com; www.bankrate.com; http://money.cnn.com/markets/bondcenter
	Long Term Government Bond Yields	www.finance.yahoo.com; http://money.cnn.com/markets/bondcenter
	Corporate Bond Yields	www.bondsonline.com
	Implied stock market volatility	www.bondsonline.com
Capital Market Behaviors	Interest rates	www.bankrate.com; http://money.cnn.com/markets/bondcenter; www.finance.yahoo.com; www.economagic.com
	Multi-market exchanges	www.wsj.com; www.ft.com; www.fese.be
	FDI	www.fdixchange.com

(*continued*)

(*continued*)

Subcategory	Value Drivers	Sources
Trade/ Industrial Policies	Transportation industry stock valuations	http://quicktake.morningstar.com; www.valuationresources.com, www.finance.yahoo.com
	Acquisitions and mergers	www.corporateaffiliations.com; www.wsj.com; http://biz.yahoo.com
	Total consumer credit	www.economagic.com; www.finance.yahoo.com;
	Market growth	www.ft.com; www.finance.yahoo.com; www.stockcharts.com
	Export of Goods Growth Rate	www.gpoaccess.gov; www.global-production.com; www.census.gov;
	Import of Goods Growth Rate	www.census.gov; http://europa.eu.int;
	Balance of Trade	www.ita.doc.gov; www.census.gov;
	Index of Import Growth Rate	www.usitc.gov
	Index of Export Growth Rate	www.cbo.gov; www.usitc.gov
	Level of Protectionism	www.cbo.gov; www.freetrade.org; www.cato.org
	International Currency Exchange Rates	www.newyorkfed.org; www.bloomberg.com; www.finance.yahoo.com
	GATT and other agreements by the WTO (World Trade Organization) Recent decisions	www.wto.org
	Balance of payment accounts	www.gpoaccess.gov; www.census.gov; www.digitaleconomist.com
	Oil price	www.oil.com; www.eia.doe.gov
	Oil production	www.oil.com; www.eia.doe.gov; www.opec.org; www.ipaa.org
	Technical requirements of transportation industry	www.dot.gov; www.fmcsa.dot.gov; www.iata.org;
	Mechanism of the oil production	www.oil.com; www.eia.doe.gov; www.opec.org
	Trade policies	www.wto.org; www.bls.gov/home.htm
	Euro exchange rates	www.ecb.int; www.x-rates.com; http://finance.yahoo.com
	Private consumption and disposable income levels	www.oecd.org; www.bls.gov/home.htm; www.cbpp.org;
	Trade volume	www.wto.org; www.bls.gov/home.htm; www.ita.doc.gov; www.cbo.gov
	Trade regulations	www.wto.org; www.cbo.gov
	% of business owned by the government	www.cia.gov; www.worldbank.org; www.imf.org
	Number of tourists	www.world-tourism.org; www.bea.gov
	Personal and business travel	www.world-tourism.org; www.bea.gov
	Hiring and Firing regulations	www.worldbank.org; www.dol.gov; www.bls.gov
	Weekly hours	www.ecct.com; www.bls.gov
	Employment Cost Index	www.dol.gov; www.bls.gov
	Hourly Compensation	www.bls.gov/home.htm;
	CPI	www.newyorkfed.org; www.bls.gov/home.htm;

Subcategory	Value Drivers	Sources
Labor Markets	Unemployment Rates	www.neatideas.com; www.newyorkfed.org; www.cnn.com; www.bls.gov/home.htm; www.imf.org; www.forecasts.org; www.cbpp.org
	Employment rates	www.bls.gov/home.htm; www.census.gov
	Labor costs	www.bls.gov/home.htm
	Labor Productivity	www.bls.gov; www.newyorkfed.org; www.nber.org
	Diversity of human resources possibilities	http://bls.gov; www.uww.edu/Adminaff/hr/hr.htm;
	Productivity	www.bls.gov; www.newyorkfed.org; www.ncpp.us
	Regulations	www.dol.gov; www.bls.gov
	Compensation per employee	www.dol.gov; www.bls.gov
	Employment growth rate	www.bls.gov/home.htm
	Hourly compensation costs	www.bls.gov/home.htm; www.cbpp.org
	Average hourly earnings	www.bls.gov/home.htm
	Social changes	www.cbpp.org; www.census.gov
	Labor market	www.bls.gov/home.htm; for analysis: www.digitaleconomist.com
	Training costs in %	Company specific
	Poverty Level	www.bls.gov/home.htm; www.cbpp.org; www.census.gov; www.whitehouse.gov
	Discrimination in the work place	www.worldbank.org; www.dol.gov; www.bls.gov
Income Distribution	GDP per capita	www.newyorkfed.org; europa.eu.int; www.worldbank.org; www.cia.gov; www.whitehouse.gov
	GDP per Employed Person	http://www.whitehouse.gov/fsbr/income.html; www.newyorkfed.org; europa.eu.int; www.worldbank.org; www.cia.gov; www.census.gov
	Difference in earning	www.bls.gov/home.htm; www.census.gov
	Labor cost index	www.dol.gov; www.bls.gov; www.census.gov
	Union	www.unions.org; www.global-unions.org
	Wages and labor productivity	www.bls.gov; www.newyorkfed.org; www.nber.org; www.ncpp.us
	International income statistics	www.fedstats.gov; www.bea.gov; www.worldbank.org
	Spending habits of emerging economies	www.imf.org; http://europa.eu.int
	Future purchasing power of different regions	www.cia.gov;
	Income per capita	www.cia.gov; www.whitehouse.gov
	Income disparities	www.bls.gov/home.htm; www.cbpp.org
	Population	www.cia.gov; www.census.gov; www.unfpa.org
	Population below poverty level	www.bls.gov/home.htm; www.cbpp.org; www.whitehouse.gov; www.unfpa.org
	Purchasing power parity index	www.bls.gov/home.htm

REFERENCES

Anders, D., and Bryant, A. 2004. "In-Depth Look at the Luxury Lodging Segment." *Merrill Lynch In Depth Report*, 2–29.

Choi, J. G. 2003. "Developing an Economic Indicator System (a Forecasting Technique) for the Hotel Industry." *International Journal of Hospitality Management* 22, no. 2: 147–60.

NOTE

1. M. D. Olsen, *Into the New Millennium: The IHA White Paper on the Global Hospitality Industry: Events Shaping the Future of the Industry* (19 pp.) (International Hotel Association, 1995).

C A S E   S T U D Y

Impact of Remote Environmental Factors on the Hospitality and Tourism Industry

The travel and tourism industry is particularly vulnerable to severe business downturns during periods of terrorist activity, political uncertainty, military conflict, and health-related crises (*Asia Africa Intelligence Wire* 2003). A generally poor global economic slowdown, a legacy of 9/11, the outbreak of severe acute respiratory syndrome (SARS), the war in Iraq, and even recent high oil prices have all hurt demand for travel services around the world. Dealing with these radical impacts has become a major challenge to the hospitality and tourism industry (Pine and McKercher 2004). In Asia, the hotel industry has weathered many years of trouble—the Asian financial crisis of 1977–1978, political unrest in a number of Southeast Asian countries, and the Bali bombing, all of which hurt travel through Asia.

During these troubled times, the industries with the biggest job losses were catering, hotels, wholesale and retail trades, transport, amusement, and recreational services. The World Travel & Tourism Council (WTTC) urged government leaders around the world to recognize the severe negative economic and employment impacts experienced by the travel and tourism sector and to develop strategic-policy measures to offset the long-term consequences to the industry and regional economies.

TERRORISM AND TOURISM

The terrorist attack in the United States on September 11, 2001, sent a shock wave throughout the airline and tourism industry (Pratt 2003). The disastrous events had a significant adverse impact on the world airline industry. Worldwide commercial passenger traffic fell by 18% in October 2001. The U.S. airline industry was hit the hardest, with its commercial passenger traffic declining 40% during the same time period. Needless to say, this placed a great financial burden on the already weakened condition of the airline industry.

Similarly, the impact of terrorism on tourism has been felt in the slowing growth of travel services, such as hotels, airlines, and tour operators, from averages approaching 3% to 4% to 15% immediately following 9/11 and subsequent invasions of Afghanistan and Iraq. In the United States, which depends mainly on domestic tourism, people are taking shorter breaks, staying closer to home, and even downgrading their vacations to camping trips. Hospitality operators remain concerned that such attacks can severely damage tourism and tourism-related businesses (Sangster 2005).

The negative impact just described is particularly severe for those developing countries that depend heavily on the tourism industry for economic development. Take the examples of the Bahama Islands and Jamaica. Tourism accounted for over 70% of the Bahama Islands GDP and about 65% of its employment. For Jamaica, tourism contributed about 8% to Jamaica's GDP and 160,000 jobs (Pratt 2003). Prior to 9/11, both the Bahamas and Jamaica had adopted aggressive sales and marketing strategies to capture a significant portion of the tourism market for the Caribbean area. The United States was the major tourist market for both countries (Pratt 2003). An emergency action plan that involved partnerships with hotels, tourism promotion boards, government and nongovernment organizations was devised in these countries to avert a potential economic disaster and to recapture the tourist traffic lost from the U.S. market in the wake of 9/11. Hotels in the Bahamas were persuaded to reduce proposed massive layoffs by coming up with creative ways to share work schedules (Pratt 2003).

The tourism industry in the Bahamas a year later showed total recovery in visitor arrivals. In Jamaica, the first half of 2002 showed arrivals were 11% less compared to 2001. The Jamaican Tourist Bureau plans to diversify and expand Jamaica's tourism client base in Europe and Latin American, for instance (Pratt 2003). An important lesson to be learned from the Bahama Islands is that a country assumes extreme risks to its economy if it depends on a single industry. Jamaica is a little better off because it has been diversifying its economy.

Terrorism threatens the hospitality industry more than any other sector of society due to the nature of the business. Many of the most destructive terrorist incidents have struck at hospitality, tourism, and travel-related businesses. For instance, the car bombings in Bali, the bombing of the Marriott Hotel in Jakarta, bombings in Morocco, bombing of the Moscow subway, railway bombings in Spain, and in 2005, the bombing of three hotels in Amman, Jordan, and bombings in London. This is important for hospitality providers because of the threat itself as well as the effect it has had on travelers. In a 2003 survey, when planning a vacation or convention, domestic visitors gave safety an average rating of 8.9 on a scale of 1 to 10, with 10 being the most significant.

Terrorism is evolving in three ways: it is gaining a wider base of support, it is becoming decentralized, and it is aiming increasingly at civilian targets. Experts predict that these trends will increase the terrorist threat to the hospitality industry throughout the world. Hospitality operators must place safety first and increase their spending on security. Security begins with people. Employees should be screened thoroughly before they are hired. Screening should also extend to suppliers, builders, and service contractors of hotels. Other suggestions include installing metal detectors in the entrance to the hotel. Since the September 11 attacks, Marriott International has added preparation for a terrorist attack to its list of routine security procedures. The company uses a system of color coding to signify the threat level for particular properties, with red the highest. In condition red, metal detectors are used to scan people, luggage, and vehicles. Other measures include surveillance and guest profiling (Sangster 2005). Hospitality security need not be taken to extremes to accomplish its purpose. Vigilance and deterrence remain the best weapons against terrorists (Sangster 2005). Hotels just need to send a message to discourage would-be terrorists.

IMPACT OF OIL PRICES

After two years of slow growth, the world economy registered a 2.6% expansion in 2003, which is expected to accelerate to 3.8% in 2004. The recovery has been driven largely by the U.S. economy and has enabled fast expansion in East Asia and South Asia. However, optimism must be balanced with caution as uncertainties about oil prices, exchange rates, and the relative health of the U.S. economy become the norm (*World Sources Online* 2004).

U.S. crude oil hit over $50 a barrel in 2004, the highest price since the New York Mercantile Exchange began trading crude oil futures 21 years ago (Yunus 2004). This price paled when compared with the near $70 per barrel prices in 2006. With transportation being central to the tourism industry's survival, sustained high oil prices will have negative impact for the industry in the long run (Yunus 2004). Tourism in Thailand experienced the negative impact of high oil prices during the first Gulf War period in 1991–1992 and suffered for more than a year. At the time, the number of foreign arrivals dropped by between 10% and 20% (*Bangkok Post* 2004). The airline and the tourism industries will be the hardest hit if the current increase in the price of crude oil persists for several years (Yunus 2004).

Fuel ranks just behind labor costs and accounts for between 10% and 20% of expenses for airline companies, according to the Air Transport Association. U.S. airlines will pay more than $28 billion in fuel costs in 2005, rising by $6.7 billion from 2004 (Baker and Field 2005). To control the fluctuations in fuel costs, many carriers have expanded hedging of energy purchases with the goal to control energy costs, maintain low airfares, and not imposing the jet fuel surcharges being levied by air freight companies (Austin 2004). Companies such as Southwest Airlines considers oil futures contracts, or hedges, its "insurance policy" against higher fuel prices. This practice allows airlines that hedge to lock in the prices they will pay for oil products months or even years in advance by buying contracts on the open market (Austin 2004). The airline industry faces the issue of to what extent it can pass the extra fuel costs to the traveling public. In the United States, airlines have rarely imposed a fuel surcharge but have offered the rising price of oil as their rationale for raising domestic fares in general (Baker and Field 2005). However, in Europe and Asia, leading carriers such as Cathay Pacific pass much of the extra burden on to the passengers through fuel surcharges.

As estimated by the Asian Strategy and Leadership Institute, oil price increases would negatively affect the airline industry, which has just started to rebound after recently being knocked down by SARS and several wars (Yunus 2004)). However, budget airlines, for instance, AirAsia of Malaysia, do not have immediate plans to increase airfares in view of the oil price increase. But the political situation should also be taken into consideration, rather than market forces alone. This is because the price increase is partially due to the current situation in Iraq and Palestine (Yunus 2004). If the United States remains in Iraq, it is expected that high oil prices will prevail over time. Even though air traffic has been strong, earnings growth remains a problem for large carriers as American, Untied, Delta, America West, Alaska, and others (Austin 2004). Five of them—Delta, United Airlines, US Airways, Hawaiian Airlines, and National Airlines—sought bankruptcy protection due to their continued insolvency and huge financial losses related to the 9/11 terrorist attacks and the U.S. economic downturn. In fact, in 2005, four years after the September 11 incident, the travel industry was still experiencing its after effects. The U. S. airline industry faces a number of challenges in addition to high fuel prices, such as lower fares due to intensive competition, and a weak dollar, which could discourage international travel.

THE OUTBREAK OF SARS AND ITS IMPACT ON TOURISM

The outbreak of the SARS in 2003 had a profound impact on tourism around the world, mainly through loss of inbound traffic, a decline of personal and business travel, and the postponement of capital investment. Hoteliers across the globe were faced with the unprecedented challenge of operating in an environment that put people at the mercy of a mysterious illness. For these hoteliers, battling health concerns, frequent single-digit occupancies, and the worldwide perception that travel to their countries just was not safe has taken an emotional toll on all (Strauss and Weinstein 2003).

The emergence of SARS became the single most important event to impact tourism in Asia in 2003. It not only affected the destinations under the World Health Organization (WHO) travel advisories, but all of the destinations in the region. SARS first appeared in China's Guangdong Province before emerging in neighboring Hong Kong. The WHO issued the first official SARS global alert on March 12, 2003, followed by an emergency travel advisory on March 15.

In Hong Kong, the Metropole Hotel was identified by the Hong Kong Health Department as a link in the chain from mainland China for the SARS epidemic. The hotel's ninth floor was discovered to be the place where the illness was passed from one traveler to another. As a result the infection spread outside of China to countries such as Singapore, Vietnam, Canada, Ireland, Germany, and the United States. The management of the Metropole reacted and attempted to be open with their staff as they established a crisis management team. A letter was distributed to all their guests to inform them of the occurrence before they made the public announcement. The announcement of the Department of Health created a furor. Within a few hours the hotel's lobby was chaos. The media reports rapidly spread panic in Hong Kong and the surrounding region. The Metropole's management maintained morale by keeping their usual hygiene maintenance and openness to its staff. The hotel's management was very visible during the crisis. The inspectors from the WHO came to the hotel three times and completed a detailed examination of the building.

On April 2 the WHO issued the first SARS Travel Recommendation, stating that Guangdong, China, and Hong Kong were areas where travelers should consider postponing all but essential travel. Tourist arrivals in Hong Kong, Singapore, and Taiwan decreased by half or more as compared to the same month the previous year. Various other destinations in the region—Japan, Korea, Macau, Australia, Thailand, Indonesia, and the Philippines—were also severely affected. This entire region was strongly dependent on air travel that had to pass through a hub in one of the affected countries. Many tourists were also reluctant to travel because initially there was a lack of information, and the subsequent uncertainty associated with the epidemic reinforced travel phobia.

In late May, the World Health Organization lifted its ban on travel to Hong Kong. By June 24 the WHO lifted its last remaining travel advisory concerning travel to Beijing. Taiwan was the last territory on the WHO warning lists to go the mandatory 20 days without reporting a new case of the virus. On July 5 WHO announced the SARS outbreak was contained worldwide. The highly contagious virus spread from Asia to as far as South Africa and Canada, killing more than 800 people. SARS infected more than 8,000 people around the world.

Following the outbreak of SARS and subsequent travel warnings from the WHO, four Asian destinations in particular suffered: China, Hong Kong, Vietnam, and Singapore. The impact of SARS on these countries has been four or five times the impact of September 11 on the United States, according to information provided by the WTTC.

Impact upon Tourism in General

The impact on the worldwide travel and tourism industry can be assessed by dividing the world into three geographical zones according to their exposure to the crisis. The countries or areas directly affected by SARS (China, Hong Kong, Singapore, Taiwan, and Vietnam) may have lost more than 30% of their travel and tourism employment, whereas their neighbors (Australia, Fiji, Indonesia, Kiribati, Malaysia, New Zealand, Philippines, Thailand, and others) in Southeast Asia and Oceania lost an estimated 15%. The rest of the world faced an average loss of 5% in tourism employment.

The economic effects of the virus were felt across Asia. The pressure on hoteliers in Hong Kong, Singapore, Beijing, and other Asian destinations devastated by SARS was immense. With occupancies plummeting to single digits, meetings and banqueting business all but drying up, and people scared to leave their homes to go out to dine, hoteliers were living a nightmare that stretched on for more than two months. Hotels across Asia experienced a 4.6% decline in revenue per available room. The travel and tourism industry was expected to lose US $20 billion of economic activity; for Singapore, travel and tourism was expected to lose US $2 billion of economic activity. Vietnam's loss from travel and tourism was expected to be US $220 million.

Hong Kong and Singapore were some of the regions poorest performers in March 2003. The Hong Kong economy was severely affected by the outbreak of SARS. All industries were affected. Tourism, which is among the pillar industries of Hong Kong, experienced the greatest drop. In 2003 Hong Kong's travel and tourism industry expected to lose over US $3 billion of economic activity as a result of SARS. This included jobs and gross domestic product. A number of airlines had cut their routes in the region. The International Air Transport Association (IATA) estimated that bookings to destinations such as the Hong Kong area were down between 30% and 40%. Passenger traffic at Hong Kong International Airport saw a year-on-year decline of 80% to 565,000, compared with more than 2.5 million in May 2003.

Because of the impact of SARS, the transportation market fell by 9% to HK $560 billion. This substantial decline was led by the severe downturn of the air transport and cruise sectors. The total number of arrivals dropped by 7% to 10 million. The only positive impact of the disease was the increased demand for local tours. Retail sectors in particular were badly affected as people avoided crowded areas in regions where incidents of the virus were high. Tourism continued to decline drastically in response to increasing numbers of SARS cases but also returned quickly when the disease was brought under control from May onward (Pine and McKercher 2004).

Many conventions were cancelled and companies called off business trips. Hong Kong started promoting local tourism to offset the loss of travelers from the mainland and overseas. There were government campaigns to stimulate demand among locals in both Singapore and Hong Kong.

Impact upon Hotels

Hotels were hit especially hard by the SARS outbreak, with occupancy rates around 25% during the month of April. Hotels started to cut costs. In May occupancy rates of some hotels fell to 15% or lower compared with 83% or more a year earlier (Pine and McKercher 2004). Many had even fallen to single-digit occupancies. In June the occupancy was 32%, as compared to 78% in June 2002. The industry had been on a steady upward trend during the period of 1999–2000, in line with the development of tourism. It fell by 32% in 2003, to HK $13.6 billion. At the peak of the outbreak, a number of hotels closed entire floors of their properties to reduce operational costs, or they took advantage of the downturn to carry out renovation programs.

The following measures showed how hoteliers coped and what survival tactics they implemented to take back some control in the uncontrollable environment (Strauss and Weinstein 2003).

Health and Safety Precautions

One major positive to come out of the crisis was the heightened awareness of hygiene throughout Hong Kong. To ensure the safety of staff and guests, a list of precautions to help prevent the spread of the virus was developed; face masks, plastic gloves and hourly cleaning routines became the norm (Strauss and Weinstein 2003). Many hotels sought advice from local health authorities about how to protect their staff and guests from the SARS virus. Security was stepped up

following the outbreak as happened after the Gulf War. Accor hotels closely followed WHO guidelines on prevention and control. Many of the hotels stopped buffet services, and back-of-the-house staff and food handlers were required to wear surgical masks and gloves at all times. Starwood increased security and safety measures and reviewed and reinforced its global emergency notification procedures. New measures included increasing frequency of cleaning maintenance processes, reinforcing personal hygiene among all associates, emphasizing associate training to recognize SARS symptoms, and increased security at service entrances and loading docks.

New Chapter in Crisis Management

With this unprecedented outbreak of SARS, there is a need to add a whole new chapter on how to deal with incidences that have much longer durations than fires or food poisonings. Part of this type of crisis management deals with cutting costs (Strauss and Weinstein 2003). Cost-cutting initiatives included staff being ordered to take annual leave immediately, no pay leave ranging from one to four days per month, terminating probationers and temporary contracts, and stopping all overtime payments. Some hotels closed swimming pools, health and fitness centers, and reduced operating hours of restaurants. The number of elevators in use was reduced to save energy. Many hotels have used "forced leave" and various creative leave-without-pay schemes to weather the storm. Hoteliers agree that these schemes must affect both management and staff equally to preserve a good working relationship once business normalizes (Strauss and Weinstein 2003).

Proactive Response

Many industry operators believed it was the time to be proactive, to perfect attitudes, service, and procedures in crisis prevention and handling. Hoteliers were forced to be innovative and use the drop in occupancy to complete major renovation, step up training programs on new service standards, and cross-train in all departments, to name a few initiatives (Strauss and Weinstein 2003). Other operators were creative with marketing campaigns designed to generate local business, especially for their food and beverage outlets or for weekend special package business that locals otherwise would not consider. For the Peninsula Group, the measures included deferring promotional activities that involved overseas travel and redirecting their advertising programs to the local market and imposing a hiring freeze for noncritical positions. The company ensured that the guest experience never suffered while cutting back-of-the-house costs, including energy and labor. No staff was laid off; they were told to clear annual leave, and some were deployed to other departments.

Impact upon Airlines

By April Cathay Pacific Airways carried just a third the number of passengers it did the same time the previous year. Passenger numbers for some airlines were reduced by as much as 80%. Cathay responded to fears that SARS spread through air travel by placing newspaper advertisements in which it pledged to do "everything in its power to safeguard the health" of passengers and staff (Pine and McKercher 2004). In mid-May Dragonair, United Airlines, and the Hong Kong Aircraft Engineering Company joined Cathay Pacific in asking employees to take unpaid leave. In so doing, the airlines tried to conserve cash while avoiding layoffs. In July Cathay Pacific resumed 70% of its scheduled services, and 90% by August. One month after the lifting of the WHO travel advisories, the region's airlines were surprised by the quick return of demand to pre-SARS levels (Pine and McKercher 2004).

Lessons Learned

In June the WHO declared Hong Kong and Beijing SARS free, and the government of Hong Kong announced a HK $1 billion package to rebuild Hong Kong's battered image so it could lure back tourists and business lost to SARS (Pine and McKercher 2004). The "Be my guest" campaign, supported by members of the Hong Kong Hotels Association, was announced right after the WHO declaration, and free airline tickets were awarded and hotels offered discounts of up to 50% on rooms, all to lure back tourists (Pine and McKercher 2004) . Business recovered with occupancies creeping back to 30% and 40% levels very quickly.

At the end of the SARS period, the world economy was still rather weak. The WTO World Tourism Barometer indicated that the effect of the Iraq conflict and the SARS outbreak was a major negative impact on the tourism industry for the first half of 2003; however, there were signs of a bounce back for the second half of the year. Various destinations managed to post good results including the most afflicted destinations in the Caribbean, South America, and South Asia. But trouble loomed. The start of the war in Iraq in March 2003 caused an immediate plunge in demand, particularly in air traffic, interregional travel, and travel to destinations perceived close to the conflict zone.

Very few destinations and sectors were immune from SARS. However, much has been gained from the experience. National tourism administrations, tourism boards, and tourism businesses are much better prepared and able to adapt quickly to changing conditions. Measures primarily focused on shifting or reducing capacity and rigorous cost control are better understood now. National tourism administrations, by backing the sector with rapid action plans in communication, promotion, and marketing, will be better able to respond in a timely and effective way should a similar crisis face the industry in the future.

Ministers from Asian nations affected by the outbreak of SARS have pledged to work together to overcome its impact on the region. They have agreed to work with the WHO to ensure that the disease, and other diseases, are kept under control. Controlling SARS requires continued vigorous surveillance and containment of new cases and intensive regional and global collaboration. China was strongly criticized for being slow to notify the WHO when the virus first emerged in its territory. One thing made very clear by this crisis is the fragile nature of the tourism business and, therefore, the need to have contingency plans for such unpredictable events (Pine and McKercher 2004)

DISCUSSION QUESTIONS

1. The hospitality and tourism industry is considered as the industry that is competing for consumers' discretionary income and time. Discuss the environmental factors that affect this industry in both positive and negative ways.
2. What lessons can we learn as an industry from these factors, and what can we do to tackle these threats and crises?
3. What would you recommend relative to establishing a scanning process to monitor the outbreak of infectious diseases?
4. Explain how you would go about establishing a causal link between the impact of a disease like SARS and the firm's ability to maintain cash flow.
5. What key value drivers would be important to identify to determine a causal link to the firm?
6. Based on the overview in this case, provide your own theory of how you would respond as a manager to this information.
7. Provide an understanding of how you would estimate the timing associated with this event.

REFERENCES

Asia Africa Intelligence Wire. 2003. "War May Cause Loss of Jobs in Tourism Industry." March 12.

Austin, M. C. 2004. "Hedging Helps Airlines Deflect Higher Jet Fuel Costs." *Purchasing* 133, no. 3: 13–14.

Baker, C., and D. Field. 2005. "Fare Rises Limit Fuel Pain." *Airline Business* 21, no. 9: 11.

Bangkok Post. 2004. "Travel Growth in Thailand Is Nipped by Rising Airfares." August 25.

Pine, R., and B. McKercher. 2004. "The Impact of SARS on Hong Kong's Tourism Industry." *International Journal of Contemporary Hospitality Management* 16, no. 2: 139–43.

Pratt, G. 2003. "Terrorism and Tourism: Bahamas and Jamaica Fight Back." *International Journal of Contemporary Hospitality Management* 15 no. 3:192–94.

Sangster, A. 2005. "Hospitality Faces Up to the Terrorist Bombers." *Caterer & Hotelkeeper.* December 1–7, 16.

Strauss, K., & J. Weinstein. 2003. "Surviving SARS." *Hotels.* July.

World Sources Online. (2004). "Global Recovery Underway But with Troubled Outlook." September 16.

Yunus, K. 2004. "Airline, Tourism to Be Hit If Rise in Oil Prices Persists." *Business Times.* May 17, 4.

Environmental Assessment

Scanning the Environment

From Chapter 6 of *Strategic Management in the Hospitality Industry*, Third Edition, Michael D. Olsen, Joseph J. West, Eliza Ching Yick Tse. Copyright © 2008 by Pearson Education, Inc. Published by Pearson Prentice Hall. All rights reserved.

Environmental Assessment
Scanning the Environment

Upon completing this chapter, you will:

1. Develop an improved understanding of the relationships between the remote and task environments.
2. Be capable of establishing the appropriate domain definition for the firm.
3. Achieve a greater understanding of the structure of the industry, including customers, competitors, suppliers, regulators, and potential competitors.

- Causal relationships between the remote and task environment
- Domain definition
- Industry structure
  - Customer
  - Competitor
  - Supplier
  - Regulator

Chapter Purpose

The forces in the remote environment ultimately begin to have a causal effect on firms through a framework often referred to as the *task environment*, which consists of the following subcategories: customers, competitors (which include substitute products and/or potential competitors), regulators, and suppliers. How each of the forces emerging out of the remote environment impact each of the subcategories of the task environment is subject to the theories formulated by the manager. These theories revolve around the causal relationships that exist between the remote and task environments.

In this chapter we seek to understand the nature of the causal relationships and accurately assess the impact they may have on the firm. In doing so, we suggest how important it is to estimate the timing of the impact and how the firm may actually be affected. What must be recognized here is that the impact will be different for each of the general categories of the task environment. In other words, some forces will impact suppliers more than competitors or regulators more than customers, and the timing of the impact may be different as well. As can be imagined, the challenges become more complex and will really test the manager's ability to formulate theories about the firm.

This theory testing will be even more challenging as the manager attempts to assess how these relationships will impact the cash flow streams of the firm. In other words, events occurring in the task environment will have a more direct relationship to the firm's overall cash flow stream and the flows of each competitive method. This connection is demonstrated in Exhibit 1 where again we draw your attention to the symbol representing the environment with special focus in this chapter on the task environment. It will be up to the manager to use probabilistic estimates regarding how each cell in the cash flow worksheets of the firm will be affected by these events. Although difficult, we trust the remaining sections of this chapter will assist in this effort.

The Domain

The first step to consider in assessing the task environment is defining the domain. The domain is the context in which the organization or firm competes. This would include such industry categories as budget airlines, luxury hotels, or casual theme restaurants, among others. Each industry sector is defined by the leading firms in that sector as well as the customers, suppliers, regulators, and competitors who conduct business daily in that domain.

Additionally, firms within a domain can be grouped according to their common characteristics. These characteristics include the critical success factors (CSFs) that are common to all firms and are necessary to compete effectively in that industry domain or sector. The assumption here is that firms who compete in the same domain will have to invest in CSFs if they expect to be able to attract the same customers that all firms within this strategic grouping are after. This also includes similarities among the competitive methods used by each firm in the strategic group. This analysis extends also to similarities relating to pricing practices, distribution, marketing and advertising, regulatory matters, and so on. In other words, the firms all function within a similar set of conditions that will affect their performance and growth.

EXHIBIT 1 Strategic Management Model

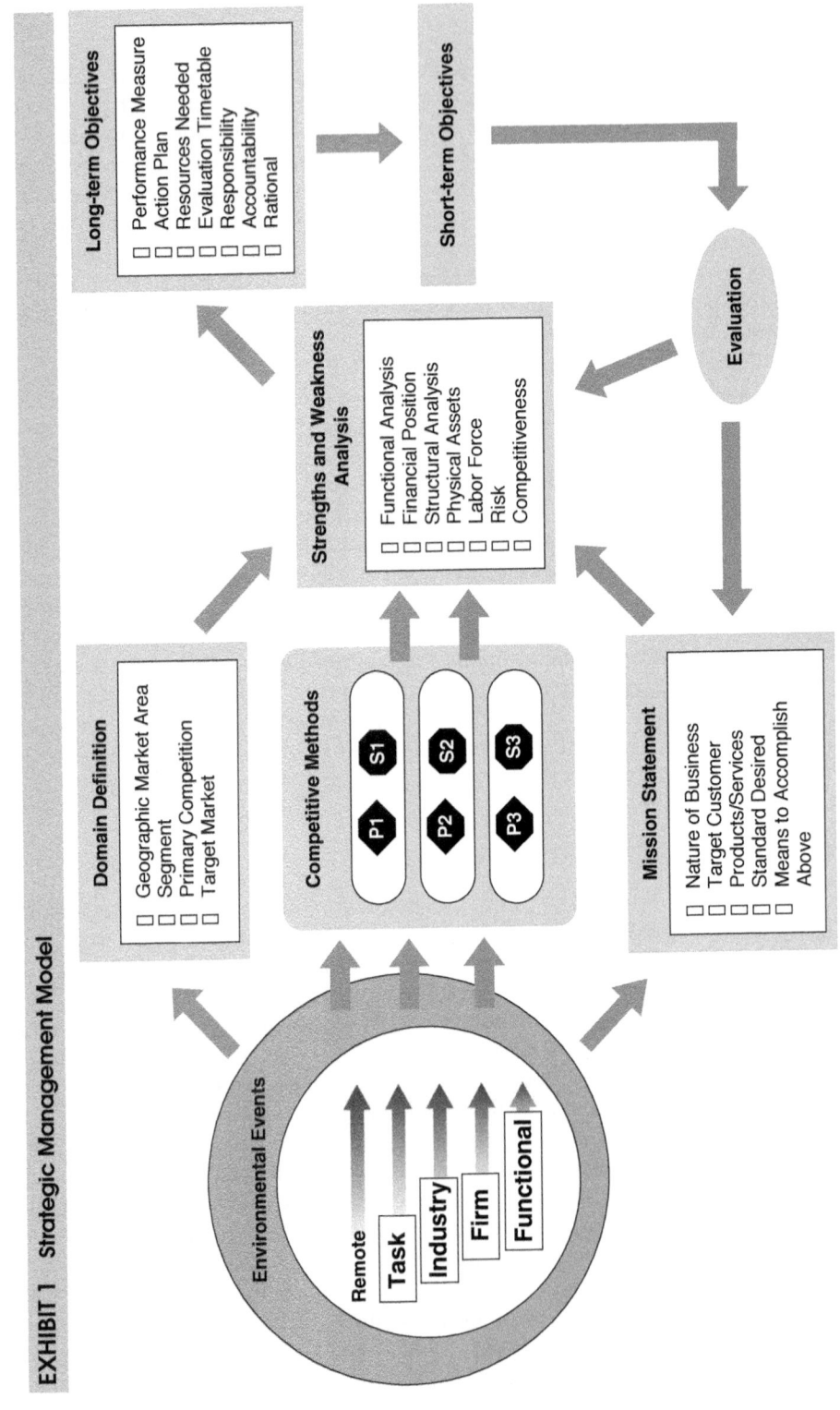

It is important to recognize that forces in the remote environment are likely to affect the elements of the task domain differently. For example, in the airline industry many events in the remote environment have had a significant impact on the future of the industry. Oil price volatility, terrorism, and infectious diseases have impacted travel, and the cost of fuel is a major value driver for all airlines. In terms of market demand, all airlines were hit with the same declining demand problem after September 11, 2001. This impact was immediate. However, regulators did not respond to the terrorism problem for many months, and then it was over a year before the airlines began to experience new regulatory requirements regarding security. In another example of causality, many of the low-cost airlines engaged in fuel hedging practices that allowed some to buffer their fuel costs in 2004 after significant price increases in oil while others felt the burden of these increases that they could only pass on to the customer or absorb themselves. Those with the hedging contracts clearly had a competitive advantage over those that did not.

These examples point out how different players in an industry sector can be impacted in different ways and with different timing to the same forces emerging from the remote environment. Yet understanding the impact of these causal relationships is important in determining the strategic direction for the firm.

Note that the domain definition is often one with gray boundaries. It would be nice to be able to have a degree of precision in this case, but it is generally not possible in free market settings. Thus the boundaries can change, and it is the task of those performing the environmental scanning process to assess changes and factor them into strategic decisions. Continuing with the airline example, many of the legacy airlines did not include the low-cost carriers in their domain. As the low-cost carriers began to make strong inroads, it is now generally agreed that it was a mistake not to expand the domain boundaries these legacy carriers were using because low-cost carriers are now redefining the structure of the entire airline industry.

The Customer/The Demand Curve as a Domain Parameter

In defining the domain, the manager must begin with the customer analysis. The first question the manager must ask is "Who is my customer?" The second question is "Do the broad forces driving change in the remote environment affect my customer?" The manager will want to understand the causal relationships between the remote and task environments to formulate theories to guide decision making regarding in which competitive methods to invest to meet the customer's wants and needs most effectively as shaped by forces in the remote environment. Most importantly, these theories will have to begin with understanding how the total demand for these competitive methods will change as a result of these causal relationships.

The first step in assessing these relationships is to know what constitutes the demand curve for the firm. We define the *demand curve* as the sum total of all the customers who will purchase the products and services offered by the firm. This definition has two dimensions. The first is the current demand, and the second is the future demand. In this case, the future demand will represent those who will purchase both the current and new products and services the firm offers. Both dimensions are measured by numbers of customers.

The challenge of determining the number of customers requires accurate estimates of the total numbers in the target customer group. For example, in the luxury or very high end segment of the lodging industry, the question is "How many travelers are there who will be willing to pay the high daily rates required by hotels in this sector?" There are many variables that can be used to estimate this number. They include such items as average income and occupation type. Demographic variables such as country of origin, age, and educational accomplishment also can help. Is the individual paying personally or will these expenses by paid by an employer or client? Is there an imbalance between supply and demand resulting in too many luxury hotel rooms or too few?

There is no exact science that will provide the definitive answer as to the numbers of possible customers, leaving the manager the task of gathering as much information as possible to assist in this effort. One of the first steps is to determine where the customer comes from and the geographic distance traveled. In some cases this is relatively simple for a local independent restaurant because its clientele may only come from the immediate area encompassing a 20-mile radius around the restaurant. It becomes more difficult if the firm is a hotel in the Caribbean and mode of travel is the airplane. In this case, it is possible that potential customers can then come from anywhere in the world.

Knowing how the customer gets to the establishment is also essential here. Mode of travel can greatly influence total demand. Continuing with the Caribbean example, if all the available airline capacity for a particular island is 4,000 seats per day, that is likely to be the daily influx of customers, assuming the planes are full. However, some customers may also arrive by ship. Interestingly, after the terrorist attacks of September 11, 2001, hospitality firms operating in the Caribbean became painfully aware that 95% of travelers to their destination arrive by air, and they faced significant demand challenges due to the decline in air travel resulting from people's fear of flying. The key in this and all other situations is to know exactly what determines or constrains demand because it makes no sense to invest in more supply if there is no way to increase demand.

Another way to look at this demand challenge is to consider the number of restaurants in the United States today compared to the number of inhabitants in the country. Assuming by 2008 there will be approximately 900,000 restaurants and an estimated 300 million people, this translates into 1 restaurant for every 333 citizens. This poses a serious question: With a ratio of restaurants per capita so low, can the industry continue to expand when the total demand is likely to be so low per restaurant? In contrast, the National Restaurant Association reports on its website that 46.4% of the U. S. food dollar in 2003 was spent in restaurants. If this trend continues to grow, the population per restaurant may not be as significant as the percentage of the food dollar spent in restaurants. The question to be answered is "Are we approaching a time when there are too many restaurants or not?"

Exhibit 2 illustrates how the analysis of the demand curve may be approached in terms of identifying key target market descriptors or variables (value drivers) used to estimate demand. This example, based on an analysis of company documents, is for the gaming industry, and the firm in this case is Harrah's Casinos, one of the leading gaming firms in the United States. Descriptors represent criteria used to help understand all the characteristics of the demand curve. These descriptors can include such labels as demographic age groupings, income levels, psychographic profiles, or reasons for travel, such as business, leisure, or groups. What is important here is that each descriptor reflects accurately the nature of the demand and helps pinpoint with greater accuracy the total potential customers in the demand curve.

EXHIBIT 2 Example of Target Market Descriptors for Harrah's Casinos

Primary criteria used to describe target market[1]	Describe in detail the specifics for each criterion at left
Preference for gaming and travel	Since the late 1980s, gambling has grown considerably in the U.S., a large portion of it occurring while Americans are traveling. Seven percent of all U.S. domestic person-trips included gambling as trip activity in 1999, accounting for 72.8 million person-trips in total. Since 1994, the number of gambling trips by Americans has increased 20 percent. According to the Harrah's Survey 2002, it is evident that support of casino gambling among U.S. households is growing. Casino gambling industry attracted more than 52.3 million people (27% of adult population) making a total of 303 million visits to casinos in 2001, on par with visits to amusement and theme parks. Gambling is expected to gain in popularity this decade as casino properties expand and enhance their facilities and new casinos are opened.
Travel Purpose	According to the Travel Industry Association of America's Profile of Travelers Who Participate in Gambling, 2000 Edition, like most travelers in the U.S., a majority of gambling is for leisure purposes (83%). Thirteen percent of gambling travelers cite business as the main purpose of trip. Gambling travelers are also more likely than U.S. travelers overall to travel by air (24% vs. 18%), include a stay at a hotel, motel, or bed and breakfast establishment (76% vs. 52%), and have higher trip spending levels.
Age	Americans ages between 51 to 65 with more discretionary time and income than others are more likely to have gambled at a casino in the last 12 months (year 2001) than seniors and those in younger age groups. Compared to the whole U.S. population, the median household income for casino gamblers is 20% higher than the national average—U.S. population ($41.343), U.S. casino gamblers ($49,753).
Income	It is likely that Americans with higher incomes visit casinos than those with low-income levels. Thirty-five percent of Americans with annual household income levels above $95,000 gamble in casinos, while only 22% of adults in homes earning less than $35,000 are casino players.
Occupation/Education	According to the Harrah's Survey 2002, casino players are more likely to hold white-collar jobs. Also, casino gamblers are slightly better educated.
Gender	More women are involved in gambling now than ever before. Especially, women more than men like to try their luck at slot machines and other electronic games (80% vs. 66%) according to the Harrah's Survey 2002.

Prepared by: Yeasun Chung, Kyungmin Lee, Hayung Lee, and Marion Mangin, 2003, Virginia Tech.
[1] Criteria can include demographic or psychographic information or categories such as leisure or business traveler.

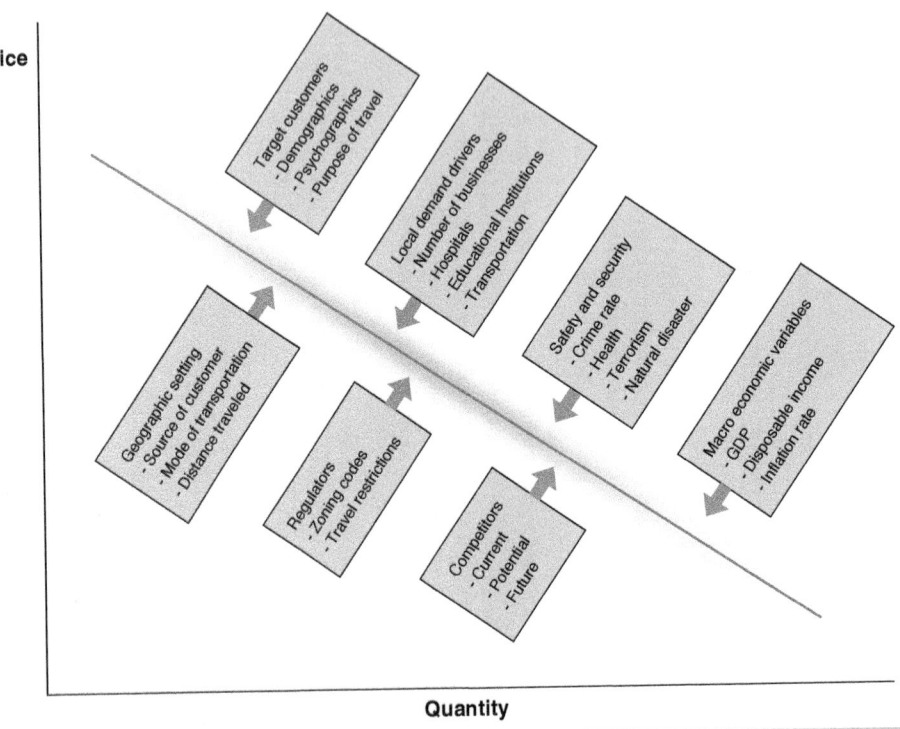

EXHIBIT 3 Variables Influencing the Demand Curve

As the discussion on demand thus far suggests, the demand curve is a complex construct that consists of many probable variables (value drivers) that managers must consider when trying to estimate the future number of customers accurately. Exhibit 3 presents a conceptual map of the probable variables that must be considered when seeking to prepare a forecast of the future cash flows of the firm. The graphic implies that there are a great many forces that can impact the overall demand of the firm, and it suggests that managers must work hard at trying to estimate what these are and their impact on overall demand as well as the demand for individual competitive methods.

The Relationships Between the Customer and Forces in the Remote Environment

Upon completing the analysis of the demand potential for the firm, the next step is to try to understand the cause-and-effect relationships between the remote and task environment in terms of the customer. In other words, it is essential to try to determine how the customer is affected by forces in the remote environment. For example, the growing use of personal digital devices further connects the customer to the e-commerce world, making it easier and quicker to make purchases with greater transparency in terms of pricing. Also, the growing consumer concern over safety and health in the context of travel is another causal relationship that will have impact on the travel industry. Managers are expected to work toward improving their understanding of these relationships to make investments in competitive methods that will add value to the firm over the long term while meeting customer needs now and in the future. Some examples may help to illustrate this.

As we have acknowledged elsewhere in the text, technology has been an important force affecting the lives of everyone. In particular, the Internet has become a significant factor in the buying and selling of goods both for business-to-business activity and business-to-consumer activity. In terms of the hospitality industry, this force can be seen playing out in the increase in the number of Internet or e-commerce purchase transactions regarding travel initiated by the customer. This growing acceptance of online travel arrangements by the customer has had negative impacts on travel agents and providers of hospitality products and services. This shift in how travel is searched and purchased began with the widespread use of the Internet coupled with the consumer's familiarity with using computers and their desire for convenience and control over the purchase transaction.

As this example serves to point out, the evolution of technology, and particularly the Internet, brought about new freedoms for the consumer in terms of how they obtain information about their travel needs and how they are booked and purchased. This causal relationship between a force in the remote environment and the customer has been well documented and will continue to affect all aspects of the hospitality industry for some time to come. The question for the manager now is "Where is this causal relationship headed, and how will it impact the firm?"

Similarly, as this second example points out, the global and/or national problems brought about by outbreaks of mad cow disease, Asian bird flu, or severe acute respiratory syndrome (SARS) have made the customer more aware of health and safety concerns when they travel. The direct impact of this was the decline in customer demand for travel in those parts of the world most directly affected by these events. Additionally, terrorist bombings in Bali, Indonesia, Kenya, Egypt, Jakarta, and other trouble spots from 2000 to the present have been cause for the consumer to stay away. The devastating destruction of the World Trade Center on September 11, 2001, frightened many away from air travel permanently and exacerbated the global recession. The manager is expected to be able to draw the necessary linkages between and among events such as these in the remote environment and their impact on the customer. It is only when these are accurately and intently considered that management can make effective investments in meeting the future needs of the customer. In this case, those investments would be enhanced safety and security measures that would help alleviate guests' fears regarding these matters.

It should be recognized that much of the information about the customer is gathered and maintained by those with sales and marketing responsibilities within the firm. Additionally, market research about the customer can be purchased from the thousands of market research firms existing across the globe. What is important to remember here is that the manager must know what questions to ask or what objectives are to be obtained. These questions come from the theories that managers build from their observations of the environment around them. So once again we stress the importance of proper theory building with respect to the causal relationships between the customer and the remote environment and how this will impact the firm.

When all the analysis of the demand curve is completed relative to who the customers are and what they want, the manager must still reach a point estimate of the number of customers to be expected. This is not something that will be precise; it more likely will be a probable range. Regardless of the difficulty in performing this estimate, it must be made because it will be required for purposes of estimating the changes in revenue resulting from investments in competitive methods. This estimate will be required when cash flow worksheets are prepared in analyzing the investment so great care and responsibility must be taken by those faced with this task.

The Competitor-Industry Analysis

The domain definition continues with the analysis of *the competitor(s)*, which can be thought of as the major firms that are leading the industry within the domain of analysis. In the case of national or international chains, the leading companies become the competitive set,[1] In contrast, in the immediate radius of a local restaurant, the leading restaurants within that radius become the competitive set. In this case there is often little confusion about who these firms are. A firm's competitive set, or strategic group, sets the competitive pace and must be monitored in any task environment analysis. In the following subsections we explore what is important to the scanning effort here. We begin the description of monitoring activities in the strategic group by using the concept of the CSFs.

Critical Success Factors

The leading firms also shape the boundaries of the industry sector. One way of doing so is by their performance on industry CSFs, those bundles of products and services that are absolutely necessary for a firm to invest in if it expects to compete in the sector. Exhibits 4 and 5[2] include examples of CSFs in the lodging and restaurant industry sectors. From a careful examination of these lists it should become clear that any firm seeking to enter these sectors must perform at industrywide benchmark levels in a majority of the CSFs if not all of them. In fact, one of the strategic decisions management must make is at what level the firm will seek to compete on each of the CSFs.

Lodging Industry Critical Success Factors

Critical success factors represent the common competitive methods that have become accepted within an industry sector and all firms must invest in if they are to compete successfully in that sector. For example, at one point in time, a reservation system was essential to the success of a lodging firm that wanted to compete nationally. That system has gradually evolved into both telephonic systems and electronic ones. Similarly, loyalty programs have become essential as ways to ensure repeat business. In scanning the task environment, managers must develop an understanding of what the industry CSFs are and perform a careful analysis in comparing their firm against the industry in this crucial element of performance. Exhibit 6 provides an example of one way of performing this task. As can be seen, the CSFs are listed in the first column and key competitors head each column thereafter. The objective for the manager is to be sure that each cell is completed and reflects which of these firms is performing the best on each

---

Critical success factors of the multinational lodging industry

1985–1994

Customer Products and Services
- Frequent guest programs
- Special service for frequent guests
- Amenities
- In-room sales and entertainment
- Business services

Technology Development
- Technology innovation
- Database management
- Computer reservation systems

Marketing Efforts
- Branding
- Niche marketing and advertising
- Pricing tactics
- Direct to consumer marketing

Market Expansion
- International Expansion
- Strategic alliances
- Franchising and management fee

Operation Management
- Cost containment
- Core business management
- Service quality management
- Travel agency valuation
- Employee as assets
- Conservation/ecology programs

1995–1999

- Rapid information technology development
- International expansion and market cooperation
- Relationship management
- Customer-oriented products and services development
- Structure reengineering
- New marketing initiatives and campaigns
- Quality Control
- Social awareness and environmental protection

EXHIBIT 4 Lodging Industry Critical Success Factors

CSF. Upon completion of this analysis, the manager will have to make strategic decisions on what resources are to be deployed to what CSF to ensure the desired competitive position on each.

Each industrywide CSF becomes a focus of the manager's scanning activity. Someone in the organization must be assigned the duty of following activities and developments for each CSF. It becomes important that this activity concentrate on those firms that are leaders with respect to each CSF, so any investments or moves made by competitors can be assessed in terms of the strategic decision to follow, lead, or stay close. It goes without saying that some firms seek to become the leader in a majority of CSFs, believing that if they lead the industry, customers will follow.

In understanding each CSF, managers must attempt to determine how and what resources are allocated by competitors to each. In performing this scanning analysis, managers must rely on industry-related news articles, discussions with suppliers, private discussions, industry trade shows and conferences, and research conducted by scholars and consultancies. Only after a thorough gathering of this information can a

EXHIBIT 5 Critical Success Factors in the Restaurant Industry

1985–94

Expansion Overseas By Multinational Foodservice Chains
- Franchise/master franchise: A franchiser grants a licensed privilege to a franchisee to use its brand name, standard production, operation, and management systems to do business. A master franchise is a licensed franchisee that has the right to do business in the whole country or an entire region. It is a popular method in the quick service industry sector.
- Management contract: A management team signs a contract with the owner of the facility and provides its expertise for a management fee. It is a commonly used vehicle in institutional, leisure and sport food management outlets.
- Strategic alliance/Joint venture/Partnership: The terms are often used interchangeably. Related or non-related businesses may form a business partnership. Such an agreement can require either financial or non-financial involvement. Co-branding- another form of partnership, which links foodservice companies with related or non-related brand names to form a joint customer service effort.
- Merger and Acquisition: Merge and acquire related or non-related businesses to capture market share or reach financial objective.

Utilization of Technology as Competitive Methods
- Internet communication with target market: Through www, communicate with customers about the product, services, job offers, etc.
- Management Information system: Installation of management information systems to integrate operation and management functions.
- Production and service oriented technology: Utilization of newly designed production equipment and service software to improve the quality of production and service.

Improving Internal Competency
- Quality management: Procedure and measurement to manage product and service quality
- Employee training and retention: Enhancing employees' production and service skills through training programs and retaining employees through various incentive programs.
- Organizational restructuring: Through organizational restructuring a company seeks to maintain effectiveness and efficiency.

Product/service Development
- Modifying the menu to adapt to local needs: Add local appealing products and ingredients, and eliminate products that do not fit the needs and demands of local patron.
- New product/concept/theme development: Develop new food products, concepts or themes to tailor the needs and demands of the customers.
- Safety and cleanliness: Stress the importance of safety and sanitation in food preparation and services. Establish procedures and measurement for food sanitation and safety training and practice.
- Chain and brand name domination: Maintain the chain and brand name image, capture market share and dominate the marketplace.
- Facility renovation: Renovate facility to create an appealing eating environment.

Target Marketing
- Heavy advertisement: Invest millions of dollars on TV commercials and other media.
- Internet advertising and promotion: Advertise menu items and service through www and promote a chain and brand images.
- Database marketing

EXHIBIT 5   *continued*

- Sponsorship, community service and charity—public relations efforts
- Environmental awareness: Initiate plans or programs to involve in environmental protection activities, such as, waste reduction, energy efficiency program or use of recycled product.

Pricing
- Price/value relationship: Through price discounting, provide value products.
- Discounting war: Compete to offer discounted price among rivals to attract customers.
- Coupon: Offer coupons to interested customers to increase sales

manager attempt to estimate the future direction of each CSF in the context of the task environment and competitive action within the strategic group.

Generally, the firm that initiates a new competitive method that leads the industry will find that key competitors will soon follow; translating what was an industry-leading competitive method (CM) into one that is now a CSF. This is often the case in the service industry where innovations, often involving easy-to-copy service dimensions, can be effortlessly replicated by all firms in relatively short periods of time.

In studying the competitor it becomes essential that this analysis include a detailed look at the financial strength of the competition. Knowing the financial resources of each competitor helps the manager to estimate whether or not any or all competitors can maintain their current position with respect to each CSF. In other words, not all firms have the financial resources to maintain their status on each CSF 100% of the time. Knowing their financial strength, who is leading, and whether or not the lead can be maintained will help managers decide what CSFs they should invest in.

Industry Value Drivers

Value drivers were defined in the previous chapter as they pertained mostly to the remote environment. Value drivers are also present in the task environment as they relate to a specific industry sector or strategic group. Thus we consider them under this heading of competition or strategic group because we know they are likely to affect all firms the same way within the sector.

From the firm's perspective, the key value driver with respect to revenues is the demand curve. This was discussed earlier in this chapter when the customer category of the task environment was presented. Put another way, the primary driver of revenue is the number of customers multiplied by what they spend. We call this *revenue per available customer*. This value driver affects the cash flow streams of the firm from what is often referred to as the *top-of-the-line* perspective.[3] Revenues result from the competitive methods the firm invests in based on the opportunities it sees in the environment. Because the customer's purchasing patterns are affected so much by events in the remote environment, management must work hard to develop the proper causal understanding between this and firm revenue over time.

The next set of value drivers is often associated with the cost structure of the firm, or *below-the-line* items. When looking at the service industries in general and the hospitality industry in particular, labor stands out as one of the most significant costs affecting cash flows. There is a strong link between the national labor cost indices and

EXHIBIT 6 Industry Strategic Group Comparison on Lodging Industry Critical Success Factors*

CSF	Marriott	Hilton	NH Hoteles	Four Seasons	Choice Hotels International
Loyalty Program	Industry leader	Improving	Trouble putting a good one together	Does not feel the need for one	Ok
Location	Feels it is the leader	No where near the market presence	Growing but a long way to go	Leading the luxury segment	Strong market presence
Reservation system	Once a leader now keeping pace only	Investing heavily to become the leader	Seeking to gain strength	Ok	Ok but not a market leader
Revenue Management System					
Technology utilization					
In room amenities					
Brand strength					
Market presence					
Brand portfolio					
Operating management system					

*Completed cells are examples only and do not represent actual conditions.

those of the firm. These causal linkages become part of what the manager must monitor and anticipate in order to plan properly.

Cost of goods sold, such as food, often represent the second most important internal value driver. Here the challenge is monitoring all the key ingredient costs associated with producing the products of the hospitality enterprise. It becomes very important here to know what the competitors are doing to ensure low cost with each of the key raw material products that are purchased. Long-term purchasing contracts, fuel hedging programs, and quality control from *farm to fork*[4] are some examples of how hospitality and tourism enterprises achieve competitive advantage within a strategic group. Exhibit 7 refers to a recent study in which key value drivers affecting the casual theme restaurant industry were investigated.[5] The results indicate that four key economic variables are able to explain the variance in an index of operating cash flows pertaining to eleven of the leading publicly traded restaurant companies over the period of 1994 to 2003. In fact, as the graphic shows, 67% of the variance in the index of cash flows is explained by these four key drivers.

What is significant to note in these results is that seafood became the value driver with the highest level of influence pertaining to the variance in operational cash flows. The other variables are more external and reflect the overall condition of the economic environment of the United States over the period under study. What is demonstrated in the study is that over 105 value drivers were analyzed and assessed in terms of their impact on the firm. This assessment included cross correlations, causality (timing), and regression analysis, pointing out that key tools of analysis can be applied

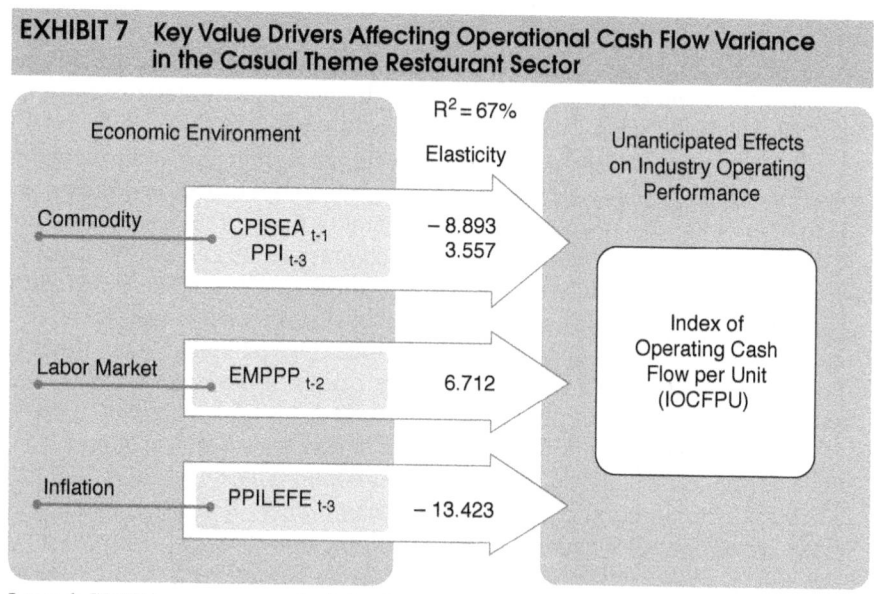

EXHIBIT 7 Key Value Drivers Affecting Operational Cash Flow Variance in the Casual Theme Restaurant Sector

Legend: CPISEA = consumer price index for seafood (CPISEA), PPI = producer price index for all commodities, EMPPP = employment population ratio, PPILEFE = producer price index less food and energy, $t-1$ = the observation in the preceding time

Source: Chung, Yeasun (2005). *Identification of Economic Value Drivers Impacting on Operational Cash Flows in the Casual Theme Restaurant Industry.* Unpublished Master's thesis, Virginia Polytechnic Institute and State University. Blacksbura. Virainia.

to any number of elements in the task environment. The study also points out empirically the causal nature of value drivers with firm performance, an argument we have been making throughout this text.

Other costs, such as insurance for liabilities, terrorism, or natural disaster, are important value drivers. Energy costs represent another of the more significant drivers that managers must incorporate into their scanning systems and then spend time assessing the causal relationships that exist between their movement and the cash flow streams of the firm. Knowing how their competitors are addressing these value drivers is another extremely important scanning activity.

Competitors and the Demand Curve

Competitors help carve up the demand curve of the firm. As indicated earlier in this chapter, managers must be able to estimate the overall demand curve properly for the industry as well as their firm. Too few competitors generally mean that the firm can continue to grow in revenues because not all of the demand is being met with the current level of supply. Too many competitors and the demand curve becomes too fragmented.

Understanding present and future competitors provides managers with a better understanding of what percentage of the total market share they are able to capture. A simplified example may help illustrate this point. Let's assume that over a one-year period, the total number of visitors to a destination is 100,000 and each visitor will stay in a hotel for approximately six nights. The overall demand curve is then 600,000 room nights. Let's also assume there are 50 hotels with an average of 50 rooms, each which results in a total supply of 912,500 room nights available (50 rooms · 50 hotels · 365 nights). This suggests that the average occupancy for each hotel is 65%. If the manager determines that the hotel's overall occupancy is below 65%, the hotel is not reaching its potential demand. If it exceeded 65%, the manager can take some comfort in the fact that the hotel is achieving more than its fair share.

It is important to recognize in the preceding example the total demand for the destination and how that is distributed among all competitors. In this case we are most concerned with what percentage of the total demand a firm is able to capture. This allows the manager to determine what is necessary to gain additional market share and what value that additional share will create for the business. This information is useful when considering expansion into new markets as well as investment of additional resources in an existing market. Keep in mind, as we have said many times before, that the environment is far more complex than this example suggests. However, demand, whether present or future, must be understood if businesses are to succeed.

Another example may help. Let's assume you are a hotel developer and are thinking about building an all-suites hotel in a particular city. One of the first questions you would ask is what the total demand for a suite hotel in that city is and how many suite hotels are already in the marketplace. Based on your prior experience, you understand that in any given metropolis that meets certain characteristics of business or leisure travel, the municipality can support an all-suite room supply of 12% of the total rooms inventory in that city. When you conducted the feasibility study you discovered that the city already had 12% of its inventory in suites. The question about whether to make the investment or not, based on this simple assessment, would suggest there is no room for another all-suite hotel. Although this seems straightforward enough, we have already indicated that such decisions are very complex and involve a number of value drivers and critical success factors as well as the personal reasons often guiding this process.

Competitive Methods

Competitive methods have been defined as a unique bundling of goods and services by the firm that cannot be easily duplicated. They differ from CSFs in that they are unique to the firm in a strategic group. They have either not been copied already or they cannot be copied. A competitive method brings the firm competitive advantage and significant value. The manager must know everything there is about each competitor firm's CM and must be able to estimate the value contribution made by each. At the risk of sounding repetitious, this is not a simple task. It requires a lot of good investigative work by the manager and also reasonably good estimation capabilities.

Identifying the competitor's CMs can be fairly straightforward. Customers may talk about them, and managers can observe or experience them for themselves. The firm's own marketing and advertising program may present an analysis of the competitor's key CMs. Financial reports may reveal it. Suppliers or their salespeople may discuss it. Once identified it requires more careful examination in terms of the products and services that make it up. Here is where things may become more difficult because the exact bundling of products and services may be challenging to determine, and it may not be clear exactly what competencies and resources the firm utilizes in delivering the CM. Exhibit 8 is a hypothetical example of one such analysis of Marriott International Corporation, along with Exhibit 9, also a hypothetical comparison, of the competitive methods of Four Seasons Hotel and Resorts against its primary competitors.

For the manager, the hardest part of this scanning effort is to determine the exact value contribution that is made by the competitive method for each competitor. For example, questions such as "What proportion of the demand for the firm results from that CM, what is the life cycle of the CM, and what stage is it in?" Some of the answers to these questions result from knowing industrywide value drivers and CSFs. Again, the manager is asked to develop theory here and draw conclusions from difficult to obtain and/or too little usable information.

Efforts at understanding the cost structure of a competitive method may prove useful in understanding the value contribution of each CM for each competitor. Industrywide value drivers are similar for all firms in a strategic group so managers should have some idea of what these are and thus develop a better look at what the below-the-line numbers may be for all competitors. It may be assumed in some cases that the competitor may have achieved some cost advantages through volume purchases or other agreements with suppliers, and these must also be determined by managers if they are to make accurate estimates of the value of each competitor's CM.

Resources and Capabilities

Also essential in the competitive analysis is the investigation of the key resources and capabilities of each competitor. This must begin with an understanding the competitor's financial position. Depending on the domain, the strategic group may be publicly traded companies, in which case standard financial performance data are available through many sources. In other cases, such as when competitors are privately or closely

EXHIBIT 8 Example Competitive Analysis of Marriott International Corporation*

Competitive methods	Length of time employed	Competitive advantage	Estimate of value added	Key innovations in the last five years	Expected future actions to enhance method	Vulnerabilities to exploit
Loyalty Program: Marriott Reward	Launched in 1983 as Honored Guest Awards and then in May 1997 transformed in Marriott Reward	• First Player • Largest program in the hotel industry	NA	• Allow point redemption for merchandise • Elite levels of membership • Visa USA Inc. and Marriott International Inc. have announced that they will offer double points for Visa cardholders and Marriott Rewards members • Points Awarded through all Marriott's brand	More Partnership with similar companies (Airlines, Rental Car, etc.)	All actions to reinvigorate the Loyalty Program are easily copied by competitors and all actions erodes revenues
Procurement Services for the Hospitality Industry: Avendra LLC	In January 2001 Marriott and Hyatt Corp. formed a joint venture, to be an independent professional procurement services the hospitality market. Six Continents, ClubCorp USA, Inc., Fairmont Hotels & Resorts joined Avendra in later stages	Avendra creates purchasing programs that offer its customers the right product and service at highly competitive prices	NA	• B2B technology platform • Internet-enabled purchasing system streamlines processes and easily integrates with other enterprise systems	Encourage all Marriott hotels and franchisees to use the procurement company	Not all Marriott Hotels are using the services offered by Avendra.

Marriott Revenue Management System for Revenue enhancement	1999	Developed RMS that isolates the different market segment and provides a comprehensive understanding of those segments' reservation behavior, price sensitivity and stay patterns	NA	• Current system evolved from earlier Yield Management System • Fully integrated with the reservation system • It provides overbooking recommendations for each property	A fully integrated system that cover all property needs and communicate extensively with headquarter and other hotels.	Still a lot of Revenue progress is needed for the competitors to match Marriott level. Marriott should then keep this advantage.
Intranet Information Sharing	1999 by Courtyard	• Assists users in expediting routine task • Provide timely and accurate information to solve hotel problems	NA	• 20 regional technology leaders trained Courtyard managers on the Intranet system • Intranet information resource that organizes information into single, easy to use property resource technology to replace manuals and other printed information • 2 Desktops at every hotel	Extend Intranet Info Sharing though all the other brands	Knowledge is power; even low paid staff should have the opportunity to access the Intranet.

*Information in cells is meant to be examples only and not representative of actual facts.

EXHIBIT 9 Competitive Methods Analysis of the Four Seasons Corporation against its Competitive Set

Four Seasons' competitive methods	Primary competitive methods offered in the segment by leading competitors				
	Ritz-Carlton	Fairmont	Mandarin	Peninsula	Shangri-La
Technology utilization (Good achievements: wireless . . .)	Good achievements (wireless, management systems)	Good achievements (wireless, EMS)	(Leader): IT plan, ERP, KM, HMS	(Leader): own R&D department, in-room innovation	Great achievements (Yield, PMS, . . .)
Sustainable policy (no special actions)	No special actions	Leader (various commitments, awards, systems)	Good involvement (partnerships, member IHI)	Good involvement (partnerships, member WWF)	Good achievements (ISO 14001)
Security commitment	Good achievements (online security, departments)	Not involved (only security guards)	Food focused (HACCP standards)	Not involved	Leader (systems, department, online policies)
Location (Leader)	Close to leader (various great locations)	Strongest in NA, weak around the world	Great locations (city, resorts)	Great locations	Great location
Loyalty Program/CRM (Weak: just alliances)	Leader (Marriott rewards)	Great program (President's Club)	Weak: just airlines alliances	Weak: just airlines alliances	Great program (Golden circle)
Culture (Leader)	Great Culture (gold standards)	Good culture	Strong culture	Good culture	Good culture
Business services (good services)	Leader	Good services	Specialized services	Leader (state of the art)	Great services (online meeting planner)

	(Leader): RC spas	(Leader): Willow stream	Great services	Great services	Great services
Spas (Leader)					
Service quality "Golden Rule"/Awards (Leader) Premium in ADR/OR/RevPAR (Leader)	Close to Leader (numerous awards) Follower (++)	Good achievements Follower(+)	Great achievements (standards) Follower (+)	Good achievements Follower	Good achievements Follower
Social commitment Great achievements	Leader (in best employee list)	Great achievements (part best Canada's employers)	Good achievements	Good achievements	Good achievements
Management contract (Leader:55 years)	Basic performance	Great achievements (40 years, Legacy help)	Good achievement (limited equity participation, Minor	Basic performance	Basic performance
Diversification (Residences) Leader	Leader "The residences", Marriott expetrise	Minor (golf, spas)		Small investment in residences (2)	Minor (country club)
Training (Good achievements)	Leader (leadership management center . . .)	Average achievements	Average achievements	Good achievements (training programs)	Good achievements

185

held firms, it is not easy to obtain. What every manager must be interested in is whether or not the competition has the financial resources to maintain its competitive position on industry CSFs or the funds to invest in new competitive methods. This knowledge is essential in that it helps managers determine how best to allocate the resources of their firm relative to the competitors.

The financial analysis should be cross sectional among firms in the strategic group as well as longitudinal so that key trends with respect to the performance of each competitor can be determined. Cross-sectional analysis focuses on the comparison of all competitors on key performance indicators. Some of the key indicators include return on invested capital, free cash flow from operations, revenues, operational profits, market capitalization, share price, and weighted average cost of capital. There are others that are more related to the industry, such as revenue per available customer, occupancy rate, revenue per available room or seat, customer satisfaction indices, and so on. The purpose of the cross-sectional analysis is to get a glimpse of who is leading the industry on these key indicators.

More beneficial is the examination of these key indicators over time, or a longitudinal analysis. This gives managers a better look at the trends regarding these indicators not only for key competitors but also for the industry strategic group. Careful analysis of these trends helps provide insight into how competitors are going to handle future needs with respect to financial resources and are they capable of implementing key strategic investments when necessary. Exhibit 10 is one example of this type of analysis using return on invested capital of three multinational hotel companies. In the second graph in this exhibit the same performance metric for four gaming companies is displayed only using a graphical form of display.

Exhibit 11 is a competitive analysis worksheet. This is designed to capture the key financial indicators relative to each competitor to be used by the manager to analyze the financial position of the competitors in the strategic group. In addition to the financial information, the worksheet also asks for information on the business model of the firm. The business model includes the key features employed by the competitor to achieve competitive advantage. For example, in the airline industry, low-cost carriers have several common features in their business models, which include use of secondary airports where takeoff, landing, and gate charges are lower than primary airports, the use of a single type of aircraft, direct city-to-city route structure as opposed to a hub and spoke system, lowest fare pricing, Web-based booking, and so on. Similarly, a company like Outback Steak Houses employs the following characteristics of their business model: open only for dinner, using secondary real estate locations, strict financial rules when investing in new locations, and limiting number of guests per server.

The examples used as part of the business model in the preceding paragraph may seem like key competitive methods of these firms. Indeed, there is no fine line between competitive methods and business model when used in this context. These concepts are often used interchangeably. What is important for the manager in this case is to try to understand how all these characteristics or CMs fit together for a particular firm in order to establish their business model and ensure sustainable competitive advantage. It is also essential for the manager to understand which CMs are the most important in terms of driving value for that competitor. Therefore, the worksheet asks for an analysis of the value created by each competitive method along with the length it has been

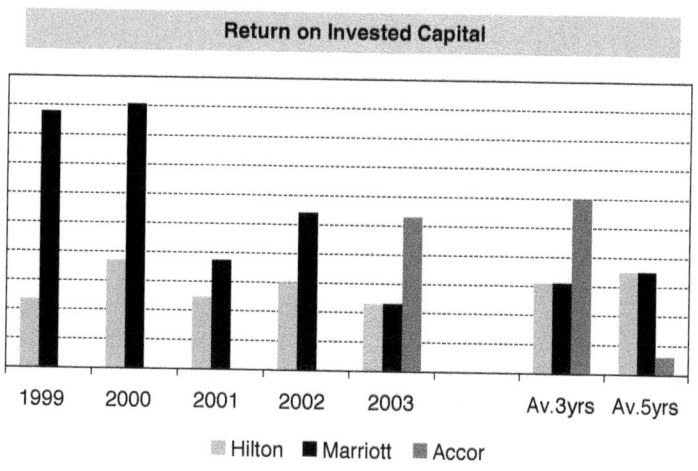

Return on Invested Capital

Hilton ■ Marriott ■ Accor

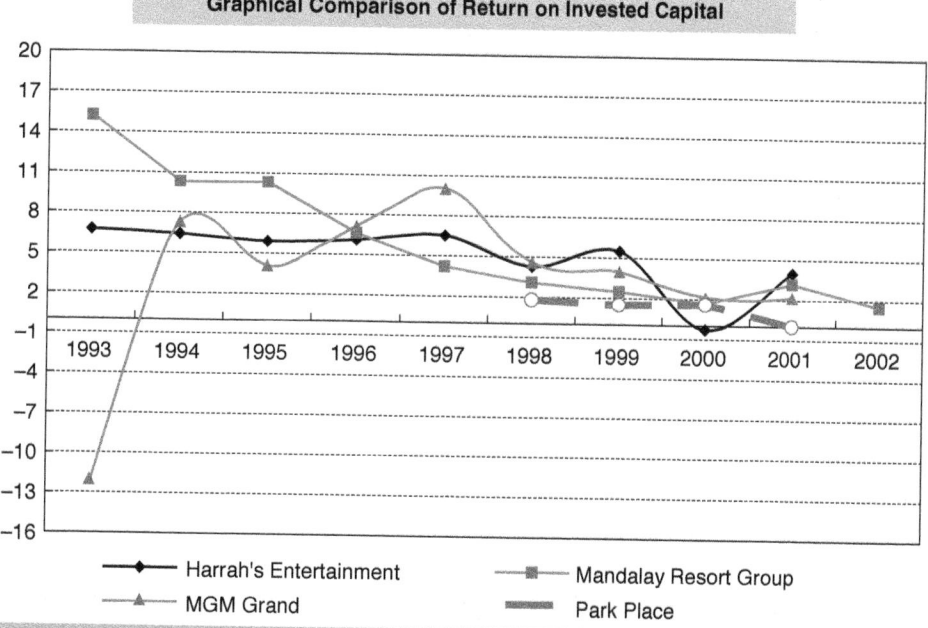

Graphical Comparison of Return on Invested Capital

—◆— Harrah's Entertainment   —■— Mandalay Resort Group
—▲— MGM Grand   ▬▬ Park Place

EXHIBIT 10 Comparative and Longitudinal Analysis of Major Multinational Hotel Companies

employed, what competitive advantage does it have, what has happened to it in terms of key innovations in the past five years, what can be expected in terms of improvements or changes, and where is it vulnerable to competitive attack.

Some examples may help to understand the importance of this dimension of competitor analysis. Let's assume that the manager completes an assessment of how his or her firm is doing on industry CSFs. Recognizing there are 10 CSFs to which all

Competitive analysis worksheet

Name of competitor
1. Graph the last five years of the following:
   a. Return on invested capital
   b. Free cash flow from operations
   c. Sales
   d. Operational profits
   e. Market capitalization (average)
   f. Share price (average)
   g. WACC
2. Describe their primary business model
3. Primary market
4. Describe the financial position of this company relative to its ability to meet its growth needs

Competitive methods	Length of time employed	Competitive advantage	Estimate of value added[1]	Key innovations in the last five years	Expected future actions to enhance method	Vulnerabilities to exploit

Comments:

EXHIBIT 11   Analysis of competitors

[1]This estimate must be the NPV of this competitive method as well as your estimate of what proportion of the firm's total market capitalization is derived from this CM.

firms are paying strategic attention, the manager concludes that the firm is ahead on two of the ten but well behind the competition on all the others. In planning the next capital expenditures budget, this manager must decide which of the eight CSFs to invest in, given the available resources for this purpose. It is generally assumed in cases such as this that every firm faces some form of capital rationing where there are not sufficient resources available to do everything desired. This includes investing in new competitive methods. The manager completing this analysis will have a much better idea of where to invest scarce resources.

If, through effective environmental scanning, the manager can determine where the competitors are directing their resources, this will serve as important information in terms of where the firm must invest to keep pace or take the lead. It would be very helpful if, through a thorough analysis of the competitors' financial position, the manager could more effectively allocate resources to achieve the greatest competitive advantage for the firm. This example also helps to point out how important it is for the manager to continue scanning developments surrounding industry CSFs and value drivers. They serve as key beacons in the decision-making process.

Another important use of the financial capabilities analysis of the competitor is to determine whether they may have the resources to copy a new competitive method created by the manager's firm. If management determines that the competitor has little investment capital available to copy a new industry leading competitive method, then the decision to go forward may be easier. This would be especially true if this condition allows the firm to achieve a one- or two-year advantage on the competition. A one- or two-year lead can make a big difference in the net present value of this investment.

What is important here is that firms cannot compete without financial resources. Knowing the financial position of all competitors in the strategic group gives the manager a clear view of what the competitive landscape will look like in the future. This clearly serves the manager well in deciding important resource allocation decisions. Beyond the financial analysis and comparison, managers must look also at all the other functional areas of the business to determine who is the strongest relative to marketing, human resources, operations, administration, and research and development. In other words, managers must invest in learning what key performance indicators are in each of these functional areas and how his firm compares.

Buying Groups

This portion of the chapter conforms to more traditional task environment or industry analyzes as suggested by Michael Porter in his now famous industry analysis model and further shapes the domain definition of the firm.[6] In this analysis managers seek to determine the key buying groups that will impact their firm and what is happening in terms of trends in each group. For example, in the hotel industry, several buying groups exist, such as tour operators, travel clubs, professional associations and meetings planners, church groups, and corporate clients. These groups constitute important parts of the demand curve of a hotel. The manager should know each well and, more importantly, try to determine the trends occurring within each. It is known, for example, that immediately following the terrorist attacks on the World Trade Center buildings on September 11, 2001, many corporations all over the world refused to allow key personnel to travel. This brought about increased use of teleconferencing and Net-based meetings, which perhaps have permanently altered the demand structure of the industry. In this case, the corporate client, as part of a significant buying group, is now reshaping how the hotel must do business as well as anticipating where this trend is headed.

Similarly, in the foodservice industry, buying groups also exist, but in many instances they are less well defined than in the hotel industry. These buying groups may include civic clubs who hold luncheon or dinner meetings at restaurants or sports clubs or other specialty organizations who include dinner or luncheon meetings as part of their organizational activities. Charitable organizations such as those who manage programs like meals on wheels where food is delivered to elderly or ill individuals who are unable to leave their homes represent another type of buying group. In some cases, local merchants produce discount coupon books, which are then sold within a local community. The purchaser of such a coupon book then expects a percentage discount on purchases in all types of retail establishments, including restaurants. These groups are not as well organized as the others mentioned in the paragraph but still represent a group buying effort that must be monitored. Similarly, those that hold individual establishment credit cards or loyalty cards, along with major credit card holders, represent potential buying groups.

Buying groups, like any component of the task environment, undergo shifts in the way they do business and thus must be watched to see if any trends are taking place in each case. If any of these buying groups represent good contributions to the firm's value-generating capabilities, then the manager must make every attempt to set up scanning systems to monitor their activities. For example, because of recent changes in how travel agencies conduct their business in light of the growing level of e-commerce transactions in travel, managers of firms who depend on travel agents for their business must begin to assess what this trend will mean to their revenue streams going forward. Exhibit 12 is an example of just such an analysis, indicating buying groups identified with the lodging industry.

Suppliers

The analysis of the supplier category of the task environment can begin broadly with a look at capital, human resources, and raw materials. Each of these general categories can be further broken down into subgroupings as we do below. In addition, there is a variety of additional suppliers that can be included here. These would include those items that appear on the firm's cash flow statement as expenses. Examples such as energy costs, occupancy costs (rent, leases, etc.), and insurance premiums are a few. Managers should look at those categories that have the greatest impact on cash flow and then pursue serious scanning efforts to be sure they are aware of all the trends occurring in each.

Capital Supply

Capital is necessary for all businesses and can either be in the form of equity or debt. Thus stockholders, owners, and others with money to invest must be thought of as important components of the task environment to be monitored. As trends in investments occur, often linked to activities of stock market indices, or as the risk propensity of investors shifts, the ability of managers to obtain a supply of needed equity capital to make investments in competitive methods will depend on how well they scan the equity markets' investment climates. Similar scanning is necessary if the manager needs to borrow money to cover current cash flow needs or to assist in investments in competitive methods. In this case, the manager can use many of the value drivers identified under the economic category of the remote environment to assist in this process.

For example, if the U.S. Federal Reserve is changing interest rates resulting in an increase in the prime rate, the manager may want to consider the firm's borrowing needs for the next year or two to be sure that necessary debt can be obtained while rates are still low or seek other sources of funds. Further, if there are wide swings in the performance of the stock market indices in terms of return, it may not be in the best interests of firms to seek new equity capital. The overall industry performance would also be another consideration in terms of seeking equity capital. If the industry is performing poorly,

Name	Brief description of products and services offered. What are the key trends you have observed for each major buying groups.
Tour operators	They buy hotel rooms and create packages which traditional travel agencies will then distribute. They are the "wholesalers" of the travel market.
	Trends: Some predict that tour operators will move the booking systems out of travel agents in favor of their own web-based online systems. Doing so, tour operators will reduce their overheads, eliminate commissions.
	A survey made in March 2002 by Atinera, a subsidiary of Amadeus, shows that the distribution methods used by the US tour operators are far from taking advantage of the technologic inventions.
	According to this survey, only 19% of these tour operators make 5% of their sales on line and 62% of them make more than 50% of their sales via travel agencies.
Travel agencies	Trends: The traditional travel agent is under threat as traditional suppliers are reducing commissions and finding alternative distribution methods. Traditional travel agencies will continue to lose share as hotel sales move online. They will represent just 18% of hotel sales in 2005, down from 21% in 2001.
	To stay in the business, traditional travel agencies have some choices to make: they can decide to provide alternative low-cost distribution channels as call centers and internet, but they can also develop very good relationships with hotel rooms suppliers and adopt the position of a tour operator in creating their own flexible packages.
Trade associations	Trade associations represent a large buying group. Trends include expectations for more complimentary rooms and meals with each meeting booked, greater expectations with regard to audio/visual media capabilities.
Corporate travel managers	Large contracts with major corporations are important sources of value. Since the terrorist attacks of September 11, 2001 the trend is for less travel and greater levels of security demanded.
Travel clubs	Increasing becoming price sensitive, while looking for more amenities at lower prices.
Meeting planners	Demand is growing for more complimentary rooms.

EXHIBIT 12   Task Analysis of Buying Groups for the Lodging Industry

efforts to obtain equity would carry premiums on the cost of capital that may make it too expensive. This type of performance would have been identified in the analysis of the task environment when the manager would have investigated the strategy group the firm is a part of and the assessment of key industry performance indicators.

Labor Supply

The labor supply situation is very critical for service industry firms. This is especially true for the hospitality industry, which must depend on both low- and high-skilled labor to perform effectively. Here again, the manager would begin this process by going back to the economic category of the remote environment to look at the labor supply-and-demand information that they obtained from the scanning process. This effort will also yield information on wages, benefits, and working requirements that would serve useful in making forecasts relative to this important supply. Here, the manager would be required to make causal judgments regarding how broad movements in the labor supply would impact the actual labor cost of the firm.

The remote political category would also be useful in this analysis because government efforts to raise the minimum wage or impose health care insurance requirements on businesses would clearly affect the supply and cost situation. The technological environment would be another important area to develop theory with respect to how new advances in technology will impact the skills and supply of labor needed. Often, new technology introductions into an industry are limited due to the lack of skills within firms to make use of it. These are issues that management must anticipate if it is to address the labor cost and supply needs of the industry and firm properly.

Raw Materials

In the foodservice industry, raw materials constitute essential supplies and as such become important contributors to firm cash flow. This was pointed out in the earlier discussion in the chapter regarding value drivers. Beef, dairy products, and other protein items make up the largest cost categories of the raw material grouping. Recent global challenges with respect to the safety of the beef supply due to so-called mad cow disease along with Asian bird flu represent environmental events that ultimately affect the supply and cost of these raw materials, especially for multiunit firms that base their menu on either or both of these items. Because they are important elements of the firm's cash flow, managers must do their best to develop data that track these important value drivers and then to understand their causal relationship to the firm.

Although the primary source of supply is important, that is, the producers of raw materials, it is also important to look at how the entire supply chain is functioning and in some cases controlled. To illustrate, there are relatively few processors of some key supply ingredients to the foodservice industry. For example, one product used widely across the sandwich sector of the industry is mozzarella cheese. If you think of all the pizza restaurants and sandwich shops across the United States, it is easy to see that this product is in large demand. Yet there are only a few producers of this product, and thus price and supply can be easily affected by actions taken by these producers or in the event of something happening to destroy the supply chain.

This is also the case with fuel oil and the airline industry. Currently the demand for oil is high, in part due to the growth in developing countries like China and India, but also because a key element of the supply chain, the refiners, who process raw crude oil into gasoline have limited production capacity and thus the supply is reduced raising the overall cost. For the airline industry this has had a significant effect on their profitability.

Part of the supply chain is made up of those who distribute the raw materials used by all segments of the industry. Certainly, the fuel cost problem just mentioned for the airline industry is also critical to those who must transport the raw materials from the farm to the producer to the end user. These costs will percolate through the supply chain, raising the overall cost of raw materials for all participants in the supply chain, including the customer. Consolidation in the distribution part of the industry supply chain has also occurred and affected firms in terms of the cost of the raw materials as well as the ability of the hospitality enterprise to acquire the specified quality of products desired to meet the internal quality needs of the firm.

Knowing how the supply chain is organized, how goods are produced, priced, and transported, are all important dimensions of the scanning process with respect to suppliers. Although much information can be obtained through discussions with producers, manufacturer representatives, sales personnel, and transport drivers, keeping track of the forces that impact the supplier is just as important as knowing the forces that impact the firm itself. For example, tomato ketchup is one commodity utilized by all foodservice enterprises. Tomatoes are produced in growing cycles across the United States with heavy production occurring in the state of California. For a large firm like McDonald's, which is probably the largest purchaser of this product across the world, if anything were to happen to California's tomato crop it would have enormous impact on this company.

Therefore, not only must McDonald's seek to ensure supply (although drought or terrorism would be out of their control), they must work within the supply chain to be sure they can get the supply they need because they cannot replenish their needs until a new harvest is obtained, which could be as long as a year away. In other words, the causal links throughout the supply chain must be understood by all players to be sure that contingency plans are available.

Other costs, such as energy, occupancy, insurance, and so on, have the same considerations. Each is part of a supply chain, and the hospitality industry has experienced considerable problems in the recent past with respect to each. The energy crisis in California recently is a good example where supply-and-demand mismanagement resulted in large increases in the cost of energy for large users of electricity like hotels. Hotels were forced to charge customers a surcharge to cover this increase. Part of this crisis was related to unscrupulous business practices by large producers such as the Enron Corp., along with the fact that few seemed to be watching what was happening in the category of the supply environment.

A similar situation has occurred in the insurance coverage available to the industry. Subsequent to the terrorist attacks on September 11, 2001, hospitality enterprises have had difficulty obtaining insurance coverage for terrorist-related activities, and even if they could, they would not be able to afford it. This problem is made even more acute because many terrorist activities have been directed at so-called soft targets that have been primarily tourism or hospitality enterprises. Other insurance-related matters, such as liability for foodborne related diseases or workplace violence, are also issues that are serving to drive this cost forward, which is likely to create additional long-term risk problems for the firm. Knowing the trends unfolding here will help the manager decide what courses of action to take in terms of investments that must be made to protect the firm.

As with every category of the task environment, the primary objective of the manager is to understand what will drive the future trends associated with each of the supply groups related to the firm's cash flow stream. Fortunately, ample information is maintained and reported in all categories. It should also be recognized here that although the examples just given no doubt have greater impact on large multiunit firms, these same issues do affect small- and medium-size hospitality enterprises. The challenge is that many of the larger firms do scan and correctly anticipate these forces, leaving the small enterprise out in the cold in terms of being able to respond quickly. Although the small firm cannot afford to invest in internal scanning activities like their larger counterparts, they cannot afford to be out of the loop in terms of anticipating key forces driving change. Exhibit 13 includes an analysis of suppliers relative to the restaurant industry.

EXHIBIT 13 Task Environment Analysis of Suppliers

Name	Brief description of products and services offered. What are the key trends you have observed for each major supplier.
Labor	**Labor Statistics** **Employment Characteristics of Families in 2002** In 2002, 79% of black families had at least one employed member, down by 0.9% point from the prior year. The proportion of white families (82.6%) and Hispanic families (86.5%) with an employed member decreased by 0.3 and .7% point, respectively. Among married-couple families, 83.5% had an employed person, little changed from 2001. The proportion with an employed member fell from 77.7% to 77.0% over the year from families maintained by women and from 86.2% to 85.1% for those maintained by men. **Trend** The hospitality industry does have a high turn over rate, so it is hard to determine the true amount of current employment rate in reference to the number of people currently employed. As the economy is recovering, restaurants are starting to build again, so jobs will start to be created in the food service industry. We believe we will see an increase in employment rate by the beginning of 2004, especially in the restaurant industry. Another indicator of the increase in performance for the restaurant industry is the National Restaurant Association Restaurant Performance Index for June 2002.
Financial Market	**Stock Market** A report showing a jump in consumer confidence (April 2004) didn't trigger any immediate selling patterns, unlike other upbeat recent economic reports. Analysts said investors are increasingly optimistic that business is improving, and that stock prices will continue to advance. Recent buying followed a few weeks of declines over interest rates. With the economy improving, many on Wall Street are nervous that the Federal Reserve will begin raising rates sooner rather than later. Higher interest rates would make it more costly for businesses to borrow money, leading some investors to worry that business expansion will slow.

Electronic Energy

Bond Market

Over the past month or so, yields on American Treasury bonds have risen more sharply that for 20 years. After hitting a ten-year low of 3.1 percent in the mid-June, ten-year bond yields hit 4.5 percent on July 31st, before easing slightly. Bond yields in Europe and Japan have also risen, but by more modest half of a percentage point. This could be a healthy sign: higher yields might reflect growing confidence that the global recovery is now well underway. Yet it could equally be a cause for concern: higher borrowing costs could cause the recovery to grind to a halt. There are other positive indicators for the market to become a positive performer. The U.S. GDP grew by 2.4% at an annual rate in the second quarter, well ahead of the average forecast of 1.5%. As tax cuts boost spending, more economist now expect GDP to grow by an annual rate of 3.5% in the second half of this year and in 2004.

Electricity

In 2002, the United States generated 3,836 billion kilowatt-hours (Kwh) of electricity, including 3,673 billion Kwh from electric power sectors plus an additional 162 billion Kwh coming mainly from combined heat and power facilities in the commercial and industrial sectors. For the electric power sector, coal-fired plants accounted for 52% of generation, nuclear 21%, natural gas 16%, hydroelectricity 7%, oil 2% and geothermal and "other" 1%. On a national level, the average retail price of electricity during 2002 averaged 7.25 cents per Kwh, down slightly from 7.32 cents per Kwh in 2001. Electricity prices in the United States fell every year between 1993 and 1999, but this trend reversed in 2000 and 2001.

Natural Gas

As of January 2003, the United States had estimated proven natural gas reserves of 183 trillion cubic feet (Tcf), or 3.3% of world reserves (6th in the world). For all of 2002, U.S. production of dry natural gas is estimated at 19.0 Tcf. Natural gas consumption is estimated at 23.2 Tcf, and net imports at around 3.5 Tcf (15% of total demand). Around 94% of U.S. natural gas imports come from Canada, mainly the western provinces of Alberta, British Columbia and Saskatchewan. Overall, the United States depends on natural gas for about 24% of its total primary energy requirement (oil accounts for 39% and coal for 23%).

195

Regulators

Regulators represent elements of the task environment that emerge out of laws designed to protect all elements of the task environment. Health departments, taxing authorities, and fire and police departments all represent organizations that promulgate regulations to be followed by businesses and individuals. Governments, whether national, state, or local, continue to pass laws that affect hospitality enterprises. Ignorance of such laws is no excuse for not following the regulations that result from such legislation. Managers must develop scanning systems to assist them in this challenging task. Fortunately, most industry trade associations do an excellent job in tracking the development of legislation and take an active role in seeing to it that an industry is protected. However, managers must take an active role in this process to be sure they are able to anticipate the impacts that any current or new regulations may have on their firms.

Regulators may also operate internationally based agreements made between nations as they seek to compete globally. The World Trade Organization (WTO), International Monetary Fund (IMF), International Organization for Standardization (ISO), and International Labor Organization (ILO) are examples of organizations that seek to impose some form of regulatory environment for businesses that compete internationally. These become important determinants of the manager's scanning window.

An example of how important it is to monitor trends in the regulatory environment relates to the food supply. As foodborne-related diseases have been on the increase due to the globalization of the food supply, governments have passed many regulations. These include requirements for training and certification of food handlers, tougher inspections of food production facilities, and the overall establishment of standards from the production to the service of food. The introduction of the Hazard Analysis Critical Control Points (HACCP) process is one example now being mandated by governments across the globe. This process puts requirements on the handling and storage of food throughout the preparation and production activities, including time and temperature regulations.

Recent examples from the terrorism activities of extremists have forced airlines to install steel doors in airplane cockpits to prevent hijackings under U.S. federal government guidelines. Similarly, under the Americans with Disabilities Act, hospitality enterprises, like other businesses, have been required to invest in facilities for those who fall under the protection of this law. The regulatory environment of all businesses is subject to new laws addressing new problems or changes in old issues and can be expected to continue to evolve. The scanning system of each firm cannot afford to ignore this important scanning function. Exhibit 14 indicates some of the key regulators affecting multinational hospitality companies.

Potential Competitors and Substitute Products

Potential competitors we define as those organizations that operate within the same domain or strategic group but have not yet become serious competitors. They may include smaller firms that have not yet emerged to compete on a full-scale basis because they are underfunded or have not yet been able to come up to standards on

EXHIBIT 14 Task Analysis of Regulators for Companies Operating Internationally

Name	Function	Brief description of area of regulation affecting segment. What are the key trends you have observed for each regulator?
ISO (International Organization for standardization) http://www.iso.ch/iso/en/aboutiso/introduction/index.html#one	ISO develops voluntary technical standards which add value to all types of business operations. ISO standards contribute to making the development, manufacturing and supply of products and services more efficient, safer and cleaner. They make trade between countries easier and fairer. They provide governments with a technical base for health, safety and environmental legislation. They aid in transferring technology to developing countries. ISO standards also serve to safeguard consumers, and users in general, of products and services as well as to make their lives simpler.	Services industry and the hospitality industry are subject to standards set by ISO. ISO sets standards not only for food quality but also for computers, safety and many other fields that competitors, suppliers and others must respect. Trends: Also the *widespread adoption of International Standards* means that suppliers can base the development of their products and services on specifications that have wide acceptance in their sectors. This, in turn, means that businesses using International Standards are increasingly free to compete on many more markets around the world. *The demand for ISO standards has never been greater.* ISO is called upon to lay down a solid and equitable foundation for the global exchange of goods and services, incorporating all the key elements required by market and societal forces: rationality, practical applicability, environmental protection for sustainable development, safeguards for safety and health, and equal opportunity to engage in world trade. ISO is in a unique position to support and equilibrate the continuous development of world trade. For consumers, conformity of products and services to International Standards provides assurance about their quality, safety, and reliability. *(continued)*

197

EXHIBIT 14 *continued*

Name	Function	Brief description of area of regulation affecting segment. What are the key trends you have observed for each regulator?
World Trade Organization http://www.wto.org/	A global international organization dealing with the rules of trade between nations. The goal is to help producers of goods and services, exporters, and importers conduct their business.	The WTO's global system lowers trade barriers through negotiation and applies the principle of non-discrimination. The result is reduced costs of production (because imports used in production are cheaper) and reduced prices of finished goods and services, and ultimately a lower cost of living. Negotiating agricultural trade reform is a complex undertaking. Governments are still debating the roles agricultural policies play in a range of issues from food security to environmental protection. Food security and environmental protection are two major issues for the hospitality industry. Trends: About 100 of the WTO's over 140 members are developing countries. They are expected to play an increasingly important role in the WTO because of their numbers and because they are becoming more important in the global economy. The WTO agreements take account of these countries' interests in a number of ways. Technical cooperation is an area of WTO work that is devoted entirely to helping developing countries (and countries in transition from centrally-planned economies) operate successfully in the multilateral trading system. The objective is to help developing countries create the capacity to build the necessary institutions and to train officials. The subjects covered deal both with trade policies and with effective negotiation.

industrywide CSFs. They may have some of the CSFs and are working on others but have not quite got there yet. They may also have many competitive methods that are similar to the leading competitors in the group but may also have some new ones that are just beginning to emerge as serious efforts to reshape industry performance.

For example, Southwest Airlines was a potential competitor when it began but was no doubt dismissed by legacy airline executives as something that would not last. We now know how wrong they were and how the competitive methods they developed would reshape and restructure the airline industry globally. Similarly, Holiday Inn Corp.'s reservation system from the 1960s was also a key competitive method that caught other competitors in the industry off guard. This potential competitor back then is still one of the world's leading multinational hotel companies today, in part because it led the industry on key CSFs.

Substitute products and services are far more difficult to identify because they may indeed emerge from outside the industry domain. Some examples may illustrate. Long before the terrorist attack on September 11, 2001, many corporations were making use of various forms of teleconferencing as ways to reduce travel costs. As the technology improved, so did the number of users and meetings held by this medium. Post 9/11 this form of communication became even more popular. This teleconferencing trend became very quickly a substitute product and service replacing travel and hotel room stays.

Home replacement meals may also qualify as a substitute product. The nation's retail supermarkets now serve prepared meals similar to those obtained in restaurants, and this move hurt future growth in the restaurant industry. The industry responded with takeout as well as delivery, and no one questions the continuing threat of home replacement meals sold by supermarkets as substitute products for eating out. Similarly, online gaming serves as a substitute product for traveling to a casino in one of the many gaming destinations in the United States and overseas. This is especially so as many worry about the potential terrorists threats associated with travel. Exhibit 15, reflecting the restaurant industry, illustrates an example of this analysis.

EXHIBIT 15   Substitute Products as identified for a typical Steakhouse Corporation

Name	Brief description of why you feel these are possible substitute products and services. What trends are occurring here to support your identification of these substitutes?
Ethnically diverse menus	The Census Bureau predicts net immigration to the population from 1995 to 2050 would result in four of every 10 people added will be Hispanic, three in 10 will be Asian and Pacific Islander, two in 10 will be non-Hispanic White, and one in 10 will be African American. Immigration trends will cause a change in the restaurant industry that can be seen in the workforce and consumer preferences of food. The shift in demographics will be a driving force of a change in consumer preferences. This trend will affect what people eat, how much they spend and where people will eat.
Greater restaurant choice	The restaurant industry continues to grow. There is expected to be approximately one million restaurants in the USA by 2010 increasing competition.
Menu's offering healthier food choices	Restaurants are responding to consumer demands of greater menu choice. With a diversifying population restaurants are diversifying to meet these demands. To cater for the health conscience consumer restaurants across the country are offering

(continued)

EXHIBIT 15 *continued*

	special menu items for those counting calories, fat intake and those who generally want to know the nutritional value of menu items. A growing percentage of table service operators feature menu items which specify nutritional value.
Cooking at home	The typical American age 8 and older consumes an average of 4.2 commercially prepared meals per week (2000). Though the trend leads more towards increased commercially prepared meals, there is a current focus on family (especially since September 11) which is refocusing consumers towards food prepared in the home and food brought externally into the home to be consumed.
Home Meal Replacements	Boston Market is the brand which is most associated with HMR. More recently quick casual such as Panera Bread are also appealing to the HMR market. Currently the HMR market is focused toward the comfort food market. However with the increasing consumer demands for healthier food this trend is set to diversify.
Personal Chefs	Current trends show greater demand for personal fitness trainers, personal shoppers and personal financial planners. Personal chefs are professional chefs who come into the customer's home and cook and store a weeks worth of food. Personal chefs do what their clients would do if they had the time, shop for groceries and prepare meals. Personal chefs will cook for several families or individuals. The increasing demands for consumers to save time yet have healthy balanced meal accompanied by quality family times makes personal chef's a realistic option for many.

SUMMARY

In this chapter we looked at the task environment and the subcategories making up each. Our mission here is to point out the importance of knowing every detail possible about the trends affecting customers, suppliers, regulators, and competitors. This also includes paying careful attention to potential or emerging competitors and a wide range of possible substitute products. We recommend a careful definition of the domain of the firm, so scanning can be managed effectively while encouraging the manager not to be too definitive for fear of excluding possible new forces developing in the environment. We have stressed how important it is to understand the causal relationships between the remote and task environment. These causal relationships impact the financial situation of the industry and the leading firms within it. Thus we stress how essential it is to understand the financial strength of each competitor in the industry context and how changes in the supply chain, regulatory situation, and customer trends are likely to impact the cash flow streams of the firm. All these relationships represent a significant level of complexity that demands from management the ability to formulate theories about them that will serve to guide the firm to long-term success. Most importantly, they should serve to enhance the decision making regarding what competitive methods the firm must invest in to achieve this succeed.

DISCUSSION QUESTIONS

1. Provide an overview of how the remote and task environments can be integrated in support of the manager's responsibility to make effective investments in competitive methods.
2. Discuss the challenges with estimating the demand curve of the business. What value drivers do you propose to assist in this difficult task?
3. What is the manager's most important priority in assessing the competitor?
4. Discuss how you would go about comprehensively estimating the financial position of those firms in your strategic group or competitive set.
5. How would you go about establishing environmental scanning for the regulator, supplier, and competitor categories of the task environment?
6. After reading and studying the environment summarize what you believe to be the most important learning contributions regarding the environment.

NOTES

1. Investment research firms often actually identify the competitive set and provide this information in their reports or websites.
2. M. D. Olsen, J. Zhao, A. Sharma, and P. Chathoth, *A White Paper on the International Restaurant Industry* (International Hotel and Restaurant Industry, 1999).
3. This common reference to the cash flow statement of the firm refers specifically to revenues.
4. This is a metaphor referring to the fact that food begins with farm production and is processed through a value chain that ultimately ends up on the fork of the consumer.
5. Yeasun Chung, Unpublished master's thesis, Virginia Polytechnic Institute and State University, Blacksburg, 2005.
6. Michael Porter, *Competitive Strategy, Techniques for Analyzing Industries and Competitors* (New York: Free Press, 1980), Chapters 6–8.

CASE STUDY

The Leader of Casual Dining: Darden Restaurant

THE IMPACT OF THE EXTERNAL ENVIRONMENT ON THE CASUAL DINING SEGMENT

Tougher economic times, busier lifestyles, an aging population with more discretionary income (despite higher oil prices), rising interest rates, and the continued growth of women in the workforce[1] are value drivers within the remote environment. These changes are big drivers that influence the entire foodservice industry and more specifically the casual-dining segment.

In 1989, 8% of all restaurant meals were bought in casual-dining restaurants. It has grown every year since then.[2] In 2002, despite the nation's economic downturn that continues to challenge the restaurant industry, casual-dining operators are surviving and even prospering.[3] They did it by borrowing ideas from other foodservice segments. In 2003 the sector was at its peak year, with 11.3% of all restaurant meals. For the most part, growth has occurred at the expense of midscale family-style restaurants. Twenty years ago, midscale family-style restaurants were a growing segment.[4] Since then America has moved upscale. The future of the $62 billion casual-dining industry, which continues to grow at a healthy 5% to 7% annual rate, will belong to those companies that can master multi-brand casual dining.[5] Although the tough economy has forced some overextended multiconcept casual-dining operators to shrink their portfolios, a number of top casual-dining operators nonetheless are ambitious about expanding the emerging brands that they own.[6]

COMPETITIVE STRATEGIES AT THE CASUAL-DINING SECTOR

Casual dinner house chains used to specialize in easily recognizable so-called comfort foods. Now, across the country, these chains are expanding their offerings by providing takeout menus and special pickup areas for customers on the go. Some of the chains continue to incorporate a wide variety of elements traditionally offered by higher-end restaurants,[7] such as exploring more sophisticated ingredients and offering extensive wine lists and upscale preparations[8] of menu items in an effort to differentiate themselves from a host of competitors. Many of the operators are refocusing on bread-and-butter brands; others are pushing the expansion of less proven, younger concepts.[9] In other words, as the customers' expectations for convenience and value continue to increase, operators are continuing to look for ideas from any segment to increase their cash flow efforts.[10] Specifically, these strategies include the following.

Introduce Higher-Priced Menu Items

With fierce competition with fast-casual, fine-dining, and other casual-dinner house concepts,[11] casual chains are going upscale. For instance, Applebee's has introduced several upscale menu products, including its blue-cheese-crusted steak.[12] It has also started to offer fixed-price three-course dinners, including an appetizer, an entree, and a dessert for about $11 in most markets.[13] Bennigan's introduced some higher-priced items to its menu.[14] The company wanted to maintain the low-end, value-oriented menu items[15] but at the same time to introduce new items. Several of the chains repositioned themselves as chef-driven concepts; others have partnered with culinary organizations to enhance the quality and authenticity of their concepts.[16]

Not only have the operators paid attention to food quality, but also the overall visual impact of the dish has received attention. At the same time, an increasing number of chefs and professionally trained culinarians are entering the segment.[17] The focus on ingredient quality and culinary authenticity reflects heavy competition within the segment, which is forcing chains to work harder at keeping the concept fresh.[18] This is also because of the growing sophistication of diners. With people traveling more and becoming familiar with a world of different cuisines, they are more adventuresome in the kinds of food they try and enjoy.[19] They are interested in fresher and lighter dining. Operationally, when the chains are going through rapid expansion, sometimes they may not put too much effort on improving the concept. However, there is always the risk in pushing a concept too far upmarket and thus alienating the core customer base.[20]

Expand on the Wine Lists

Nationwide, not only are these casual-dinner houses featuring upscale entrees, they also offer better wines and wine by the glass to capture the trade-down from finer dining concepts. With the gross profit on a glass of wine at about 60%, California Pizza Kitchen rolled out a list of 20 wines at dinner along with a new menu.[21] Darden has upgraded and expanded the wine offerings at its Red Lobster and Olive Garden concepts.[22] Olive Garden began a revitalization of its casual Italian concept in 2000, instituting partnerships with Italian companies and developing new wine program initiatives.[23] Darden's new concept, Seasons 52 offers more than 110 wine selections, half of which are available by the glass.[24] The idea is to enhance the whole dining experience with food and wine pairings.

Curbside Takeout

Increasingly, curbside takeout and separate entrances for carryout business are appearing throughout the casual-dining segment.[25] Outback Steakhouse Inc. promoted its Curbside Take-Away program[26] with national television advertising spots. Romano's Macaroni Grill started a similar initiative in 2001.[27] Takeout sales in all categories passed $60 billion in 2002, and casual-dining carryout has been growing at the 10% range.[28]

Investing in New Growth Vehicles

It is extremely difficult to identify the magic combination of elements that enable a concept to reach the billion-dollar mark, which is why there are only a few billion-dollar casual-dining concepts in America.[29] Hurdles include getting a brand to work in a wide range of regions and markets by appealing to a mass audience[30] while keeping up with changing consumer tastes. As their primary concepts continue to grow at healthy paces with solid sales results, companies such as Darden Restaurants Inc., Outback Steakhouse Inc., Brinker International Inc., and O'Charley's Inc. are making bigger investments in expanding their smaller or recently acquired brands.[31] In response to upgrading, Darden Restaurants Inc.'s newest concepts are at the upper end of the casual-dining spectrum such as Bahama Breeze, its Caribbean concept, which was launched in 1996.[32] In 2003 Darden opened the first unit of its test concept Seasons 52, which features fresh, low-calorie[33] seasonal American menu items with a wine bar. It is positioned as a "casually sophisticated" grill and wine bar.[34]

Divest and Concentrate on Core Brands

At the same time, however, operators such as Carlson Restaurants Worldwide have been or will be paring down their portfolios to devote their resources to expand their core brands in order to gain a stronger financial footing.[35] To respond to this trend, Carlson Restaurants Worldwide (parent of T.G.I. Friday's) has sold or divested nearly all of the 21 units in its upscale-casual, emerging-brands group.[36] The company is focusing on the growth of the 713-unit T.G.I. Friday's and 83-unit fast-casual Pick Up Six concept.[37] O'Charley's Inc. expanded the 80-unit Ninety-Nine Restaurant and Pub chain by 10 units in fiscal 2003,[38] at the same time

continuing to grow its namesake brand at a steady pace.[39] California Pizza kitchen Inc. will follow suit on their new up-scale-casual restaurant concept, L.A. Food Show bar-and-grill concept, in an effort to bank on the increasingly sophisticated palates of consumers.[40]

The Leader in Causal Dining: Darden Restaurants

In 2006 Darden was the nation's largest casual-dining company, with more than 1,380 casual-dining restaurants, including 679 Red Lobster unites; 563 Olive Gardens; 104 Smokey Bones Barbeque and Grill outlets; 32 Bahama Breeze restaurants; and three Seasons 52 units.[41] As one of the best run companies in the industry, Darden has more than 150,000 employees.[42] For the fiscal year that ended May 29, 2005, Darden Restaurants reported net earnings of $290.6 million, up 16% from the previous year.[43]

Darden Under the Leadership of Joe Lee

Joe Lee helped open the first Red Lobster restaurant in 1968. In 1970 General Mills purchased Red Lobster and named Joe Lee president and chief executive of the chain in 1972.[44] In 1971 Red Lobster established an in-house department for purchasing seafood worldwide that worked directly with the producers instead of depending on the limited number of distributors available around the coastlines.[45] It also established a microbiology laboratory in 1976 to ensure quality assurance of its seafood supply. Lee was appointed president of General Mills Restaurants in 1979, where he was responsible for the major national expansion of both Red Lobster and Oliver Garden.[46] In 1984 he was elected to the General Mills board of directors. In 1991 Lee became executive vice president of General Mills Inc. and was appointed chief financial officer a year later, when he was elected a vice chairman of General Mills.[47] He has been chairman and chief executive of Darden since its 1995 spinoff from General Mills Inc. General Mills spun off its restaurant division as an independent entity, and Darden Restaurants was born. Darden then held an initial offering of it shares to become a publicly traded company.[48]

Internally Developed Concepts

Darden is the only company in the industry with two popular brands, generating more than $2 billion each in annual sales.[49] Darden's internal development of its Olive Garden, Smokey Bones, Bahama Breeze, and Seasons 52 concepts is uncommon in the industry.[50] Most chains obtain a new growth vehicle by acquiring an existing chain or acting as a venture-capital outfit by investing in a concept.[51] Not many companies have the core competency and consumer research and development abilities that Darden possesses.[52] Positive results from its prototype Seasons 52 restaurant have spurred Darden Restaurants to take the health-conscious concept to the next level of testing.[53] The company will open two new locations in 2004.[54] The concept was debuted in 2003. The company considers Seasons 52 the best of its new concepts, which also includes Bahama Breeze and Smokey Bones BBQ.

Red Lobster The brand is more than 35 years old.[55] The first Red Lobster was opened in 1968 by Bill Darden. Red Lobster contributes more than $2 billion of Darden's $5 billion in yearly sales and about half of its profits.[56] Red Lobster is aiming to reinvent itself as a "significantly better seafood restaurant."[57] To do so, it has simplified the menu with the highest quality seafood it can offer at its midrange prices, abandoned its tropical themes in restaurants for a crisp, clean look with white-shirt-and-black-pants uniforms, added northeastern coastal imagery

to its menu and website, and trained staff to expound upon the freshness of its offerings.[58] Red Lobster is committed to a multiyear, five-part strategy in an appeal to a broader range of consumers.[59]

The primary challenge is to restore guest traffic increases and profitable sales growth at Red Lobster.[60] Although Red Lobster's turnaround is not complete, the real pain is behind them.[61] Menu changes and operational improvements, such as better staffing, cleaner restaurants, and serving hot food hot, are paying off.[62] The company will reposition its marketing and advertising for the chain to achieve its growth potential.[63] It began testing revamped menus and advertising campaigns in 2006 to further broaden its appeal to consumers.[64] Red Lobster had gotten onto solid footing after a very shaky fiscal 2004 and 2005, when the concept posted four consecutive quarters of negative same-store sales.[65] So far in fiscal 2006, Red Lobster has recorded positive same-store sales in each quarter.[66]

Olive Garden The Italian-themed Oliver Garden chain is going strong 24 years since its launch. Performance at Olive Garden has not faltered since Darden's initial public offering, and the 10.5% rise in same-store sales in the latest quarter of 2005 marked the 42nd consecutive quarter of growth.[67] The concept continues to post strong same-store sales.[68] New unit openings will total between 30 and 35 units in fiscal 2007.[69] Darden expects both top-line growth and cost savings in this concept.[70] With Red Lobster, these two concepts constitute the majority of Darden's 1,100-plus units.[71] They are proven performers.[72]

Bahama Breeze The first Bahama Breeze was opened in 1996. The company thought that Bahama Breeze was moving into a stage of sustained, steady growth, and President Heckel was ready for another challenge like launching another Bahama Breeze.[73] Bahama Breeze buildout is projected to be limited to the 100- to 200-unit range. This is due to the complexity of the Bahama Breeze concept as well as the real estate and zoning challenges associated with its large outdoor deck and live entertainment, which place restrictions on the concept's site selection.[74] Bahama Breeze generates average unit volumes in the range of $5.5 million to $6 million, placing it at the upper end of casual dining in terms of individual-unit sales.[75] In developing the brand, the company went through a process to better understand how consumers respond.[76] They learned that the concept performs best in high-quality densely populated sites, in more mature trade areas.[77] The new Bahama Breeze prototype is smaller in area and less costly and complex to build.[78] Analysts consider Bahama Breeze a viable long-term concept,[79] although it does not have the very broad appeal of an Olive Garden.[80] Its higher per person average check attracts a higher-income customer than does Red Lobster or Olive Garden, and a younger clientele.[81]

Smokey Bones After its launch in 1999, casual barbecue concept Smokey Bones has emerged as the company's hottest growth vehicle, nearly doubling its unit count (27 to 53) and more than doubling sales ($55 million to $116 million) in 2003 to land it as the only barbecue chain in the Top 25.[82] To ensure high-frequency visits, the company broadened Smokey's appeal to include a new lineup of nonbarbecue entrees in 2003.[83] It also offers friendly, high-energy service to differentiate itself from its competitors. It also replaced "Sports Bar" on signs with family-friendly "Grill." Although many chains are fine-tuning menus and marketing while continuing to add new units in 2006, Darden Restaurants Inc. has decided to slow expansion of its

Smokey Bones brand until the concept can be reimaged and margins improved.[84] The concept could be retooled and with perhaps even a new name. It will downplay its barbecue-centric image so that it will appeal to a broader audience.[85] The company projected Smokey Bones has the potential to become as large as Olive Garden or Red Lobster, in the 700- to 800-unit range.[86] Smokey Bones averages unit sales of $3.5 million to $3.9 million.[87]

Financial Performance

Darden has recently decided to divest itself of this concept. In the third quarter ended February 2003, Darden's experienced a 7% earnings decline. This is after the company spent an additional $10 million in incremental marketing expenses to drive same-store sales increases in the face of a tough economic environment and tough year-to-year comparisons.[88] The decline in earnings also reflects the soaring insurance costs that affect many restaurant operators.[89] Darden, reporting on its recent performance, cited higher costs and geopolitical uncertainty[90] as the drivers behind the less than projected growth in fiscal 2003 earnings per share (5% to 10%). That was substantially below the company's long-term growth target of 15% to 20%.[91] Analysts thought that it will be difficult for Darden to achieve its long-range target of 15% growth on a consistent basis.[92] Darden posted fiscal 2002 EPS of $1.30.[93] It also reported a 16% decline in fourth-quarter net income.[94] However, Darden's total revenues climbed 6.6% in 2003, despite a decline in sales for the seafood chain, due to sales growth at the company's other chains.[95]

In an aim to boost sales at Red Lobster and Olive Garden, Darden continues to explore strategies that address brand positioning.[96] Darden is more dependent than its counterparts on same-store sales growth for driving top-line growth.[97] Darden's earnings model is more sensitive to sales than its counterparts because the company owns and operates 100% of its restaurants.[98] Red Lobster had some of the strongest growth in 2000 and 2001 and into 2002.[99] This was during a rejuvenation program for both the Red Lobster and Oliver Garden brands.[100] With the remodeling and refreshing of the brand, they drove the average check up, introduced some higher-ticket items, and repositioned the brand.[101]

In 2004 Darden Restaurants Inc. scored a 10.7% increase in fourth-quarter sales to $1.36 billion, aided by 19 new Olive Garden, 30 new Smokey Bones restaurants and Olive Garden's 5% rise in same-store sales for the quarter ended May 30.[102] Red Lobster experienced sluggish sales, but the new president, Kim Lopdrup, was confident that sales would increase as Red Lobster extracted benefits from new nutrition-oriented marketing tactics and improved guest satisfaction scores.[103] The chain had completed its strategic review and had made progress in sharpening brand identity while planning sales pitches focused on the nutritional and low-carbohydrate attributes of seafood.[104] Seafood is very low in carbs, fats, and calories. Red Lobster is using a disciplined approach testing new food to ensure it drives high guest satisfaction, fits the desired brand image, and also works well operationally in its restaurants and is not dilutive to margins.[105] This year, Darden Restaurants Inc. shut six underperforming locations (four Bahama Breezes, one Olive Garden, and one Red Lobster) and shifted emphasis toward a new, smaller prototype for future expansion of the chain.[106]

In 2005 Darden reported surprisingly strong fiscal third-quarter results and boosted the earnings outlook of its fiscal year ending in May.[107] This is because Olive Garden achieved record profit growth and the second consecutive quarter of gains in same-store sales at Red Lobster, the first time that had happened in more than a year.[108] In other words, Darden seems to be regaining momentum. Its shares have climbed about 14% to $30.[109] After months of uneven same-store sales results and inconsistent sales promotions, Darden Restaurants Inc.'s flagship Red Lobster seems to be experiencing the continuation of the turnaround of the brand in 2005.[110] In an attempt to broaden the appeal of the concept, it is retooling its menu by adding more midpriced items and simplifying operations.[111] Red Lobster's turnaround appears to be working as profitability improves and as the concept benefits from strong traffic gains as a result of its focus on value and improving the image of the restaurant.[112] They also plan to better align annual promotions in terms of timing and type.[113] Darden also will continue its cost-control campaign.[114] Darden reported record operating profit and returns at the Olive Garden chain and near-record operating profit at Red Lobster from the quarter ended February 2005, and it raised its estimate for earnings growth for fiscal 2005 from 19% to 21%.[115]

DISCUSSION QUESTIONS

1. Discuss the changes in the industry structure throughout the decades and how this affected the growth of the casual-dining segment.
2. How does Darden define its domain throughout its company history? Briefly discuss how the company performance was affected due to these changes in the remote and task environment.
3. Darden is one of the few foodservice organizations that commit to internally developed concepts, whereas other competitors turn to mergers and acquisitions for their growth vehicles. Discuss the pros and cons of the two approaches.
4. Identify the key determinants of the demand curve for each of Darden's current

concepts. Discuss the similarities and differences as you see them.

5. Determine who the key competitors are for each of Darden's key concepts.

6. In assessing the key competitors, identify those with the necessary financial resources to compete with Darden's investments in new products and services.

7. Considering the Red Lobster chain, discuss the key elements of the supplier, regulator,

substitute, and potential competitor subcategories of the task environment.

8. What do you conclude from the analysis of Darden regarding the nature of the casual theme restaurant industry sector, and how do you anticipate it changing over the next five years?

NOTES

1. S. Ward, "A Better Recipe," *Barron's* 85, no. 15 (2005): 20–21.
2. E. Duecy, "Casual Dining's Not-So-Casual Approach," *Nation's Restaurant News* 38, no. 5 (2004): 39–44.
3. R. Ruggless, "Full-Scale Effort: Chains Carry Out Fine-Dining, QSR Ideas to Drive Sales," *Nation's Restaurant News* 36, no. 44 (2002): 1, 39.
4. Op. cit., no. 2.
5. Op. cit., no. 1.
6. J. Peters, "Great Expectations: Chains High on New Brands, Old Flagships," *Nation's Restaurant News* 37, no. 21 (2003): 1, 47.
7. Op. cit., no. 2.
8. Ibid.
9. Op. cit., no. 6.
10. Op. cit., no. 3.
11. Op. cit., no. 2.
12. Ibid.
13. Ibid.
14. Op. cit., no. 3.
15. Ibid.
16. Op. cit., no. 2.
17. Ibid.
18. Ibid.
19. Ibid.
20. Ibid.
21. Op. cit., no. 3.
22. Ibid.
23. Op. cit., no. 2.
24. Ibid.
25. Op. cit., no. 3.
26. Ibid.
27. Ibid.
28. Ibid.
29. Op. cit., no. 6.
30. Ibid.
31. Ibid.
32. Op. cit., no. 2.
33. Op. cit., no. 6.
34. Op. cit., no. 2.
35. Op. cit., no. 6.
36. Ibid.
37. Ibid.
38. Ibid.
39. Ibid.
40. Ibid.
41. S. Spielberg, "Joe R. Lee. (Darden Restaurants Inc. Appoints, Its Sales and Number of Units)," *Nation's Restaurant News* 39 (2005): 21.
42. Ibid.
43. Ibid.
44. Ibid.
45. Ibid.
46. Ibid.
47. Ibid.
48. Ibid.
49. Op. cit., no. 1.
50. Op. cit., no. 6.
51. Ibid.
52. Ibid.
53. Anonymous, "Second Seasons (Darden Restaurants Inc. to Open New Stores)," *Restaurants & Institutions* 114, no. 1 (2004): 12.
54. Ibid.
55. Op. cit., no. 1.

56. Ibid.
57. K. MacArthur, "Red Lobster Retools as 'Better Seafood' Eatery," *Advertising Age* 76, no. 34 (2005): 4.
58. Ibid.
59. Ibid.
60. R. Ruggless, "Rivera Latest to Exit Red Lobster as Chain's Sales Continue to Sink," *Nation's Restaurant News* 38, no. 3 (2004): 1, 48.
61. Op. cit., no. 1.
62. Ibid.
63. Ibid.
64. S. E. Lockyer, "Darden Pins Growth on Red Lobster, Olive Garden," *Nation's Restaurant News* 40, no. 14 (2006): 1, 9, 59.
65. Ibid.
66. Ibid.
67. Op. cit., no. 1.
68. Op. cit., no. 64.
69. Ibid.
70. Ibid.
71. J. Peters, "Darden Prexies Out as Company Retools," *Nation's Restaurant News* 36, no. 35 (2002): 1, 6.
72. Ibid.
73. Ibid.
74. Ibid.
75. Ibid.
76. S. Spielberg, "Darden Takes Wind Out of Bahama Breeze's Sails," *Nation's Restaurant News* 38, no. 21 (2004): 6, 208.
77. Ibid.
78. Ibid.
79. Ibid.
80. Ibid.
81. Ibid.
82. M. Malone, "Smoking the Competition," *Restaurant Business* 103, no. 11 (2004): 60.
83. Ibid.
84. S. E. Lockyer, "Ownership Changes, New Menu Items Fuel Dinner House Growth," *Nation's Restaurant News* 40, no. 30 (2006): 72142.
85. Ibid.
86. Op. cit., no. 71.
87. Report from University of Central Florida (2003), retrieved from http://www.ucf.edu/.
88. J. Peters, "Darden Earnings Not So Saucy, Down 7%," *Nation's Restaurant News* 37, no. 13 (2003): 1, 65.
89. Ibid.
90. Ibid.
91. Ibid.
92. S. Spielberg, "Darden's 4th Q Net Income Declines 16%; '04 EPS Off Target," *Nation's Restaurant News* 37, no. 26 (2003): 1, 211.
93. Op. cit., no. 88.
94. Op. cit., no. 92.
95. S. Spielberg, "Darden's 2nd-Q Net Sinks as Red Lobster Flounders," *Nation's Restaurant News* 38, no. 1 (2004): 11.
96. Op. cit., no. 88.
97. Op. cit., no. 92.
98. Ibid.
99. Op. cit., no. 60.
100. Ibid.
101. Ibid.
102. S. Spielberg, "Darden Posts 10.7% Sales Jump, Eyes Red Lobster Comeback," *Nation's Restaurant News* 38, no. 27 (2004): 4, 11, 54.
103. Ibid.
104. Ibid.
105. Ibid.
106. Op. cit., no. 76.
107. Op. cit., no. 1.
108. Ibid.
109. Ibid.
110. S. Spielberg, (2005). "After Some Roller-Coaster Results Darden Reports Red Lobster Now on Smoother Ride," *Nation's Restaurant News* 39, no. 14 (2005): 1, 46.
111. Ibid.
112. Ibid.
113. Ibid.
114. Ibid.
115. Ibid.

ADDITIONAL REFERENCES

Anonymous. 2004. "New Darden Chief Foresees Acquisitions." *Restaurant Business* 103, no. 13: 14.

Cebrzynski, G. 2006. "Research Firm: Brand Recognition Drives Success for Major Chains," *Nation's Restaurant News* 40, no. 36: 814.

Holmes, T. E. 2004. "Clarence Otis Named CEO of Darden Restaurants." *Black Enterprise* 35, no. 4: 28.

Peters, J. 2003. "Darden Scores Appetizing Results Despite Series of Senior-Executive Shifts." *Nation's Restaurant News* 37, no. 1: 1–11.

Ruggless, R. 2003. "Morris Quits Red Lobster Presidency." *Nation's Restaurant News* 37, no. 40: 1–54.

Spielberg, S. 2004. "Darden's Lee to Step Down as CEO in December." *Nation's Restaurant News* 38, no. 34: 3–117.

———. 2005. "2005 Pioneer of the Year: Joe R. Lee." *Nation's Restaurant News* 39, no. 38: 70–72.

Investing in Competitive Methods

Upon completing this chapter, you will:

1. Understand the role of the manager in adding value to the firm.
2. Develop an understanding of the investor's requirements for return on invested capital.
3. Relate the estimation of cash flows, cost of capital, risk, and investment to the responsibility of adding value.
4. Apply the use of the net present value (NPV) discounted cash flow technique to the adding value imperative of all managers.

- Making investments in competitive methods (CMs) that add value
- Understanding the cost of capital and the investor's imperatives
- The relationship between estimating cash flow, cost of capital, risk, and investment with the investor's return on capital expectations
- Making the right investment decision

From Chapter 7 of *Strategic Management in the Hospitality Industry*, Third Edition, Michael D. Olsen, Joseph J. West, Eliza Ching Yick Tse. Copyright © 2008 by Pearson Education, Inc. Published by Pearson Prentice Hall. All rights reserved.

Chapter Purpose

The primary purpose of this chapter is to introduce and develop the second construct of the coalignment model, strategy choice. We suggest that once opportunities are identified, making the right strategic choices requires managers to invest in CMs that create lasting economic value for the firm and its investors.

This value addition imperative implies that these CMs will provide the required returns on capital employed, compensate the investor for the risks they have to take in supplying the capital, and takes into consideration the time value of money. It is at this point in the future development of the coalignment model in Exhibit 1 where the environment and strategy choice construct come together in a synthesis of *strategic management thinking* and *financial management*. It is this blend of functional capabilities that is necessary for managers to achieve the fundamental purpose of all businesses; that is, to *add value*.

Making the Right Investments

Peter Drucker, the modern era management guru, has often been attributed to this statement: "It is more important to do the right thing than to do things right." The intent of this statement is to say that you can do things correctly, but unless they are associated with doing the right thing, this action will contribute little to the firm's long-term success. Similarly, in the reasoning behind the coalignment model, the need to scan the environment properly for threats and opportunities assumes that this will lead the manager to do the right thing, that is: *make the right investment choices that will add sustainable value to the firm*. To be sure that the investments are the right ones, managers must evaluate each investment using basic principles and concepts associated with financial management.

Making the right investment choices is necessary because investors are demanding, and sustainable strategies cannot be achieved without them. It is fully expected that a manager will adhere to *three basic imperatives* in every investment decision they make:

1. Managers will provide a return on investment that meets investor's' goals.
2. Managers will take into consideration inflation when making investments.
3. Managers will reflect the investors' need to be compensated for risk.

In meeting the investors' first imperative, an investment must earn returns that add value to the firm. Adding value mandates that a manager will not make any investment that does not add value to the firm. This means that all investments will provide returns that exceed the firm's cost of capital. Simply put, the cost of capital is what the investor expects to earn from every dollar invested. For example, if an investor seeks a return of 15% on every dollar invested, management must be sure that that dollar earns an annual return of $1.15 ($1.00 original investment plus $0.15, the earnings on that dollar). If a CM earns less than this amount, investors will not meet their objective and will likely move their investment capital elsewhere. Remember that investors have choices so if they are dissatisfied with a return on their money, they will find an alternative investment.

Regarding imperative number 2, the investor expects managers will recognize that a dollar today is worth more than a dollar in the future. This is often referred to as the

EXHIBIT 1   Strategic Management Model

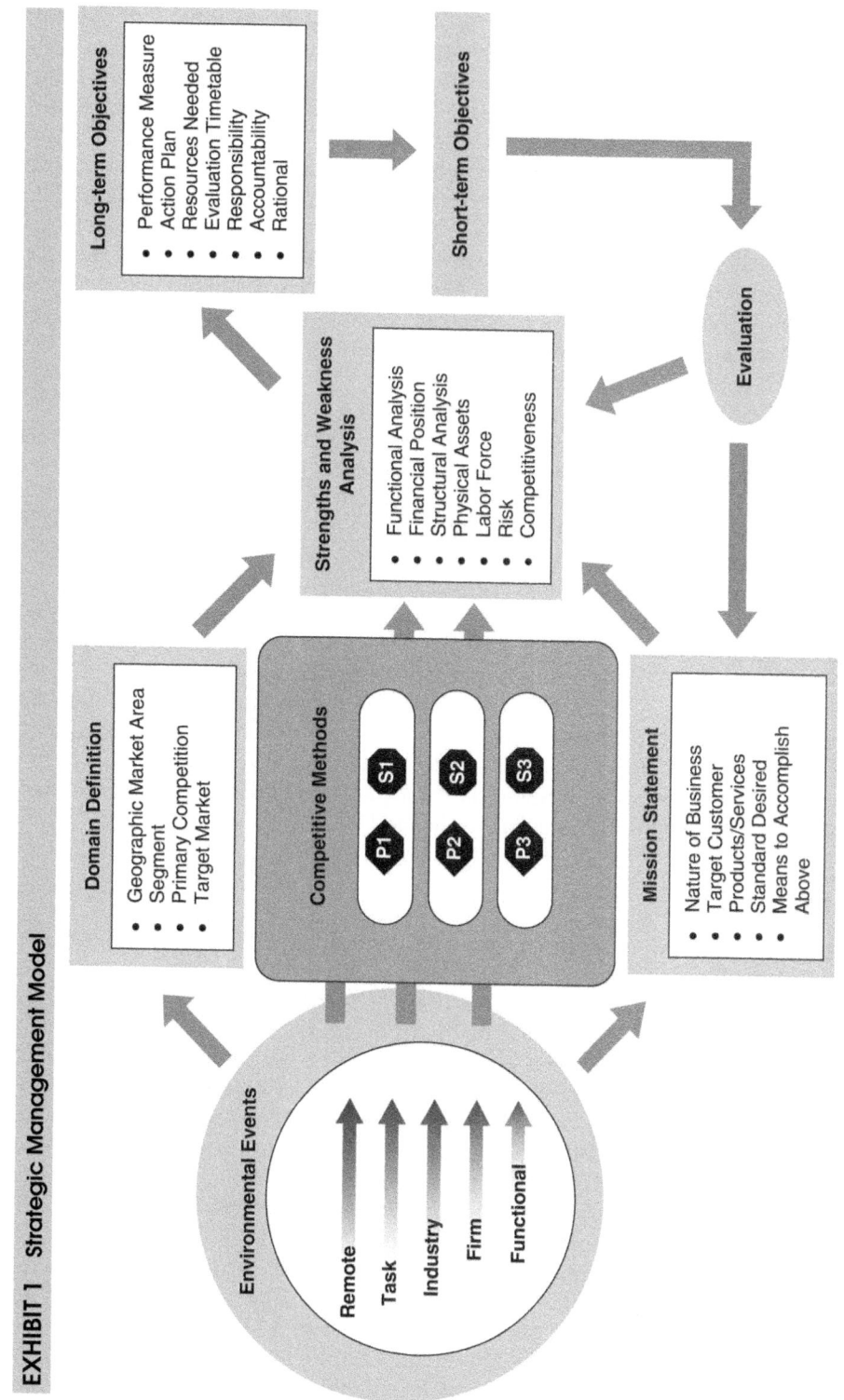

Long-term Objectives

- Performance Measure
- Action Plan
- Resources Needed
- Evaluation Timetable
- Responsibility
- Accountability
- Rational

Short-term Objectives

Evaluation

Strengths and Weakness Analysis

- Functional Analysis
- Financial Position
- Structural Analysis
- Physical Assets
- Labor Force
- Risk
- Competitiveness

Domain Definition

- Geographic Market Area
- Segment
- Primary Competition
- Target Market

Competitive Methods

P1   S1
P2   S2
P3   S3

Mission Statement

- Nature of Business
- Target Customer
- Products/Services
- Standard Desired
- Means to Accomplish Above

Environmental Events

Remote
Task
Industry
Firm
Functional

time value of money. Inflation implies that individuals are subject to rising prices for goods and services in the future so that a dollar will actually be worth less in the future than today. For the investors, this is unacceptable, and they expect managers will make investments that will compensate for inflation. This is basic common sense; no one wants their wealth to be eroded by inflation.

Investors are in general adverse to risk. If they are asked to make risky investments they demand to be compensated for this precarious effort. Think of it this way: If you had a net worth of a million dollars and you are interested in seeing that amount grow, would you be willing to invest in that business based on the *hopes* that the firm's managers would consistently make the right decisions? Not unless you had complete confidence in the leadership of that management to achieve the targeted objectives. Even then, you no doubt would want to be compensated for the risk you are taking, which is imperative number 3.

Thus, for the typical investor who seeks a 15% return on capital under normal business risk conditions, he or she would expect an additional return above this for any investments that are of greater risk than what is normally the case for a business. In other words, the percentage return required would be higher for more risky investments. This additional compensation in this case is often referred to as a *risk premium* or *hurdle rate.* Managers can help to avoid unnecessary risk by making the right investments based on their effective environmental scanning. They must never forget, however, that investors expect this third imperative to be considered in any strategic choice decision.

These three imperatives represent a basic fundamental in running any profit-oriented business. Managers' decisions each day affect how well these imperatives are met. Whether it is investing in new technology, building a new hotel or restaurant, creating new training programs, or purchasing a new piece of food production equipment, each decision must meet these three imperatives or the manager fails in his or her most important role of adding value. This point cannot be overlooked; businesses will not succeed in the long term unless managers understand the importance of financial management and proper allocation of resources to investments that add value.

What Is Capital?

Now that we have introduced the three imperatives regarding every investment, it is time to visit more thoroughly the concept of capital. In market economies there is no such thing as a free lunch. Businesses don't just emerge out of nowhere. It takes money to launch a business. That money comes from investors who expect returns and wealth maximization. Investors come in many varieties, ranging from large investment banks, institutional investors such as mutual funds and pension funds, individuals of significant wealth, friends, family, and in-laws. Regardless of how big or small, these investors will charge you for the use of their capital. Even if you use your own money, you should pay yourself a return so you are sure your money is growing according to your objectives. The money provided by this group of investors is referred to as *equity capital.* This is generally the most expensive form of capital.

Those who invest equity expect repayment either through dividend payments or through growth in the value of the business or both. It is not mandatory that dividends be paid, but it is expected that the three imperatives be met through one of these means. The penalty for not meeting the imperatives for the manager is usually a termination notice. Investors are not generally patient and may occasionally relax somewhat on the imperatives but only for a short period of time. The equity markets can be quite unforgiving and have little patience for marginal managers who make poor or high-risk investments in CMs that do not produce value.

Capital can also be obtained through debt. Businesses, like individuals, borrow funds to meet certain needs. To do so they seek to obtain bank loans or in some cases issue bonds or other obligations to those who have money to lend. For the typical individual, the cost of this money is referred to as interest and the obligation is to pay back the lender on a regular basis. If you have ever had a friend lose their car or even worse their home, you know that unless the interest, and usually the principal, is paid, the lender takes your property as compensation.

Debt capital has an advantage of lower cost primarily for two reasons. Unlike the equity investor, the lender secures the loan through an agreement that permits them to take your property or assets if you don't make your payments. These assets are referred to as *collateral* and thus reduce the risk for the lender. The other advantage of debt is that the interest paid is tax deductible. Consequently, the cost of debt is usually lower than equity. However, the dangers for investors of equity regarding the firm's use of debt are that as the amount of debt capital increases relative to equity capital, the risk increases because the chances of the manager being able to pay higher amounts of interest expense decrease, especially when business conditions turn bad. Thus even lenders assess the risk of the business and will charge more for the money they loan if they feel conditions warrant this.

Most businesses use a combination of debt and equity to finance the purchase of assets necessary to make the business productive. In the context of the coalignment model, assets are CMs that include products and services and the equipment, buildings, land, and human resources necessary to run the business. One of the manager's key responsibilities is to manage the balance of debt and equity, which is why one of the most important accounting ratios, debt to equity, is so important.

This leads us to suggest that, based on our discussion so far, the manager must manage the balance sheet of the business with just as much attention as the profit and loss statement. Every business has a balance sheet with assets on the left and liabilities and equity on the right-hand side. From basic accounting it is well known that assets equal liabilities and equity. From our preceding discussion we know that liabilities and equity funds have a cost, and the use of the assets must result in covering that cost according to the imperatives listed earlier. The key is to be sure that the manager effectively balances the debt and equity to keep the overall cost of the capital low and risk minimized.

The simplified example of a balance sheet in Exhibit 2 tells the story.

This hospitality property (which could easily represent a business class hotel or resort property) has total assets valued at $43.5 million. This means that the investors in this property have purchased assets of this value to generate a return that meets their objectives. To purchase these assets. they borrowed $23.5 million from long-term lenders and used short-term credit for purchasing labor and materials to deliver the CMs offered. The stockholders (equity investors) invested $20 million.

When looking at the balance sheet, it is important to first assess the cost of the various sources of capital. This is done to determine the firm's cost of capital. The cost of capital is what the firm must pay to obtain the money to invest in the assets listed on the left-hand side of the balance sheet. In the case of debt, because this firm has a bank

Assets		Liabilities & Stockholder's Equity	
Current assets		Current liabilities	
Cash	$100,000	Accounts payable	$250,000
Inventory	300,000	Wages payable	300,000
Accounts payable	100,000	Interest payable	50,000
Total current assets	$500,000	Total current liabilities	$600,000
Fixed assets		Long term liabilities	
Land	3,000,000	Bank loan	10,000,000
Buildings	25,000,000	Bonds	12,900,000
Equipment	5,000,000	Total long term liabilities	$22,900,000
Goodwill	10,000,000	Total current and long term liabilities	$23,500,000
Total fixed	$43,000,000	Stockholders equity	$20,000,000
Total current and fixed assets	$43,500,000	Total Liabilities and stockholders equity	$43,500,000

EXHIBIT 2   Hospitality Co. : Simplified Balance Sheet

loan and several bonds, it must be determined what the firm is paying for each. In the case of the bank loans, this information is easily obtained from the agreement signed and is also reported in the 10K reports of publicly traded companies. In the case of bonds, the cost of this money is generally referred to as the yield to maturity (YTM). This information can be found by investigating several types of financial websites that report on bond values. In the case of Hospitality Company, the long-term cost of debt is the weighted average of the cost of debt. In this example, we assume this cost to be 5% after taxes.

The cost of equity is not as easy to determine. We could say that it is simply what the investor expects to earn relative to the three imperatives. However, many companies have millions of investors who can own from one to millions of shares. Therefore it is impossible to find out what returns each one wants. In trying to answer this question, several scholars have created methods to assist in this case. The capital asset pricing model (CAPM) and the arbitrage pricing model are two well-known examples.[1] Although they offer help in estimating the cost of equity, no foolproof method really exists. It is beyond the scope of this text to explore this topic further, but note that managers are expected to try to provide as accurate an estimate as is possible of the cost of equity.

Because the hospitality industry is primarily one of small and medium-size enterprises, cost of capital estimates can even be more daunting. One advantage does exist, however, because there are generally fewer stockholders so it may be possible to actually gain a sense of what return expectations are. When all scientific approaches fail, the manager can always determine the returns on equity that the firm has been earning and assume this is acceptable to investors. This implies that the investors will expect these returns to continue into the future, and thus this becomes the cost of equity. Another approach would be to take the average return on equity generated by the firm's competitive set or strategic group and use this as the benchmark estimate of equity. Let us assume this is the approach we have used for the Hospitality Company and that return on equity is 12%.

Now that the cost of each type of capital has been determined, it is an easy step to determine the firm's cost of capital. It is simply the weighted average of the cost of debt and equity. The figures in Exhibit 2 are used for this purpose. We begin by determining the proportion of debt and equity in the balance sheet. We ignore current debt because it is expected that this will be paid within a year. Therefore, the total of long-term liabilities and stockholder's equity is $42.9 million. The total amount of the long-term liabilities is $22.9 million. The proportion of debt to total capital is 53.4% ($22.9 million/$42.9 million). The proportion of equity to total capital is 46.6% ($20 million/$42.9 million). The weighted average cost of capital (WACC) is then determined as follows:

Proportion of debt (53.4%) × the cost of debt (5%)	=	.0267
Proportion of equity (46.6%) × the cost of equity (12%)	= +	.0559
WACC		.0826

This WACC becomes Hospitality Company's *cost of capital*, and every investment that the management of this firm makes must equal or exceed this cost of capital or the management will destroy the wealth of this firm. *This is the return on investment figure that was identified as the first imperative earlier.* Note that this example is simplified, and the actual estimate of the cost of the various sources of capital can be quite complicated.

Being a value-adding manager for Hospitality Company means that every dollar invested must earn a return of 8.26%. It does not matter whether the investment is in buildings, equipment, or CMs; the manager's job is to be sure that every investment provides this return. It is typical for the manager of the firm to use the firm's cost of capital to value all investments that reflect the normal CMs associated with the firm and its industry. However, when the manager engages in creative thinking and innovative activities and invests in CMs that may create risk, it is possible that a higher cost of capital should be used to ensure that the compensation for the risk imperative is met. We discuss this further under the heading of risk in this chapter.

Strategic management is about being sure the right investments are being made to sustain the organization's economic life well into the future. To accomplish this, managers must be sure that they invest in those CMs that create the greatest value and that resources in the firm are allocated to those methods. Again, value in this context means that all investments equal or exceed the firm's cost of capital. Therefore, the manager's decision-making focus should constantly be on making sure that each CM achieves its return expectations.

In this section we have introduced the manager's responsibility for managing the balance sheet with respect to investments in CMs. It is important to point out here that it is also the manager's responsibility to be sure he or she manages the balance between debt and equity. Put another way, it is a strategic decision by management to determine the proportions of debt and equity. In looking at the balance sheet of Hospitality Company, it can easily be seen that if a larger proportion of equity is used with its attending higher cost, the firm's WACC increases. The opposite is true if more debt is used. But this is true only up to a point at which the firm's cash flows cannot sustain debt payment obligations. Then the firm is at risk of insolvency, and lenders and investors will raise their costs of capital to compensate for the risk.

From Balance Sheet to Cash Flows: Adding Value with Competitive Methods

This brings us to the next point regarding the synthesis of financial management and strategic management. We will go from the balance sheet to the cash flows of the firm. Exhibit 3 presents graphically the merging of these ideas. In this exhibit we introduce a cash flow statement with the detailed version of the coalignment model overlaid. This illustrates how the decisions made by managers from a strategic perspective link to the cash flow streams of the firm. In other words, the investment decision in CMs and the allocation of resources to those CMs result in cash flows for the firm.

EXHIBIT 3 Synthesizing Coalignment Theory with the Realities of the Firm's Need to Produce Cash Flow: The Value-Adding Model

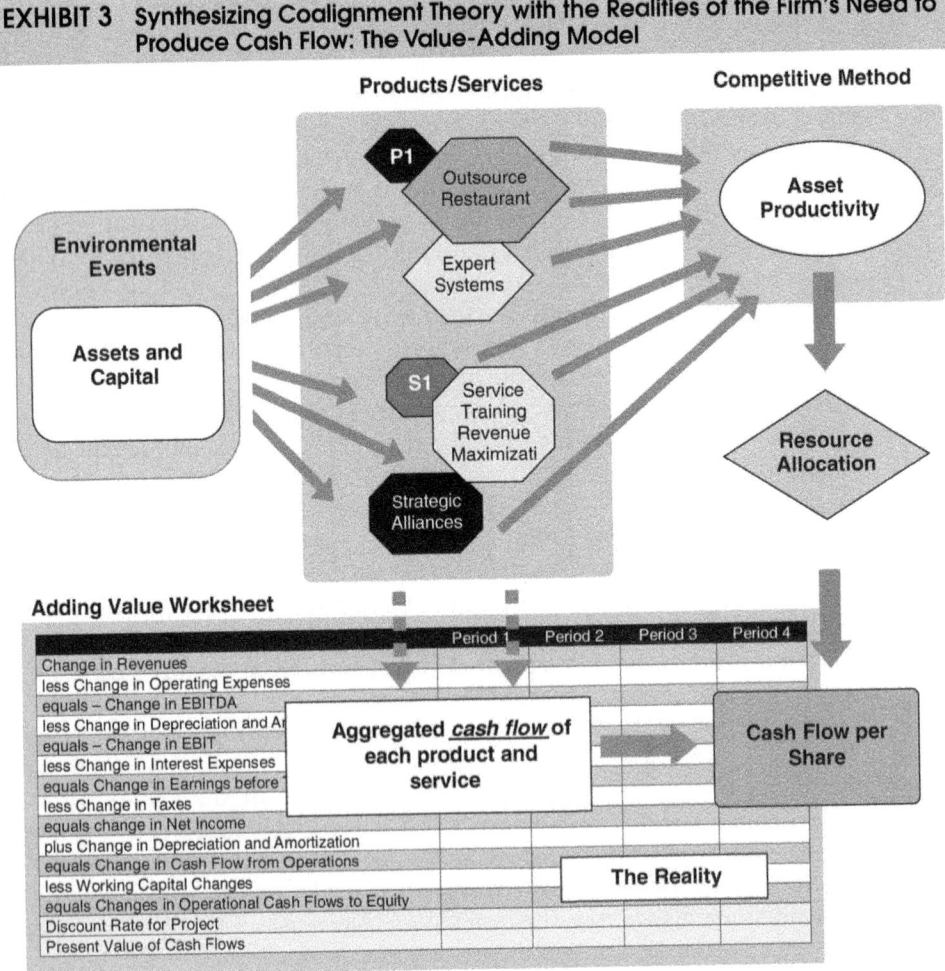

For the manager, *every* CM must be valued by the cash flows it produces. Our focus here is on the manager's need to add value by investments that enhance return on capital employed. We will not focus on the manager's need for managing cash flows from financing and investments. Those topics are best left to textbooks that focus specifically on strategic financial management issues. Our attention here is strategic investments that ensure the best products and services that meet the needs of the customers in the demand curve of the hospitality enterprise.

Drawing attention once again to Exhibit 3, the purpose of this blending of concepts is to be sure the manager recognizes that strategy is all about making investments that add value, and the coalignment model offers a way of looking at this challenge. Put differently, cash flows will not be maximized unless each investment is evaluated based on the long-term strategic consequences to the firm. The goal here is to focus managerial attention on the cash flows generated by CMs for the simple reason that you can only put cash in the bank. No bank that these authors know of will accept price earnings ratios, earnings per share numbers, or profit and loss statement results in lieu of cash. It is the cash that becomes the number in determining the return on investment as discussed in the previous section. This important point must become part of the manager's daily thought process.

At the risk of being a bit repetitious at this point, let's revisit the coalignment model to be sure the conceptual leap from ideas to reality is clear. First, opportunities are observed from environmental scanning activities conducted by the firm. These opportunities are then considered as strategic choices to be made by the firm. The strategic choices are products and services bundled together into CMs. Each CM produces a cash flow stream much like that outlined in the form in Exhibit 3. If management is performing its role properly, it will allocate resources to those CMs that generate the highest value as measured by cash flows. Managers must then be sure to allocate those resources consistently to the highest cash flow producers until such time that the CM no longer produces the desired value.

Exhibit 4 provides an additional and more detailed look at this concept. CMs are portfolios of products and services bundled together in unique ways. Yet each product (P1–P3) and service (S1–S3) has a cash flow stream associated with it. Each product and service, in other words, is a separate investment. Management bundles them

EXHIBIT 4   Aggregated Value of a Portfolio of Products and Services

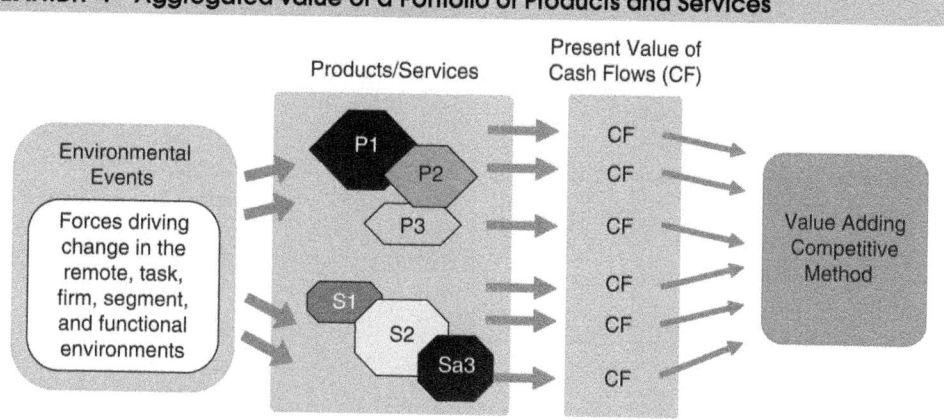

together to achieve a level of inimitability to help it ensure the maximum economic life and value. As this graphic illustrates, these cash flows from each product and service when aggregated help to create the overall value of the CM.

Cash Flows and the Pillars of Value

The cash flow form in Exhibit 3 is a standard one found in most accounting or finance textbooks. Unfortunately for the student reading that text, the cells in cash flow spreadsheet are already completed by the author(s). No where in the real world of business have the authors of this chapter found forecasted cash flow statements filled out and ready and waiting. They must be completed by the manager and this is no simple exercise. Our purpose therefore in this chapter is to focus on how the manager goes about estimating those numbers going forward because that is what managers are paid to do. Thus, for each cell in the cash flow form, a manager somewhere has had to make estimates for the numbers that are in it. This estimation process is no simple task and, as we point out, is based on the environmental analysis discussed in the previous four chapters.

Several approaches can be used in the cash flow estimation process. The purpose here is to focus only on the investment that is made in CMs and the changes in cash flow resulting from these investments. Thus, as you can see in the form, each line or row in the form is titled, and each title is preceded by the term "change in." This means that as a result of this investment there will be changes in revenues and changes in expenses. What we are interested in knowing is the value added as a result of the change or investment. Remember that investments in new CMs are expected to add value in addition to the value provided by all the existing CMs that the firm offers to its customers. Thus our interest in looking at changes in value.

The measure of value we use in this text is referred to as net present value (NPV). The choice of this financial management technique is based on accepted theories of finance, and it incorporates all three imperatives as outlined at the start of this chapter. Simply put, it takes into consideration the future cash flow stream associated with an investment, considers the time value of money, the cost of capital, risk, and the overall investment in the CM. We look at each of these elements, which we refer to as the pillars of value creation. These are illustrated in Exhibit 5.

Estimating Cash Flows

As stated throughout this text, managers must be forward thinking, always on the lookout for new investment ideas to grow the firm and its value. Although accounting information is useful for helping us understand the business, it is always about the past. The previous period's balance sheet and cash flow statements are about what went on yesterday, not what is expected to go on tomorrow. Of course this historical information is useful in making forecasts, but it should not be relied on as the only approach to looking at the future. Managers can use it to formulate theories about how new CMs will perform, but if similar methods have not existed in the firm, then historical data is of little use.

Cash flow estimation begins with looking at the change in revenue resulting from an investment. Here is some underpinning for this important process. First, the demand

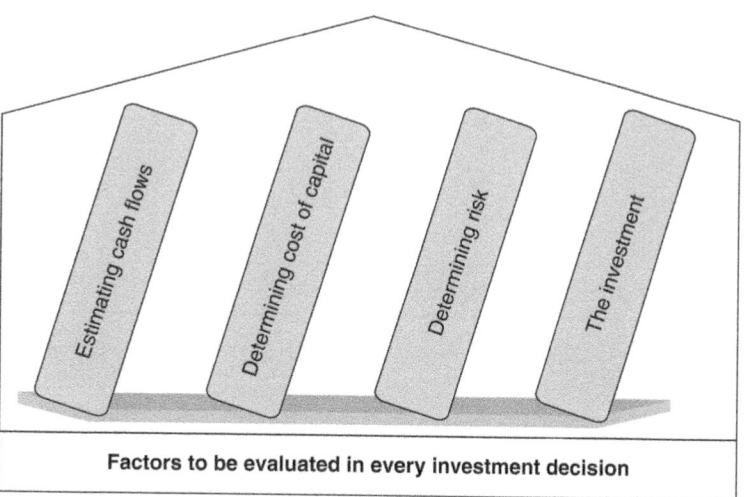

Factors to be evaluated in every investment decision

EXHIBIT 5   The Pillars of the Investment Decision in Competitive Methods

curve for a CM must be estimated. Target market descriptors, industrywide critical success factors (CSFs), competitive analysis, and key value drivers from both the remote and task environments are used to estimate the demand. These are estimates and are based on how the manager analyzes, interprets, and synthesizes information from a complex set of sources of information. Yet it is essential that managers use all the information possible and deliberate carefully to yield a set of assumptions that will be necessary to forecast the future cash flow streams of current and new CMs.

In expected value analysis, the manager is asked to determine a range of probable future demand possibilities. The manager, based on his or her theory and analysis of how a certain CM will sell, can elect to have any number of possible outcomes to include in the analysis. Then, based on a review of the competitive situation, the firm's performance on industry CSFs, and key value drivers, he or she should be capable of assigning probabilities to each outcome. Exhibit 6 provides an example. The demand possibilities in column **(a)** represent the manager's thinking based on his theory of how this new CM will result in increased sales of units to be offered to the customer. The actual units sold in column **(b)** represent the possible range of demand. The probabilities in column **(c)** reflect the manager's judgment and theories supported by his or her assumptions regarding value drivers, industry CSFs, and the competitive situation. It might be said here that this is how managers earn their salaries, by using their experience and cognitive skills to make estimates that are accurate.

This example suggests that a similar level of analysis and thinking must be performed for every cell in the change in revenue row of the cash flow worksheet. This brings out another important challenge for the manager, that is, what the actual life of the investment is because the cash flow worksheets must be completed for the useful life of the CM going

Demand possibilities (a)	Actual units sold (b)	Probability of sales (c)	Expected value (b)*(c)
Excellent	10,000	.10	1,000
Good	8,000	.30	2,400
Favorable	6,000	.30	1,800
Encouraging	4,000	.20	800
Marginal	2,000	.10	200
Total expected unit sales resulting from new competitive method			6,200

EXHIBIT 6   Expected Value Analysis of Possible Demand for a New Competitive Method

forward into the future. Here again, the manager is engaged in a process of estimation. It is impossible to predict the useful economic life of a CM, but it is necessary if accurate cash flow estimates are to be produced and new CMs approved. It is also necessary for managers to evaluate the life expectancy of current CMs to determine when it is time to consider ending resource allocation to them.

Estimating the useful economic life depends on proper environmental scanning. As was indicated in the previous four chapters, managers are asked to identify value drivers in the remote environment that would indicate the need for new CMs or the removal of current ones. Understanding the causal effects of these value drivers on consumer wants and needs helps in the process of estimating life. However, managers must not forget to factor in current and future competitive action and all the analysis performed in the task environment. Once again, the manager is asked to formulate a theory and support it with appropriate assumptions.

Once the revenue stream has been estimated and the life of the CM is also estimated, the manager must make the estimates associated with the changes in costs related to this CM. Here again, every cell in the cash flow worksheet should contain an estimate. Expected value techniques can be used here as well. The important point to make is that each estimate is serious business from the point of view of the investor. The expectation is that each estimate represents the best practice with respect to environmental scanning, demand estimation, life cycle determination, and costs. Careless or serendipitous behavior here can seriously affect the growth in value of the firm and the return the shareholder is expecting. It is safe to say that managers are not permitted to make many mistakes in this area if they expect to hold their jobs.

A word of caution is necessary here. Estimating is as much an art as it is a science. Estimating techniques like expected value calculations, scenario building, sensitivity analysis, regression analysis, and other multivariate techniques help with the science part of this. The art comes from the ability of the manager to use inductive and deductive thinking to formulate cause-and-effect theories about the performance of future cash flows. It is in the art part of the equation where those who seek to promote the investment in a CM can from time to time be overly optimistic. This becomes even more the case if someone really wants the project to be accepted. In this case, everyone involved must guard against the emotional links to these optimistic forecasts. Likewise, those who do not want to see a project move forward are likely to advocate a more conservative forecast and hopefully a lower value. In either case, managers must be objective and challenge the assumptions behind the forecasts of those who are promoting investments in CMs.

Estimating the Cost of Capital

We have provided some discussion on this matter already in this chapter, so let us return to this topic further. At the risk of again being somewhat repetitious here (we know hospitality students in general would rather deal with people than finance), the cost of capital is what the firm must pay for the money it uses to conduct day-to-day business and investments in CMs. The balance sheet in Exhibit 2 and the discussion that followed provided the background for understanding this important strategic financial management tool. Now let us look at this matter a bit further.

The cost of capital issue is probably one of the most illusive of all concepts in finance for several reasons. First, it is taught in basic corporate finance courses as somewhat of a static concept. That is, the assumption is that once one has an understanding of how to calculate the WACC, the work is done. That is not really true. Cost of capital can be a very dynamic concept, especially when a firm is growing rapidly and using many forms of capital to finance this growth. Although the topic of financing and its impact on the cost of capital is best left to a more complete discussion in a financial management text, we must recognize that the manager's decisions on what CMs to invest in can have an impact on the firm's overall cost of capital.

The second reason why cost of capital is such an illusive concept is that the literature in finance has not provided one, consistent, and universal definition. Exhibit 7 illustrates just a few of the expressions of the cost of capital that have been pulled from various texts in finance, and as you can easily conclude; confusion is not far behind this problem. When looking at the legend alone, you can see duplication of terms and sometimes several meanings to the same or similar term. And that is not all. The cost of capital is also often referred to as the discount rate, cap rate (or capitalization rate), even hurdle rate. Therefore, to combat this confusion in terms, it is best for the

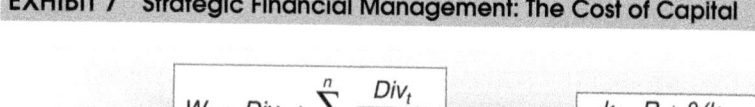

EXHIBIT 7 Strategic Financial Management: The Cost of Capital

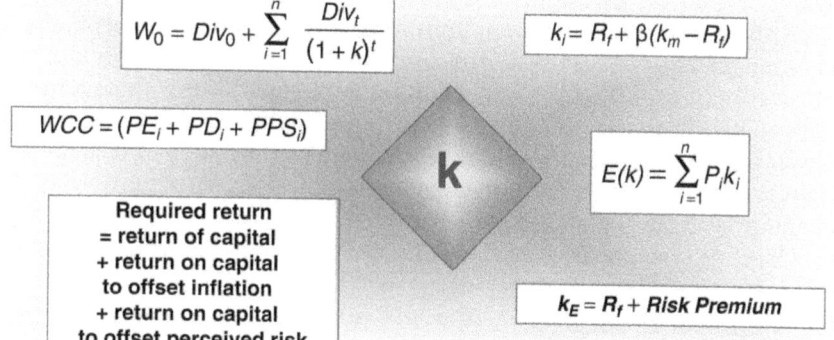

$$W_0 = Div_0 + \sum_{i=1}^{n} \frac{Div_t}{(1+k)^t}$$

$$k_i = R_f + \beta(k_m - R_f)$$

$$WCC = (PE_i + PD_i + PPS_i)$$

$$E(k) = \sum_{i=1}^{n} P_i k_i$$

$$k$$

Required return
= return of capital
+ return on capital
to offset inflation
+ return on capital
to offset perceived risk

$$k_E = R_f + Risk\ Premium$$

manager to learn the concept and know the principles behind value addition result from investments that earn returns in excess of the firm's cost of capital, regardless of how it is labeled.

The third reason for the confusion of this term revolves around what number to use. As we point out shortly, the WACC is used to employ discounted cash flow techniques to the valuation of investments in CMs. In general, the firm's overall cost of capital is used to discount investments in most CMs, but occasionally a method may depart from the normal types of investments that a firm makes in industry CSFs or current CMs. However, when a new CM is evaluated, those reviewing the investment decision may attach a risk premium or hurdle rate to a specific investment. This means that they may add to the firm's WACC a percentage that they feel compensates them for the risk, which is one of the three imperatives introduced earlier in this chapter.

There are no rules or norms as to what percentage to add for risky projects, so it usually falls within the purview of the individual responsible for finance to decide this based on his or her experience. For example, in one research project that the authors are familiar with, development executives of multinational hotel companies were asked what percentage they would add on to hotel investments in the Caribbean region according to the political and economic risks of certain countries. For high-risk nations the risk premium or hurdle rate was 6%; for medium risk, 4%; and low risk, 2%.[2] In other words, these executives had already determined a priori hurdle rates based on past experience.

Note here, as it was in the section on estimating cash flows, that the challenge in estimating the cost of equity is subject to the same caveats. Too much optimism or pessimism can cause firms to make incorrect decisions about an investment in a CM. What is important is that managers seek to obtain the best estimates possible and to hold all those working on the estimates to the same high standards.

Taking Risk into Consideration

When it comes to the future, nothing is certain. Therefore, every investment into the future is subject to some risk. Risk is a normal part of life. Risk results from the failure of management to develop solid cause-and-effect theories about events in the environment and their impact on the firm.

The first step in taking risk into consideration is to agree to a definition. For our purposes here, *risk* is defined as the probable variance in the future cash flow streams of a business or CM. *Variance* is a statistical term that suggests forecasts will vary around an average. Investors prefer that that variance be at a minimum.

Risk begins with bad assumptions made by management. This happens when the manager fails to assess the environment completely and relies on bad or incomplete information regarding what opportunities or threats lurk in the environment, which leads to bad investments. Failure to capture the correct value drivers, identify the relevant CSFs, or misinterpreting competitors' actions all lead to incorrect decisions. Therefore, the manager and investor must first be comfortable with the idea that scanning has been performed effectively.

Once the scanning is done, the cash flows are estimated. This process was discussed earlier, but remember that if the demand curve is not properly determined, the life of the project is not well thought out, especially in the context of competitive action, or the actual changes in revenues or costs have not been properly estimated and so there is a greater level of risk associated with this investment. Here again, we point out how important it is for the manager to use the appropriate information and make the correct assumptions about it. Failure to uphold a high standard is likely to mean the firm will not make its projections, which in turn signal to the investment community probable risk.

Of course, not all investments in new CMs fit this rigorous standard. In some cases information is not always available to guide the estimation process. New creative ideas about what the customer may want in the future may not always fit the normative thinking frameworks of those involved in making the decisions. In other words, investors or other managers may not be receptive to new ideas. They may not appreciate thinking "out of the box," as the phrase goes. This is a very common dilemma: Either a manager is creative and seeks industry-leading innovative CMs or maintains the status quo, always seeking to perform on the CSFs and the firm's CMs. The best solution to this paradox is that risk is a function of balance between doing the same old things and becoming creative. As long as the investor can feel confident in the manager's logical thinking ability, scanning capability, and reasoning, risk can be tolerated. If not, the manager is increasingly viewed as having a high-risk profile, which may end up being the wrong reputation to have.

That reputation ultimately affects how bankers and investors view the decisions and proposals made by the manager. If the manager is perceived as risk averse, the hurdle rate applied by these stakeholders as described in the previous section will be less punishing to the investment's chances. If the opposite is true, then a much higher hurdle rate will be applied, which can have negative effects on the ultimate approval of the investment project.

The reason this discussion of risk and the cost of capital is important is that it is the denominator in the NPV formula, which is the ultimate measure of value added by an investment.[3] If projects are to be valued properly based on realistic cash flow projections, the forecasted cash flows that represent the numerator in the formula must be divided by the best approximation of what the cost of capital should be. A few examples may help. Assume for the moment that an investment in the remodeling of the restaurant can be expected to bring in additional cash flows over a five-year forecast period of $2.5 million. Further assume that the firm's cost of capital is estimated to be 10%. Using a simple feature in a basic spreadsheet computer program, the present value of those cash flows is approximately $1.9 million. Now, if management feels that this project is risky and decides to use a risk premium of 2% added on to the firm's present cost of capital of 10%, the revised present value is approximately $1.8 million, or $100,000 less. What this example points out is that if you raise the denominator, the present value of the future cash flows declines.

Why is it important to know this? Assume the firm had to invest $1.9 million to do the remodeling, add kitchen space, and purchase extra land to accommodate more parking. The first example suggests that the firm will have a NPV of $0. This means that the firm has at least earned a return on capital and adjustments for inflation. However, in the second example, the firm is actually destroying $100,000 of value because the NPV is that far below the investment in the remodeling program. In this latter case, the managers or decision makers have destroyed wealth, which is quite the opposite of the three imperatives outlined at the beginning of this chapter.

What our examples and discussion reveal thus far is that it is critical to be sure the cost of capital is accurately estimated because good investments could be ignored or bad ones accepted simply by a decision on what to discount the future cash flow streams of the investment by. As stated previously, a full discussion of corporate finance is beyond the scope of this chapter; however, it is important that managers recognize that risk is an item that must be managed. The risk factors we are referring to relate to the industry and the firm.

As a brief reminder, a key risk factor is the demand curve. Proper estimation of the probable demand for the CMs considered for investment is essential. All elements of the remote and task environments impact demand, and they must be considered when estimating cash flows. Cavalier approaches to estimating demand create risk, and the manager must be capable of convincing investors that these estimates are well grounded in assumptions supported by scanning data.

Risk is also related to operating leverage. This type of leverage refers to the change in cash flows relative to given changes in revenue. Exhibit 8 illustrates this point.

Company A has a relatively low break-even point compared to company B as can be seen by the dotted line extending from graph A to B. The primary difference between the two companies is that company B has a much higher level of fixed costs. There are several probable reasons for this, such as more expensive leasing costs associated with the locations obtained by company A. It is not uncommon for companies in the midst of growth strategies coupled with the difficulty of finding good locations to engage in leases that perhaps are too expensive or force the firm into seeking a higher level of sales. The point to recognize here is that if the firm locks itself into a higher fixed-cost requirement, it will have to generate many more sales dollars compared to a company like A. If this is the case, greater risk results simply because if company B experiences any type of sales decline there is a higher probability that they may not be able to have sufficient cash necessary to meet its current obligations.

As this section indicates, managerial decisions bring about risk, and thus each decision must be made considering this important component of the investment analysis process. Although our focus is on strategic managerial decision making, we must not forget that risk is also driven by key industry value drivers that affect the cost structure of the firm. Therefore, the importance of monitoring these value drivers is

EXHIBIT 8   Operating Leverage and Risk

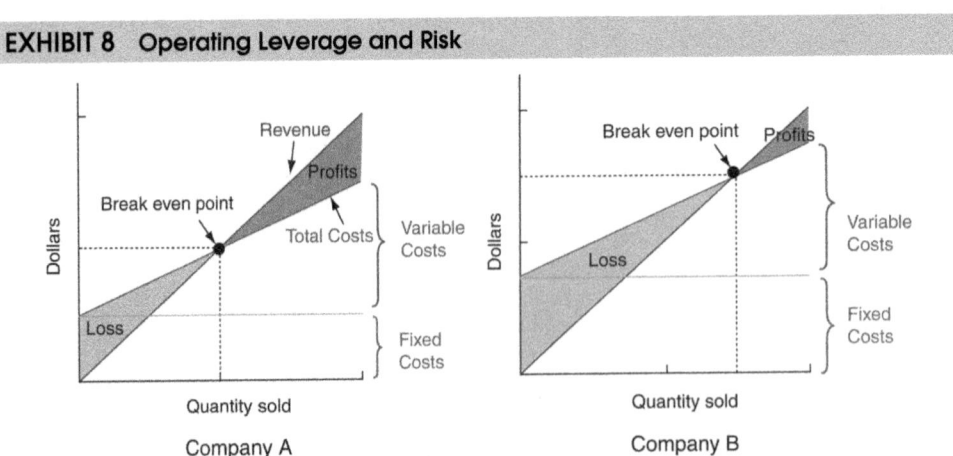

reemphasized here so that any forthcoming changes in previous patterns of any driver can be quickly noted and managers can then react strategically rather than at the last minute. For example, significant changes in the cost of meat, seafood, energy, or insurance can have significant impact on operational cash flows. Knowing well in advance of possible problems will assist management in buffering this impact and consequently reduce the probable variability in cash flows resulting from such changes.

The Investment Decision

The last of the four pillars to be explored is the actual investment required for each CM. In other words, most CMs require an immediate (and perhaps future) outlay of cash. In some cases the outlay is directed at intangible matters such as patents or copyrights. Large-scale investments in human capital such as training or education activities are additional examples of such intangibles. Buildings, equipment, land, and other tangibles reflect the second major type of investments that are the result of strategic decisions. Regardless of whether or not they are tangible or intangible, the total investment can have significant impact on the return on invested capital.

Exhibit 9 provides a list of the factors to be considered when valuing investments. The first item to consider is the capital outlay required. For example, in adding room capacity to a hotel, estimates are usually based on a "per room" cost. It is not uncommon for this figure to range from $40,000 to $1 million based on the type of hotel. As demonstrated in the following section, this estimate and ultimately the actual costs can have a significant impact on the return realized from this investment. Incorrect estimates of the actual investment cost can turn a CM from one of providing desired returns to one of taking value away from the firm.

Evaluating the quality and life of investment materials often falls to the manager to evaluate. Staying with our example of new hotel rooms, the quality of carpeting, wall covering, bathroom fixtures, and so on, often requires the manager to negotiate with suppliers, designers, owners, and other stakeholders regarding the cost, quality, and life of product determinants. Here again, if the cash flows are estimated to be a certain life but the products and materials will not hold up for that period, then the investment valuation will be incorrect. The manager's consideration here should be that all materials are in alignment with the customer's needs, the owner's pocketbook, and the operational crew's ability to clean and maintain. Bad judgment here will result in an investment that underperforms expectations.

Assessing the state of the art of technology and materials is always going to be a challenge for management. The environment in which we live and work is changing. These dynamic times will continue to enhance the advancements in technology and

---

EXHIBIT 9   Factors Affecting the Investment Decision

- The capital outlay required
- Evaluating quality and life of investment materials
- Determining state of the art technology and materials
- Sourcing materials
- Design, engineering and construction:

materials. To ensure the right choices here, managers can be expected to remain somewhat current on developments through their scanning efforts but must also recognize that they will have to rely on experts to assist in this effort. Once again, the overall impact of the investment is affected by the right choices made by managers in this regard.

The issue of sourcing materials refers to the manager's need to be sure to find the right source of supply for all items making up the investment. This is a task related to risk management in which the manager must work with individuals who have a substantive knowledge of the materials and how best to obtain them at the right price. This relates to the discussion in the preceding paragraph in which the life of the materials is important to ensuring that the cash flow projections can be met realistically. In many cases, especially with regard to investments in technology or safety and security, the manager is not always familiar with the distribution channels or manufacturers. However, this lack of familiarity should not stop the manager from seeking advice here because as in the other factors of the investment we have discussed, mistakes here can be costly.

The design, engineering, and construction related to investments must be left to the professionals. As in all factors regarding the investment decision, the manager's task here is to ensure that the professionals do their jobs properly. That is to say, best practices must be followed, credentials must be established, and a track record of success must be determined if projects are to proceed as planned. If the manager cuts corners on any of these elements, the potential cost overruns are many and threatening to the returns projected for the investment.

Discounted Cash Flow and Adding Value

Discounted cash flow techniques refer to forecasting the cash flows of a CM into the future. As we have discussed with regard to the four pillars, the manager must begin the evaluation of an investment by forecasting the future cash flow streams of that CM. However, based on the fact that a dollar is worth more today than in the future, the forecasted cash flows must be brought back to today's value because we are going to invest in today's dollars. In other words, you cannot compare the dollar invested at today's value with dollars that will be earned in the future because this value will be reduced due to the time value of money. Thus the process is referred to as the *discounted cash flow technique.*

There are two primary discounted cash flow (DCF) techniques employed by investors. They are referred to as net present value (NPV) and internal rate of return (IRR). They both measure the same thing: the return on an investment. We prefer the NPV method because it measures the return in absolute dollars. The formula for NPV is illustrated in Exhibit 10. The exhibit displays the formula found in most corporate finance textbooks, and as you will notice, each element of the formula corresponds to one of the four pillars we have just discussed. To provide the links to the prior discussions, CF_n represents the cash flow forecast presented as pillar 1. The cost of capital was discussed as pillar 2, and this along with the discussion on pillar 3, risk, constitutes the firm's cost of capital adjusted for any risk that is likely to occur. Pillar 4 was the investment required for this particular CM.

As we have outlined in each of the preceding subsections, the manager's role is to make appropriate estimates regarding each pillar and then plug those estimates into the spreadsheet and the formula to determine the NPV of a specific investment in a

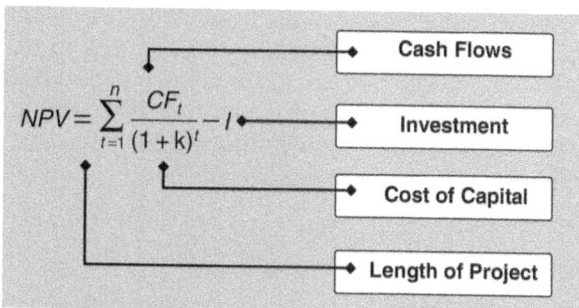

$$NPV = \sum_{t=1}^{n} \frac{CF_t}{(1+k)^t} - I$$

- Cash Flows
- Investment
- Cost of Capital
- Length of Project

EXHIBIT 10 The Net Present Value Formula

CM. The advantage of the NPV method is that it incorporates the three basic imperatives outlined at the start of this chapter. The return on capital imperative is accomplished through the use of the WACC in the denominator of the formula. The time value of money is incorporated in the denominator as well because that denominator for each period is raised to the specific power of that period. By doing so it brings the value of the numerator to today's dollars; thus inflation is taken care of. Additionally, any risk premium on the cost of capital is also incorporated into the denominator.

When the results are calculated if the NPV is zero or greater, the manager can make the investment because all three imperatives are met. A zero value means that the project's cash flows discounted back to present value exactly equal the investment cost based on the firm's WACC.

In many firms the need is to make several investments in a given fiscal year so managers would rank the projects from the highest to the lowest NPV. In most cases those projects with the highest NPV get the go-ahead for the investment. This then leads the manager to conclude that he or she is truly a *value-adding manager* because only those investment decisions with the highest NPV are permitted to proceed.

The NPV is also a useful tool in helping managers determine how a CM will impact the share price of the firm. A very simple calculation is to take the number of outstanding shares of stock and divide that into the NPV of a CM to estimate the impact it has on a firm's share price. For example, if a firm had a current share price at the close of trading of $25 and the firm had 1 million shares of stock outstanding and the NPV of the proposed CM was $1 million, the probable share price increase would be $1 (1 million/1 million), making the new share price $26. This is, of course, a theoretical estimate because investors must have confidence in management's decision, the investment world must legitimize this by suggesting that the share price will increase as a result of this investment, and sales of shares of stock will attract more investors.

SUMMARY: THE VALUE-ADDING MANAGER

As you may be concluding at this moment, this entire chapter has been about making estimates of key determinants of the firm's value. These estimates are underpinned by a thorough and effective environmental scanning system. Each of the estimates related to the four pillars is linked to the value drivers, CSFs, demand curve projections, competitor actions, and activities in the task environment. Therefore, one of the most essential skills the strategic manager must possess is to be able to take all of the complex factors and information related to them and synthesize them into appropriate theories of cause and effect relative to the firm. The stronger the manager's ability here, the more probable the right decisions will be made and that investors will have growing confidence in that manager.

DISCUSSION QUESTIONS

1. Provide a thorough understanding of what you understand to be the three imperatives all investors seek from investments in competitive methods.
2. What is a competitive method?
3. Explain how you would go about estimating a firm's cost of capital.
4. What is meant by operating leverage?
5. Link the process of estimating cash flows to the chapters on environmental scanning.
6. Discuss the role of risk in estimating the NPV of investments in competitive methods.
7. Indicate how you interpret the four pillars related to the investment decision.

NOTES

1. For more detailed discussions of these approaches, see any corporate finance textbook.
2. Desna Turnbull, "The Influence of Political Risk Events on the Investment Decisions of Multinational Hotel Companies in Caribbean Hotel Companies" (PhD diss., Virginia Polytechnic Institute and State University, 1996).
3. See Exhibit 10 for the complete formula.

CASE STUDY

Internet Merchant Model: The Internet and E-Commerce and Forces Driving Change

The Internet became part of many people's lives in the mid-1990s. E-commerce swept across the business horizon quickly, and for the hospitality industry, it became one of the major forces driving change. One of the key drivers within this force was third-party Internet booking sites. They increasingly are becoming the bane of the industry up through the early 2000s. Despite the fact that the industry was forewarned, the new intermediaries took control of large blocks of hotel room inventory and drove prices down. The industry is trying to recover by investing in competitive methods to combat this trend.

INTERNET CHANGES HOTEL INVENTORY

The Internet has changed the way how hotels sell their products. Travel is the number-one product sold online.[1] According to the Travel Industry Association of America's (TIA) latest Travelers' Use of the Internet study,[2] more than 64 million online travelers used the Internet in 2003 to attain information on destinations or to check prices or schedules.[3] Of that group, 42 million actually booked travel online. Greater use of the Internet seems to be changing travel patterns.[4] The enhanced accessibility of last-minute specials via the Internet, as well as low prices on last-minute travel, is stimulating later booking patterns.[5] Airline tickets continue to be the most frequently purchased travel products online, reported by 75% of all online travel bookers. This is followed closely by accommodation at 71%, increased from 57% in 2002.[6] Online travel bookers spend an average of $2,600 online in a year, up from $2,300 in 2002.[7]

Electronic hotel bookings show a continued dramatic growth, and there is the continuing importance of global distribution systems (GDS) e-commerce for hotel brands and chains.[8] Internet reservations received at central reservation offices (CROs) of major hotel brands grew 34% in 2003 versus 2002, according to TravelCLICK.[9] An estimated 66% of the brands' centrally booked Internet reservations[10] were made through the brand websites. According to Forrester Research, online hotel bookings will double from $6.9 billion in 2002 to $14.7 billion in 2006.[11] Six Continent's Lowest Internet Rate Guarantee promises that if a consumer finds a lower rate publicly viewable and bookable on another website on the Internet for the same hotel and same dates within 24 hours of booking on Six Continents' site, Six Continents will honor the lower rate and even provide a discount.[12]

Hoteliers describe a third-party online booking with three basic models: the mer-chant model, such as hotels.com and Expedia's Travelscape; a commissionable model offered by all three GDS; and opaque sites such as Priceline and Hotelwire.[13] With the merchant model, hotels assign inventory to third-party sites, which mark up the rooms and sell them.[14] The commissionable model typically pays the seller a 10% fee.[15] Consumers who purchase rooms on opaque sites buy a hotel of a certain quality level in a certain area without knowing the brand until after they pay for it.[16]

INTERCONTINENTAL TO REGAIN ITS INVENTORIES

Hotel companies have been very slow to react to this challenge. They have been criticized for not taking advantage of all the online opportunities that were out there, which has allowed several online intermediaries to come in and establish first-mover advantage.[17] The online distributors, like Expedia, Priceline and Travelocity, and other third-party online bookers, are becoming agents rather than suppliers. They provided much needed volume during the recent troubled years following 9/11 by filling up distressed inventory and ensuring much-needed cash flow.[18] There has also been considerable industry consolidation, with certain intermediaries becoming more powerful and starting to dominate the sale of travel online.[19]

In defending its position against the new intermediaries, global hotel giant Intercontinental Hotels Group (IHG) decided to take control with its *Best-Rate Guarantees* and a range of other promises aimed at making the consumer book directly with the company.[20] It promised to match any third-party online distributors' rates for consumers who booked on the company's websites.[21] The promises included the lowest rate, no booking fees, and privacy.[22] Management thought that if people book online through an intermediary, they have control of the customer and they will probably book there again.[23] For hotel companies, this means that they would lose the chance to interact and engage in customer-relationship management.

Global hotel groups are getting tough in their fight to regain their inventories from online third-party bookers.[24] IHG was the first chain to cut ties with Expedica.com and sister company Hotels.com.[25] This was followed by a stern warning to the online merchants from Hilton International.[26] Intercontinental is a manager of brands, it franchises more than 90% of its hotels.[27] To protect the value of its brands, IHG established a set of certification criteria in 2004, which developed the rules that third parties must adhere to when distributing its inventory online.[28] In so doing, IHG wants to make sure that the business is incremental business to justify the commissions paid to the online brokers.[29] About 70% of its businesses are racked, which leave the remaining 30% for third-party intermediaries.

The hotels would like to see online brokers share the risk over the inventory and payment terms as traditional travel agencies, such as American Express and Carlson Wagonlit, do.[30] IHG has adopted a new standard for its portfolio of brands for selling or reselling room inventory "via any and all online travel companies."[31] IHG will work only with distributors who agree to display all available room inventories, ensure reservations are guaranteed through an automated and common confirmation process, respect IHG's trademarks, and not engage in confusing and potentially unclear marketing practices.[32] The binding standard also means that room inventory at all IHG brand properties will not be accessible to distributors that are not certified. The group certifies Travelocity and Travelocity Business as third-party distributors for its more than 3,500 hotels worldwide.[33]

Similarly, Hilton International has introduced guidelines for working with online providers on "supplier-friendly terms" with lastminute.com and Travelocity, and it is in continuing discussions with Expedia.[34] Less than 20% of Hilton International's business comes through third-party online intermediaries.[35]

THIRD-PARTY INTERMEDIARIES

Smith Travel Research estimates that $1 billion in profits has changed hands from suppliers to online intermediaries.[36] The top-ten third-party websites sharing in this profit for hotel bookings to brands were Priceline, Expedia, Travelocity, Orbitz, Hotwire, TravelNow, USA Hotelguide, Lodging, Woldres, and Southwest.

From the perspective of the Internet intermediaries such as Expedia, most of their business goes to independent hotels,[37] but they also would like the partnership with the brand names and hotel chains, such as Marriott, Le Meridian, and Disney. The online intermediaries consider that they add value to independent hotels, and perhaps less to the chain hotels, and that they assume a huge marketing risk.[38] They may own the customers the first time,[39] and after that hotels have the same access to the customers as the online brokers. They consider themselves as a normal travel player with the same type of costs of any other travel player.[40] It is just different from offline players because their customers shop online and while they pay less on brochures because it is online, but they claim that they pay more for advertising on the Internet.[41]

While the major hotel chains are struggling to regain lost ground and revenues, the smaller players, such as midsize global groups Le Meridien Hotels & Resorts and small regional players including Jumeirah International,[42] regard the online intermediaries as welcome partners to give them the visibility online and enable them to compete on a level playing field. These smaller firms do not have the marketing funding or the expertise to cater to customers who like booking online. Third-party online distributors enable them to reach market and customers that they do not have access otherwise. The online business is allowing them to maintain their independence in a world that is brand conscious.[43]

THIRD PARTIES UNDER THREAT

In 2004 there was considerable growth for brand websites, at the expense of merchant and opaque websites.[44] Of all the reserva-tions made through websites, 30.7% were made through the Internet in 2004. This is compared to 27.1% in 2003. Internet reser-vations include brand websites, retail websites, and opaque websites. The remain-ing 69.7% of the reservations were made through GDS-linked travel agents, elec-tronic, and voice means. Third-party web-sites have lost their share of Internet reservations booked on hotel company websites.[45] Because hotel companies have fought back against third-party intermedi-aries, they have stemmed the tide. The key question then becomes "Are these efforts truly adding value to the enterprise?"

DISCUSSION QUESTIONS

1. Explain why the hotel companies' responses to third-party intermediaries are considered competitive methods.
2. Identify the key value drivers used to deter-mine the cash flow streams associated with investments of this type.
3. What factors may influence the cost of cap-ital associated with investments of this type?
4. Are there any unique risk factors to be considered with investments of this type?

5. How would you effectively determine the life cycle of this investment?
6. Examine whether or not the intermediaries have the same value drivers as the hotel companies.
7. Discuss the similarities and difference between the independent hotels and the chain hotels regarding the investment in competitive methods.
8. Discuss the challenges with identifying cash flows associated with such a complex com-petitive method.

NOTES

1. S. Shellum, "Friends or Foes?" *Hotel Asia Pacific* 6, no. 2 (2005): 16–20.
2. Travel Industry Association of America, "Online Travel Booking Jumps in 2002, Despite Plateau in Online Travel Planning" (2002). Retrieved from http://www.tia.org.
3. Travel Industry Association of America, "TIA Shows Continued Growth in Online Travel Bookers; Nearly One-Third Book All Their Travel Online" (2004). Retrieved from http://www.tia.org.
4. Ibid.
5. Anonymous, "Online Booking Continues to Grow (Focus: Business Hospitality)," *Westchester County Business Journal,* February 9, 2004.
6. Ibid.
7. Ibid.
8. J. Macharia, "Online Reservation: The Path to Tread," *The African Executive,* 2007. 21–28 February.
9. Ibid.
10. TravelCLICK. "Major Hotel Chains Grew Internet Reservations by 34% in 2003; TravelCLICK Reports eTRAK Results from 30 Leading Brands" (2004). Retrieved from www.travelclick.net.

11. "Six Continents Touts Online Initiatives" (Online Marketing), *Lodging Hospitality,* February, 2003.
12. Ibid.
13. R. Shaw, "Booking Sites Create Challenges, Opportunities," *Hotel & Motel Management,* 2002.
14. Ibid.
15. Ibid.
16. Ibid.
17. Op. cit., no. 1.
18. Ibid.
19. Ibid.
20. Ibid.
21. Ibid.
22. Ibid.
23. Ibid.
24. Anonymous, "Global Giants Get Tough with Online Merchants," *Hotel Asia Pacific* 5, no. 6 (2004): 26.
25. Ibid.
26. Ibid.
27. Op. cit., no. 1.
28. Ibid.
29. Ibid.
30. S. Shellum, "Small Mercies," *Hotel Asia Pacific* 6, no. 3 (2005): 22–24.
31. Op. cit., no. 24.
32. Ibid.
33. InterContinental Hotels Group, "InterContinental Hotels Group Certifies Travelocity; Discontinues Relationship with Expedia and Hotels.com" (2004). Retrieved from http://www.ichotelsgroup.com.
34. Op. cit., no. 30.
35. Ibid.
36. Op. cit., no. 1.
37. Ibid.
38. Ibid.
39. Ibid.
40. Ibid.
41. Ibid.
42. Op. cit., no. 30.
43. Ibid.
44. Anonymous, "Major Hotel Chains Grow Internet Reservations over 22% in 2004, Brand Websites Increase Volume of Reservations over 31%," April 5, 2005. *Internet Wire.* http://www.activatordesk.com/IWire9202000
45. Ibid.

ADDITIONAL REFERENCES

Anonymous. 2003. "Six Continents Touts Online Initiatives." *Lodging Hospitality* 59, no. 2: 42.
———. 2005. "Hotel's Branded Sites Clawing Back Online Bookings." *Hotel Asia Pacific* 6, no. 4: 28–29.

Shellum, S. 2004. "Online Bookings Soar." *Hotel Asia Pacific* 6, no. 3: 30.

Choosing Competitive Methods

Portfolios of Products and Services

Choosing Competitive
Methods

Learning Objectives

Upon completion of this chapter, you will:

1. Define a competitive method (CM) as a portfolio of products and services.
2. Understand the role of CMs in adding value to the firm.
3. Evaluate the CM as an investment in the future.
4. Understand the nature of the economic life span of a CM.
5. Be capable of conducting an analysis of current and future CMs.
6. Have an appreciation of the challenge of limited resources when many investments in CMs are needed.
7. Understand how investments in CMs affect the market value of the firm.

Key Concepts

Defining the competitive method (CM)

Choosing CMs

CMs as investments

The value-adding role of CMs

Life cycle of CMs

From Chapter 8 of *Strategic Management in the Hospitality Industry*, Third Edition, Michael D. Olsen, Joseph J. West, Eliza Ching Yick Tse. Copyright © 2008 by Pearson Education, Inc. Published by Pearson Prentice Hall. All rights reserved.

Chapter Purpose

In this chapter we define the competitive method and elaborate on its role in achieving strategic success for the hospitality enterprise.

Investing in Opportunity: The Choice of Competitive Methods

This chapter focuses on the choice of competitive methods (CMs) that the firm decides will make up its overall strategy as it seeks to compete effectively in the environment making up its domain. This component of the coalignment model is illustrated in Exhibit 1 in the symbol that is magnified. The overall strategy of a firm begins with the decisions management makes regarding what type of business it wants to be in. In the hospitality industry this could include competing in the quick-service or casual theme restaurant segments of the foodservice industry, in the economy or luxury segments of the hotel industry, or in some element of the tourism industry. This decision on what segment to compete in is determined by the analysis of the environment. Once the segment is chosen, success competing in this environment is determined by the total array of CMs that the firm invests in. This chapter focuses on the concepts underpinning CMs.

Defining the Competitive Method and Related Concepts

A CM is a portfolio of products and services bundled in such a way that it attracts those customers from within the overall demand curve of the industry. Service industry firms offer a large number and variety of products and services creating many unique CMs. Many of the CMs are intangible and difficult to produce consistently over time, but by and large represent the firm's unique offerings as it tries to compete within its domain. Each CM must however reflect the fact that it is linked to the opportunities and threats within the environment and at the same time produce the needed returns sought by investors. Exhibit 2 illustrates this relationship.

Unique Bundles of Products and Services

Exhibit 2 stresses the alignment between the environment and the CMs while pointing out that in service industry settings, firms attempt to bundle products and services together in unique ways. It is this unique bundling that offers firms the opportunity to sustain competitive advantage and is very much a part of the strategic thinking process. Examples may include such concepts as room service in the hotel combining products such as menu items with individualized services when the items are brought to the room. Some hotels have adopted the individual butler concept where the customer only interacts with one customer contact employee throughout his or her stay. The butler combines the unique products and services the customer desires. In the travel

EXHIBIT 1   Strategic Management Model

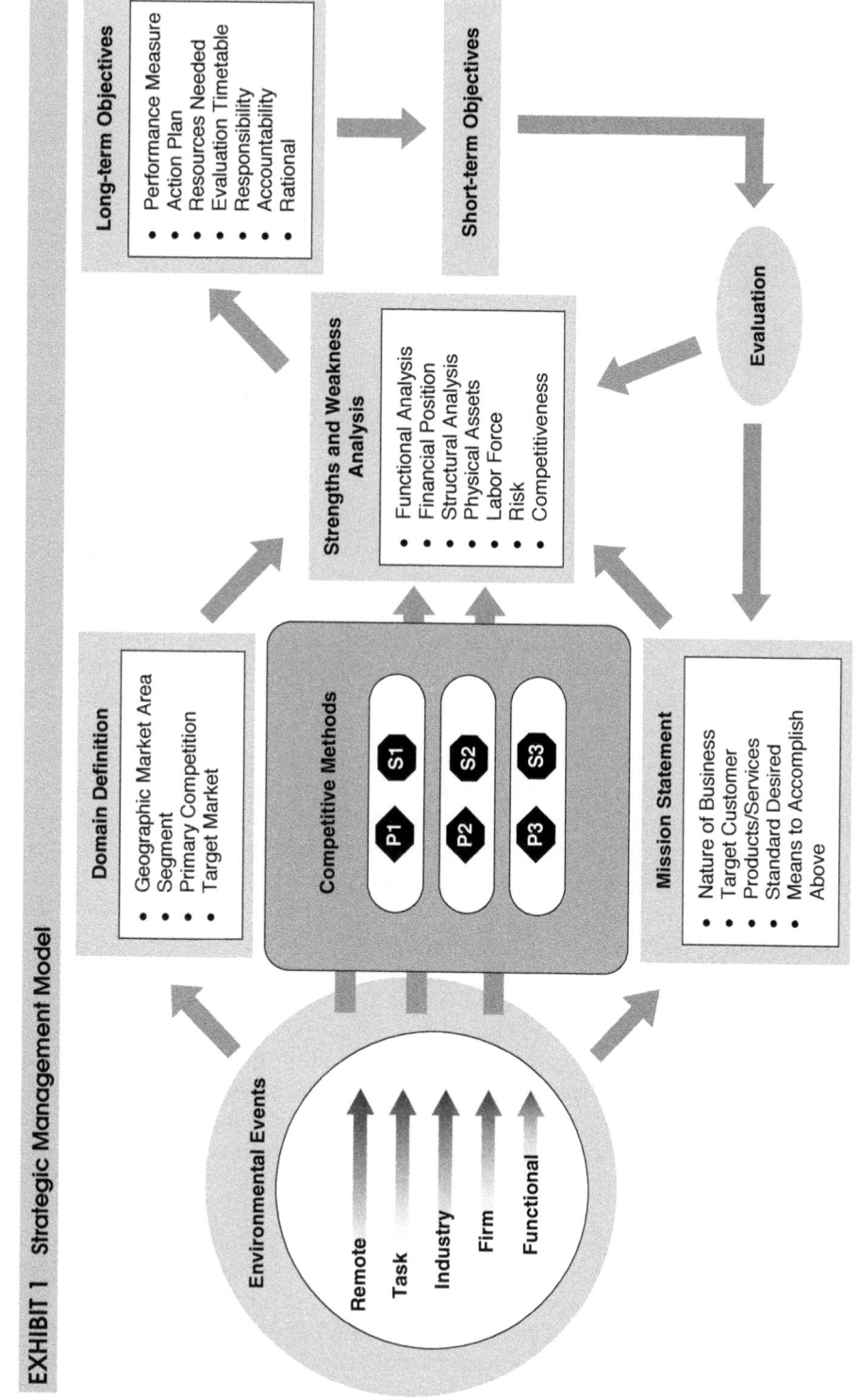

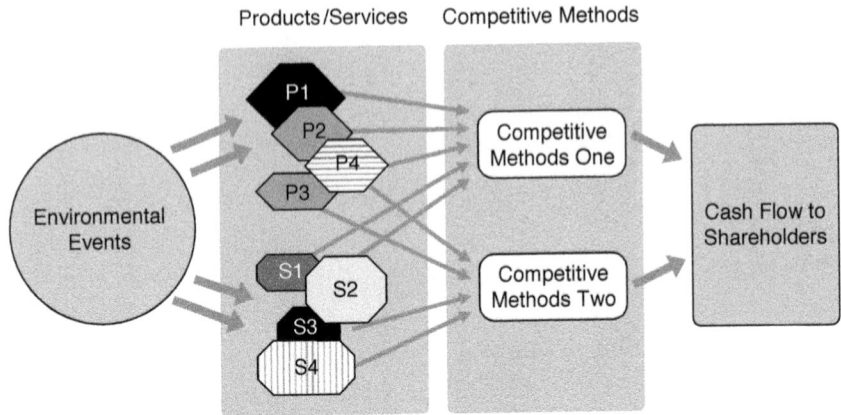

EXHIBIT 2   Competitive Methods as Combinations of Goods and Services

industry, firms like Expedia, the online travel agency, have moved toward packaging complete trips for individuals based on their desires for certain services and products.

Because many service enterprises offer numerous, perhaps hundreds of possible combinations of products and services, the CM becomes the primary way that they can differentiate themselves from other firms and seek to achieve sustainable competitive advantage. In fact, the more a firm is able to bundle its products and services into truly unique CMs, which others will find hard to duplicate, the greater the chance of achieving profitable and sustainable advantage.

The concept of CMs, therefore, is not a simple one. Bundles of products and services, both tangible and intangible, do not lend themselves to precise definitions. The approach taken within this text to try to address this challenge is that a CM must result in increased revenue for the firm. That is, each CM must appeal to the customer in the marketplace and serve as the main reason why that customer is willing to part with his or her money. Its outcome is directed toward top-of-the-line performance.[1] In other words, *the CM is a revenue producer that has strong market appeal and can offer the firm competitive advantage.*

A CM must be unique to the individual firm. Therefore, industry critical success factors (CSFs) cannot really be included in the explanation of a CM because by the definition given in earlier chapters, CSFs are essential to all firms in an industry if a firm expects to compete successfully in an industry sector. A manager of a service firm must perform well on all or most CSFs. Because all firms have them, they cannot be thought of as unique revenue generators that offer the firm competitive advantage. In fact, if the firm does not possess them, they may actually experience a decline in revenues.

A firm that seeks to achieve industry leadership with respect to one or more CSFs can then claim that these CSFs are performing as CMs because they are outperforming the industry in this case and presumably bringing about increased revenue streams as a result. For example, for many years Marriott International has claimed leadership in loyalty programs and reservation systems, both of which are considered industrywide CSFs. And because Marriott has enjoyed better performance on occupancy and average daily room rate compared to others, it can really consider its investments in both as CMs. *For a firm to consider a CSF as a CM it must lead the industry, and this leadership must result in improved return on invested capital over time.*

CMs have distinct economic lives. Seldom is it the case that a service firm develops unique CMs that are not immediately copied by all those who are in the sector, especially if they have proven to be good revenue and cash flow generators. The life of a CM is linked to several key variables such as the forces driving change as identified in the remote environmental analysis (and demonstrated in Exhibits 1 and 2), value drivers, competitor actions, and demand curve makeup.

The Life Cycle of Industries, Organizations, and Competitive Methods

If firms are to continue to add value, management must understand the concept of life cycle. This biological metaphor suggests that industries, firms, and CMs have finite lives. Although unlike humans, it is possible to sustain the life cycles of these entities for extended periods with good planning and future-oriented management. Exhibits 3 and 4 illustrate the application of this concept to organizations. As can be seen in Exhibit 3, most entities begin with the inception phase and move to transition and then toward decline. The transition stage can consist of either growth or decline.

Inception usually begins with a great idea or concept by entrepreneurs who turn it into reality. Ray Kroc of McDonald's is a good case in point. From a single-unit restaurant serving hamburgers, he took a concept through growth and made it into the largest retail foodservice company in the world. This company has enjoyed unprecedented growth for over 50 years. Today, it continues to lead the industry in many ways and sets the pace with respect to industrywide CSFs and CMs, which help it to enjoy a long and successful life.

EXHIBIT 3 Organization Life Cycle

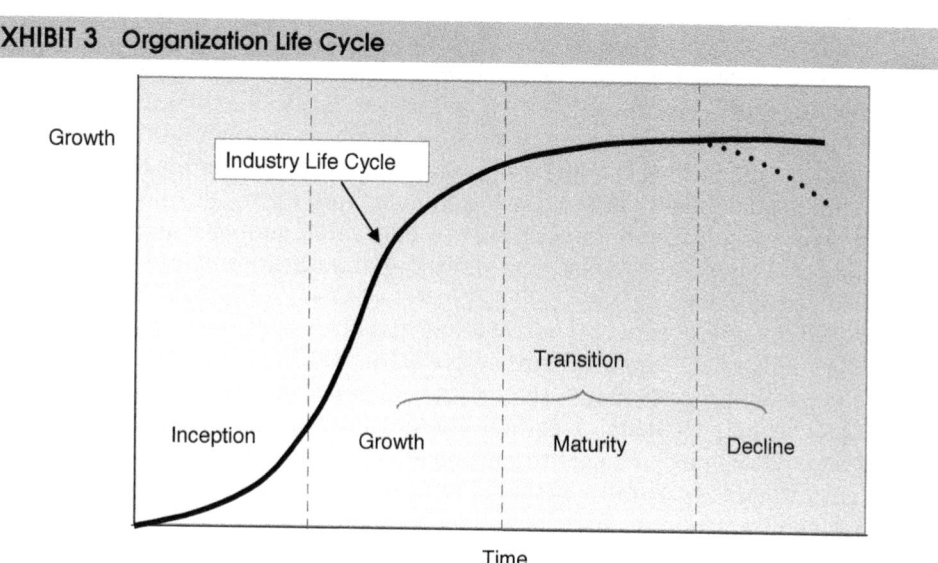

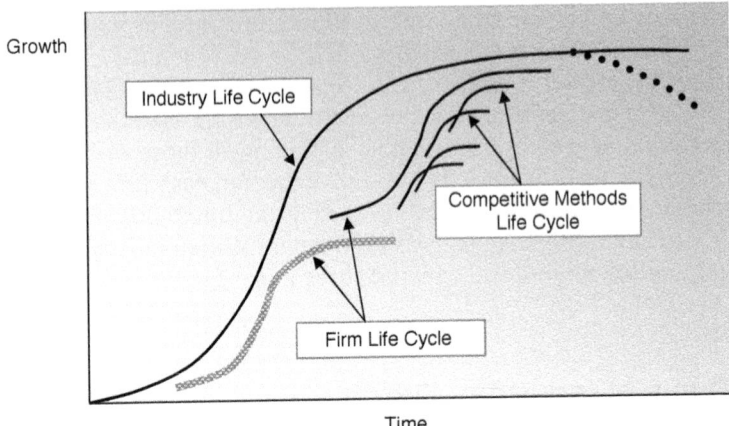

Growth

Industry Life Cycle

Competitive Methods
Life Cycle

Firm Life Cycle

Time

EXHIBIT 4   Industry, Organization, and Competitive Method Life Cycles

McDonald's led the development of the entire quick-service restaurant industry, always enjoying competitive advantage by maintaining its leadership position. It was in an ideal posture: an innovative firm, leading the development of an entire industry. Its CMs were always at the forefront of industry ideas. By being able to lead the industry it was always able to extend the life of its CMs, which in-turn allowed the organization itself to enjoy a healthy, value-adding life. This was accomplished in part by the regular introduction of new products and services that led the industry.

After being responsible for creating the quick-service restaurant industry, McDonald's must now compete in it along with many firms. The growth that was experienced in the early stages has now given way to maturity, creating an extremely competitive environment for all players. This environment is seen as actually shortening the life cycles of all the firms unless they work hard at staying ahead of consumer demands. This generally means creating new CMs more often. Exhibit 4 illustrates this relationship.

The quick-service restaurant industry curve is illustrated as the largest curve covering the longest period of time. In the case of McDonald's, it can be said that this company initiated this curve and industry. As other firms entered the industry, they too enjoyed a life cycle depending on how early, or late, they entered. Obviously, the earlier the entry, the longer the potential economic life cycle to be enjoyed. As the industry became crowded, maintaining growth and value-adding capability became more difficult. Exhibit 4 is simplified to show only the relationship of two firms in this very crowded industry.

The smallest set of curves represents the lifespan of the CMs of each firm. As the figure illustrates, the curves are nested under the curve of the firm. Observing this relationship suggests that as the industry matures, the ability of a firm to grow value is increasingly challenged, and the lives of the CMs it invests in grow increasingly shorter. Thus the challenge for management in this environmental context is to recognize where their firm is situated and to make investment decisions in CMs that reflect this position. For firms that find themselves in mature industries with extended life cycles, the more the strategic emphasis of management must be on investing in industry-leading CMs because so many of the previous CMs have now turned into CSFs. This puts greater strain on management to be creative in how it plans to compete in the future.

The concept of life cycle provides a useful link between the elements of environment and strategy choice in the coalignment model. For it is the importance of the environment and the ability of the firm's management to scan that environment correctly that will allow it to identify the industry-leading CMs that will add value early in the cycle and allow it to maintain it over the longest life possible. Therefore, knowing where the firm and its CMs are relative to the industry and all competitors is a fundamental necessity for tomorrow's manager.

The concept of the life cycle is a very intangible one. Judging the length of life of new ideas, investments, firms, or industries is full of uncertainty. There appear to be no scientific rules to guide this activity, thus leaving the estimation process up to management. As you will recall, we briefly mentioned life cycle in the chapters on the environment, and as a tool to assist in the process of scanning we introduced the concept of value drivers. We once again suggest that they can be useful in assessing the life cycles of CMs as well as firms and the industries they compete in. In doing so, managers must seek to always understand what value drivers are most closely linked to the analysis in question.

For example, research has indicated that there are four specific value drivers that have a high degree of association with the operational cash flow stream of casual theme restaurants. By tracking these value drivers, it is expected that managers would begin to understand how they could impact the firm in both the short term and long term, with the long-term analysis being linked to the possible life cycles of certain menu items or the restaurants themselves. The key here is to always be vigilant as to what the value drivers are and then track them over time to study their impact on life cycle. This is another example of the strategic thinking that managers are expected to perform when making the correct investment decision.

It must be remembered that the life cycle is an important determinant relative to estimating the cash flow streams associated with an investment in a CM. In looking at a typical cash flow estimate, management must indicate the number of years or periods that the investment will cover. This is, in fact, the estimate of the life cycle. Failure to estimate the cash flow stream accurately may result in investments being accepted by management that actually produce negative value or could underestimate the value addition they bring. Life cycle estimation and the accompanying cash flow streams often require the manager to rely on scientific processes and techniques as well as a little good luck because it is very difficult to accomplish successfully. Here again, value drivers can assist managers in this difficult task.

Exhibit 5 provides a look at how the life cycle may be assessed and estimated. This form helps management organize its thoughts as it seeks to do the difficult work of estimating the life cycle of a CM. As can be seen, the second column asks the manager to identify the value drivers that are linked to a specific CM. These value drivers would have been identified in the scanning process and serve to help the manager decide that there is opportunity associated with an investment in a particular CM. The column heading specifically calls for industry value drivers because it is important for the manager to determine where his or her firm is at relative to the industry so the manager can determine the potential life. As indicated in Exhibit 4, if the investment

EXHIBIT 5 Estimating the Life Cycle of Competitive Methods

Competitive method	Indicate industry value drivers supporting this life cycle estimate and their forecast	Implementation		Competitor response/capability Be sure to include financial capability to respond	Number of periods
		Market lead time	Set up time		
Cleanness and Food Safety	Health and food safety related issues being one of the major forces driving change. • Suppliers are pressured to deliver hazard free products. • Governments appeared as the main regulators for the quick service restaurant segment. • Growing reliance on HACCP regulations • Growing incidences of food borne related diseases Globalization of the food supply	McDonald's was quick to respond to food chain quality control immediately following the outbreak of mad cow disease. It was at least 6 months ahead of the competition.	It took at least one year to achieve chain wide implementation across 30,000 units.	Yum Brands Taco Bell responded quickly. It has sufficient free cash flow to make the necessary investments and therefore becomes the primary competitive threat to the McDonald's program.	This will be a continuing life CM since it is already an industry CSF. Since McDonald's has taken the lead in this regard the forecast period is only 2 years given the response by Taco Bell and the fact that many regulatory authorities will make it a requirement within the next 2–5 years.

in a CM comes late in a life cycle it will not enjoy a very long economic life, resulting in the potential of insufficient returns.

Column 3 is headed "market Lead Time and Setup Time," which refers to how long the firm has to bring an idea to the marketplace. Setup time refers to the time it takes to actually implement the CM across the firm and its units. Market lead time includes the market research and testing that normally accompanies a CM. This can range from a few weeks in the case of a simple menu item to more than a year if a firm is bringing out a new hotel or restaurant brand. During this market lead time the manager should expect that competitors will already be looking at what the firm is doing to be sure that they do not fall too far behind on the competitive landscape.

Setup time can often take years. For example, with McDonald's having approximately 30,000 units worldwide, any new CM must be introduced into that many markets. This involves company owned or managed units and those of franchisees. If construction or investment is involved, this could stretch the time horizon because there is a chance that permits will have to be secured and financing found. Then there is training time. These are important dimensions of the life cycle because the CM may not be producing positive cash flows during these two critical periods.

Column 4 refers to anticipated competitor response. As we have stated elsewhere in this text, strategy is not only about what the firm intends to do, it is also about how the firm responds to competitors or how competitors respond to the firm's actions. There is no easy way to approach the information needed for this column because it is almost impossible for managers to get all the competitive intelligence they need about each and every competitor. However, there are ways of making educated guesses. Using all the information obtained in the analysis of the task environment, managers can improve their assessment here. Of particular importance is the financial capability of the competitor. They may desire to copy a CM, but if they do not have the financial resources then this should give the firm a little more life to the CM.[2] Here is where effective environmental scanning will really become important.

Given the information in the exhibit and some good inductive thinking, the manager should then be able to make better judgments about the potential life cycle of any CM. Realizing that this estimation process is still more of an art than a science, managers should do all that they can to gather as much information (as detailed in the task environment analysis) as possible to have a stronger underpinning to their estimates.

The Process of Choosing and Evaluation of Competitive Methods

The natural flow of the thinking associated with the coalignment model suggests that after the manager has thoroughly assessed both the remote and task environments, decisions must be made regarding what CM to invest in within the context of its domain, especially those that will drive future value. There are two reviews that must take place in this regard. First, the firm must determine whether or not it is currently providing CMs that meet the three investor imperatives. Secondly, is the firm maximizing the value from existing CMs, or does it need to work on unleashing value that may be trapped in each?

Before engaging in the evaluation process of determining new CMs, managers must perform a thorough evaluation of how they are performing on the industry's list of CSFs. We do want to stress how essential it is to conduct a cash flow analysis of each CSF because investments in maintaining performance on each CSF requires the use of the firm's resources. Each CSF must be evaluated and ranked according to how much it contributes to firm value so management can make informed decisions on how best to invest its limited funds.

The process of evaluating CMs begins with a careful review of each CM and the current level of cash flow that it generates. The original assumptions behind investing in the CM in the first place must be questioned. Does it still reflect forces driving change? Have the value drivers underpinning it evolved? Has the competitive situation changed? In other words, is this CM still in alignment with the environment? Additionally, the cash flows originally forecast should be compared to the actuals to determine if projections have been met. The life cycle must also be evaluated.

If the CM is performing well, then management must probe further to be sure all the value that was originally forecasted has actually been achieved. In this case investigation into the internal resource allocation process takes place to see if costs of implementing the CM can be improved. Additionally, the question must be asked: If demand is still strong, can more revenue be achieved or must new markets be explored? The processes to produce, inventory, and sell the products and services related to the CM must also be looked at to be sure they are reflecting the current best practices in the industry.

The evaluation of current CMs should be an ongoing process with individuals having responsibility for one or more CMs required to update their value-generating potential at regular intervals. Exhibit 6 contains a sample format for this type of evaluation. As can be observed in the exhibit, it is a comprehensive look at current CMs but one that has a strong future orientation to it. As is evident, this is a summary analysis that is used for review and decision-making purposes and it would be supported by sufficient data and research. This form should serve as a guide to all managers who have been given the responsibility for managing a CM. It requires a constant review of all of the products and services bundled into the CM to be sure that they are all still relevant and producing the value expected. This review is done in the context of the forces driving change along with the key value drivers (external and internal) that are causally associated with the force. The estimated stage in the life cycle is also asked for here to be sure that managers are staying on top of the events affecting that life cycle.

Of course, the form also calls for an evaluation of the CM in terms of key performance variables including cash flow and NPV. Other performance indicators are also included in this analysis with specific emphasis on future performance. It is recommended that such analysis be performed at a minimum on a quarterly basis. Given the performance of each CM, it is useful to perform this review on a more regular basis, making sure that all personnel responsible for the CM are given the opportunity to have input into this analysis.

Once the current CMs are evaluated and decisions made regarding their future, then it is up to management to determine what new CMs should be considered. The same type of evaluation occurs here as with current CMs. The objective always is to maximize value, and thus only those that provide the best value over the long term should be considered.

EXHIBIT 6 Evaluation Form for Current Competitive Methods

Name of competitive method:
Bioengineered and genetically modified food products

Products and services:
- Products:
  Vitamin enriched beef patties and beverages, excellent tasting French fires with low transfatty acids and cholesterol reducing, ice cream high in calcium but low in fat
- Services:
  Online nutritional rating of all menu items, custom designed menu format so the customer can individualize the choice of products according to dietary needs

Changes in remote and task environment regarding:
- Forces driving change:
  Aging of the population; shortage in labor force; higher rate of women in the work force; public opinion and health consciousness related to high rate of obesity; decreasing proportion of children; growing scarcity of water resources; increasing global population; demand for healthy food, especially by the aging.
- Value drivers:
  Growing demand for healthy products, links between cost of health insurance and eating habits including weight gain; growing quantity of land devoted to production of modified food products; growing demand for improved agricultural output in the developing world; growing concern over the quality of the global food supply; need to have products withstand the stresses of global shipping; need to reduce variability in the cost of key food ingredients as world demand grows; aging population and demographics leading to demand for this type of food product
- Critical success factors:
  Few established factors at this stage; need to insure sources of supply comply with normative health and safety standards; research and development capabilities; marketing and consumer relations capabilities
- Life cycle:
  This CM is in the initial stages of this life cycle with an estimated life of at least 30 years.

Changes in cash flow estimates and NPV
- Original estimate: $2 billion
- Current performance: negative flows supporting R&D, current NPV is -$250,000

Assessment of the future performance of this competitive method including all key performance indicators
- Given the value drivers underpinning this CM the value adding potential of this CM should meet the original estimate over a 10 year period of time. The key performance indicators here will be consumer acceptance which implies an active consumer research and communication program, strong scientific evidence of the value of these fortified foods including longitudinal data; consumer acceptance with respect to taste, mouth feel and other sensory criteria; will represent 15% of menu item sales by 2012.

Investment Resource Limitations Must Be Considered

When performing this type of analysis, the manager will often find a situation where capital rationing will be present. That is, there is hardly ever enough resources to meet all the investment needs of the firm. The challenge that the manager will face is whether or not to invest in CSFs where the firm is weak or to ignore those needs and go with new ideas that will provide new advantages. These are the types of choice

Investments in *CSFs*	NPV $	Investment required $	Investments in *CM*	NPV $	Investment required $
CSF1	10,000	50,000	CM1	5,000	25,000
CSF2	100,000	40,000	CM2	20,000	150,000
CSF3	1,500,000	800,000	CM3	6,000,000	3,400,000
Total	$1,610,000	$890,000	Total	$6,025,000	$3,575,000

EXHIBIT 7 A Comparison of NPV and Investment Requirements of CSFs and CMs

decisions that managers must make regularly. They are important decisions because resource allocation decisions must go toward those CMs and/or CSFs that create the greatest value. Exhibit 7 contains a look at the firm in which the project list exceeds the resources available.

An examination of the table is revealing. There are three CSFs that management has identified that need investment and three CMs. The total investment required for the CSFs is $890,000 and for the CMs is $3,575,000. If management could make all the investments, the total amount required would be $4,665,000. However, under conditions of capital rationing, the manager only has a budget for all investments this coming year of $1,100,000, considerably less than what is needed.

The manager is now faced with a dilemma. Should he or she invest in CSFs or CMs, or some combination of both? Under the premise that we have put forth so far in the text, investments should be made only in those items that bring in the greatest value. In this example, CM3 is out of the question if only current funds are to be used (this assumes the manager does not seek to raise new debt or equity capital). CF3 will use up a little over half the budget. It appears as though that investment would be made first because it has the highest NPV, followed by CSF2, and then CM2. CSF1 and CM1 would round out the investments using the current budget, leaving $35,000 excess. Of course, the manager could decide to seek additional equity capital as well as debt funds to finance the investment in CM3, but for the moment we assume this is not possible. In this case, all investments can be made except for CM3. If the budget would be lower, the manager would have to make choices, and the simple response would be to go with only those investments that add value by rank according to NPV.

These choice decisions create many challenges for regular businesses and complicate matters for some aspects of the hospitality industry. One of the unique features of the hospitality industry is that hospitality companies very often do not own the assets they are managing. Through a variety of management contracts and lease arrangements along with licensing and franchising agreements, hospitality companies must respond to the needs of the owners of these assets. This includes requiring the manager to understand the needs of the owner with respect to the returns on capital associated with key CMs.

An example may help. When the manager of a hotel operating under a well-known brand was asked why the audiovisual media equipment package was very out of date and why new investments had not been made, his response was that the owner of the hotel would not authorize the investments. Instead, he insisted that new marble sinks be put in the bathrooms of the sleeping rooms of the hotel. When further quizzed as to where most of his business comes from, he was quick to say that 80% came from meetings and conventions. Given that this customer type is very dependent on media to communicate effectively during these events, the logic of the owner's decision seems quite inappropriate, yet the manager was unable to communicate the importance of this CM to the value-generating needs of that owner.

In the preceding example, media capability is really an industry CSF, and in this case it would seem only logical that investments in state-of-the-art technology should be made. However, this manager was ineffective in communicating this to the owner. Although there are several possible reasons for this lack of ability to communicate, a few may help us to understand the situation. First, many managers are not equipped to communicate with owners because they often have no experience as owners themselves and they have accepted a role as an operations manager rather than a value-adding manager. Secondly, they may not possess the necessary conceptual tools to translate their operational needs into investment projects. These two reasons alone account for many of the problems between management companies and owners.

As our example illustrates, there is much to be considered when managing any business and the CMs that serve as the value generators. Here again, the manager is concerned about the best use of the firm's resources both now and in the future. This is part of the strategic thinking that managers must perform daily if they expect to guide the firm successfully into the future. In this type of analysis, any sign that any one of the CMs is not going to continue generating value must be a call to action for managers. Any hesitation here can be troublesome for the firm's performance overall and cannot be tolerated by any of the firm's stakeholders.

Summary: The Value Question Revisited

We now turn to a discussion of the cost of capital and the three imperatives that the manager must address with regard to the investor after having defined the CM within the context of the firm and industry. We address the contribution that each CM makes to the overall value of the firm. In doing so we point out that the job of the manager is to know and understand what CMs add the greatest value now and in the future, and the greater this understanding, the more comfortable investors and employees can feel regarding the direction in which the management is taking the firm.

In revisiting this value-adding dimension, let us remind you that each CM is expected to produce economic value over its entire life. We are also reminded that a firm will have several CMs that make up the strategy choices of the firm. Each of these CMs is valued using the discounted cash flow technique referred to as net present value (NPV). When the NPV of each CM is added to the others, this total should, in a perfect world, add up to the total value of the firm.

Some examples may help. For a corporation like Marriott International, Accor, and other hotel management companies, the discounted cash flow value of all their management contracts are aggregated, and this then approximates the market capitalization of the firm.[3] Put another way, the market views each contract as a separate CM, and when they are aggregated that is what the firm should be valued at, at the present time. Similarly, for publicly traded restaurant firms, the NPV of each restaurant, when aggregated, becomes the market value of the firm.

In the case of a specific hotel or restaurant, the portfolio of CMs within the firm, when aggregated, becomes the determinant of the total value of the firm. Thus, when the management of the firm is thinking of selling, it should try to convince the potential buyer that the firm has some outstanding CMs, each with long lives, and when added together should be considered the selling price of the firm. In terms of current practices in the industry, a similar approach is used by those who appraise businesses (often real estate appraisers), and it is referred to as the market value of the business (another form of discounted cash flow analysis). In this case those doing the valuation of the business simply take figures related to sales and costs and discount that back to present value. In many cases this is acceptable for simple businesses, but we feel it has the potential of not properly representing what drives the value of the hospitality enterprise.

Let's use Exhibit 8 to illustrate the point. The total value of the firm (using our definition of market value of the firm) is represented by the large circle. Think of it as a silver dollar. Remaining consistent with the symbols in use throughout this text, the ovals within the silver dollar are CMs, and their size is proportional to the NPV provided by each. That is, the total market value of the firm is an aggregate of the NPVs of each CM. As you can easily see, there is some blank space within the silver dollar. This suggests that not all of the firm's value can be easily explained by the NPVs of each CM. This is because it is relatively difficult to determine the exact value of all CMs because so many are intangible and thus make it difficult to determine the NPV precisely.

Regardless of the difficulty of estimating the intangible value of CMs, for the manager, it is essential that the value determinants be well understood because part of the coalignment thinking process mandates that management allocate resources to those CMs that create the greatest value. Owners and investors expect managers to know this and to ensure the cash flow generation capability of the CM. Strategic thinking in this case is always directed toward a consistent allocation of resources to those CMs that create the greatest value.

Investors would like to see the silver dollar completely full of CMs because this would imply little risk related to the true value of the firm. That is, the total value of the firm is explained by the CMs used by the firm, leaving very little guesswork as to what creates this value. But most managers would not prefer this transparency because this would suggest that it would be easier for their competitors to better understand how they have created value. This could affect their ability to maintain sustainable competitive advantage and leave the firm vulnerable to competitive attack.

If, for example, competitors knew that a particular CM of their chief rival firm was the primary determinant of the firm's value, but the life of that CM was growing short, they could exploit this opportunity to try to take competitive advantage away from that firm. Similarly, decisions about what CMs to invest in can be improved if competitors had a more complete blueprint of the value determinants of their own firm compared to others.

This type of analysis leads to the heart of the strategic thinking process. That is, firms must make choices regularly as to where to put their resources. Knowing how value is created within the firm and in those of the competition enhances the decision-making process. It must be stressed here that estimating value of each CM and that of the competitors is just that, an estimation process with great potential for error. Some of the error can be minimized if that manager really knows his or her industry and can make proper assumptions about the value drivers underpinning each CM.

Exhibit 8 also indicates the presence of a dotted line around the silver dollar. That dotted line represents the imperative that investors seek. Simply put, they expect that dollar to grow in value on a consistent basis. This implies that managers are expected to grow more value out of each CM and add new ones when possible. Consequently, *the coalignment process is dynamic in the sense that managers must manage each CM to be sure that it continues to generate cash flows and each CM grows in value.* This means a constant scanning effort regarding each CM and a continual evaluation to be sure the CM receives the necessary resources required to allow it to produce and grow. This implies that if the CM is no longer viable, it should be eliminated from the portfolio as soon as possible and replaced with new ones.

Successful CMs often are those that are difficult to imitate by competitors. As Exhibit 8 indicates, there is some overlap among the CMs. This should be viewed as a positive strategic move. First, by allowing this overlap it is possible that firms can leverage resources across several CMs. Second, this overlap keeps the competitors from completely understanding how value is created, thus making it difficult for them to copy. This is especially important in service firms where many services can be copied easily.

In trying to understand fully the value of any firm, financial analysts often comment on the difference between the book value of the firm and its market value. They look at the balance sheet and see an accounting value of say $100 million but when they multiply the number of shares outstanding times the share price the value is $800 million. How is the difference of $700 million explained? As suggested earlier, part of this may be the intangibles such as patents, licenses, copyrights, intellectual capital, and so on. The gap, however, is large, which would make investors nervous. They would continue to apply pressure to managers to explain this difference. This of course was

EXHIBIT 8   Market Value of Firm as Estimated by Aggregating NPVs of CMs

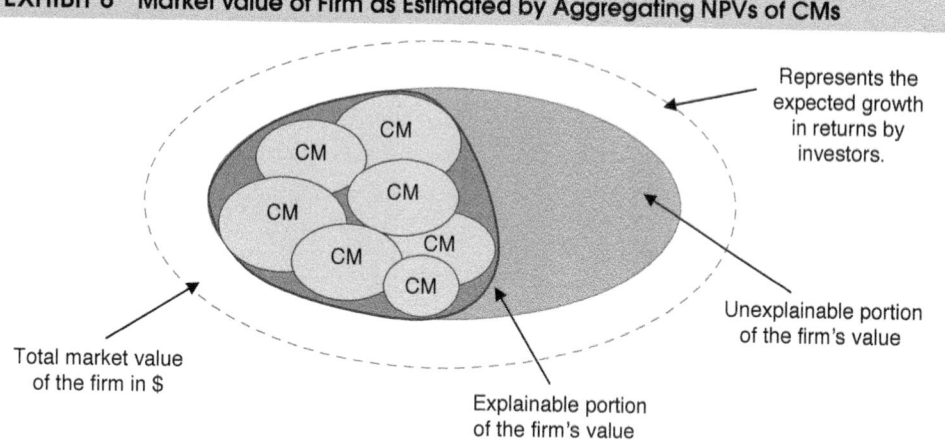

the problem in the so-called dot.com valuations of the late 1990s and now has investors very skeptical about such gaps.

The difference between book and market value is usually treated as goodwill on the balance sheet and most often results from mergers, acquisitions, or buyouts. This difference is often a reflection of the difference between what the firm was valued at and what it was actually sold for. This difference, if it was higher, is referred to as a *premium*. Whatever the cause, investors like to see more of that silver dollar filled in than not. Thus managers must communicate to all stakeholders how value is created and how they expect to maintain and grow that value.

To sum up this subsection and to use an overworked phrase, the "bottom line" here is that managers must meet the three imperatives if the "silver dollar" metaphor is to become reality. Growth is mandatory for those companies whose shares of stock are traded in the public equity markets; otherwise investors will look elsewhere. This can only be accomplished through wise investments in CMs that have sustainable value.

DISCUSSION QUESTIONS

1. Define competitive methods
2. Provide a definition of the life cycle of a competitive method and link the life cycle to environmental scanning.
3. Discuss managements role in reviewing the performance of current competitive methods.
4. How should the manager make a choice among, CSFs, current CMs and future CMs in the context of scarce resources?
5. Explain how a firm can explain its market value using the concept of competitive methods and the NPV.
6. How can management achieve the growth in market capitalization desired by investors?

NOTES

1. Top of the line is a metaphor for the cash flow statement in which top of the line refers to sales or revenue figures.
2. This type of analysis is often referred to as "gaming theory" where executives try to anticipate the competitive responses of their competitors as they seek to reach an important CM decision.
3. Market capitalization is simply defined in this case as number of shares of stock outstanding times the share price of that stock.

EXHIBIT 9 Relationship of Value Drivers Making Up a Force Driving Change and Competitive Methods Chosen with Subsequent Impact on the Cash Flow Stream of the Firm

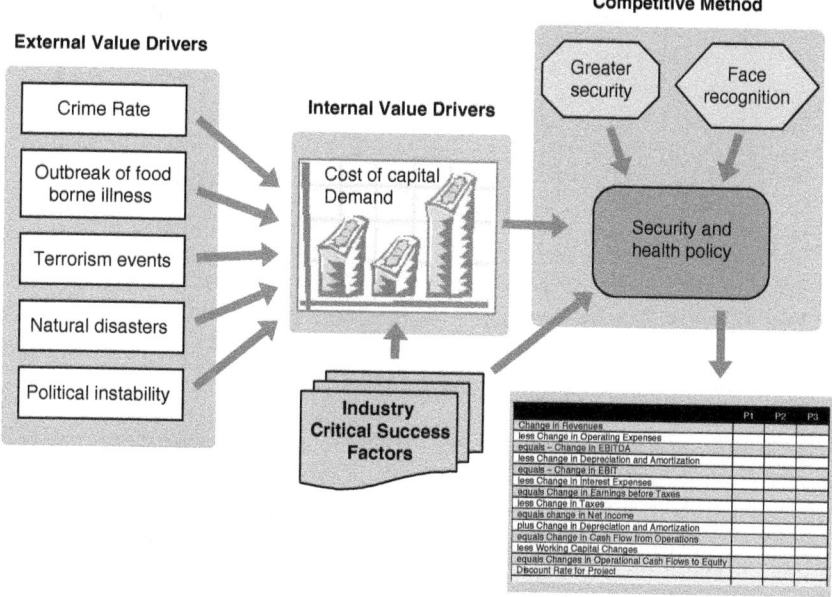

CASE STUDY

Accor Expansion Strategy in Asia

ASIA AS THE KEY FOCUS OF HOTEL EXPANSION

As North American and European markets reach saturation with fierce competition, leading players of the hotel industry are targeting Asia for their future growth. This is because the Asia Pacific region offers excellent growth prospects, with China as the driving force. According to the World Tourism Organization, China will become the world's top tourist destination by 2020. China's National Tourism Administration statistics indicates that inbound arrivals in China will reach 210 million within the next two decades and total tourist income will be about US $302 billion, or 8% to 11% of gross domestic product. In other words, China offers the greatest potential for future growth in inbound, outbound, and domestic travel.[1]

The Pacific Asia Travel Association (PATA) 2004 statistics indicated that arrivals of international visitors to 30 Asia Pacific destinations increased 21%, with an additional 15.3 million visitors to the region. The severe acute respiratory syndrome (SARS) effect was devastating to tourism; however continued economic growth in the region, especially in China, has promoted more business travel and given its people more leisure time and disposable income for travel. According to MasterCard's MasterIndex of Travel in 2004, confidence has returned among travelers and the tourism industry. Travelers continue to engage in both personal and business trips, increasingly within the Asia Pacific region, with Singapore, Thailand, and China emerging as the top destinations.[2]

Following the SARS outbreak in 2003, the travel and tourism industry has worked hard to recapture the pre-SARS momentum in bringing back business travelers and investors to the area.[3] Major global hotel companies began to implement aggressive expansion plans for the region.[4] After years of competing in the high-end segment of the mainland market, some international hoteliers are looking to penetrate the budget sector, which is growing strongly due to domestic travel increases.[5] Hilton International plans to become a major player in the region's leisure market by increasing the number of Hilton Worldwide Resorts to 13 properties.[6] It announced that it will accelerate its expansion with new hotels in Sydney and Kuala Lumpur, Malaysia, that were previously slowed down due to the SARS health crisis.[7] InterContinental is also expanding its diversified hotel brands of luxury and budget brands. InterContinental operates about 3,300-plus properties worldwide under the InterContinental, Crowne Plaza, Holiday Inn, and other brands.[8] It also launched its Holiday Inn Express budget brand in Shanghai and Beijing. IHG is targeted to open at least 80 hotels in Asia in 2005, half of which were slated for China, including properties at the upper upscale, upscale, and midprice price points.[9]

Best Western plans to boost its number of budget hotels to 100 by 2007.[10] Best Western has identified Asia, specifically

China, as the key geographic region for significant brand growth.[11] Its plans project more than 50 new hotels in 2004 and 2005. Its ambitious plans call for 100 hotels in China by 2007.[12] Hyatt, which operated four hotels in China in 2003, has seven more under construction,[13] which includes Hyatt Regency and Park Hyatt brands. By 2013 Hyatt is aiming to have 38 hotels in China, Hong Kong, Macau, and Taiwan.[14] Marriott is focusing on international brand expansion, and Asia is a key to boosting revenues from outside the United States.[15] The JW Marriott brand will continue to move into secondary cities in Asia.[16] In 2003 Marriott operated more than 500 hotels outside the United States, compared with just 16 in 1991.[17]

ACCOR THRIVES IN HARSH TIMES

In 2003 the lodging and tourism industry experienced a decline in reservations around the world due to a combination of global economic downturn, the SARS epidemic, and the war in Iraq.[18] Most companies, such as the Hilton Group, Marriott, and InterContinental, experienced a sharp drop in sales due to the decline of luxury tourism and high-end business travel.[19] The uncertainty in the external environment brought on by these incidents convinced management of the dangers of relying solely on a network of five-star hotels and an international clientele.[20] Accor has recorded better sales than its rivals. Accor's achievement is primarily due to its diversified portfolio strategy with emphasis upon budget properties. While traditional hotel markets were suffering a decline, budget hotels and the backpacker market was actually increasing. With more than 90% of its business coming from low- and midpriced hotels, including Europe's Ibis and America's Motel 6 and Red Roof Inns, Accor has been able to achieve balanced growth despite uncertainty in the environment.[21]

SIZE AND SCOPE OF ACCOR

A recent survey undertaken by MKG Consulting ranked Paris-based Accor as the fourth largest international hotel group in the world. Accor was established in 1966 when French entrepreneurs Paul Dubrule and Brad Pelisson built their first hotel, a 60-room property.[22] Ever since, the company has revolutionized the French domestic market. Accor's corporate philosophy is to maintain a balanced portfolio of hotels ranging from first class to economy.[23] Today, Accor's brands, which include Sofitel (deluxe), Novotel (first class), Mercure (a multitiered midmarket brand), Ibis (economy class), Formule 1 (budget), All Seasons, Urbis, and Pansea cover the full spectrum of accommodation needs from two star to five star in most business and leisure destinations,[24] although there is not a single hotel that carries the name Accor. In 1990 it bought the 550-motel group Motel 6 in the United States, making its room supply total 160,000 rooms.

In 2007 the Accor group has close to 4,000 hotels and resorts globally, and 453,403 rooms in its portfolio. In fact, Accor's hotels spread across 90 countries. Of the approximate 4,000 hotels, Accor operates about 2,500 in the economy sector, generating about a third of the group's revenue and 50% of its profit.[25] Accor, along with other key players in the industry such as Marriott and Starwood, shares the view that they are consumer product companies. Unlike other big brands, such as Promus and Hilton, they concentrate on lodging and engage their expertise in managing an array of different brands.[26] Thus, in addition to operating hotels, Accor also diversifies into a full range of tourism services around the world, with casinos, travel agencies, restaurants, catering, convention center management, and even charter cruises.[27] Accor also provides services to corporate clients and public institutions.[28]

ACCOR EXPANSION IN ASIA

Increasingly, more hotel owners recognize the value of a brand and the importance of international management, which is good news for management companies such as Accor. Taking advantage of the growing middle class of the Asia Pacific area, Accor's expansion strategy aims at supplying the market with affordable accommodations. In just over a decade, Accor has established itself as the largest hotel group in the Asia Pacific region, and it is still actively pursing more acquisitions.[29] Accor has more than 200 hotels in 15 countries, namely Australia, New Zealand, New Caledonia, Cambodia, China, Indonesia, Japan, Korea, Laos, Malaysia, the Philippines, Singapore, Thailand, and Vietnam.[30] Its global reservation system, the Resinter Central Reservation Service, is one of Accor's strengths. Accor is both an owner and a manager/operator of hotels.[31] The company attempts to establish a strong management presence in key regional centers, with much of the decision making centered at the local level. The company invests in both new and existing hotel developments to secure strategic locations. Essentially, the company has built a geographic network of hotels in key commercial and leisure cities, and it has developed a multibrand strategy to satisfy market demand.

Australia

Accor first entered the Asia Pacific region in 1982, established a regional office in Bangkok in 1988,[32] and opened its first hotel in Australia three years later in 1991. In 1992 a deal between the Australian company Quality Pacific Corp. and the French-based Accor SA led to the launch of Accor Asia Pacific (AAPC). AAPC is essentially a hotel operator rather than a hotel owner, although it does have equity in some of its hotels. The company established a good network in Australia but eventually shifts its power base toward Asia.

KOREA AND THAILAND

The pace of Accor's development has increased greatly through joint-venture partnership agreements with major local companies in countries such as Indonesia, Thailand, and the Philippines.[33] Accor has a significant presence in these countries and is providing vehicles for further expansion.[34] Accor Asia Pacific also has gained success in the Korean market with its midmarket strategy. The group is also planning to develop the Ibis brand in Seoul.[35] It offers top-quality services in secure and clean hotels at reasonable prices. The company expands its operation in line with Korea's decentralization policy of moving administration-level government offices away from Seoul, which creates a greater demand for business class hotels in provincial cities such as Taejon.

Before the tragic incident of the tsunami in December 2004, Thailand was Accor's top market of interest after China because of the country's continued success at retaining tourists. Recently, Accor has added the Fortune Hotel Bangkok to its growing network of Mercure properties in Asia in 2004. The hotel is part of an aggressive expansion of the Mercure brand in Asia and is expected to appeal to Accor's customer base around the region. There are now over 750 Mercure hotels worldwide.

China's Three-Prong Strategy

China has a rapidly developing domestic market, while its outbound market is one of the fastest growing in the world.[36] Accor saw the same potential in China as it saw in the French domestic market of the 1960s. Therefore, it entered China's market in 1985. Accor plans a major expansion of hotels, including the introduction of economy hotel brands to China and Korea as part of an Asian-wide focus on building hotel networks for domestic and regional markets.[37] In 2003 Accor Asia Pacific, China National Aviation Holding Company (Air China), and its affiliate, China National Aviation Holding Travel Service Company, signed a Memorandum of Understanding[38] joining forces in sales and marketing activities, such as frequent-flying programs, packaging of product, key account sharing, and market research.[39] In addition, each party extends the partnership to hotel management and cobranding to promote their brands in both the domestic and international markets.[40]

Accor also partners with a range of well-established public and private enterprises,[41] which include the Beijing Tourism Group and JinJiang International Management Corporation.[42] The JinJiang International Group, based in Shanghai, operates 150 hotels and 32,707 rooms in China. The JinJiang agreement involves the management of the Sofitel in Shanghai and also establishes a new sales and distribution network, Accor-JinJiang Hotel Distribution, targeting key national and provincial domestic corporate accounts throughout China.[43] According to David Baffsky, chairman of Accor Asia Pacific, the agreement reflects the importance of China in Accor's future development strategy. In recognition of the impressive achievement of Accor Asia Pacific since 1993 under his leadership, Baffsky was named "Asia Pacific Hotelier of the Year" by the leading property group Jones Lang LaSalle in 2004.

Financially, Accor's expansion is funded by investors such as Colony Capital which has invested US $1.3 billion to fund European and Asian expansion in 2005, including heavy investment in the Chinese market. Twenty years after it entered China in 1985, Accor has 35 hotels under management[44]: 21 Sofitel, 12 Novotel, 2 Ibis, Zenith, and Century. In addition to Shanghai and Beijing, the group is also planning new five-star hotels in Hangzhou, Shenyang, Shijiazhuang, and Chengdu of Sichuan Province, and Anshan as well as four-star hotels in Beijing and Nanjing.[45] There will be seven Accor hotels in Beijing before

2008, one of which, Novotel, will be solely owned by Accor,[46]. This will be the first company wholly owned hotel. Accor plans that their Ibis brand hotels will eventually comprise about half of the group's operations in China.[47]

In summary, Accor devises three main strategies to facilitate its expansion in China:

- Develop the Sofitel and Novotel brands in prime business and leisure locations.
- Develop a chain of economy hotels to cater to the rapidly growing domestic travel segment.
- Identify more strategic partners in its drive to enlarge its share of the domestic and international markets.

MARKET POSITIONING AND COMPETITIVE METHODS

To position itself as an international company, Accor has developed products and competitive methods that are most adaptable to each market segment. It attempts to blend into the local culture of whatever country in which it operates. In South Africa, it started with its budget brand Formula I;[48] in Brazil, it started with its midscale hotels. In the United States, Accor is pursuing a two-pronged strategy: expanding its economy segment with Motel 6 and Red Roof Inns, with the goal of achieving leadership in the economy segment, and reaching its luxury market with Sofitel.[49] To strengthen its global market dominance, Accor continues with an aggressive expansion plan for Eastern Europe with its budget and midscale brands. In Asia, it relies on forming strategic partnerships.

Development of Economy Hotel Sector

The international hotel chains, Marriott, Starwood, InterContinental Group (the former Six Continents), and Accor, are not as focused on luxury hotels as they were when they first entered China in the 1980s. For example, Marriott's leading performer in 2002 was the midscale Courtyard by Marriott Pudong Shanghai. Still, Accor is considered the first Western hotel company to target the economy segment of the mainland's domestic business traveler market with its Ibis brand.[50] The group focuses upon the lower tier in secondary cities through the same brand.[51] Ibis was first launched in France in 1974 after Accor's founders had already revolutionized the business market with the introduction of the business-class Novotel brand.[52] Ibis changed the industry structure in Europe where most budget accommodations were small independent hotels or bed and breakfasts.[53] Some of these accommodations had poor facilities, were small and unbranded, and offered inconsistent product and service quality.[54] Ibis plan is to capture the economy market with high-quality standardized products and services that can be delivered at a cost of 30% below the competition.[55] Growth in the economy hotel sector has accelerated sharply with the rise of discount airlines[56] such as Ryannair, and Accor is focused upon this group of travelers.

Accor believes that the market in Asia is similar to France, where the hotel markets are similarly mixed and inconsistent. It decided to expand its economy hotel division in Asia Pacific as it recognized the changing travel patterns in the region.[57] This includes a rapidly growing domestic travel market, growth in intra-Asian business/ leisure travel, and a worldwide move away from top-end accommodation in preference for midmarket and economy hotels.[58] There are no internationally branded three-star brands operating in the Chinese market, although there are some good independent domestic three-star hotels.[59] However, these domestic hotels lack brand recognition among international travelers, network support, Internet and reservation distribution systems, and global management expertise.[60]

There are growing signs of an emerging class of business travelers in China, including intra-Asian travelers,[61] who are price conscious with an expectation of international quality standards. Accor also considers the timing ideal for the company to construct a substantial hotel network in China as well as a hospitality infrastructure to respond to the country's economic expansion.[62] It claims that it has learned from past experiences and plans to broaden its hotel base in Asia with the launch of the Ibis and Formulae 1.[63] Accor now has 100-plus Ibis hotels in Asia.[64] The recent openings of Ibis hotels in Seoul, Korea, and Tianjin and Chengdu, China, have highlighted the demand for such hotel products.[65]

Furthermore, Accor is expanding in new directions and has introduced a different type of lodging product under its umbrella of brands. Base, which caters to backpackers, is a fresh new approach in New Zealand. This brand provides its customers basic consistency, security, and predictability of experience. Backpackers stay on average 40 nights and spend more than US $2100 per person in New Zealand, making this a very lucrative market segment. The backpacker market is more resilient and profitable than other market sectors. The average backpacker stays in Asia Pacific for three months and spends an average US $10,000, whereas the average tourist stays for one week and spends US $2000.

Use of Technology as a Competitive Method

Accor focuses upon its reservations and technology to gain competitive advantage: It commits itself to centralizing yield management and streamlining reservation systems. For instance, Accor's two U.S.

economy brands share one reservation system, and its European brands, including Formula 1, Ibis, Novotel and Sofitel, share another.[66] The company's goal is to eventually merge the European and U.S. reservation systems and to incorporate a global yield management system.[67] The new system will create economy of scale and allow Accor to cross-sell all its brands. Synergies occur when the system moves customers up and down the value chain in lodging and when it creates the potential to sell them time-share, holiday vacation or cruise packages.[68]

To further emphasize its focus, Accor developed an online booking engine that features instant confirmation and shows daily rates for a 60-day period, reportedly the first international hotel group to do so.[69] In 2002, in recognizing that the intraregional travel market represents 70% of Accor's business in Asia, it launched a multilingual booking platform dedicated solely to Asia, accorhotels-asia.com.[70] In fact, the company was the first to launch a Chinese-language booking engine dedicated solely to China's massive domestic travel market, followed by a Japanese version.[71] Allowing Asian customers to automatically link to welcome pages in their native language. The

website is designed to suit the unique and diverse language needs of Asia.[72] This is one of the many ways that the company commits time and resources in building its bases and the corresponding infrastructure in China for a substantial expansion.

CHALLENGES AND FUTURE PLANS

As China and Asia continues to attract and offer opportunities to European and North American investors, there will be a day when the market becomes oversupplied. The challenge for these operators is to survive and thrive in a mature market. The implication is that lodging operators will need to focus on accommodating the emerging lifestyle trends and needs of the fast-growing group of Asia travelers, especially the rapidly expanding urban middle class.[73] Accor is confident that it has the vision to take its business further with innovative new products and ideas and hard work. By 2010 Accor plans to expand to 5,000 hotels (2,700 in Europe, 1,500 in North America), representing some 600,000 rooms. Needless to say, Asia, especially the Chinese market, is a key focus for Accor, which now operates 110 hotels in Asia Pacific in 2005 but plans to increase the total to 250 by 2010.

DISCUSSION QUESTIONS

1. How do the changes in the environment influence international hotel players to adapt their expansion strategy?
2. What factors allow Accor to establish itself as a successful key international hospitality organization?
3. How does Accor adapt its competitive methods in each country/region it enters?
4. What are the competitive methods that contribute to Accor's success?
5. When considering the value proposition offered by Accor's various brands, estimate the share price implications of each.
6. What is Accor's WACC, and how is it affected by the risks associated with entering into emerging markets?
7. What political and economic risks do you find Accor facing, given its strategy of pushing into China and Asia in general?
8. What aspects of Accor's strategy do you believe to be most sustainable?
9. Compare Accor's technology utilization with their competitors. How do they perform on this industry CSF, and what actions should they pursue, if any?

NOTES

1. B. Serlen, "Accor, Hilton, InterContinental Expanding in Asia Region. (Asia Pacific)," *Business Travel News* 16 (2003): 21–22.
2. Anonymous, "Singapore, Thailand Top Asian Tourist Destinations," *Asia Africa Intelligence Wire*, 2004.
3. Op. cit., no. 2.
4. Ibid.
5. J. Lau, "Hotelier Targets Chinese Budget Sector," *The Financial Times,* October 10, 2003.
6. S. Shellum, "All Eyes on Asia!" *Hotel Asia Pacific* 4, no. 6 (2003): 16–21.
7. Op. cit., no. 2.
8. Op. cit., no. 7.
9. Op. cit., no. 2.
10. Op. cit., no. 6.
11. Op. cit., no. 7.
12. Ibid.
13. Ibid.
14. Ibid.
15. Ibid.
16. Ibid.
17. Ibid.
18. C. Matlack and L. Cohn, "It's Time for Accor to Get Some Respect," *Business Week* 3850 (2003): 32.
19. Ibid.
20. S. Shellum, "Asia Pacific Hotel Leaders Michael Issenberg, Miguel Ko, Patrick Imbardelli and Koos Klein Look at What Lies Ahead; The Greatest Challenge Is Uncertainty," *Hotel Asia Pacific*, 2004.
21. Op. cit., no. 19.
22. C. Wolf, "World Domination, Niche by Niche," *Lodging Hospitality* 56, no. 4 (2000): 34–37.
23. Op. cit., no. 21.
24. Anonymous, "Accor Asia Pacific-World's Leading Hotel Group," (Accor Tourism Award) [Brief article], *Business Asia*, 2003.
25. J. Lau, "Accor Expanding Presence in China Hotels," *The Financial Times*, 2003: 25.
26. Op. cit., no. 23.
27. Op. cit., no. 21.
28. Anonymous, "Accor to Manage Nine New Hotels in China," 2003.
29. Anonymous, "Accor Premiere Vacation Club Launches Web Site; Now Includes 10 Properties," *The Timeshare Beat*, 2001.
30. Op. cit., no. 25.
31. Op. cit., no. 30.
32. Ibid.
33. Op. cit., no. 30.
34. Ibid.
35. Op. cit., no. 26.
36. "Accor Asia Pacific Joins Forces with Air China—Air China Agreement Complements Accor's Major Expansion in China" (2003). Retrieved February 20, 2007, from http:/ /www. accorhotels-asia. com.
37. Op. cit., no. 21.
38. Op. cit., no. 37.
39. Ibid.
40. Ibid.
41. Op. cit., no. 21.
42. H. Mahtani, "Accor Checks in to China," *Hotel Interactive*, 2003.
43. Op. cit., no. 21.
44. Anonymous, "Accor to Invest CNY 1.8n in China," *SinoCast China Business Daily News,* January 16, 2006: 1.
45. Op. cit., no. 26.
46. Anonymous, "Accor Expects to Own 7 Hotels in Beijing Before 2008," *SinoCast China Business Daily News*, November 22, 2005.
47. Op. cit., no. 26.
48. Op. cit., no. 23.
49. Ibid.
50. Op. cit., no. 26.
51. Ibid.
52. Op. cit., no. 21.
53. Op. cit., no. 19.
54. Op. cit., no. 21.
55. Ibid.
56. Op. cit., no. 19.
57. Op. cit., no. 29.
58. Ibid.
59. Op. cit., no. 21.
60. Ibid.
61. Op. cit., no. 2.
62. Op. cit., no. 29.
63. Op. cit., no. 21.
64. "Accor Opens 100th Hotel In Asia as Asia Pacific Chairman David Baffsky Wins Major

Award" (2004). Retrieved February 20, 2007, from http://www.accorhotels-asia.com.
65. Ibid.
66. Op. cit., no. 23.
67. Ibid.
68. Ibid.
69. Op. cit., no. 25.

70. C. Kolle, "Accor Website Goes Multi-Lingual," *Asian Business* 38, no. 2 (2002): 69.
71. Op. cit., no. 21.
72. Op. cit., no. 71.
73. Op. cit., no. 3.

ADDITIONAL REFERENCES USED FOR BACKGROUND BUT NOT CITED

Anonymous. 2005. "Accor Expands, Carlson Consolidates." *Lodging Hospitality* 61, no. 7: 12.
———. 2005. "Colony Invests 1B in Accor." *Real Estate Finance and Investment*, 1.
Issenberg, M. 2003. "In the Footsteps of a Legend." *Hotel Asia Pacific* 4, no. 5: 40–44.

Shellum, S. 2004. "Asia Rising." *Hotel Asia Pacific* 5, no. 5: 18–23.
Wolf, C. 2000. "World Domination, Niche by Niche." *Lodging Hospitality* 56, no. 4: 34–37.

Analyzing Core Competencies

From Chapter 9 of *Strategic Management in the Hospitality Industry*, Third Edition, Michael D. Olsen, Joseph J. West, Eliza Ching Yick Tse. Copyright © 2008 by Pearson Education, Inc. Published by Pearson Prentice Hall. All rights reserved.

Analyzing Core Competencies

Analyzing Core
Competencies

Upon completion of this chapter, you will:

1. Understand the role of core competencies in executing the delivery of competitive methods.
2. Grasp the importance of the linkages between core competencies and competitive methods in creating sustainable competitive advantage.
3. Utilize frameworks for assessing the strengths and weaknesses of the firm's competencies.

Core Competencies

The service exchange

Linking core competencies

Service production competencies

Product production competencies

Functional competencies

Visioning competencies

Organizational structure competencies

Branding competencies

Physical asset competencies

Integrating competitive methods and core competencies

Chapter Purpose

The coalignment process proceeds from the scanning of the environment to the selection of competitive methods. *The next step in the strategic thinking process is to ensure that resources are consistently allocated to those competitive methods that are determined to add the greatest value to the guest and, by extension, to the firm.* This next part of the alignment process is significant and every bit as challenging as the alignment between the *scanning* and *choice* phases. In the model (Exhibit 1), this construct is indicated as *firm structure*. In general, we can describe firm structure in more detail by looking at Exhibit 2. As this conceptual map illustrates, four key elements are relevant to understanding structure. The right-hand side of the graphic focuses on the analysis work the manager must do to begin the process of matching competitive methods (CMs) with core competencies (CCs). To begin, there is a need to have a way of looking at CCs to try to understand them. We offer such a framework in the first part of this chapter. Secondly, it is important that the core competencies are assessed in terms of their strengths and weaknesses relative to the CMs, which constitutes the second half of the chapter.

Having completed the analysis portion, the manager must then work toward determining the degree of alignment between each CM and the firm's CCs, which is the focus of the first half of the next chapter. Once this is completed the action to be taken is either to maintain successful alignments or set objectives necessary to accomplish this, which is where the implementation process becomes essential. The implementation plan becomes the link to the business plan and operating budgets of the firm and is the second half of the next chapter.

As a reminder and underpinning for this and the next chapter, the focus of the coalignment model is the CM. Recalling the definition provided in the previous chapters, a CM is a unique combination of goods and services that is sustainable and creates value for the firm. The entire effort of ensuring proper implementation and execution of each CM should be directed at the point of transaction between the customer and the firm. That is, the firm's resources must be utilized to achieve the maximum performance of each CM relative to the customer and the customer experience.

The first part of this chapter is organized around the transaction between the customer and the customer contact employee and how resources should be directed to this important unit of analysis. In particular we emphasize the CCs that are essential for the delivery of these products and services and the peripheral competencies that aid and support this process. We close the chapter with an overview of several frameworks useful for assessing the strengths and weaknesses of the firm's CCs.

A Framework for Assessing Firm Structure

To bring some type of order to the complexity of this construct, we have attempted to capture the essence of the service industry by focusing on the firm's *core competencies (CCs)* presented in the model in Exhibit 3. This model provides a useful framework for viewing this important connection between strategy choice and resource allocation. The model can be viewed as three concentric rectangles. At the heart of the model is the transaction that occurs between the customer contact employee and the guest.[1] This transaction is referred to as the *exchange process* where all the products and

EXHIBIT 1 Strategic Management Model

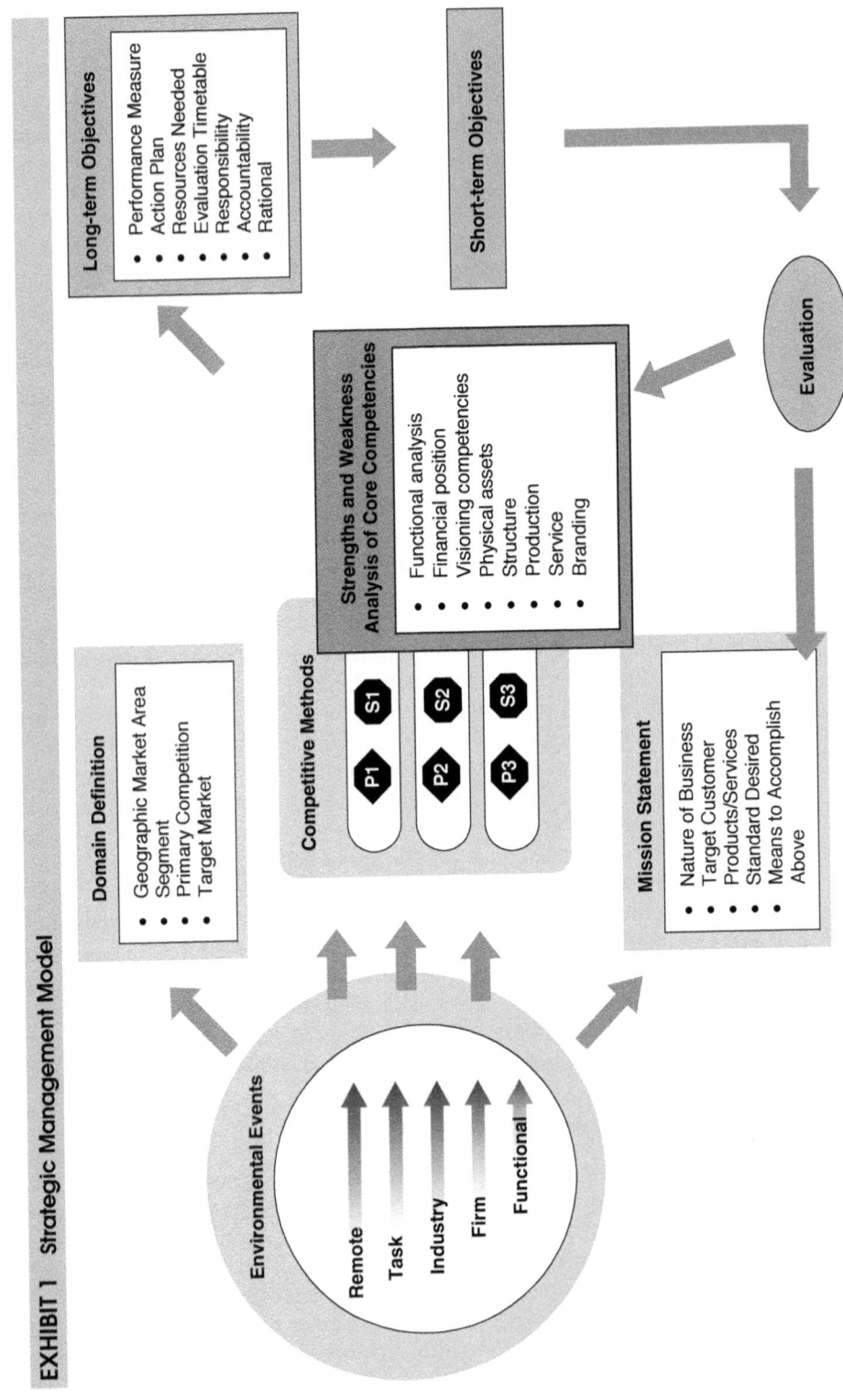

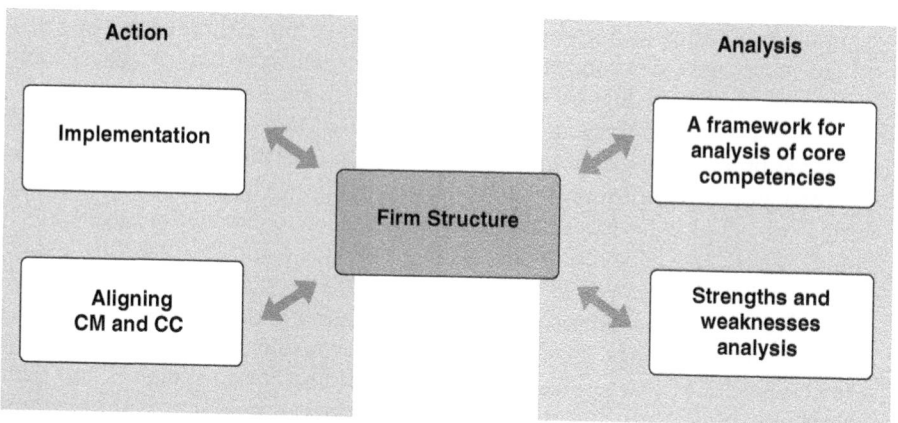

EXHIBIT 2 Conceptual Map of the Structure Construct

services that have been carefully created by the firm, and blended together into a specific competitive method, are presented to the customer by a customer contact employee. To accomplish this successfully, the enterprise has to develop a set of CCs, as represented in the model by the second concentric rectangle. It is these CCs that must receive the bulk of the firm's resources if these CMs are to be implemented properly. The third rectangle reflects the *peripheral competencies (PCs)* that are necessary to achieve a masterful exchange while maintaining normal business functions.

The model conveys the complexity faced by managers of service firms as they try to create the means to deliver their products and services. Not only must they create

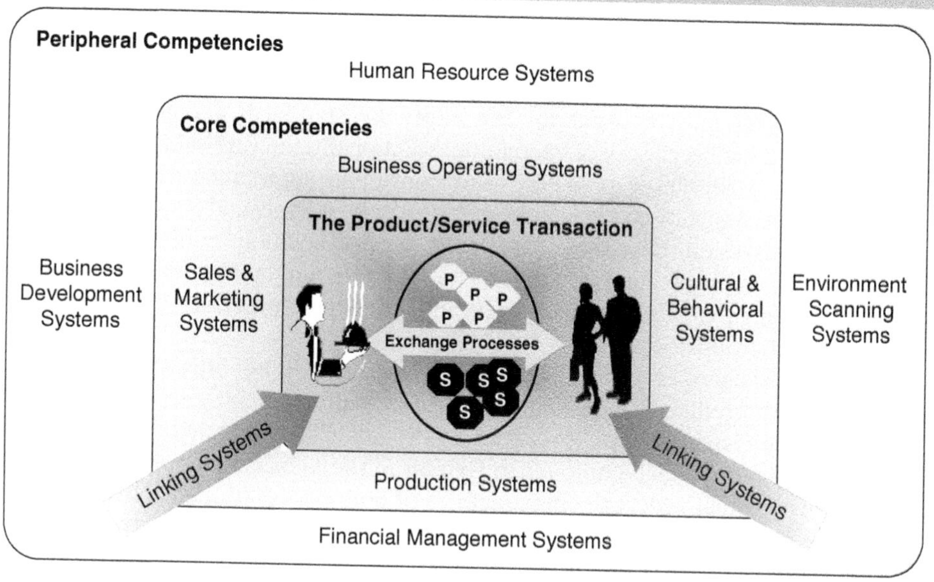

EXHIBIT 3 Competency Model of the Hospitality Enterprise

superior abilities to accomplish this delivery to the customer at the right time and place, they must also concentrate on integrating the core and peripheral competencies so as to achieve the highest standards of performance and value.

The *exchange process* is often referred to as the *moment of truth* in the normative service literature. This metaphor suggests that it is the point in time when all of the efforts put into choosing the right product and service mix (CM), and the development of the CCs to deliver them, come together to execute a *transaction* that meets and, ideally, exceeds both the demands of the guest and the cash flow expectations of the owners.

The transaction that occurs between the guest and the customer service employee is a complex exchange process. The complexity results from the uncertainties inherent in the nature of the service experience itself and the production and technological processes involved in producing the physical products the customer seeks. Furthermore, each party to the exchange has certain expectations that they seek to have met. How well these expectations are met is a function of the many resources and capabilities each participant brings to the transaction. Although the hospitality enterprise can develop its own resources and capabilities to ensure proper execution on its part, it can do little to develop those of its customers, thus creating significant challenges for the firm.

The transaction is also made complex because each step in the exchange process is made up of several systems. Purchasing, food production, communication, information exchange, and feedback are examples of systems supporting each transaction. Each has its own inputs, processes, and outputs, which are not always easily combined in any specific transaction. The more numbers of products and services included in the transaction the more systems needed, and thus the more complexity the firm must face. In this context, managers must review every system of the exchange to determine what competencies are required to execute each product and service offered at the desired level of perfection.

The hospitality manager is further challenged in this effort because of the intangible nature of the service portion of the transaction. Therefore, the technologies used to produce the desired level of service must consider the intangible and perishable nature of the service provided. Because service is most often a perceived experience, the technologies must account for the imprecise standards and heterogeneous nature associated with each service encounter. Additionally, the very short distribution channel, that is, the service is produced and consumed simultaneously, creates significant challenges in quality control if standards are to be reliably and consistently achieved with each transaction. Lastly, because many service encounters involve a live exchange between employee and customer, the technologies must address the uncertainties surrounding the information transfers and task uncertainties that undoubtedly will result from each transaction.

This exchange between customer and employee is not only about the products and services offered; it is also a function of the actual human interactions that occur during the entire transaction as illustrated by the double-headed arrow linking the guest to the customer contact employee in Exhibit 3. These exchange processes are behavioral dimensions that reflect the personalities of both parties to the exchange and are influenced by the context of the situation (modes, atmosphere, etc.) surrounding the transaction. These processes include attitudes and perceptions influencing the behavior of both parties to the exchange, communication skills, information analysis and search by the employee regarding the needs of the transaction, role formation and playing, the development of trust between the parties, and adherence to norms and standards. These processes are a reflection of the culture, training, and development programs within the firm in addition to the expectations of the customer who is participating in the exchange. Although it is more difficult to identify the competencies associated with each of these processes, it is nonetheless essential that the interaction be accurately assessed and performed if competitive advantage is to be achieved.

To help reduce the uncertainties associated with the complexities of each transaction, the firm must therefore invest wisely in the choice of CCs. As Exhibit 3 illustrates, these competencies focus on several systems. Business operating, cultural and behavioral, production, and sales and marketing systems serve to shelter or buffer the exchange processes from the uncertainties associated with producing products and services. The challenge for management is to develop or choose the appropriate systems within this CC rectangle to deliver the products and services critical to the firm. This execution effort cannot be done unless the firm has also chosen the best qualified individuals to carry it out. Management's responsibility here is to be sure that the necessary resources are channeled to the most value-producing competitive methods.

Business operating systems focus on the accounting, budgeting, planning, controlling, and coordinating activities the firm utilizes. They also include management information systems, risk reduction (as associated with insurance coverage for liabilities or natural disasters), and legal activities. Cultural and behavioral systems serve to structure the set of beliefs and values established by the firm to ensure consistency across all transactions. Production systems include all the technologies associated with the conversion of raw materials into finished goods. Sales and marketing systems function to reduce uncertainty by helping shape the messages and expectations for the customer about what she or he is likely to receive in the way of products and services. It also assists in eliminating, to some degree, the workflow uncertainty often found in hospitality organizations. Developing these competencies must be viewed as absolutely essential. They must be completely integrated into the effective delivery of the portfolio of products and services comprising the firm's competitive methods.

An example may help to illustrate this. McDonald's is faced with considerable challenges to ensure proper delivery of its products and services worldwide. Ensuring a continuing supply of safe beef products is perhaps the most critical competency this firm has had to develop. Incorporating strict evaluation and control of supply, delivery, processing, and production systems is a CC that is essential in this case. Similarly, transitioning to oils that do not rely on transfats for flavoring french fries requires an effective core competency in research and development. These CCs are essential if McDonald's is to serve the best products possible to an increasingly demanding customer.

Peripheral competencies (PCs) as indicated in Exhibit 3 serve to support the continuing development and maintenance of the CCs. The ability to acquire essential resources such as labor and capital is especially important in the contemporary environment of the hospitality industry. Similarly, it is necessary to develop and maintain the effectiveness of the environmental scanning systems of the firm. These systems support the business development activities that are so necessary if the firm is to take advantage of new opportunities in the complex and dynamic nature of the hospitality industry environment.

It is not enough to develop both CCs and PCs without building the linking or integrating systems that are essential to ensure success. These systems, as represented by the arrows moving inward from the peripheral competencies to the exchange transaction in Exhibit 3, include many organizational structure issues: for example, those involving decision making regarding resource allocation, or the development of management information systems that result in the efficient and effective sharing of strategic information among all organizational units. Planning activities, evaluation of performance, and communication of that measurement to interested stakeholders, reward systems, process improvement efforts, and leadership processes also constitute important linking systems necessary to achieve competitive advantage. The greater the linking and integration among CCs and CMs, the greater the likelihood that the firm can achieve advantages that are not easily copied by other firms. These issues are covered in greater detail in the latter part of this chapter.

Exhibit 4 provides a closer examination of the product–service exchange introduced in Exhibit 3. It identifies several possible CCs that are necessary for the successful execution of the delivery of the products and services contained in the portfolio referred to in the exhibit as competitive method A. This example demonstrates the need for management to view each CM from the perspective of which CCs are needed to execute and achieve the level of quality desired and then assess its performance against their standards and those of the industry. This matching process is essential if a firm is to achieve any level of competitive advantage, and it is facilitated through the use of integrating or linking systems. The list of competencies in this example also supports the point made earlier that the exchange process is a complex one requiring important resource allocation decisions by management.

The ability to execute CMs successfully is very challenging in the service industries for several reasons. First, the intangible nature of the service experience makes it hard to execute perfectly each time simply because the customer and customer service employee

EXHIBIT 4 Resources and Capabilities Model of the Hospitality Enterprise

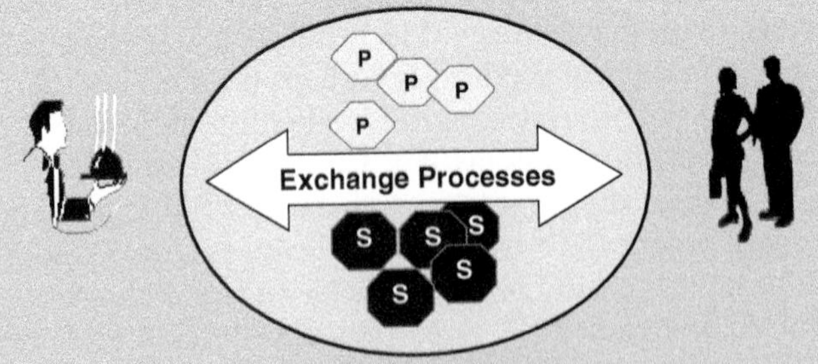

Competitive Method A

Sample list of core competencies for competitive advantage

Superior execution   Quality control
Behavioral performance skills   Service training programs

produce and consume the experience together, and this is likely to be different for each exchange. Secondly, for those firms that have multiple units, achieving execution 100% of the time in each unit and for each transaction is nearly impossible. There are just too many variables to contend with in multiple-unit businesses. This then creates a degree of variability in the execution of strategy that challenges managers and demands their attention in relation to developing the best competencies and resources possible.

Frameworks for the Analysis of Core Competencies

There are many different ways to look at the competency issue. We provide several generally accepted frameworks for assessing the firm's competencies with the goal of having you assess the firm's strengths and weaknesses using the one that best reflects its array of CMs. Remember that the assessment process must be focused on how well the competencies ensure the proper execution of those CMs that create the greatest overall value for the firm. Only those competencies necessary to accomplish this important goal should be considered. Those that do not match any CMs are in most cases to be considered expendable because they contribute little to the value-adding potential of the CM.

The potential number of CCs in a hospitality organization can be numerous. To provide a comprehensive overview of all the possibilities for assessing the strengths and weaknesses of each, several frameworks are introduced in the following subsections. The choice of the framework will be contingent on the CC, so it is possible that one or more frameworks may be used for this purpose. The point is that managers will always be on a quest to improve CCs so they can assure investors of a consistent delivery of a CM. The first framework used to identify possible CCs will focus on the predominant theme in this text, that is, the service and product mix.

Service Production Competencies

As illustrated in Exhibits 3 and 4, the service transaction is essentially a complex set of processes that involve both the customer service employee and the customer in the production and consumption of the service experience. As such, the hospitality enterprise must concentrate on building CCs according to the types of service transactions provided by the firm and listed in Exhibit 5.[2] The information in this table classifies the probable types of service exchanges that are likely to occur in a typical hospitality or service enterprise. Each of the categories of service listed requires varying sets of CCs depending on the level of service the firm chooses to provide.

A closer look at the descriptions in the table suggests that the CCs required to achieve a successful service transaction consist of several dimensional features: (1) the type of contact that occurs between employee and customer ranging from self-service to personal interactive, (2) the type of information exchanged during the transaction ranging from simple to complex, (3) the communication processes utilized, (4) the behavioral dimensions that must be enacted, (5) the degree of contact time between customer and employee, (6) the extent of customer participation in the production of the service, (7) the atmosphere of trust and customer attachment surrounding the transaction, (8) the feedback systems used by the employee to complete the transaction successfully, (9) the decision-making ability of the employee in meeting the customer's needs (often referred to as *self-management* or *empowerment*), (10) the

Type of Service	Description	Examples
Self service	Minimal customer contact, simple service process, oriented towards speed and convenience, little behavioral needs from customer	Quick service restaurants
Maintenance Interactive	Customers seek employee contact only when needed to solve problems, expect only limited assistance if needed, no need for customized service, customer seeks little recognition	Casual theme restaurants, limited service hotels
Task Interactive	Focus is on customized professional level of service, the need for trust exists, customer seeks recognition above basic elements of the service exchange, expect service personnel to make decisions on the spot	Full service hotels, and restaurants
Personal Interactive	High customer attachment to service experience, high attachment to service employee by customer, high levels of information input, high level of trust, highly customized	Travel agent specializing in custom trips, concierge, consultant, masseuse, personal tour guide

EXHIBIT 5   Categories of Service Transaction and Their Definition

degree of customization required by the transaction, (11) customer recognition needs, and (12) the degree of capital, asset, and labor intensity.

Each of the 12 dimensions requires the investment of resources to achieve the competitive advantage management is seeking. Investments in the CCs for each of these groupings must be evaluated using maximizing cash flow per share of equity. Each competency can impact the cash flow of the firm because it can either add costs and/or revenues to each transaction. Because the service transaction is more uncertain with respect to costs and revenues, the cash flow variance associated with each exchange can be high. Thus careful selection of CCs regarding the service experience can greatly reduce this variance.

Exhibit 6 lists examples of CCs in the service transaction area. As the list implies, the service transaction is steeped in complexity and uncertainty. The CCs, when considered individually, can be easily imitated unless firms are able to weave them together in such a way that competitors find it extremely difficult to duplicate them. In an era of growing customer expectations about the level of service and the value received for the price paid, creating sustainable advantage will prove to be an illusive target for all firms, unless they are able to combine several competencies together and execute them better than their competitors.

As the examples in Exhibits 2 to 4 suggest, the unit of analysis to be used to identify CCs is the transaction between the customer and customer contact employee. In this context, many of the competencies reflect the behavioral elements present in the transaction, suggesting the importance of investments in training and development. This training and development will naturally have to focus on the behavioral skills needed to complete the transaction, but it will also have to concentrate on helping the

• Transaction cost efficiency	• Degree of asset intensity per transaction
• Speed of transaction	• Number of special skills needed per transaction
• Training in behavioral skills	• Complexity reduction in service delivery process
• Training in communication skills	
• Degree of Self-management required by employees	• Degree of task uncertainty reduction per transaction
• Access to effective service personnel	• Degree of workflow uncertainty reduction per transaction
• Degree of service culture	• Employee loyalty
• Employee attitudes	• Internal services marketing effectiveness
• Services marketing effectiveness	• Responsiveness to customer needs
• Consistency or reliability of service performance	• Meeting of safety and security needs of customer
• Degree of sensitively to customers special needs	• Appropriate service capacity at each point of service delivery
• Convenience of access to service	
• Customer loyalty	• Technological assistance to the service transaction, i.e., information technology, expert systems, artificial intelligence
• Degree of intangibility	
• Degree of job autonomy	
• Clarity of service standards	
• Degree of people intensity (employee and customer) per transaction	

EXHIBIT 6   Examples of Core Competencies Related to the Service Transaction

service employee manage the uncertainties associated with providing the service level desired. Thus communication skills, information processing, self-management, and quality control become processes that must be learned and applied to the heterogeneous nature of the service transaction.

Product Production Competencies

Unlike the service intangibles, products represent the tangible portion of most portfolios. The traditional systems model of inputs, transformation, and outputs provides a useful framework to use in understanding CCs with respect to products. The systems model in Exhibit 7 provides an illustration of the relationships in the model and examples of CCs regarding this important element of competitive advantage.

The *inputs* represent the mix of raw materials, labor, and capital that are necessary to produce the desired end product. The quality of those inputs is determined by the amount of resources the firm commits to each of them. In addition to the level of resources expended for high-quality inputs, the firm must also develop the capability to acquire those inputs. Usually, a firm is able to achieve more advantage if it has superior access to the inputs it needs and can influence the nature of the supply-and-demand relationships that exist in their business domain. For example, large-volume purchasers of some products are able to influence the price, timing of production, and even the overall quality of a product resulting from that production. In some cases, firms have been known to require their suppliers to guarantee that they will receive the products they need at the specification level desired, 100% of the time. Therefore, purchasing systems, inventory systems, cost control systems, and all systems designed to acquire the best inputs represent important core competencies that must be developed by the firm at the input stage.

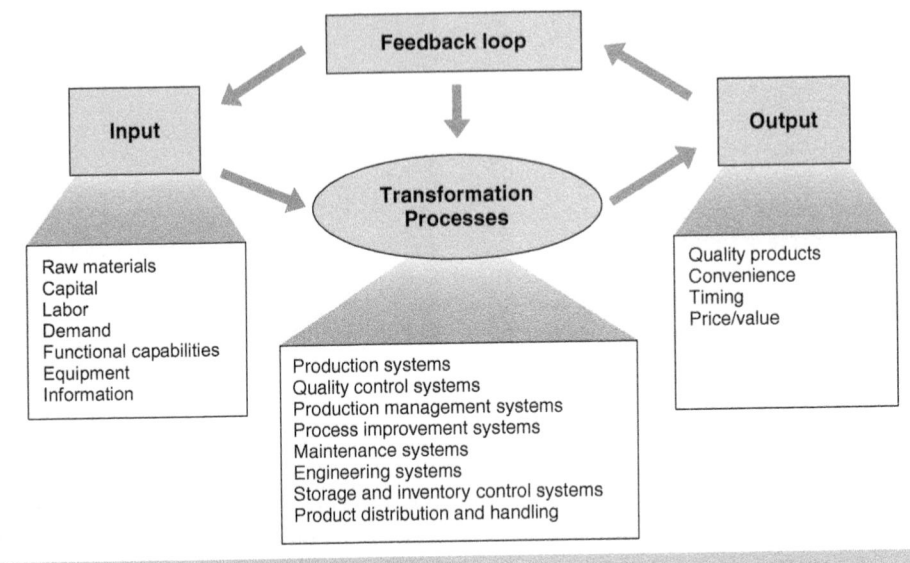

EXHIBIT 7 The System Model of Production

The *transformation* process requires specific technologies to bring about the conversion of inputs into outputs. It includes those systems that are used in the process. Food production systems, quality control systems, production management, and engineering systems, cost control systems, and management information systems are a few examples of processes that are integral to converting the inputs into the desired outputs. Each process utilizes specific technologies purchased or designed to produce the products and services offered by the firm. Management must focus here on what capabilities are necessary to be sure the technology is able to assist in executing each process to perfection. An important consideration here is that the employees must be able to use the technology as it was designed. In other words, the systems must all be functional. Only if the systems are fully functional can management attempt to consider them as CCs.

The recent emphasis in the management literature on reengineering and continuous process improvement and quality control concepts such as Six Sigma suggests that if firms are to be successful today, they must be engaged, on a constant basis, in efforts to streamline the processes used to produce goods and services. This emphasis suggests that firms must review each and every process involved with producing goods and services. In this review, each step in the transformation process is carefully evaluated to see if it is the most efficient and effective. If it is not, the process is redesigned to achieve the desired goal of perfect execution. If this goal can be achieved, it can then be claimed that management has achieved competitive advantage.

The *output*s of the systems model are the products and services that are produced to the desired standard for every customer and add value for the owners of the firm. This standard will have been determined by the environmental scanning activities, which have identified tomorrow's opportunities for those firms who seek to be industry leaders. As has been mentioned frequently in this text, achieving the desired execution and standard in the service industry is no easy task. It does involve a large number of

CCs working in harmony. Thus feedback systems must be carefully designed to alert management when this is not the case. That is to say, feedback systems themselves become important CCs. The popularity of what is referred to as the Balanced Scorecard[3] illustrates how important it is to determine performance measurements for all competencies necessary in executing the firm's CMs. These systems must, however, reflect the uncertainties and complexities of the exchange process. Whatever feedback system employed, it must be built around the performance of the CM.

In looking at CCs using the products and services framework, management will need to focus its attention on the processes utilized in the production of both. As this overview suggests, services must reflect the exchange process between employee and customer. This exchange is very complex and often very uncertain. Its success is as much a function of reality as it is perception. Human factors, including emotional processes, are involved in achieving success here. With respect to the production of goods, the processes are more tangible and require systems that must be functional 100% of the time. In this case, the skills and capabilities needed are a little easier to define. In both settings, however, the processes are dynamic and subject to a fair amount of workflow uncertainty as well as task uncertainty. What is essential in this case is that management must blueprint each process to determine what systems and standards are needed and then seek to develop or acquire the CCs necessary to achieve the desired degree of success.

Functional Framework

Management is often viewed as a series of functions to be performed. For example, business school curricula have focused on enhancing student skills in what is referred to as the functional areas of management. These functional areas are most often grouped into the categories listed in Exhibit 8. This view represents another way of looking at CCs. It begins with identifying which tasks must take place within each function and what competencies are necessary to perform them.

EXHIBIT 8 Functional Areas for Core Competencies Development

Functional area	Key components
Finance	Asset management, capital budgeting, capital structure, financial analysis and planning, financial control and budgeting, asset valuation
Marketing	Product development, promotional activities, distribution, pricing, internal marketing, external marketing, communications, public relations, market research
Human resources	Organizational behavior, labor relations, hiring, developing, compensating, leadership, educating, high performance work practice systems
Administration	Accounting, management information systems, strategic planning, legal, risk/insurance, communications, resource allocation and control
Operations	Cost control systems, production systems, production management, quality control, process improvement
Research and Development	New business opportunities, competitive intelligence, product testing, feasibility studies, business valuation

Once this is determined, the next step is to employ the people with the competence to perform each task at a level above the competition. This implies that firms are able to recruit, hire, and maintain the most skilled staff in each area or are able to buy this expertise from consultants and other providers.

Once the right people have been employed, the firm must provide an environment that promotes opportunities for them to function at a level that motivates them. They must be provided with the resources necessary to achieve the level of competency that puts the firm ahead of its competition. These resources include the systems and capital necessary to achieve superiority. The right culture is also necessary.

In addition to hiring the right people and providing the right environment, management must be sure that it is utilizing the best practices that are being developed in each functional area. This means that management must scan the functional environment to be sure that it is staying ahead of the best developing practices. The concept of continuous process improvement fits well within this activity. If management is to develop CCs, it must also concentrate on improving them continually.

Essential to the functional analysis must be management's perceptions of how each function links and is integrated into each CM. Staying true to the principle that resources must be allocated to key CMs, functional capabilities must demonstrate their linkage to those CMs that add the greatest value. For example, in the contemporary world of hotel financing today, private equity firms and hedge funds have emerged as key sources of financing. Because obtaining financing is a key core competency necessary to grow hotel chains (growth is often considered as a key CM), expertise in this element of finance is essential. It is necessary for negotiating deals, estimating cash flow streams, and arranging contracts necessary to launch new deals.

Other Competency Frameworks

Visionary/Creativity Competencies

Capabilities that do not fit conveniently into the product–service or functional frameworks but, according to leading thinkers in the area of CCs, are important to achieving competitive advantage include such skills as creativity, vision, leadership, and innovation. Trying to capture the essence and intangible nature of each these capabilities and weave them throughout the organization's culture is one way of achieving this competitive advantage. And many firms are seeking to do just that in this world of rapid change and growing complexity. The primary challenge here is to try to define each of these competencies so that they can be developed and/or acquired. The problem is that these competencies, although easy to describe conceptually, are difficult to make tangible. Thus they tend to be illusive competencies that can best be described by the phrase *you know them when you see them.* However, trying to break them down into key elements for the purposes of training and development is not so easy. Nevertheless, there is growing belief that they do represent one of the most important frameworks for achieving competitive advantage.

A sample of the skills and capabilities within this framework and often stated as needed in tomorrow's hospitality industry is provided in Exhibit 9. Looking at this list points out how important leadership is to the organization and the new types of

- A Visionary employing value adding strategies
- Using and managing knowledge and technology for competitive advantage
- Spanning boundaries of cultures, business environments and management know-how
- A synthesizer and blender of skills and knowledge in a fast changing environment
- A leader in a dynamic and complex setting
- A manager and motivator of the knowledge worker

EXHIBIT 9 Skills and Capabilities Essential to Tomorrow's Hospitality Manager

competencies managers must develop to compete effectively in the future. The challenge for all types of hospitality firms will be to find not only those who have the potential or already possess these capabilities, but also to identify those who can educate and train managers to use them. Despite these challenges, many are convinced that these will be the most important CMs of tomorrow.

Organizational Structural Competencies

Other competencies often mentioned in the hospitality industry include organizational factors such as span of market share, market coverage or geographic dispersion (often referred to as site location advantage), and economies of scale. *Span of market share* reflects what percentage of the potential market the firm is capturing. In the hospitality industry, this is usually a function of how many units the firm is able to place in key locations within specific market areas. *Market coverage or geographic dispersion* refers to the number of markets the firm is in and doing well. *Economies of scale* reflect the classic definition of spreading costs over many units versus just a few. Evidence of how important these examples of competencies have recently become is the continuing race by all firms to become the largest (as measured by number of units), either nationally or internationally in the industry. From McDonald's to Marriott, expansion programs are underway in aggressive fashion.

The thinking behind this approach goes beyond the obvious marketing reasons; it also focuses on how size can give the firm the ability to achieve superior access or control over its resources. Prevailing thinking by many industry pundits is that there will only be a few major firms dominating the industry, and everyone appears to be making the attempt to be one of those few or is at least thinking along such lines. Although it remains to be seen if this consolidation does occur, it is clear that the quest for market share and economies of scale will continue to be sought after for their value in providing competitive advantage.

Cost advantage is also considered to be an important competency that large firms have attempted to develop. In this regard, technology, or, more appropriately, the overall cost efficiencies realized by investments in technology are seen as increasingly providing firms with competitive advantage. The ability to be the low-cost producer in an industry is an enviable position. McDonald's and Econolodge are well-known brands that have achieved high degrees of success through being low-cost producers. Low cost is in part a function of size and buying power, which in turn allows better access to resources. Thus many firms seek to obtain technological advantage so they can develop the competencies to become low-cost producers.

Two recent additions to the literature on competency-based strategy are the concepts *of organizational learning* and *social awareness*. The concept of organizational learning suggests that firms can achieve competitive advantage by creating an organizational environment that encourages the firm, and its employees, to reinvent themselves. The concept of reinvention refers to the ability to generate new products and services on a regular basis. In other words, this is similar to the points made in the chapters on the environment. That is, firms must seek to renew themselves in the context of the dynamic and complex nature of today's business environment. Today's champions of this theory provide plenty of evidence to suggest that this is what will determine a firm's future. Social awareness is increasingly becoming an important competency. Whether the issue is the environment, poverty, or other forms of social consciousness, many firms are seeking to develop capabilities in these areas. Companies such as Ben and Jerry's have achieved some success in this area. The developing synergy between the growing power of buyers and the firms they interact with in efforts to improve on social awareness is likely to see a growing importance of this capability, requiring firms to develop this capability today and in the future.

Branding

The power of the brand has long been considered an enormously valuable competitive advantage. And indeed, no one can argue with the recognition given to Hard Rock Cafe, McDonald's, Regent Hotels, Ritz Carlton Hotels, Shangri-La Hotels, Singapore Airlines, and Hertz Rent-a-Car. The value of the brand in the hospitality industry has become an important resource for many companies and is now considered an important value-generating competency.

The *power of the brand* concept has long been associated with customer loyalty. It is supposed to symbolize specific attributes of the products/services identified with the brand and that the customer desires. These are a function of the firm's ability to deploy its resources and capabilities. Thus the brand is supposed to reflect the standards, quality, value, and consistency in product/service delivery and output. The brand is designed to assist the customer in differentiating among a range of products and services. It reduces consumer uncertainty in the product/service choice decision.

Inherent in the branding process is product and service consistency. Firms that are able to make use of a few manufacturing facilities to produce consumer goods such as detergent or toothpaste can achieve this uniformity relatively easily. However, this is not the case in the service industry and especially the hospitality industry. As mentioned frequently throughout this text, this industry consists of thousands of mini-manufacturing facilities. Whether it's McDonald's growing array of over 30,000 units worldwide or Marriott International's 2,000-plus hotels, being able to achieve the degree of consistency called for by the notion of branding is next to impossible without a superior collection of competencies. This standard, most would agree, cannot be easily achieved.

It is this concern that has resulted in many industry observers suggesting the power of the brand may be overstated in this industry. In fact, many argue that branding in this business has confused the customer because there are so many brands and the consistency both within and between them is poor. Although this debate will be played out over the years, it does suggest that the branding concept can achieve success only if firms are able to define the key elements of the brand and what competencies they possess to ensure their consistent delivery. Failure to do this adequately will create brand dilution and erode the usefulness of the concept in achieving competitive advantage.

Physical Assets

The hospitality industry is well known for producing magnificent hotels, restaurants, and resorts. Well-known architects such as John Portman and I. M. Pei have designed outstanding physical assets. The atrium lobby became for many years synonymous with the Hyatt chain of hotels. It clearly was an important resource to the Hyatt image. Although it still is most associated with the Hyatt name, other hotels have successfully copied the idea. Nevertheless, it is still viewed by some as an important internal resource creating a specific identity for the hotel to use in its competitive efforts.

Similarly, Disneyland and Disney World and their branded resorts in Hong Kong and Europe are resort and entertainment complexes that provide inimitable advantage. The Greenbrier Resort in West Virginia or the Breakers Resort in Florida are other examples of unique physical assets that cannot be easily duplicated. Exclusive resorts the world over seek to reach this inimitability to give them the drawing power to sustain competitive advantage in this highly competitive industry.

The ability to design and construct unique physical assets reflects a core competency that not all firms can accomplish. This is even more important if this process can accomplish beauty and difference without creating inordinate operating and maintenance costs. Given the capital and labor intensity of the industry, this is really an important core competency.

Dimensions of Firm Structure

Basically, the construct of firm structure refers to how an organization allocates resources throughout the firm and is made up of several dimensions. It includes decision-making authority (centralization of control), the number of rules and regulations (formalization), and the number of specializations or specific job functions (complexity) and how they all fit together to make the firm work (configuration) along with being able to react quickly to changing environmental forces. Additionally, communication systems (within the firm and with external entities and individuals), formal and informal leadership activities, control systems, and other business-related systems make up structure.

In looking at firm structure, the manager must decide if the degree of formalization, centralization, complexity, and configuration along with flexibility are in alignment with the environment of the firm and the CMs that it uses to meet the imperatives of the investor. In the subsections to follow we briefly describe these concepts and encourage the manager to employ an analysis of these in relationship to understanding the strengths and weaknesses regarding the resources and capabilities of the firm.

Formalization refers to the degree to which the rules and policies that guide action at all levels of the organization are defined, understood, and adhered to. As Exhibit 10 suggests, formalization is often associated with the control function of

- Standardization
- Policies chart
- Procedures
- Rules
- Performance reviews channels
- Controls systems
- Resource allocation systems
- Employee handbooks
- Policy manuals
- Operating instructions
- Communication
- Management info
- Budgets

EXHIBIT 10
Organizational Structure
Formalization

management. For the organization to stay on course toward its implementation objectives, it is necessary to build in some formality to ensure that all the processes work as they are designed. Although the concept of formality has been part of management thinking for quite some time, in today's dynamic business environment it is management that is increasingly challenged to achieve the right balance between too many rules and regulations and too few.

Centralization refers to the hierarchical relationships that define the lines of communication, responsibility, and authority throughout the firm. This definition extends to the resource allocation decision processes used all through the enterprise for all types of investments that it makes. It also refers to the firm's adherence to the chain of command or formal communication linkages between vertically adjacent management levels. Put simply, centralization defines the power relationships that exist in a hospitality enterprise. In the traditional one, especially a hotel, the power relationships were well defined with the general manager poised at the top of a pyramid with many levels cascading down from there. In many instances the hospitality manager has always focused on the importance of control and the necessary power to go along with it. That is not the case today because the changing workforce, workplace, and business environment require a greater sharing of the power, authority, and accountability necessary to meet the most demanding needs of the guest (Exhibit 11). This is especially important in a service organization where the customer contact employee is so integrally involved in the implementation of those goods and services that constitute the most value-adding competitive methods of the firm.

- Locus of control
- Power
- Authority
- Accountability

EXHIBIT 11
Organizational Structure
Centralization

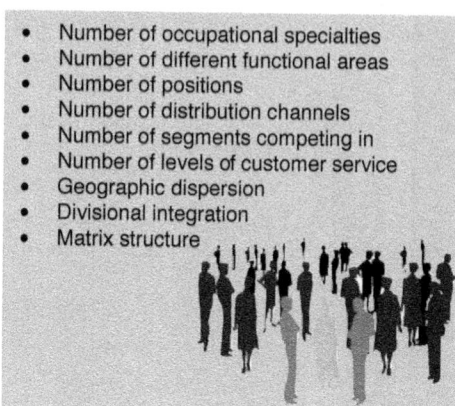

- Number of occupational specialties
- Number of different functional areas
- Number of positions
- Number of distribution channels
- Number of segments competing in
- Number of levels of customer service
- Geographic dispersion
- Divisional integration
- Matrix structure

EXHIBIT 12
Organizational Structure
Complexity

Complexity refers to the number of specializations within the organization along with the degree of task complexity within all jobs (Exhibit 12). Obviously, the more the specializations and task complexity that exists, the more significant will be the challenges to achieving effective implementation. The number of positions, distribution channels used to sell products and services, and the variety of brands or segments a firm competes in represent variables that will influence the overall complexity of the firm. The more complex the firm, the more challenges that management must face if it is to achieve successful implementation. The number of functional areas and linking mechanisms among them also add to the overall complexity of the enterprise. However, it is intuitively obvious that if the firm is more complex, it will have to rely more heavily on these linking mechanisms if it is to achieve success in implementing its strategy.

The dimension of configuration represents a similar challenge to management. *Configuration* refers to the actual spatial arrangements that exist in an organization and affects not only the transactions between workers and customers but also entire divisions within the firm. This is an especially important implementation dimension in multiunit firms where operations are dispersed geographically. In many ways, it is a dimension that is the outcome of the decisions made by management regarding formalization, centralization, and complexity.

Once management considers these dimensions, they must then actually be used to design how the organizational relationships will be formed. Exhibit 13 illustrates how a number of organizational units like those found in the common organization chart are

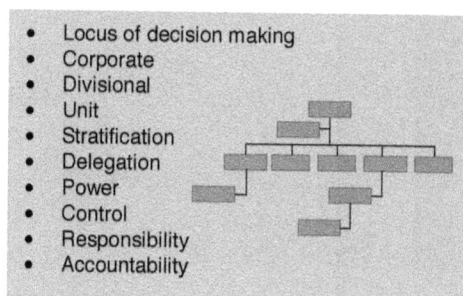

- Locus of decision making
- Corporate
- Divisional
- Unit
- Stratification
- Delegation
- Power
- Control
- Responsibility
- Accountability

EXHIBIT 13
Organizational Structure
Configuration

arranged. Although the standard organization chart is often outdated the moment it is drawn in these fast-changing times, nevertheless, some display of how the pieces, power, responsibility, and control of the organization is arranged is necessary to ensure proper implementation. Failure to spell out these relationships and communicate them to all employees is a sure recipe for trouble.

Flexibility is a dimension of structure because it refers to the firm's ability to change quickly in these dynamic times. This dimension increases in significance the larger the firm grows in number of units. Generally, the more units and wider dispersion, the less flexibility the firm has in reacting to change.

We have made the point all along that hospitality firms exist in a constant state of change. If this is so, then firms must be able to change when needed. This means that they must be flexible. Many management thinkers have suggested that firms should guard their CCs and buffer them from environmental influences (Exhibit 14). Although this thinking was fine in a stable environment, it is not so in today's volatile marketplace. The need for flexibility represents a paradox for management. On the one hand, creating core competencies and protecting them is important to achieving competitive advantage; on the other, hanging on to them too long can mean that others could possibly develop new competitive methods and competencies and thus achieve their own advantage. The ability of management to design firms that can achieve a set of highly developed competencies while still being flexible enough to strike quickly when new opportunities present themselves will be management's most significant challenge in the decade ahead.

The dimensions of structure constitute one of the most important variables used in trying to understand strengths and weaknesses. They are complex, consisting of several variables each that will impact the degree to which a firm will be able to execute CMs. It must be remembered that these dimensions should follow the firm's choice of CMs. It should not be the other way around, that is, where they drive the choice of methods. This is a very significant issue in multiunit hospitality firms because they are so complex, especially those with thousands of units. These large firms find it difficult to respond to change because their structures can be so inhibiting. Management must recognize that this is a problem and guard against it. Only then can it make the necessary decisions to achieve successful implementation. To help management with this process, the questions outlined in Exhibit 15 can serve as a guide for this important framework for evaluating CCs. These questions are followed by the structural dimensions that we outlined earlier. Although the list of questions is not exhaustive, it should serve to assist in the process of taking the concept of structure and applying it to the real-world setting.

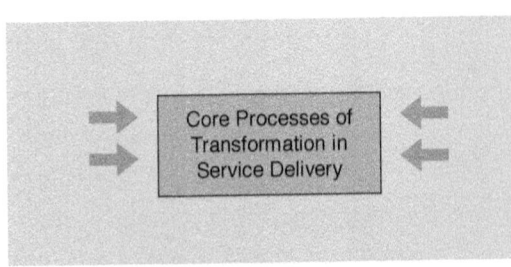

EXHIBIT 14
Organizational Structure Flexibility

1. Do you think that the policies & rules of operation in your organization are clearly spelled out? Formalization
2. As a manager at your level, are you allowed to make decisions about any of the following? Centralization
   * product or service offerings
   * operations
   * marketing strategy
   * research and development
   * capital budget decisions
   * long-term strategy decisions
3. Would you prefer the channels of communication of your company to be more open, more informal, or less so? Centralization
4. As a manager at your level would you say that access to financial and operating information is limited or unlimited? Centralization
5. Do you always follow the formal chain of command in your company when you communicate to managers at other levels or to employees? Formalization and centralization
6. When you receive orders from upper level management is the formal chain of command followed? Centralization
7. If the formal chain of command is not followed, from whom do you receive orders? Centralization
8. Do you talk informally to managers at other levels or with managers at your level? If so, how often? Complexity, formalization, configuration and centralization
9. Are there mechanisms in place that allow you to respond to market changes as quickly as needed? Flexibility
10. Are there linking mechanisms in your organization that allow you to communicate problems or concerns that you experience as you try to maintain competitive advantage? Formalization

EXHIBIT 15   Checklist of Variables to Assist in Evaluating the Firm's Structure

Financial Competencies

Although assessing financial competencies might appear last in this section, it actually deserves special attention. We have suggested under the functional framework that managers must look at all the functions of management, and this view has not changed. However, managing the balance sheet and its strength becomes perhaps one of the most important overall competencies.

A manager must be constantly taking a measurement of how the firm is doing regarding key financial indicators to be sure that capital can be raised when necessary and the reputation of the firm with respect to risk and return is strong. This is management's imperative, which should be in alignment with that of the owners of the firm.

SUMMARY

In this chapter we have looked at concepts to help us understand the illusive construct of structure. As illustrated in Exhibit 2 the construct has two major dimensions, analysis and implementation. We have attempted here to present ways for the manager to try to analyze and understand the total array of competencies that a firm must use to execute the implementation of CMs successfully. As you will no doubt agree, this analysis is an intellectual exercise of significant challenge. Our goal here was to provide several ways in which the firm's competencies can be analyzed. And as has been stated, the manager may use one or all to assist in trying to understand what the competencies are and how they interact with the successful delivery of CMs.

DISCUSSION QUESTIONS

1. Provide your interpretation of the service exchange and illustrate its importance in adding value to the firm.
2. Define what is meant by core competencies; peripheral competencies and linking systems.
3. Discuss the various frameworks for understanding the strengths and weaknesses of the competencies of the firm.
4. Describe organizational structure and its dimensions. Indicate how they may affect hospitality firms based upon the type of service level that they deliver.

NOTES

1. We consider this to be the focal point for all operational strategic thinking activities in the firm and to represent the one most important differentiating feature between the manufacturing and service industries.
2. Adopted from C. Becker and M. D. Olsen, "Exploring the Relationship Between Heterogeneity and Generic Management Trends in Hospitality Organizations," *International Journal of Hospitality Management* 14, no. 1 (1995): 39–52.
3. R. S. Kaplan and D. P. Norton, *The Balanced Scorecard* (Harvard Business School Press, 1996).

Appendix 1

Concepts of Service

The hospitality industry has changed dramatically. Intense competition, sophisticated consumers, revolutionary changes in information technology, as well as globalization, have forced hospitality managers to seek sustainable competitive advantage. Unfortunately, reliance on easily copied tactics results in only momentary advantage. What is today's unique atrium lobby is tomorrow's fact of life. What wows the guests today, bores them tomorrow. Therefore, managers today must seek to emphasize those value-adding competitive methods (CMs) that are difficult for competitors to duplicate and continues to impress guests. Quality service is one of those methods. Service quality depends on proper training, execution, and quality control as well as sufficient resource allocation to attain and maintain leadership.

As noted earlier, services possess characteristics that make them different from products, thus requiring a different strategic mindset. To gain competitive advantage through outstanding service, the firm's managers must focus on those core competencies necessary to ensure that the service transaction is completed successfully. Sustainable competitive advantage is only achieved when a firm is able to prevent its competitors from easily duplicating its portfolio of products and services. Thus managers must understand that service, when well conceived and executed, is a weapon capable of both providing sustainable competitive advantage and creating value for the firm in the form of cash flow per share. Service must be an activity that provides added value to both the guest and the firm. It satisfies a need of the guest, for which he or she is willing to pay the firm at a level greater than it costs the firm to provide it, thereby creating a positive cash flow per share. The challenge to management is to ensure that the millions of daily service encounters (moments of truth) are executed in a manner which ensures that guest expectations are met or exceeded at a price that meets the return required by the firm. Therein lies the rub! To meet this challenge managers must:

1. Understand how guests derive utility from the service
2. Understand how the organization can produce and deliver that utility
3. Understand how the organization must be managed to add value and produce the rate of return required
4. Enable the organization to meet its objectives to both guests and owners

Successful execution of the service encounter depends on the ability of the firm's managers to implement the chosen strategy.

To be capable of accomplishing this, leaders must undergo a dramatic shift in managerial thinking:

1. From an all-devouring attention of controlling costs (internal focus) to attention to the results of good performance (external)—cash flow per share
2. From a focus on making jobs employee centered (structure) to a focus on both the employee and the guest (process management);
3. As well as developing a total understanding of the roles of operations, marketing, and human resources in the delivery of service.

In accomplishing this there results a change in focus:

1. From product focus to total guest experience
2. From short-term to long-term relationships with guests, employees, and suppliers
3. From technical quality of core product outcomes to quality of the overall relationship with both guests and employees

It is important to understand the manner in which the delivery of a service is different from the delivery of a product. Researchers over the past two decades have espoused many differences between the nature of products and services. The prevailing evidence suggests that services are different from products in the hospitality industry because of the following characteristics:

1. Service is a performance not a physical object (intangible)
2. The guest is involved in production
3. Service delivery management—the guests desire to be served when and where they choose
4. Quality control is difficult

SERVICE AS A PERFORMANCE

Due to its very nature, service in the hospitality industry is a performance where guest and service provider interact in a complicated process. Because it is a performance involving people who may or may not have the same shared vision of the desired result, it is extremely challenging to manage. Survey after survey reveals that a woeful minority of travelers in the United States rate the service they receive in hotels and motels as either excellent or very good. This is after years of Total Quality Management and other programs designed to provide guest satisfaction. It becomes apparent that managers must understand the guest's desired outcome as well as the costs they are willing to bear to achieve it. In addition, the manager must be able to communicate this vision to the service employee to ensure alignment. Beyond this, the manager must also realize the costs associated with providing the service to ensure the long-term success of the firm.

By viewing service as a performance, important service dimensions are illustrated. The first is the idea of role playing. Each participant in the service encounter has a role to play. It is when there is a misconception of these roles that ambiguity and discontinuity degrade the service delivery. If the restaurant server does not recognize that a guest ordering wine is an expert and treats the person as a novice, explaining all the wine characteristics in great detail, there is a great possibility that the guest will perceive the service encounter as less than satisfactory. In this instance the server did not read the proper cues from the guest as to the guest's expectation of his or her role. It is the role of management to act as a director and train the employee to read the various cues given by guests. Of course, service employees must also be trained not only in how to play the various roles but also how to know which is appropriate for the situation. The idea is that of a service repertory where a

service employee reads guest cues, chooses the correct role, and plays it to the satisfaction of the guest. Management must also provide guests with cues as to what role they are expected to play. This is done through market communication. In restaurants, for example, the guest must be given clues as to the type of service: quick, limited, or full service; formal or informal; and so forth. An extensive wine list gives the impression to the guest that the server may be relied on to provide assistance in choosing a wine. If in fact management has not trained the server adequately, a perception of poor service is the probable outcome of the service performance.

The second concept is that of front stage versus backstage. Employees who come into contact with guests must recognize that they are "onstage." Actions, words, and gestures of all employees shape the guests perception of the performance. Housekeepers, bus persons, and maintenance employees must be trained to understand that when they are in the presence of guests, they are as much a part of the performance as the bellmen, servers, and front desk personnel. In short, everything perceptible to the guest must be thought of as being a visible component of the service. Personnel who are backstage, as it were, are just as important because they support the people onstage. If they fail to perform correctly, the results of their actions will also be apparent when the room is not ready or the menu item is not available.

GUEST INVOLVEMENT IN THE SERVICE PROCESS

In the hospitality industry, the guest is involved in the process. This involvement impacts not only their perception of the service but also other guests' perceptions. This characteristic requires that managers design service systems that are guest friendly as well as choose market segments that are compatible. Again we must focus on the development of the core competencies (CCs) that enable the firm to manage the exchange process in a manner that differentiates it positively from its competitors. The exchange is made more complex by the interaction of the guest in the delivery process.

There is guest involvement is every service system. In hotels from the time guests enter the system either through the reservation system or the check-in procedure, they are a part of the process. The same applies to restaurants, attractions, car rental agencies, and cruise lines. The manner in which the system is designed impacts directly on guest satisfaction. The simple concept of finding the front desk can often be a challenge to the guest: Multifloored lobbies with no signage are a perfect example. Extensive menus often slow down service when a guest has difficulty in choosing among all the selections. In designing the system, guest needs must be considered. If quick service is desired, choices must be limited. If expedited check-in is desired, only that information absolutely necessary should be sought.

Given the diversity of our global environment, the idea of a single homogeneous market segment is passé. Therefore when choosing market segments to serve, managers must ensure that they are compatible. Different market segments have different needs, and it is very difficult for one firm to fulfill all of these needs, particularly if they are too diverse. Also it must be remembered that guests impact not only their own service, but also that of those around them. The crying baby next to the couple celebrating a special occasion will probably result in dissatisfaction on the part of the couple. The philosophy of selling to any group (just put heads in beds) may have negative implications when two disparate groups interact in the hotel. Upscale guests may resent the impact on their hotel stay by tour groups. If

management desires to sell to disparate groups, it is best that they attempt to keep them separated during their stay.

SERVICE DELIVERY MANAGEMENT

Manufacturing firms have the ability to inventory their products as a means of adjusting to fluctuating market demand. Barrington and Olsen[1] found that the uniqueness of the hospitality industry is in part due to the fact that guests must be provided with the correct service when and where they want it, consistently. Hospitality firms, however, are unable to inventory their service. This characteristic can have a great impact on the profitability of the firm. Hospitality managers must utilize their productive assets (labor and physical facility) in the most efficient manner to assure sufficient cash flow per share. Because guests demand the service where and when they want it, the concept of service delivery management is important. In a market where demand is constant, management of service delivery is relatively simple. It is only when demand fluctuates that service delivery management is a concern. When discussing service delivery management in the hospitality industry, we mean the management of the physical facility, with its accompanying equipment, and labor.

The question of how much physical capacity to build is a concern because of the impact of fixed costs on cash flow per share. Hospitality managers faced with excess capacity are often tempted to offer discounts in an attempt to cover as much fixed cost as possible. This practice is usually disastrous. The same problem faces all hospitality decision makers: Too much capacity with its attendant high fixed costs during periods of slow demand reduce profitability; not enough capacity during periods of peak demand and potential sales are lost, again exerting a negative effect on available cash flow. Capacity management is critical in the management of service delivery systems.

Staffing is problematic when demand fluctuates. Although daily staffing requirements are often difficult to determine, one must also consider the size of the total staff. The addition of personnel to the organization inflicts costs. People must be hired and trained, and payroll taxes must be paid. These costs are the same whether we are hiring full-time or part-time employees. Overscheduling personnel can result in high labor costs and reduced cash flow, whereas underscheduling can result in lost sales and guest dissatisfaction due to poor service.

As may be seen, because our industry is capacity constrained with heavy fixed investments and substantial fixed labor costs, even small improvements in service delivery can have a significant impact on cash flows. In addition to the impact on cash flows, good service delivery also results in guest satisfaction and return visits.

QUALITY CONTROL

The fourth characteristic, quality control, is the cause of the failure of many hospitality organizations. In manufacturing, quality control is relatively easy to manage. Technical measurements, tests, detailed specifications, and robotics all contribute to a consistent, high-quality product. The fact that these procedures occur out of the sight of the customer is another plus. Do any of us know how many times an appliance we have purchased has been sent back by quality control personnel until it has met specifications? With manufactured goods, most corrective efforts are not discernible to the customer.

This is not the case in the hospitality industry. The short distribution channel—a hospitality service is produced and consumed simultaneously—creates significant challenges to quality control. Because guests are involved in every encounter, they are immediately aware when the service is not being performed correctly. Therefore management of the process, including the development of standards of delivery, is critical. Due to the heterogeneous nature of services—it is a transaction perceived by different personalities—allocation of resources to training is imperative. Managers must be aware that it is impossible to have a disgruntled guest forget what has occurred. The best that can be expected is to mollify them through quick and positive recovery actions. It must be understood by all managers that quality in the hospitality industry is not an added-on inspection function. It is an ongoing process that must be designed into the service delivery system because any breakdown in quality is immediately discernible to the guest. It is through the investment in core competencies that the firm reduces the uncertainties of the moments of truth and attains a level of quality service that separates it from its competitors.

Proper management of these four interrelated characteristics is what differentiates successful companies from their competitors. Successful service managers understand that there is a need to redefine jobs as well as retrain managers and employees. They understand that guests come to them with unsatisfied needs looking to them for fulfillment. Whatever these needs are, the guest desires hassle-free solutions at a reasonable price. Their problems are our problems. The Ritz-Carlton Hotel company understands this and trains their employees to think and act appropriately. It is a part of their service philosophy. Espoused as number 8 of *The Ritz-Carlton Basics* Exhibit 1A) see, it is clearly stated that "Any employee who receives a customer complaint *owns* the complaint". According to Ed Staros, former vice president operations, each Ritz-Carlton employee "is empowered to (1) break away from their routine duties; (2) apply immediate positive action with a $2,000 spending authority; (3) document the incident for future analysis; and (4) snap back to their routine." Although firms competing in other hospitality industry segments may think they cannot afford to empower employees to solve guest problems, the truth is that they must. The dollar limits may vary, but the concept is valid for all market segments: The loss of customers through the delivery of improper service is more expensive than remedying the problem.

In the previous section, we presented an overview of service including its importance as a differentiating competitive tactic. We also discussed the characteristics that make services more difficult to manage than products. In the next section we explore the concept of quality and its place in the management of service.

EXHIBIT 1A The Ritz-Carlton Basics[1]

1. The Credo will be known, owned and energized by all employees.
2. Our motto is: "We are Ladies and Gentlemen serving Ladies and Gentlemen". Practice teamwork and "lateral service" to create a positive work environment.
3. The three steps of service will be practiced by all employees,
4. All employees will successfully complete Training Certification to ensure that they understand how to perform to The Ritz-Carlton standards in their position.
5. Each employee will understand their work area and Hotel goals as established in each strategic plan.
6. All employees will know the needs of their internal and external customers (guests and employees) so that we may deliver the products and services they expect. Use guest preference pads to record specific needs.
7. Each employee will continuously identify defects (Mr. BIV) throughout the hotel.
8. Any employee who receives a customer complaint "owns" the complaint.
9. Instant guest pacification will be ensured by all. React quickly to correct the problem immediately. Follow-up with a telephone call within twenty minutes to verify that the problem has been resolved to the customer's satisfaction. Do everything you possibly can to never lose a guest.
10. Guest incident action forms are used to record and communicate every incident of guest dissatisfaction. Every employee is empowered to resolve a problem and to prevent a repeat occurrence.
11. Uncompromising levels of cleanliness are the responsibility of every employee.
12. "Smile – We are on stage." Always maintain positive eye contact. Use the proper vocabulary with our guests. (Use words like – "Good Morning," "Certainly," "I'll be happy to" and "My pleasure").
13. Be an ambassador of your Hotel in and outside of the work place. Always talk positively. No negative comments.
14. Escort guests rather than pointing out directions to another area of the Hotel.
15. Be knowledgeable of Hotel information (hours of operation, etc.) to answer guest inquiries. Always recommend the Hotel's retail and food and beverage outlets prior to outside facilities.
16. Use proper telephone etiquette. Answer within three rings and with a "smile". When necessary ask the caller "May I place you on hold." Do not screen calls. Eliminate call transfers when possible.
17. Uniforms are to be immaculate. Wear proper and safe footwear (clean and polished), and your correct name tag. Take pride and care in your personal appearance (adhering to all grooming standards).
18. Ensure all employees know their roles during emergency situations and are aware of fire and life safety response processes.
19. Notify your supervisor immediately of hazards, injuries, equipment or assistance that you need. Practice energy conservation and proper maintenance and repair of Hotel property and equipment.
20. Protecting the assets of a Ritz-Carlton Hotel is the responsibility of every employee.

[1] Ayala, G., Staros, E., and West, J. J., "Marketing quality in the hotel sector", in *Service Quality in Hospitality Organizations*, Olsen, Teare and Gummesson eds, 1996, Cassell: London.

MANAGING QUALITY

The importance of the effective delivery of quality service is becoming more evident throughout all aspects of the service sector and especially in the hospitality industry. The management of quality is essential in that it directs the firm's goals and has a profound influence on the functions of individual employees. It must be imbedded in the corporate culture and communicated clearly to all members of the organization.

There are many definitions of quality; most are more appropriate to manufacturing than to service. Juran[2] notes that many companies have defined quality in terms such as conformance to standards or specifications. He thinks that these work well in the ongoing production of services at the operations level, especially where employees may have difficulty in identifying guest needs, but they are dangerous at the higher levels of management. At those levels it is important that management identify the products and services that respond to customer needs, as well as recognize that conformance is only one of many measures needed to ensure quality. It must be remembered that quality is a target that moves as guests' needs change. The organization must design services that are capable of modification or complete change as dictated by guest needs, either now or in the future. It must be design services with the future in mind: Management must possess a future orientation. Juran, who along with Deming is recognized globally as the founder and leader of the quality movement, defines quality along two dimensions: (1) features that respond to customer needs and (2) freedom from defects.

Gronroos,[3] in his research in service quality, states that quality is what guests perceive. He notes that top managers must define quality the same way the guest does. It should always be remembered that "what counts is quality as it is perceived by customers." Gronroos defined quality along two dimensions:

1. Technical or outcome related—what the guest actually receives is extremely important to them. If the steak is not cooked as ordered or the hotel room is dirty, the guest immediately makes a judgment as to the quality of the product based component of the firm's product. In many companies this is their only definition of quality. However, this is only one dimension, it is what the guest is left with and can be measured objectively by both the guest and the management;

2. Functional or process related—this is how the guest actually receives the service from the organization. A steak may be cooked to perfection but if it is served by a surly service employee, the guest's perception of quality will be adversely affected. Functional quality is more than simply the interaction of the service employee with the guest, it is also the design of the process to satisfy guest needs. A caring, empathic service employee cannot overcome a poorly designed service system. If one of the guest's expectations is convenience, then the system must be convenient for the guest to arrive at a feeling of good quality. The functional dimension is much more difficult to measure as it is a subjective judgment made by the guest based upon how they received the service and how they experienced the total service delivery process.

Drawing on the previously cited works of Juran, who found that the definition of quality was too rich to be defined along one dimension, and Gronroos, who partitioned service quality into two components, technical and functional, we define quality in the hospitality industry along three dimensions—doing the

1. right thing—here we are following Juran's dictum of providing products/services that respond to guest needs. If the guest desires in-room checkout for convenience, then it will be provided. If there is a need that other competitors are not serving, then the firm will attain a competitive edge in being the first to provide it: *competitive methods*;
2. right—here we combine both Juran and Gronroos in that the service must not only be free from defects (technical dimension), the service delivery process must be designed in such a manner as to provide for all guest needs, such as convenience, good interpersonal relationships with service employees, and so on:—*core competencies*;
3. consistently—here we recognize the need for the organization to be able to deliver its service/product delivery process the same way through millions of service transactions. Inconsistency is the bane of hospitality firms. The public does not desire to be surprised and associate a desired outcome with a brand. When the brand falls short of those expectations, a negative judgment of the quality of the experience is made by the guest: *good implementation.*

As we suggested earlier in the chapter, to gain a sustainable competitive advantage there must be a linking of CCs and CMs. Nowhere is this dictum more obvious than in our definition of quality as *doing the right thing, right, consistently*. It is incumbent on management to create these linkages when it is designing the service delivery system. Our definition also recognizes the marketing aspect of quality with the idea of providing guests the utility they desire at the level of their expectations every time we serve them.

PERCEIVED QUALITY VERSUS PERCEIVED VALUE

It is easy to confuse perceived quality with perceived value. In fact, the two are very different concepts. The essence of the definition of quality as stated earlier is the correct identification of guest needs and the correct satisfaction of those needs consistently: In short, performing at a level that meets or exceeds guest expectations. Research by Boulding[4] has concluded that individuals enter the service encounter with two types of expectations: what will happen and what should happen. After the service encounter, the guest develops a cumulative perception of the delivered service based on initial expectations and actual experiences. Therefore perceived quality is a subjective judgment of the matching of expectations with experience. If there is no negative gap between the two, then a positive perception of quality is experienced. As the gap widens in a negative direction, the perception of quality is decreased. A wide positive gap is as inappropriate as a wide negative gap. If the firm is consistently exceeding expectations to a high degree, they are probably losing money either through higher costs or lost revenue due to lower prices. They are basically overserving the needs of the market. Although this may be an effective short-term approach to gain market share, it is not sustainable in the long term. The law of cash flow will eventually come into play and the firm will be required to cut service or raise prices.

Perceived value is a cost-based relationship. To put it algebraically: $PV = b - c$. Perceived value equal benefits minus costs. In every service encounter in our industry, the guest receives benefits and bears costs. Exhibit 2A lists examples of the various costs and benefits in the service experience.

As seen in Exhibit 2A, guests may perceive a lunch of poor technical and functional quality as a good value if it is convenient and inexpensive. What is illustrated is that the

EXHIBIT 2A	Perceived Value	

Perceived Value	Benefit	Cost
Good	Lunch	inexpensive; poor technical quality; poor functional quality convenient
Poor	Lunch	expensive; excellent technical quality; excellent functional quality; inconvenient.
Good	Lunch	moderately priced; good technical quality; good functional quality; convenient

benefit received is greater than the cost the guest had to bear, thus a positive perceived value. Many of us have purchased either meals or other services that we considered to be of poor quality, but the reduced cost influenced our decision. Oftentimes consumers agree that the service is of low quality, but they were influenced by an overbearing need such as convenience due to time constraints or budget. In this scenario, the low-quality producer enjoys a competitive advantage that will last only as long as they are not faced with competition from a higher quality firm entering the market. If this does occur, the new entrant will immediately attain market dominance. In the case of the firm that possesses both good technical and functional quality but is both expensive and inconvenient, management should reconsider their strategic marketing plan. Perhaps they should not be competing in the lunch market and should focus only on dinner. Outback Steakhouse has followed this strategy to great success; they recognize that good dinner locations are not necessarily good lunch locations. Desiring to maximize their cash flow per share by lowering investment and increasing margins, Outback management has positioned their restaurants in secondary markets that are easily accessible to their dinner guests while

eliminating the lunch day part completely. Many casual dining theme restaurants located in excellent lunch locations are beginning to experience a decline in dinner traffic as more competitors follow the Outback marketing strategy. The third firm that is meeting the needs of the marketplace at a reasonable cost is also perceived to be a good value and possesses a much stronger competitive position than its two rivals. Success relates to management's choice of the portfolio of products and services they think will enable them to attain a sustainable competitive advantage. In the preceding example, only the third firm seems to have made the correct choice.

PRINCIPLES GUIDING THE IMPROVEMENT OF QUALITY SERVICE

Berry[5] posits seven principles that can be used to guide the improvement of quality service. We have adapted them for the purposes of this text:

1. *Quality Is Defined by Customers:* Quality is conformance to guest expectations. Guests decide what good quality is and what they consider important in the service product. It is imperative that management understand their perspective.

2. ***Quality Is a Journey:*** Quality must be pursued constantly. The journey is for continuous improvement. Guests' needs and expectations change as they are exposed to new experiences, and the intelligent manager is constantly striving for improvement.

3. ***Quality Is Everyone's Job:*** Responsibility for quality service cannot be delegated to one individual or department. In the hospitality industry we are a collection of processes, each of which must be managed in conformance with the goals of the organization. Every service employee and moment of truth counts. The guest perceives the experience as a whole, not a collection of processes.

4. ***Quality, Leadership, and Communication Are Inseparable:*** To produce quality service experiences, employees must posses knowledge, feedback, and support from management. Management, however, must provide service leadership.

5. ***Quality and Integrity Are Inseparable:*** Service quality requires a corporate culture that emphasizes integrity. Fairness toward guests and employees must be a core value shared by all.

6. ***Quality Is a Design Issue:*** Service quality must be designed in advance. The use of technology, personnel, and guest participation must be planned in advance. The process must be designed with the ultimate goal in mind.

7. ***Quality Is Keeping the Service Promise:*** Guests' expectations are often shaped by the organization. When the organization promises to provide a certain level of service, it must keep those promises. Failure to do so results in poor perceived quality and guest dissatisfaction.

Although these principles seem to be self-evident, they are not practiced by the majority of the firms in the hospitality industry. It should be heartening to remember that the three firms used as examples in this chapter follow these principles and are leaders in their industry segment.

In this appendix we have examined the concept of quality service. We have discussed the various dimensions that make the management of service different from the management of products. We also have recognized that the hospitality industry is not a pure service industry because we produce both a product and a service for our guests. We must recognize that the service process is managed and executed by humans who are apt to occasionally make mistakes. Although this is a given, the management of the firm must always strive for complete excellence—mistake-free service. If they don't, the mindset is established to accept less than 100% excellence—a fatal mistake. Competitive advantage will be lost as guests' experiences don't match expectations and dissatisfaction results in lost sales. A rate of 95% complete satisfaction means that 5,000 guests out of 100,000 will be dissatisfied and probably not return—that is a significant amount of lost revenue!

Notes

1. M. Barrington & Olsen, M. D. (1988). *"An evaluation of service complexity measures of front office employees in the hotel/motel industry."* Hospitality Education and Research Journal, 12(2), 149–162.

2. J. M. Juran, *Juran on Quality by Design: The New Steps for Planning Quality into Goods and Services* (The Free Press, 1992).

3. C. Gronroos, *Service Management and Marketing: Managing the Moment of Truth in Service Competition* (Lexington Books, 1990).

4. W. Boulding et al., "A Dynamic Model of Service Quality: From Expectations to Behavioural Intentions," *Journal of Marketing Research* 1, no. 30 (1993): 7–27.

5. L. L. Berry, "Discovering the Soul of Service," Advance Uncorrected Proofs, The Free Press, 1999.

CASE STUDY

Use of Loyalty Programs to Build Competitive Advantage*

THE LOYALTY PROGRAM IS THE GAME OF THE DAY

The top three deciding factors that drive a guest's lodging purchase are location, brand familiarity, and loyalty or reward programs. In today's highly competitive business environment, customer loyalty programs are a way to retain repeat customers. Loyalty programs supposedly result in customer commitment and serve as a powerful inducement of return.[1] The programs have become a competitive necessity. Consumers have embraced the concept of rewards and are increasingly looking for a payoff for their spending behaviors, even as they go about their everyday activities.[2] According to Visa's USA's quarterly report, more than 81% of all U.S. households participate in at least one type of reward program; 57% of Americans own a reward card, and of those, 71% use their reward cards. Moreover, an increasingly widespread use of debit cards is reported. Consumer debit transactions totaled $11.2 billion in 2006, a 17% increase over the previous year.[3] The increased usage of debit cards has resulted in increased customer expectations.[4] From buying groceries, to filling up the car, to going out to eat, debit card use is increasing, and consumers desire "credit" for their purchases.[5]

Rewarding customers for their loyalty has become widespread in service industries and increasingly common in many segments of the travel industry, including airlines, hotels, and restaurants.[6] As a result, customers are now able to pay for goods and services with new currencies such as frequent flier miles and Diner's Club Rewards.[7] To leverage customer retention, many restaurant companies have turned to the frequency programs, and frequent flier programs now have become the most important marketing tool of the airline industry.[8]

OBJECTIVES OF LOYALTY OR FREQUENCY REWARD PROGRAMS

Companies understand that loyal customers are more profitable than nonloyal customers[9]. It is estimated to be three to five times less expensive to retain an existing customer than to attract a new one. These cost advantages are generated by reduced service costs, increased guest spending, lowered price sensitivity, and positive word-of-mouth referrals.[10]

Through loyalty programs, companies hope to achieve the following objectives:

- Increased focus on building customer loyalty: To protect the existing customer base and maintain sales levels, margins, and profits.[11]
- To deepen their customer relationships: To enhance the market share by increasing sales to existing customers.[12]

*This mini-case is written based on information available up to November 2006.

- Drive usage behavior: To enhance cross-selling the company's products and services.[13]
- To create differentiation.

LOYALTY PROGRAM IN HOTELS

The hotel industry has matured with a small number of key players. Across the industry, customer defection rates are high, which in turn decreases corporate performance. Therefore, customer retention is a key challenge for management. To achieve competitive advantage, hotels adopted frequency reward programs. Now, just as the airlines, nearly all the major hotel chains have frequent guest programs where hotels reward their frequent guests with free room stays and other perks.[14] In fact, many companies have spent much time, money, and effort in building their customer retention programs and enhancing their loyalty schemes as the most important marketing tool in an effort to compete for a shrinking pool of frequent travelers. Hoteliers consider it one of the single most cost-effective ways hotel brands can acquire new customers, retain existing customers, and drive competitive market share. Marriott International has found that members of the Marriott Rewards program more than double their number of stays after joining the program. Hotels are making it easier for their customers to claim rewards. In other words, loyalty programs of branded hotel companies are becoming a stronger influence than ever.

Hotel programs are getting generous[15] but more complex compared to airline programs. Unlike frequent-flier plans, which typically grant points for miles flown, hotel programs are usually based on dollars spent, including the cost of the rooms, food, and other services but not taxes.[16] With frequent flier programs, a customer can get free trips in the domestic United States for 25,000 points, with advance booking, and not travel on a blackout day. In contrast, hotel plans require different amounts of points for different properties.[17] So it is not easy to compare the programs between hotel chains because after a certain number of stays, participating guests can earn a higher number of points.[18] The progression in value of hotel loyalty programs has prompted a growing number of members to redeem points for hotel stays rather than transfer their points to miles toward free airline tickets.[19] Hotel points have become more valuable than airline miles.

Based on individual needs, travelers have a variety of loyalty programs to choose from among the different brands of major hotel companies covering a range of price points. Presumably, there are some important differences between plans, enough to make customers favor one over another.[20] Loyalty programs span from those offered by major international chains, to second-tier hotel operators, and all the way to independents.

Programs offered by international chains include Hyatt's Gold Passport, Marriott's Honored Guest, Starwood Preferred Guest, Intercontinental's Priority Club, and Hilton's HHonors.

Intercontinental Hotels

The group's Priority Club Rewards was the industry's first hotel loyalty program. It is the largest with a membership exceeding 27 million.[21] It provides customers with choice and flexibility. The rewards program has 3,600 properties worldwide and covers these brands: InterContinental, Crowne Plaza, Hotel Indigo, Holiday Inn, Staybridge Suites, and Candlewood Suites. The program is noted for its consumer-centric approach. The Group (IHG) has even gone as far as launching the "Any Hotel, Anywhere" option in 2005 in which members can trade their points for stays at hotels outside the chain. The company believes that this flexibility will make customers more loyal to the brand.[22] This is a partnership with American

Express Incentive Services to offer free nights at any hotel worldwide that accepts the American Express card.[23]

Marriott

Marriott's Rewards program has three "Elite" levels of membership.[24] Marriott claims that it operates the largest frequent guest program in the world. With hotels that span the various price points available, the hotelier serves guests' lodgings needs under these names: Marriott, Renaissance, Courtyard, Residence Inn, and Fairfield Inn. A study showed that the Marriott Rewards program requires fewer visits for free stays than competitors' frequent-visitor programs. The rewards program helped Marriott to remain relatively successful through the sluggish economy of 2001 to 2003.

Hilton

This hotel chain also found success in its frequent-visitor programs, HHonors, which encourages customer loyalty with the lure of benefits. One out of three guests belongs to the Hilton HHonors loyalty program. These 3.5 million active members are the most important customers for the company's nine brands, which include Hilton, Doubletree, Embassy Suites, and Hampton Inn.[25] HHonors takes the advantage of OnQ, a technology platform that enables real-time updating and access to customer profiles at all of the company's 2,200 hotels via reservation centers, customer service departments, websites, and the front desk.[26] The evolution of technology allows Hilton to get back to the basics of hospitality by finally having the means to offer customized incentives,[27] where members can earn both points in its HHonors program and frequent flier miles on an airline of their choice based on the same hotel stay.[28]

Other Programs

Starwood Preferred Guest: available at Sheraton, St. Regis, Westin, W Hotels, Four Points by Sheraton, TownePlace Suites, and SpringHill Suites.[29]

Hyatt Gold Passport: available at Hyatt and Hawthorn Suites. Hawthron Suites, an extended-stay brand that is part of U.S. Franchise Systems, set the precedent for the idea of cross-price-point partnership in 2004.[30] Frequent guests with Hawthorn Suites became eligible to redeem points for stays at Hyatt.[31]

Radisson Gold Points: available at Radisson, Country Inns, Park Inn, and Park Plaza Hotels.[32]

Members of **Choice Hotels** International and **Cendant** Hotel Group's frequent guest programs can redeem their points for stays at full-service hotels outside the Choice and Cendant portfolios of midprice and economy brands. Choice partnered with Preferred Hotels & Resorts Worldwide, and Cendants with Sol Melia Hotels & Resorts and Outrigger Hotels & Resorts.[33] Preferred Hotels & Resorts is a collection of independently owned hotels. Sol Melia has more than 330 properties in resorts like Puerto Rico and the Dominican Republic; Outrigger, with 51 properties, is a well-known brand in Hawaii, Australia, New Zealand, Fiji, and Tahiti.[34] This move allows them to compete more effectively with the industry's larger and more established frequency programs.[35] For Preferred, Sol Melia, and Outrigger, they also benefit from partnering with midprice and economy chains.[36] This allows them to generate more room nights and build brand awareness that they would not otherwise be able to do.

Nonhotel Rewards

Hotel companies such as Carlson and Wyndham are at a disadvantage in encouraging customer loyalty, given their size and distribution, compared with such multitiered competitors as Marriott International, Hilton Hotels Corp., InterContinetal Hotels Group, and Starwood Hotels & Resorts Worldwide, each of which has a multimillion member frequency program.[37] In order to compete, they provide their membership with nonhotel rewards. Carlson Hotels Worldwide allows its Goldpoints frequency program members redemption options beyond free hotel stays.[38] Travelers earn Goldpoints Plus credit for stays at any Carlson-branded hotel.[39] Carlson brands include Radisson, Country Inns & Suites, Park Plaza, and Park Inn.[40] This program allows members to have access to entertainment and shopping rewards, in addition to free lodging, products from name-brand online retailers and gift certificates, and other purchases at other Carlson companies, including T.G.I. Friday's restaurants and the Radisson Seven Seas Cruise line.[41]

Wyndham International gave members of its By Request loyalty program the flexibility to earn non-hotel-stay gifts through a partnership with American Express Other examples include companies[42] like Florida-based America's Best Value Inn, which is offering members of its Value Club who make a reservation through the company's website complimentary travel insurance.[43]

Independent Hotels

Small independent hotels can often compete on price but do not have the ability or resources to offer such reward programs.[44] Some independent hoteliers consider this unfair competition and claim that loyalty schemes are placing pressure on hotels to relinquish their independence.[45] Not surprisingly, loyalty programs have become a major challenge faced by independent hotels. These programs are a powerful motivator for booking. Independent hotels and boutique hotels also reward loyalty. They create loyalty with personalized service, for instance, tickets to ball games or preparation of their favorite foods. They reward employees for gaining information about what pleases guests. Some of them invest in more comprehensive Internet marketing. For example, 11 independents formed a joint marketing group of independents to market its website, UniqueChicagoHotels,

where visitors to the site are directed to each hotel's website.

AIRLINES, TRAVEL AND OTHER HOSPITALITY COMPANIES

Travel companies, especially airlines, are hard pressed to provide new outlets where customers can use their points, which have flooded the market in recent years as reward-generating credit cards have become more common. They also are responding to desires among members for more choice in the rewards program, how they use their points, and a range of relevant rewards that appeal to their unique preferences.[46] As airplanes and hotels fill to near-record capacities, loyalty programs are expanding the ways they let members redeem their points. In addition, especially as demand for airline seats has rebounded but airfares have remained low over the past year, airlines are reserving fewer seats for rewards customers. Jay Sorensen, president of IdeaWorks, a travel-industry consulting firm, estimates that in 1994, one mile was worth 2.4 cents, whereas at the end of 2004, its value had dropped to 1.4 cents.

For instance, American Express Co. starts letting Membership Rewards customers use their points to buy travel through the American Express Travel website. That gives members for the first time the option to directly purchase airplane tickets, hotel stays, and cruises at the travel site, a private-label version of Travelocity, which includes airlines such as AMR Corp.'s American Airlines and UAL Corp's United Airlines that are not Membership Rewards partners. The American Express Peso Platinum Card offers extensive travel-related rewards for its members, with over 40 airlines and 100 hotels within the Asia Pacific region listed in its 2006 Membership Rewards Catalogue.[47]

Whereas airlines have made it a little harder and costlier to use frequent-flier miles since 9/11, hotels have gotten more promotional.[48] Many now have tie-ins with credit cards; for instance, the use of a MasterCard to pay for stays at a Hyatt Hotels property earns a night free.[49] Many chains are also allowing guests to earn points through spending at certain restaurants and car rental chains and to exchange points for everything from Tumi luggage to gift certificates at Best Buy.[50]

Similarly, persevering loyalty is a challenge in the gaming industry because consumers are largely driven by where they win and where they lose.[51] To gain customer loyalty is not only limited to hotels. In fact, casinos excel in loyalty program effectiveness, as compared to airlines and hotels. The Las Vegas–based casino company Harrah's created its Total Rewards program with the goals of gaining a greater share of its customers' overall gaming budget and providing superior customer service.[52] It offers customers a wide range of rewards beyond merchandise, including more than 50 vacation packages and once-in-a-lifetime experiences.[53] Harrah's estimated that customers spent about 43% of their annual gaming budgets at its properties in 2002, compared with 36% before the program started in 1999.[54] The program is operated under the idea of cross-market play where customers can gain points in any of Harrah's 26 casinos when they travel. The program uses WINet (winner's information network), which connects and consolidates customer information from all of Harrah's transactional, slot machine, hotel management, and reservation systems.[55] This allows the company to identify cardholder spending patterns and create individualized markets based on their preferences and projected worth.[56] This is compared to tracking an online shopper's website behavior.[57]

HOW TO RUN AN EFFECTIVE LOYALTY PROGRAM?

The success (strength) of customer loyalty programs is measured by two components: the percentage of guests who are members of a brand's loyalty program (participation) and the importance of that program in the guests' decision to stay at that brand (effectiveness).[58] Companies invested substantial amounts of money in the introduction of loyalty programs with the aim of increasing customer retention rates. Statistics show that there is definitely value to frequent guest programs because many travelers do habitually make their travel decisions based on their memberships in loyalty programs. Moreover, firms can use reward programs to support their capacity management.[59] It is found that reward programs add flexibility for firms to adjust their capacities to market demand and avoid intense price competition during the period of low demand.[60] Loyalty programs have gone through phases, with the original airline miles programs giving way to the elite rewards packages of perks and special access.[61]

Which rewards programs is best? What kinds of rewards do customers prefer when making dining decisions?[62] Despite the large sum of investment on loyalty programs and their rising popularity, there is doubt among scholars over the effectiveness of these frequent user programs,[63] which has not yet been empirically supported because loyalty programs are mainly set up for retention purposes and not for gaining new customers. Thus companies offering rewards programs should not take things for granted. It seems that the best rewards programs are those that encourage loyalty, profitability, and an ever-deepening customer relationship.[64]

One of the elements that determine a program's value from a customer's perspective is the timing of the reward.[65] It also depends on the amount of effort needed to reach the requirements of a particular reward and the relative efficiency of monetary versus nonmonetary rewards.[66] Although special offers may be enticing, customers should find the hotel chain that best fits their travel habits and focus on its program, says Tim Winship, publisher of frequentflier.com, a travel information site.[67] That may mean staying in a hotel in the reward plan that is less convenient than one would like.[68] So loyalty programs should not be a mere points program. Loyalty programs are worth joining for more than just the giveaways of a free night. For instance, Starwood's Preferred Guest Program has a check-in service for its gold- or platinum-level members.

With all the loyalty programs around, differentiation is the key. To be different than the competitors, these programs have to show the added value and fun of being in the program.[69] In achieving this, companies are taking their rewards programs up a notch by offering more personalization and choice. Some companies increase reward options, personalized experience during their stay, and offer expanding partnerships. The information guests share through loyalty programs can determine the product and service mix offered. These experiential rewards focus on lifestyle and create unique experiences that aim at reinforcing the brand. It is important to make sure the incentive is something that customers really want, in other words, relevance to the end customer. Increasingly advanced technologies enable companies to obtain and maintain customized relationships with their customers at a reasonable price.

Consumer companies are better known for their customer incentives, whereas hotels provide guests more choices and flexibility to enhance their programs. Cendant companies include car rentals Avis and Budget and outside partners like JCPenney and Best Buy, which enable members to earn points much quicker. With an inventory of hotels, rental cars, vacation rental properties, and time-shares, TripRewards brandishes unique offerings in the travel loyalty arena.[70] For instance, Cendant TripRewards has 6,000 properties in its loyalty programs, with 4.4 million members. TripRewards include properties from Wingate Inn, Days Inn, Ramada, Super 8, Howard Johnson, and Travelodge, Avis and Budget car rental, Fairfield time-shares, Jackson Hewitt tax service, and retail partners like FTD, Eddie Bauer, and Kohl's.[71] It is aimed for leisure travelers, rather than primarily targeting frequent business travelers, and consumers who take limited trips annually. In addition, franchisees in the local properties often take the initiative to add guest-loyalty amenities of their own.[72] There is flexibility available to local operators that serves to encourage guests who are not members of TripRewards to sign up for membership at check-in.[73]

The Market Matrix Hospitality Index is based on national survey and online database to study customer satisfaction with hotels and other hospitality sectors.[74] A study has found that neither overall satisfaction nor satisfaction with the people factor was a determinant of repeat-purchase behavior; however, attitudinal loyalty, or word-of-mouth loyalty, did. In other words, guest satisfaction does not appear to have the substantive and sweeping effect on guest loyalty that has previously been assumed.[75]

Providing high levels of comfort reduces the price sensitivity of business travelers.[76] Guests define comfort in five areas: product, staff, arrival, value, and location.[77] Moreover, there are other factors that are considered important to the guests in building repeat business. Hoteliers should not assume that satisfying their guests will ensure repeat purchases.[78] It is suggested to undertake a reconsideration of the loyalty program and to put money in features such as hotel design, amenities, and quality of employee service because these have been shown to be primary drivers of loyalty. Lodging managers should continue to focus on their employees, particularly in the area of training.[79] Points may get the guest to try the product; however, it would be quality service and product that guarantee repeat patronage.

Loyalty schemes recently were challenged. The managing director of Supranational, a global representation and reservations brand, an independent UK hotel group, has brought to the attention of the European Commission the need to investigate loyalty schemes that offer air miles and other incentives run by major chains.[80] Under the loyalty program, many business travelers would choose major chains and personally benefit from the schemes. They often do not seek advice from travel agents about the most suitable or convenient hotel.[81] Small independent hotels are in a disadvantaged position, not because of their price, but because they do not have the financial support and market penetration to offer loyalty programs as the large chains do. Supranational considers this lead to unfair competition. It has no problem if hotels want to offer rebates or free nights to regular customers but is opposed to incentives not related to the hotel trade.[82] It is no longer about what a hotel can offer but is part of a whole marketing strategy.[83] Loyalty schemes are putting pressure on hotels to relinquish their independence and could be forcing them out of business in areas where major chains have saturated the market.[84] Points- and miles-based loyalty programs that appeal to Boomers and Matures (those over 60) do not resonate with Generational X or Millennials.[85] They like to explore and are much less loyal as customers.

DISCUSSION QUESTIONS

1. Briefly discuss the function of loyalty program in retaining repeat customers.
2. Explain the cost and effectiveness of loyalty program.
3. Link loyalty program to branding competencies in creating sustainable competitive advantage.
4. Loyalty programs are considered as competitive methods because they serve the role of driving top-of-the-line performance. Given this fact, identify the key core competencies that must be developed within a firm to execute this CM successfully.
5. How can you track resources allocated to this CC from studying company documents and materials?
6. What PCs do you believe a firm must have to execute a loyalty program successfully?
7. What linking mechanisms do you believe are necessary to achieve success with loyalty programs?
8. What loyalty programs are considered the leaders in various sectors of the hospitality industry, and are there common CCs within sectors?

NOTES

1. J. Barsky and L. Nash. "Customer Satisfaction: Applying Concepts to Industry-Wide Measures," *Cornell Hotel and Restaurant Administration Quarterly* 44, no. 5/6 (2003): 173–83.
2. J. Swann, "What's Perking: Banks Offer Their Special Blend of Debit Card Rewards Programs," *Community Banker* 15, no. 8 (2006): 30.
3. Ibid.
4. Ibid.
5. Ibid.
6. D. Jang and A. S. Mattila, "An Examination of Restaurant Loyalty Programs: What Kinds of Rewards Do Customers Prefer?" *International Journal of Contemporary Hospitality Management* 17, no. 4/5 (2005): 402.
7. Ibid.
8. Ibid.
9. C. Noordhoff, P. Pauwels, & G. Odekerken-Schroder, "The Effect of Customer Card Programs: A Comparative Study in Singapore and The Netherlands," *International Journal of Service Industry Management* 15, no. 3/4 (2004): 351.
10. Op. cit., no. 6.
11. Ibid.

12. Ibid.

13. Ibid.

14. B. Kim, M. Shi, & K. Srinivasan, "Managing Capacity Through Reward Programs." *Management Science* 50, no. 4 (2004): 503.

15. C. Palmeri, "Rating Frequent-Sleeper Plans," *Business Week* 3905, October 25, (2004).

16. Ibid.

17. Ibid.

18. Ibid.

19. D. Eisen, D. "Reward Hotel Nights Trumping Air Miles," *Business Travel News* 23, no. 9 (2006): 12.

20. Op. cit., no. 15.

21. Op. cit., no. 19.

22. K. Strauss and D. Gale, "IHG launches 'Any Hotel, Anywhere,' " *Hotels* 39, no. 6 (2005): 14.

23. Ibid.

24. Op. cit., no. 15.

25. M. Beirne, "Burke Customizing Hilton HHonors," *Brandweek* 45, no. 36 (2004): 17.

26. Ibid.

27. Ibid.

28. Op. cit., no. 15.

29. Ibid.

30. B. Serlen, "Choice, Cendant Offer Upscale Benefits at Other Chains. (Specialty report: loyalty programs), Business Travel News, March 7, 2005: 22.

31. Ibid.

32. Op. cit., no. 15.

33. Op. cit., no. 30.

34. Ibid.

35. Ibid.

36. Ibid.

37. B. Serlen, "Two Chains Provide Non-Hotel Rewards," *Business Travel News* March 7, 2005: 23.

38. Ibid.

39. Ibid.

40. Ibid.

41. Ibid.

42. Ibid.

43. Anonymous, "Latest Loyalty Offering: Try Free Travel Insurance," Hotels 39, no. 11 (2005): 34H.

44. L. Hayhurst, "Hotel Chain Warning," *Travel Weekly* 1772, June 3, 2005.

45. Ibid.

46. Op. cit., no. 2.

47. Anonymous, "American Express Beefs Up Rewards Program," BusinessWorld (Philippines) (2006).

48. Op. cit., no. 15.

49. Ibid.

50. Ibid.

51. M. Haeberle, "Betting on Customer Loyalty," *Chain Store Age* January 2004: 12A.

52. Ibid.

53. Ibid.

54. Ibid.

55. Ibid.

56. Ibid.

57. Ibid.

58. Op. cit., no. 1.

59. Op. cit., no. 14.

60. Ibid.

61. S. Law, (2006). "Banks Renew Focus on Rewards Programs." *USBanker* 116, no. 4 (2006): 28.

62. Op. cit., no. 6.

63. Ibid.

64. Op. cit., no. 61.

65. Op. cit., no. 6.

66. Ibid.

67. Op. cit., no. 15.

68. Ibid.

69. M. Beirne, M. "Scoring Points, Having Fun," *Brandweek* 45, no. 37 (2004): 18–19.

70. Ibid.

71. M. Beirne, (2004). "The Mother of Incentives," *Brandweek* 45, no. 4 (2004): 4.

72. R. Shaw, "Extra Perks Help Build Guest-Loyalty Programs," *Hotel and Motel Management* 219, no. 12 (2004): 4.

73. Ibid.

74. Op. cit., no. 1.

75. I. Skogland and J. A. Siguaw, "Are Your Satisfied Customers Loyal?" *Cornell Hotel and Restaurant Administration Quarterly* 45, no. 3 (2004): 221–31.

76. Op. cit., no. 1.

77. Ibid.

78. Op. cit., no. 75.

79. Ibid.

80. Op. cit., no. 44.

81. Ibid.

82. Ibid.

83. Ibid.

84. Ibid.

85. C. Wolff, "Reaching Out to Generation X," *Lodging Hospitality* 62, no. 5 (2006): 32.

ADDITIONAL REFERENCES USED FOR BACKGROUND BUT NOT CITED

Anonymous. 2003. "Marriott Cashes in on Customers' Desire for Frequent-Visitor Bonuses. *The Enterprise* 33, no. 18: S11.

———. 2004. "Choice Teams with Preferred for Luxury Rewards Program." *Hotels* 38, no. 11: 34D.

Barsky, J., and L. Nash. 2003. "Improved Loyalty Programs Target Dwindling Number of Travelers." *Hotel and Motel Management* 218, no. 12: 16.

Chang, J. 2006. "Rewarding Loyalty." *Sales and Marketing Management* 158, no. 2: 16.

Higgins, S. M. 2005. "Independent Hoteliers Free to Go It Alone." *Hotel and Motel Management* 220, no. 15: 4.

Jang, D., and A. S. Mattila. 2005. "An Examination of Restaurant Loyalty Programs: What Kinds of Rewards Do Customers Prefer?" *International Journal of Contemporary Hospitality Management* 17, no. 4/5: 402–8.

Johnson, A. 2005. "Rewards Programs Aim to Give Users Greater Flexibility." *Wall Street Journal*, p. D4.

Kim, B., M. Shi, and K. Srinivasan. 2004. "Managing Capacity Through Reward Programs." *Management Science* 50, no. 4: 503–20.

Noordhoff, C., P. Pauwels, and G. Odekerken-Schroder. 2004. "The Effect of Customer Card Programs: A Comparative Study in Singapore and the Netherlands." *International Journal of Service Industry Management* 15, no. 3/4: 351–64.

Watkins, E. 2004. "Service, Not Points, Builds Guest Loyalty." *Lodging Hospitality* 60, no. 13: 2.

Wozniak, L. 2004. "Price of Loyalty." *Far Eastern Economic Review* 167, no. 13: 58.

Leadership and Strategy: Challenges for Tomorrow's Manager

From Chapter 11 of *Strategic Management in the Hospitality Industry*, Third Edition, Michael D. Olsen, Joseph J. West, Eliza Ching Yick Tse. Copyright © 2008 by Pearson Education, Inc. Published by Pearson Prentice Hall. All rights reserved.

Leadership and Strategy: Challenges for Tomorrow's Manager

Leadership and
Strategy: Challenges for
Tomorrow's Manager

Learning Objectives

Upon completion of this chapter you will:

1. Understand the contingency relationships affecting leadership.
2. Have a full appreciation for why leadership will be different in the future.
3. Understand the visioning process.
4. Understand the process of leading change.
5. Appreciate the challenges resulting from a both changing workplace and the nature of work within it.

Key Concepts

Leadership and change

Visioning the future

Managing change

The visionary strategist

The boundary spanner

The change agent

Chapter Purpose

It is our firm conviction that to be an effective leader, tomorrow's manager must be a visionary, one who is able to translate a view of opportunity to a guiding vision. This guiding vision must be communicated to, and internalized by, all members of the organization. It is therefore our purpose in this chapter to define how individuals will take their organizations into the future by successfully leading change.

Leadership Will Be Different

The hospitality leader of tomorrow will be different from today. There will be no more autocratic "my way or the highway" approach to obtaining productivity gains from the workforce of the future. As Harold Leavitt (2005) notes, " authority . . . has never been enough to guarantee effective management, and it is certainly not enough to handle middle manager's jobs today" (58). He goes on to note that due to the fast-changing, speeding world, managers must become equipped with many more skills and competencies than were required in the past. Managers now need imaginative, persuasive, visionary, and inspirational skills—the skills many label leadership. Leavitt agrees with us: Now is the time for managers to become leaders and develop their leadership skills.

Today, human capital has become the most important asset of hospitality firms. Bill Darden, founder of Red Lobster Restaurants and the namesake of Darden Restaurants, once remarked, "I am convinced that the only edge we have on our competition is the quality of our employees as reflected each day by the job they do." His words will have even greater perspicacity for the future. Employees (human capital) follow leaders because leaders inspire them, motivate them, and encourage them to be the best that they can be. Managers must develop their leadership skills, including effective implementation of their programs, enhanced ability to solve problems, and the ability to communicate the future they desire to create.

The Quest for Leadership

In the last 50 years, scholars have attempted to understand the phenomena of leadership. We have experienced theory X, Y, and Z. We have seen transactional analysis, empowerment, management by objectives, and zero-based budgeting emerge as the popular approaches to motivating individuals. Scholars have endorsed the proponents of expectancy theory, exchange theory, path goal theory, least and most preferred coworkers theory, and other laudable attempts at understanding how people within organizations behave and work toward accomplishing goals. We have learned that leaders have traits with which they are born, that charisma is essential, and that size and attractiveness of the leader is important. In the end, they are theories that leaders can benefit greatly from understanding; but, nonetheless, they are theories that work only part of the time—thus the lasting popularity of the contingency theory illustrated in Exhibit 1 that is discussed in greater detail later in this chapter.

In examining previous approaches that attempt to understand leadership, we noted that they emerged when environments were fairly stable and simple. This is not

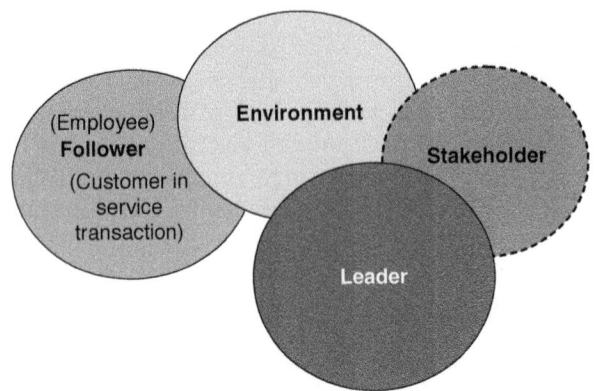

EXHIBIT 1 The Contingency Approach

the case today. Today, leaders are required to learn how to deal with the speed of change. The acceleration of uncertainty means that future managers will be expected to anticipate events in the future with more regularity and accuracy. They will be forced to become future oriented if they are to lead their firms in our tumultuous vision of tomorrow. This is clearly a change from the past.

As we look toward the continuing shift to a world based on knowledge industries, the leader must recognize that this will change the type of individual who will be employed in the hospitality industry. This shift to the knowledge revolution is similar to the shift from agriculture to the Industrial Revolution. As the Industrial Revolution changed the face of the globe, so too will the knowledge revolution. This means that workers entering during this revolution will have their value to the hospitality organization based on not only what they can do but also on what they know. For the most part, these types of individuals cannot be led by autocratic styles.

They will demand leaders who will trust them and reward them on the basis of their contributions. Leavitt (2005) notes, "Formal authority—once the most powerful of managerial tools—has become entirely insufficient, often even counterproductive, in our most complex world" (61). The atmosphere will become one where the leader is considered as "first among equals." This egalitarian approach will differ from a pure form of egalitarianism because individuals will be rewarded, often handsomely, for what they know as well as what they accomplish. They will be recognized for this knowledge and rewarded for standing above the rest, but they will enter into work tasks with the idea of demonstrating this excellence in a climate with teammates who possess the same standard of excellence. They will respect each other for their abilities and consider themselves as equals in this way. The leader will just happen to be first among them regarding the task to be performed. This is vastly different than the way it is today in the hospitality industry where frequently the leader is expected to be able to tell others how to perform.

Leadership will be different because as we generate knowledge workers who possess these special capabilities we will begin to see more unbundling of the products and services offered by hospitality enterprises. Already we observe firms outsourcing restaurants, accounting and payroll practices, housekeeping, human resource functions, and other functions that previously were always done in house. In this case, why is it necessary for the manager of tomorrow to understand these tasks? Might they not better spend their efforts learning how to determine what they should expect from these specialists, how to negotiate with them to achieve the best strategic alliances, and how to allocate their resources most effectively to the services that meet the guest's needs? In other words, tomorrow's leaders must be more adept at finding the best strategic partners along with the best hourly employees. This requires an entirely different approach to leadership than the one that the leaders of the hospitality industry embraced in the past.

The change brought on by the movement toward knowledge workers creates more complexity in the workplace. Because essential individuals increasingly possess higher levels of knowledge with respect to specific specialized tasks, it is not difficult to see that leading such employees is becoming more of a challenge. The simple rules that have guided management action in our industry will no longer work. Thus leaders will have to rely more completely on others who possess the expertise to bring about decisions that will move the organization forward. Today, it is not sufficient to predict that a certain trend will occur. Leaders require the advice and input of experts who understand the complexities associated with each variable within the trend. Knowledge workers are necessary to unravel the complexities of the competitive marketplace.

These changes suggest that the nature of work is changing in the hospitality industry. This means that although the tremendous body of knowledge of leadership throughout the previous decades has been helpful in understanding the complex role of leader, they are of little help today as we stand on the threshold of a knowledge-based world. Although leaders in the hospitality industry will still have to be sure that beds are made, dishes washed, and customers served, they will have to accomplish this in a more challenging, fast-changing, and complex environment. They cannot expect to accomplish this with the old understanding of leadership that has prevailed across the industry. They must understand that the nature of leadership has changed.

Leadership Defined

As illustrated in Exhibit 1, leadership has been defined in contemporary literature as the relationship among the leader, follower, and environment. In our view, we also included the stakeholder. Although some may argue that the stakeholder is part of the construct situation, we think otherwise. By our definition, the stakeholder is the owner or investor of the hospitality firm. These stakeholders have become an increasingly powerful voice in deciding the future of the industry. This voice, we believe, will continue to have a strong influence in how hospitality organizations are managed, and therefore should be included in the overall contingency relationship surrounding the leadership role.

We suggest the importance of the leader's understanding of the environment due to their task of creating a vision of the future and translating this vision into the fabric of the organization. Exhibit 2 contains a flow diagram to assist leaders in visioning that future.

EXHIBIT 2   The Visioning Process

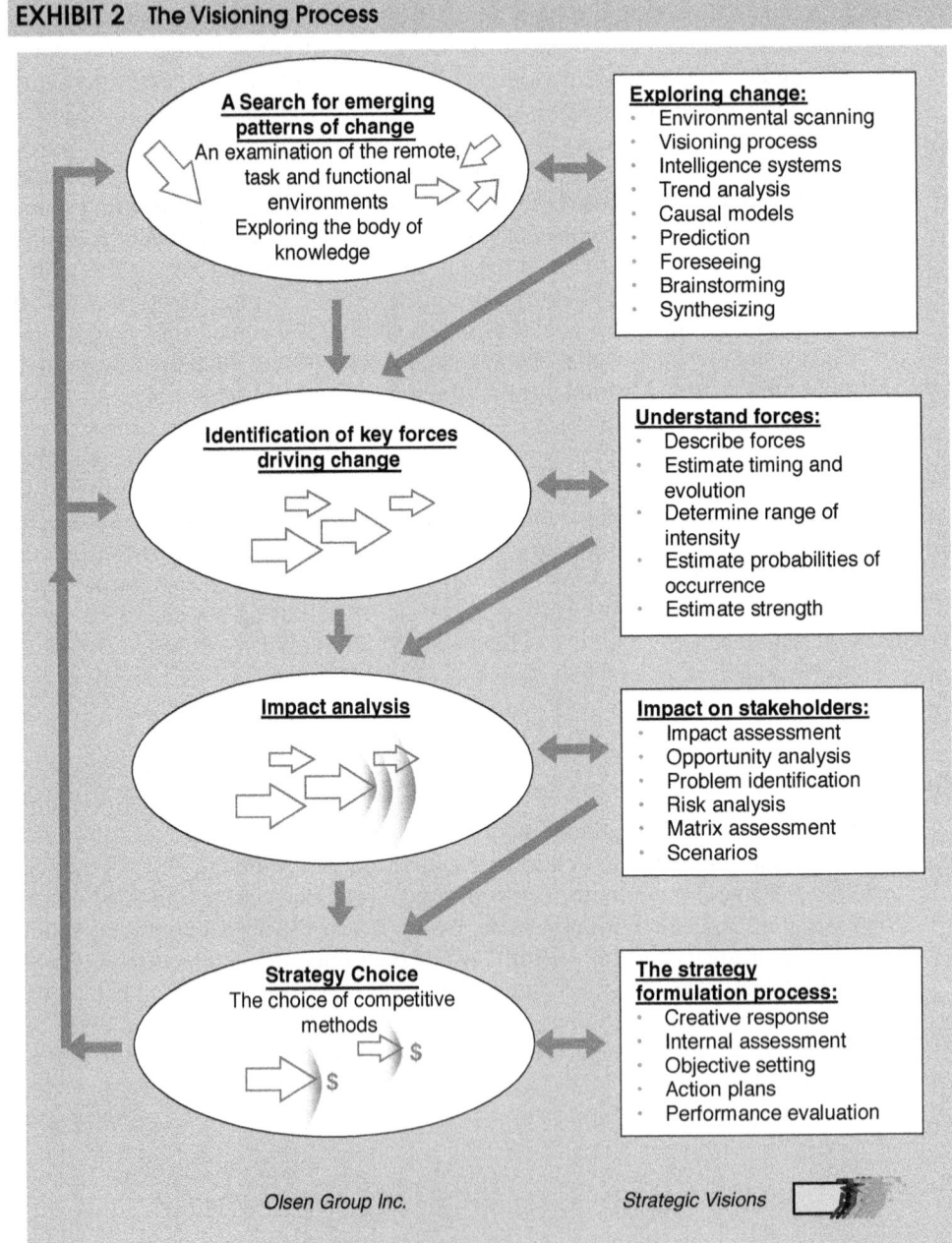

A Search for emerging patterns of change
An examination of the remote, task and functional environments
Exploring the body of knowledge

Exploring change:
- Environmental scanning
- Visioning process
- Intelligence systems
- Trend analysis
- Causal models
- Prediction
- Foreseeing
- Brainstorming
- Synthesizing

Identification of key forces driving change

Understand forces:
- Describe forces
- Estimate timing and evolution
- Determine range of intensity
- Estimate probabilities of occurrence
- Estimate strength

Impact analysis

Impact on stakeholders:
- Impact assessment
- Opportunity analysis
- Problem identification
- Risk analysis
- Matrix assessment
- Scenarios

Strategy Choice
The choice of competitive methods

The strategy formulation process:
- Creative response
- Internal assessment
- Objective setting
- Action plans
- Performance evaluation

Olsen Group Inc.   *Strategic Visions*

As you will note, the first effort that occurs in this visioning of the future process is the attempt by the firm's management to understand the forces driving change that are likely to influence the future of the firm. The multidirectional arrows represent the influences of the forces. As you can see, they are haphazard, indicating their random nature in the environment. As illustrated in the exhibit, there are a number of ways to attempt to understand this uncertainty. Trend analysis, visioning workshops, causal modeling, environmental scanning, and prediction are all techniques that have been used successfully to obtain a greater understanding of how environmental change may impact the firm. These activities are ways to explore change, always requiring a free form of thinking, commonly referred to as getting *out of the box*, a metaphor for removing the boundaries of your perceptual window and freely exploring alternative scenarios.

Once this step in the visioning process has been completed, management must identify and define those forces that they believe will impact the firm in a substantive way. They must also understand what comprises the forces and the time frame in which they are likely to remain an important influence on the organization. Managers must be capable of estimating their strength and the probability of their future. Although this often is easy to do for those forces that have been around for quite some time, it is not so easy to accomplish these important leadership tasks when new forces are at work.

Imagine small hotel operators in the resort villages of the Swiss Alps, the deserts of Arizona or Morocco, and the rain forests of Indonesia. They probably have relied for years on tour operators or travel agents to bring them business. They have not paid attention to what changes are occurring in the environmental sector relative to global distribution systems. Therefore, it is no surprise that should they be asked to determine how changes in this sector will impact them, they would probably answer not much or not at all. Although some of these operators may make this prediction with confidence, we should wonder if they answer this way because they do not understand the distribution system, let alone the changes. If the latter is the case, these individuals lack the capacity to create a guiding vision to lead their small organizations into the future.

Once they have identified the forces driving change, organizational leaders should conduct an analysis of the impact these forces will have on the firm. What is important to mention here is that the leader must now take this information and communicate it to all members of the organization. In doing so, the objective is to establish a sense of urgency about the need for change. It would be nice to assume that all personnel in an organization welcome change and are eager to face the uncertainties that it creates in their jobs and even their lives, but we would be foolish to assume this is reality. The opposite is normally the case. Therefore, leaders must be able to provide convincing proof of their understanding of these forces and their impact on the firm. Leaders must be effective communicators who are respected for their commitment to obtaining the strongest level of analysis regarding this challenge of predicting the impact of change. The importance of integrity, honesty, and ethics become more integral to the change process at this time.

Once the communication process is complete and a sense of timing established, what the firm plans to do to meet the challenges of change must be determined. This effort refers to transferring a vision of the future into the vision of the organization. In this case, tomorrow's leader must again be convincing in demonstrating where the firm is headed and how it plans to get there. Leavitt (2005) defines this as the pathfinding function of leadership. Leaders must define the future they wish to create for the organization. What we mean is the future is not history in reverse. It is not out there waiting to be excavated. Leaders must design it, create it, build it. This means identifying the future competitive methods that will assure a bright future for the organization when implemented as planned. Here, the transfer of vision to followers and stakeholders must be successful if the leader is going to be able to acquire and harness sufficient resources to implement strategic intention.

In this model, vision becomes the intangible but understandable portrait of the future the leader wishes to create. It is about what the organization is to become. It should focus the energies and the resources of all constituencies on how the organization will compete in the future. This is an enormous challenge for a leader. To be effective here, one must have established the trust of the followers and stakeholder. Here again, effective communication is essential along with a depth of understanding of each force driving change. In today's world of rapid change and more accountability, the leader must withstand the test of serious challenges to the vision. It must be defendable and feasible.

The hospitality industry has many examples of the successful implementation of the leader's vision. Caesar Ritz, Ray Kroc, J. Willard Marriott, Kemmons Wilson of Holiday Inns, and Conrad Hilton all possessed visions that guided the development of their respective firms. It was Wilson who saw the developing national highway system as an opportunity to begin a national chain of limited-service hotels catering to the emerging middle-class citizens of the United States who possessed the means and desire for travel. At the same time, Kroc saw a need to provide inexpensive food of consistent quality in a rapid service environment to this same market, and he did so by purchasing and expanding McDonald's. This permitted the large number of women entering the workforce in the 1960s and 1970s into jobs offering little time for lunch to leave the workplace to obtain a quick, convenient meal. These same women were also able to enjoy the McDonald's experience with their young families because McDonald's was designed for families when most of the other restaurants of the time catered to adults and were often less than accommodating to families who brought children to their premises. As these brief examples illustrate, these leaders were able to translate their vision of the future into a successful future for their companies.

Essential to this visioning effort is creativity. The leaders referenced in the preceding paragraph were creative entrepreneurs who built their organizations on dreams and ideas about the future. They were the idea champions that transferred creative ideas into substantive action. Creativity is an illusive concept. It is difficult to describe, but usually you know it when you see it. Many argue that only a few are creative, that it is something with which people are born. Others suggest it can be learned. We argue the latter. If we are able truly to expand our perceptual window, see patterns of change, and are motivated and excited by the thought of developing something new, it is easy to be creative. What this supposition strongly suggests is that the leader of tomorrow will be required to grow personally through the acquisition of knowledge and experience. As we move toward a knowledge or information society, this need is no longer a desirable objective; it is mandatory. Leaders must be able to use this growing intellectual power to lead creative change if they expect to remain the spiritual and rational leaders of their organizations.

Transferring Vision into Action: Getting Everyone Behind the Vision

In this contingency relationship of leadership, the best of creative thoughts and products will not occur unless they can be implemented. Jim Collins (2001) notes that leadership requires ferocious resolve, a strong determination to do whatever needs to be done. He observes that great leaders are fanatically driven to obtain their desired results. Collins finds that most great leaders display a "workman like diligence—more plow horse than show horse."

We present a model for managing change in Exhibit 3. Our model provides a framework for managing change and demonstrates how the creative visioning effort evolves into a plan to bring about realization of a vision. In other words, it is a blueprint designed to assist the leader in bringing all members of the organization into agreement about the desired future of the firm, resulting in a shared vision.

As we have already mentioned and the first step in this flow diagram suggests, there must be a recognition and acceptance of the need for change. This includes agreement on the forces at work driving change. It also requires an agreement on the sense of urgency for change. Although it may be very easy to get individuals within an organization to agree on the forces driving change, it can be perhaps quite a challenge to get them to agree on a sense of urgency. This is especially so for those organizations that have been successful and still consider themselves to be. As Collins (2001) states, "Good is the enemy of Great." He reasons that the vast majority of firms do not become great because they are good and content. It is easy for individuals in these organizations to feel quite comfortable with themselves and see no sense of urgency to do anything but continue on the same path. The phrase "If it isn't broken, don't fix it" is often used to justify the need to stay on course. This problem is exacerbated in large firms where such inertia can be punishing to any change effort.

Often, the sense of urgency is driven by crisis. In this case, there is usually little that has to be done to get acceptance on the sense of urgency. There is a very good chance in today's environment that if leaders wait until this occurs it will be almost impossible for them to correct the crisis in time. Thus leaders must be very effective communicators, especially in defining the need for change and the timing of the forces driving change. What we mean is that leaders must fully understand all the variables making up a force driving change and its potential impact on the firm. This enables them to communicate more effectively and credibly the urgency for change.

EXHIBIT 3 Managing the Change Process

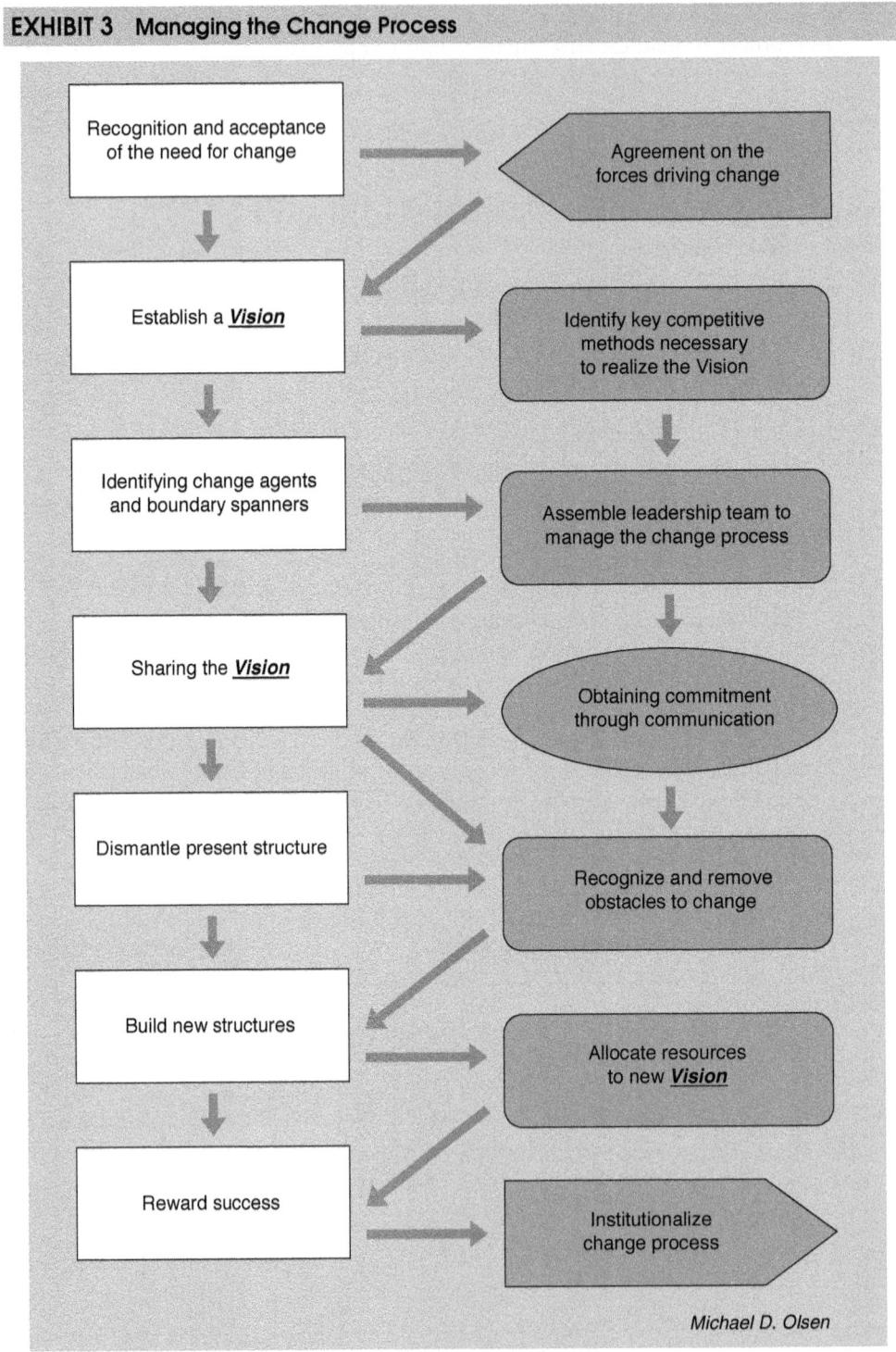

The next step in the process is identifying the vision and translating the vision into key competitive methods. In the context of managing the change process, it is necessary for leaders to provide convincing evidence that these competitive methods are correct for the situation and are feasible. If this is not done effectively, the organizational participants will shroud the process in doubt and erode the leader's ability to achieve the desired state of change. For those in the organization who support change, the leader will find little challenge forthcoming. However, for those who fear the consequences, there will be many reasons given for why change won't work. They will also become the loudest voices in the chorus saying, "We told you it wouldn't work" if such efforts fail. This is a delicate stage and will demand from the leader the proper identification of change agents to be included in this communication process.

In identifying change agents, leaders must select those associates who can effectively span the boundaries of all groups and functions within the organization. These can be either formal or informal leaders or combinations of both. Regardless of what title one places on them, they will be the essential messengers of change. Their selection requires careful thought. Often, leaders make the mistake of enlisting employees who in the past have cried the loudest for the status quo. They think that if those members are involved in the change process they will be converted and serve as effective disciples of change.

Although in a minority of cases this may be true, the primary criterion for identification and selection of change agents must be their strong conceptual and perceptual skills that enable then to develop personally effective communications to bring individuals to action. In today's world where knowledge workers play increasingly greater roles in organizational leadership, this type of change agent becomes more difficult to develop. Nevertheless, it must be the goal if change is to be managed effectively. These agents must share the vision. They must internalize it, believe in it, and have the energy to make it happen. The role of energy must not be underestimated. This is especially the case in organizations that have for too long believed they are superior. Resistance to change will be much greater here. In this case, the change agents must be credible, passionate, and spiritual in their belief of the vision. It is balancing the passion with rationality that will require a high level of intellect and understanding of the change process.

Never will this role be more important than when it comes to dismantling the current organizational structures and building the new ones essential for implementing change. It can be expected that the majority of individuals who doubt the vision or the competitive methods will do whatever they can to sustain the status quo. They will likely fear for their jobs, which is based on their uncertainty of the future. The change agent's most important objective in this organizational setting is to paint as accurate a picture of the desired future as possible. Efforts to remove doubts and their accompanying uncertainties must be priority number one.

It is natural for people to fear change. Whether it is due to their fear of the unknown or the fact that they will have to change to maintain a viable role in the organization must be understood by the change agent. Removing this uncertainty must also be a passion that becomes an important part of tomorrow's leader. If the assumptions of continuing change in the future are valid, this is probably one of the main challenges that the future leader will have.

The next step in our model, building the new structures, reflects the importance of implementation through allocating resources to the vision. Many organizations are able to create the vision and even achieve the necessary support throughout, but they fail in the long run to allocate the necessary resources to the vision. It may seem like this is a basic point and goes without saying. Yet when we consider how difficult it can be to dismantle old structures, it is easy to see how those who do not want to see change occur will effectively divert resources to old visions and to the protection of the old order. Managing the change process therefore must involve clear objectives of preventing this obstructive behavior from occurring. It must be assumed that it will occur; therefore, it is best to anticipate it early on in the change effort.

Of course, succeeding in change is essential. In our model this implies that organizations will reward the positive outcomes of this effort. To be effective here, firms must have milestones that are attainable, timely, and substantive. In other words, people must feel that they are achieving results in a timely fashion, and they must be rewarded appropriately. In organizations where the systems of reward are unclear or mitigated by cultural or negotiated impediments, this will become more difficult. However, unless all participants are involved in getting behind the vision and rewarded for success, the process of realizing the vision will deteriorate into failure.

The last element of our model is to institutionalize the change process. This is to suggest that it will be necessary for firms to create a climate and culture of change, one that is accepted by all members of the organization. For this to occur, they must have trust in the leadership, feel that they can and should contribute to the change effort, and believe in where the organization is headed. Trust becomes the most operative word here. Trust is a function of the integrity of the leadership, the belief that they will do the right thing. This trust will be earned not acquired. This requires the future leader to accept more of the moral and social responsibility for their actions and those of the organizations they lead.

What Capabilities Will the Leader of Tomorrow Have to Possess?

Now that we have demonstrated how leadership is different from management and how tomorrow's leaders must employ a vision for the future to lead change, our next task is to discuss the skills and competencies that will be required by tomorrow's leader. As the key points in the box illustrate, we have already discussed many of the skills and competencies throughout the text. We will explain each in limited detail in the sections to follow.

- A Visionary, employing value adding strategies
- Using and managing knowledge and technology for competitive advantage
- Spanning boundaries of cultures, business environments and management know-how
- A synthesizer and blender of skills and knowledge in a fast changing environment
- A leader in a dynamic and complex setting
- Ambition for the organization, possesses a sense of purpose beyond their personal success
- Relentless in their pursuit of tangible results and achievement

---

We have already stressed the visionary aspect of tomorrow's leader. In addition, we have said that value-adding activities can only come from accurate assessments of the environment. Those skills must be complemented with the leader's ability to create the vision and to persuade others to follow. To accomplish this, the leader must become a change agent, spanning the boundaries of organizations, cultures, and knowledge to create a vision that synthesizes his or her unique view of the world. Clearly, using and managing knowledge will be necessary. This capability will have to be transferred to the practical need to invest in technology to achieve competitive advantage. For, we believe, it will be technology in its broadest sense—the convergence of computing, telecommunications, and knowledge-driven content software—that will shape the future competitive strategies in the hospitality industry.

The need for vision and managing knowledge demands that the leader have strong skills in integrating and synthesizing divergent and complex concepts to create the ability to compete in the future. This is a skill not usually taught in the business schools of the world. The leader must develop the ability to detect relationships and not simply think deductively. Tomorrow's leaders must possess these capabilities if they are to succeed in the fast-changing complex world. Seeing patterns and relationships that will lead to new products and services will be a must. Leaders will not be able to do this without taking advantage of knowledge experts. They must become capable of extracting the information needed, analyzing it relative to the business domain, and translating it into competitive advantage. Success here will therefore be as much contingent on vision as it is on knowledge and its application to business problems.

Thus leadership will be required to stand the test of time in a dynamic and complex setting. Leaders must be able to use the capabilities of the best knowledge workers who will offer insight into the changing environment (remote, task, segment, firm, and function) and instill in others the confidence to reach out for this change. To do this, leaders must have earned the confidence of their followers. This is certainly a different view of leadership in our industry than has been the case in the past.

We have painted a challenging picture of the leader of tomorrow. These views not only originated from our recent work in the industry but they are also those of many of the leading thinkers on the subject of the leader of the future. As Exhibit 4 indicates,

---

EXHIBIT 4   Leaders of the future will have the following characteristics

- Extraordinary levels of perception and insight into the realities of the world and into themselves
- Extraordinary levels of motivation to enable them to go through the inevitable pain of learning and change, especially in a world with looser boundaries, in which loyalties become more difficult to define
- The emotional strength to manage their own and others' anxiety as learning and change become more and more a way of life
- New skills in analyzing cultural assumptions, identifying functional and dysfunctional assumptions, and evolving processes that enlarge the culture by building on its strengths and functional elements
- The willingness and ability to involve others and elicit their participation, because tasks will be too complex and information too widely distributed for leaders to solve problems on their own
- The willingness and ability to share power and control according to people's knowledge and skills, that is, to permit and encourage leadership to flourish throughout the organization

these challenges are many and varied.[1] They indicate one common theme: Leadership will require the extraordinary. The ability to motivate while at the same time sharing power will be most difficult. This is especially true in the hospitality industry, which has been built on a strong tradition of not sharing power. Yet this will be essential if the hospitality manager of the future is to pursue a value-adding strategy that will be contingent on followers, stakeholders, and the situation as shaped by the business environment. The challenges of tomorrow will thus bring forth a new type of leader for an industry evolving into a new century.

Leadership and Strategy

We have offered the idea that organizations can be successful if leaders can effectively align the forces driving change, make investments in competitive methods that reflect these forces, and consistently allocate resources to those CMs that create the greatest value. Although much of the leadership on the topic of strategy tends to focus on the processes and procedures regarding this strategy, we have chosen to suggest that it is a way of thinking on the part of effective leaders. We trust that you will now conclude that managing organizations is not a simple process, and it requires strong intellect, perseverance, and vision and the ability to be personally effective in leading the organization through the turbulence and uncertainty in today's world. It is a wonderful challenge for anyone to embark on.

NOTE

1. Edgar H. Schein, "Leadership and Organizational Culture," in *The Leader of the Future*, eds. F. Hesselbein, M. Goldsmith, and R. Beckhard (The Drucker Foundation, Jossey-Bass, 1996).

REFERENCES

Collins, J. 2001. *Good to Great*. New York: Harper Business.

Drucker, P. 1992. *Managing for the Future*. New York: Plume.

Ford, C. M. and D. A. Gioia, eds. 1995. *Creative Action in Organizations*. Thousand Oaks, CA: Sage.

Handy, C. 1997. *The Hungry Spirit*. London: Hutchinson, Random House (UK).

Hesselbein, F., M. Goldsmith, and R. Beckhard. 1996. *The Leader of the Future*. New York: The Peter Drucker Foundation for Nonprofit Management.

Kotter, J. P. 1996. *Leading Change*. Boston: Harvard Business School Press.

Leavitt, H. J. 2005. "Hierarchies, Authority, and Leadership." In *Leader to Leader* 37 (Summer): 55–61.

Nanus, B. 1992. *Visionary Leadership*. San Francisco: Jossey-Bass.

CASE STUDY

New Leadership Styles: Sternlicht vs. Schultz*

The changing times of the hospitality industry call for different CEO leadership styles. Two types of leaders dominate the lodging industry: those in the hotel business and those in the business of hotels.[1] For those in the hotel business, the focus is on the guest; for companies that are in the business of hotels, the focus is on the investor.[2] Once the industry was influenced by career hoteliers focused upon the guest, however, the emergence of hotel real estate investment trusts (REITs) with high-profile dealmakers such as Hilton Hotels Corp.'s Stephen Bollenbach, Patriot American Hospitality's Paul Nussbaum, Barry Sternlicht of Starwood Hotels & Resorts Worldwide,[3] and Henry Silverman of Cendant Corp., all leaders who speak the language and sell Wall Street. They are industry giants who have changed the form and substance of the U.S. hospitality business much as Holiday Inns and Marriott did in the 1950s, 1960s, and 1970s.[4] They are seen as ruthless competitors, fearless risk takers, and master tacticians. In this case, we examine two hospitality leaders: Barry Sternlicht of Starwood Hotels and Resorts and Howard Schultz of Starbucks, both of them known to move their product offerings from commoditization to differentiation.

BARRY STERNLICHT OF STARWOOD: LEADERSHIP BY RISK TAKING

Today's Starwood Hotels & Resorts is the result of Sternlicht's vision to create a multi-brand lodging industry behemoth.[5] Sternlicht is one of the youngest leaders in the hotel and leisure industry today. He was only 35 years old when he became the chairman and chief executive of Starwood Capital Group, which he founded in 1990. Sternlicht has been characterized as brash, boastful, young, smart, bright, hardworking, and aggressive. He is a visionary in a stark new era of real estate finance.[6] During his 10-year reign as chairman of Starwood Hotels & Resorts, Sternlicht has turned a small hotel company[7] into a global giant, with over 750 properties in 80 countries. The company's portfolio consists of company owned, leased, managed, and franchised hotels.[8] Sternlicht transformed a real estate investment company worth less than $10 million into a $15 billion hotel empire.[9] The company conducts its hotel business both directly and through its subsidiaries, which includes ITT Sheraton Corp., and it engaged in the gaming business principally through its subsidiary Caesars World, Inc. (no longer a part of the company).[10] Other brands of Starwood include Westin, The Luxury Collection, St. Regis, W Hotel, Ciga, and Four Points. Through these brands, Starwood Hotels is well represented in most major markets around the world.[11]

Unique Company Structure That No Other Can Match

Sternlicht graduated from Harvard Business School in 1986 and began working in a leading real estate firm where he proved himself

*This case was compiled based on the information available up to November 2006.

a gutsy and deft dealmaker.[12] His big break came when he purchased the nearly bankrupt Hotel Investors Trust in 1994, one of the three paired-shared REITs that were grandfathered from the Deficit Reduction Act of 1984. Sternlicht paid $120 million cash and other assets for a 73% stake. The company was called Starwood Lodging Trust. The company looked to others to be a money pit, yet Sternlicht saw a diamond in the rough. Starwood was already a trust that owned hotels and was paired with a sister company that managed hotels.[13] Sternlicht foresaw value in its rare paired-shared structure, in which a REIT and a standard operating company traded as one stock.[14] What is unique about Starwood is that there are two Starwoods—one which owns the hotels while the other operates them, yet their shares trade together. Only three other publicly traded companies had a similar status at the time. This structure gave Starwood major competitive advantages over its competition, both REIT and non-REIT. All other REITs must lease their hotels to separate entities that pay taxes. A paired share can own and manage the hotels as well, thus combining the flexibility of a conventional company with the tax advantage of traditional REITs, which pay no taxes but must distribute 95% of their earnings as dividends to shareholders.

King of Hotels

In 1988, when Sternlicht was 27, he led an attempt to buy Hilton Hotels which was unsuccessful. Since then, due to his swift investments and farsighted vision, he has been able to build a real estate empire from scratch. His success stems from his ability to recognize value before others as well as his understanding of the management lodging properties and the financial aspects of real estate. Sternlicht is always willing to buck conventional wisdom and invest in hotels that are due for a turnaround. He always manages to implement a complicated

financial restructuring of a nearly bankrupt asset that others do not think is possible.

Beginning in 1995, Sternlicht made a series of savvy hotel acquisitions that culminated with the acquisition of Westin Resorts & Hotels Worldwide for $780 million from the Japanese Aoki Corp. Westin was considered to be one of the best deals that had ever been made in the history of U.S. real estate. Westin's worth increased to three times its cost only a year after the transaction. Sternlicht's Starwood's hotel holdings were then taken public as a REIT.

After closing the deal, Starwood Capital began buying hotels aggressively. After the overbuilding and overleveraging of the late 1980s, hotels were being sold at 30% and 40% of replacement value in the early 1990s. In 1990, the U.S. hotel industry as a whole lost $5.7 billion. Not surprisingly, the institutional investors stayed away from this industry. But the demand for rooms had risen every year in the past 20 years. and yet supply had been constrained. Because the hotel market was recovering more slowly than other sectors in real estate, Starwood capital figured the best deals were to be found in lodging. The trust's strategy was to acquire upscale properties with significant upside potential at discounted replacement cost.

Starwood was and still is considered a deal-making shop, a real estate company. Starwood also made a white knight offer of US $14.6 billion to purchase ITT Corp., owner of the Sheraton chain and the St. Regis. The paired-shared tax break was probably instrumental in helping Starwood in this acquisition. As a result, Sternlicht, the 37-year-old whom nobody had heard of before the takeover, presided over the world's biggest lodging empire, Starwood Hotels & Resorts Worldwide Inc. ITT was a 77-year old company with $10 billion in assets.[15] Starwood acquired a company seven times its size in revenue to become the largest lodging and gaming company in the world, with a total market capitalization of about $18 billion in 1998.[16]

For Starwood, Sternlicht took a company on the verge of bankruptcy and turned it into a giant.[17] Starwood is aggressive in its acquisition strategy of repositioning properties, many of which are underperforming. These acquisitions have also been done cheaply at an average of 30% lower than the cost of constructing the properties from the ground up.[18] These acquisitions have placed Starwood in a strategic position in the real estate market because most of the company's properties are upscale full-service luxury hotels in cities where new buildings are expensive to construct.[19] The company's success to date can be attributed to its timely strategy of focusing upon maintaining a superior corporate structure with excellent operational execution. External environmental forces were also in Sternlicht's favor. He was able to finance his deals with new shares of company stock instead of borrowing money due to a bullish stock market. Barry Sternlicht became a Wall Street darling when his stock, including dividends, soared by 86% in 1996. The value of Starwood's stock rose from $12 a share to $56 in 1997, and its revenue grew from practically nothing to over $900 million.[20]

The Aftermath

Sternlicht was named chairman and CEO of the new Starwood. With an established portfolio Sternlicht turned his attention to building a corporate culture and structure. The aim was to develop an operating group to manage the substantial portfolio and maximize its potential. Starwood sought to attract and recruit talent from Wyndham, Doubletree, Marriott, and Hyatt. It desires a reputation as a company of excellence. Sternlicht may have made buying hotels look easy, but he discovered their management was much more challenging. His inexperience in lodging operations was exposed in 1997 when he earned a reputation as a

controlling taskmaster.[21] He was depicted as abrasive, egocentric, lacking operating experience, and in over his head. The company's stock sank from a high of $60.38 in 1998 to $20 in 2000. Starwood's shares had underperformed in the American stock market by 45% since the ITT purchase. Sternlicht's alleged weak leadership was not solely to be blamed because Starwood also lost its favorable tax status. In 1999, under pressure from legislators, Starwood abandoned its special "paired-shared" REIT status and became a standard corporation.

To reclaim its image and to raise company morale, Sternlicht made changes. He took the criticisms seriously and became more disciplined. He made appointments to the top management to bring credibility and discipline to the company. He sold off more than $7 billion of noncore assets to reduce debt. Starwood also sought to sell its Ciga group, a collection of 25 European luxury hotels.[22] Starwood underwent a major reorganization. It simplified its structure, in part to convince Standard & Poor's to list it in its 500-stock index.[23] All of its efforts seemed to have paid off. Starwood gained in earnings and market share over its competitors, Marriott International Inc. and Hilton Hotels Corp. As Sternlicht matured, his image as an ambitious, impatient, and self-confident hotelier was transformed into the role of CEO.[24]

Achieving the right look and feel was crucial to Sternlicht's strategy.[25] He sought to create a strong brand distinction through the quality of material and design[26] in his hotels. Sternlicht came from a deal-making background, but he also considers himself a master marketer who can simultaneously tap into the unserved needs of hotel guests while creating immense buzz in the market. He is credited for major innovations, including the W boutique hotel chain, the Westin Heavenly bed, and the practice of using branding amenities. Sternlicht also developed the successful marketing strategy for

Westin with the Heavenly Bath and Crib promotions, which pushed the chain's rate from $135 to $160 per night.[27]

Starwood has succeeded in making the hotel guest room the center of attention of the lodging experience. Sternlicht is not the originator of the boutique hotel, but he proved himself an innovator when he developed the trendy W Hotels in 1998. W signifies witty, warm, and wonderful. It is a hip boutique brand, widely regarded as one of the industry's most successful launches.[28] Sternlicht has successfully addressed consumer lifestyle needs and made W a brand that can be duplicated seemingly at will and with high profit margins. Many critics did not think that standardizing and mass producing a series of boutique-like hotels would be feasible. But Sternlicht was right. W Hotels became a hit with both travelers and locals who patronize the hip bars and restaurants in the hotels. His intention was to build a hip national branded boutique. He did so and earned one of the Marketers of the Year awards in 2005 by Brandweek. His hotels may not have been the first to offer a great bed, but they were the first to articulate it to a growing travel market.[29] The industry leaders, including Marriott, Radisson, Crowne Plaza, Hilton Choice Hotels, and Hyatt, followed suit by coming up with their versions of beddings and boutique hotels.

Beginning in 2001 Starwood, just as the other large lodging chains, was hit by low occupancy rates and bottom line pressures until business turned around in 2005 and 2006. As the majority of the brands of Starwood are heavily focused to upscale business travelers, it experienced a loss in 2003. Yet Sternlicht adhered to his principal strategy: to invest in what he believes since there will be better times ahead.[30] The company committed itself to renovating the Sheraton Hotels and Resorts and Westin Hotels & Resorts brands. In 2005 this effort resulted in operating income from Starwood's North American hotels jumping 49% to $664 million, with a 12% increase in revenue per available room among same-store units, versus the 7.8% industry average.[31]

In late 2003, Sternlicht realized that he was no longer the right person to lead the company to the next level and stepped down as the chairman and chief executive. He remains active in the company as its executive chairman, focusing on capital investment and general strategy. The biggest challenge for the new CEO will be managing capital spending and dealing with third-party websites that continued to drive down hotel rates in an already tough economic environment.

LEADERSHIP IN FOOD SERVICES

In the foodservice industry, Howard Schultz of Starbucks has developed a new style of leadership. Without Schultz's vision and commitment, coffee would just be a commodity and Starbucks would not be the international force that it is today.

HOWARD SCHULTZ OF STARBUCKS: LEADERSHIP BY COMMITMENT

The success of Starbucks is attributed to the vision and leadership style of one man, Howard Schultz, who turned coffee from a commodity into an experience while creating one of the most recognizable, dynamic and successful global retail brands in history. Howard Schulz is to Starbucks what Ray Kroc was to McDonald's. It was the vision and persistence of both men that took the original concepts of the original companies beyond their owners' vision and turned them into global icons. With Starbucks, Schultz has created an American institution.

Howard Schultz was born in 1953 and grew up in a housing project in Brooklyn, New York. He graduated with a BA in communications from Northern Michigan University. He worked for a Swedish housewares company and was introduced to one of their clients – Starbucks Coffee, Tea and Spice. Starbucks was first opened in 1971 in Seattle by Jerry Baldwin and Gordon Bowker, offering a wide selection of whole bean coffee. He was impressed by the concept and saw its potential. Schultz was convinced that Starbucks would appeal to a greater multitude if it was positioned as a coffee bar serving up espresso drinks like coffee bars in Italy. He joined the company as director of retail operations and marketing in 1982. The company tested the concept and enjoyed great success, but the owners decided not to expand the concept. As a result, Schultz left Starbucks to form his own coffee-bar company. He met Dave Olsen, who had run a successful coffeehouse in Seattle called Café Allegro. Olsen's Place was more in the European café tradition than in the style of Italian stand-up espresso bars. Olsen's Place was what Starbucks later became – a gathering place in the neighborhood. Schultz and Olsen shared both a passion for coffee and a philosophy on how to run a business. Schultz is credited for his ability to communicate the vision, raise capital for expansion, and plan for the expansion. In contrast, Olsen's strength is in the area of operations, hiring and training, and ensuring the best quality of coffee. Schultz and Olsen opened the first Il Giornale in 1986, and it was a success. Five years later, the company opened a second Seattle store and its first international store in Canada.

In 1987 the owners of Starbucks wanted to sell the six retail stores and their roasting plant. Schultz and Olsen raised $3.8 million and purchased Starbucks. They then changed the name of all their stores to Starbucks because of the stronger brand name in Seattle and among mail-order customers. Starbucks experienced quick expansion in the years to come: It opened 15 stores in 1988 and 20 in 1989. By 1992 they had 165 stores. At first, their expansion was limited to the Pacific Northwest, Chicago, and California. They espoused a strategy of market saturation and building up customer loyalty. Starbucks chose not to franchise the stores to keep the quality of their product under their control. To raise the capital to sustain the expected growth, Schultz decided to take the company public with an initial public offering in 1992. Starbucks became the first coffee company to become a public company. The initial public offering (IPO) raised $29 million for Starbucks, and the company's market capitalization stood at $273 million. This came about only five years after Schultz purchased the company for $4 million.

In 1993 Starbucks opened its first East Coast store in Washington, D.C, and expanded to New York and Boston in 1994. Today, it operates more than 8,000 locations in 40 countries around the world and employs more than 80,000 people. Starbucks possesses a 6% market share of U.S. coffee consumption.[32] Even with this size, Schultz considers Starbucks to be in the embryonic stage of growth. His dream is to continue to expand the company to make Starbucks one of the most recognized and respected brands in the world.[33] In an era of global expansion, he believes in the importance of strong local partners. He desires partners who are entrepreneurs and who understand and value people.[34] Schultz does not believe that Starbucks is suited to a franchising system. He sees franchising as nothing more than a distribution channel with access to capital. Starbucks employs a vertical integration strategy with total control of all aspects of operation, from coffee production onward. This has been a cornerstone of the Starbucks corporate culture to a greater extent than any other branded foodservice or food retail business.[35] Starbucks has restaurants, department stores, airlines, and grocery stores selling its coffee, giving the company the number-one share in America.[36]

Starbucks entered the Chinese market in the late 1990s partnering with mainland

and Taiwanese food and beverage companies.[37] In 2006 it had 165 stores across 18 mainland Chinese cities, about 120 of which are in either Beijing or Shanghai.[38] By comparison, the company has 600 or so Starbucks units in Japan.

Howard Schultz, the man who lead Starbucks from a Seattle niche retailer to global coffee-shop powerhouse, is a mixture of altruist and supersalesman.[39] He is competitive in pursuing his vision of a world-beverage company.[40] He is tough on his competitors, notably aggressive in real estate siting.[41] However, Schultz is an entrepreneur with a strong commitment to Starbucks and to the community. He has implemented a series of practices unprecedented in the retailing industry, mixing capitalism with social responsibility.

Commitment to Employees

Schultz introduced significant innovations to the U.S. foodservice industry when Starbucks provided stock options and a comprehensive health insurance for its staff[42] and their spouses in 1988, including the 65% of the firms employees who were part-timers. This policy earned loyalty and lowered employee turnover for the company. At the same time, he pursued workforce productivity through investment in information technology, matching employee staffing closely to the most profitable trading periods.[43]

According to Schultz, the Starbucks story is not about advertising, promotion or marketing. Rather it is about culture and values as well as the relationship the company has built with its people.[44] To him, great companies endure because they value their people.[45] He believes that a company cannot exceed the expectations of its customers unless the management first exceeds the expectations of its employees. Schultz set out to create a company culture that is open, participative, and caring about its employees.

Commitment to Customers

Schultz is recognized for his leadership and innovative approach in turning the coffee lifestyle company into one of the world's most recognized brands. Schultz aims at creating long-term value by balancing profitability with heart. Starbucks' success is the result of recognizing the equity among the company, its employees, and customers. Schultz maintains that the Starbucks business model is not about serving coffee. Its intimate relationship with customers is one of the key elements of the brand. In addition, Schultz does not believe one can build a sustainable brand simply through advertising and sales promotion. He believes that the success of Starbucks demonstrates that it has established an intimate connection with its customers. Starbucks creates an experience around the romance of coffee and a sense of community by establishing a true relationship with the customer—the "third space" between work and home.

Commitment to the Community

Schultz led Starbucks to adopt an environmental mission statement.[46] He embraces social responsibility in every link of the value chain. He insists that the company take an interest in the farming communities who harvest the coffee beans[47] they purchase, pledging to buy only coffee that has been organically grown. He instituted the policy that directs future profits from stores where employees are murdered in robberies to organizations working for victims' rights and violence prevention. Starbucks has built schools, health clinics, and safe coffee-processing facilities. The company works with celebrity entrepreneurs such as Magic Johnson to bring Starbucks stores to poor urban neighborhoods across the country. The Starbucks Foundation sponsors literacy programs, Earth Day cleanups, and regional AIDS walks.[48]

After being CEO for 18 years, Howard Schulz recognized it was time for him to move away from running the day-to-day activities of the company. His change of responsibility in the company reflects his focus on developing the international expansion strategy, specifically in Europe. As chairman and chief global strategist, Schultz is involved in strategic management with an immediate focus on sequencing development of international business. In 2006, Schultz announced that he intends to triple the number of stores, to 40,000, with half in the United States and half overseas. He has decided to challenge Yum Brands and McDonald's as the world's largest restaurant chain.[49] The big question is whether Starbucks can sustain the growth it has been enjoying over the past two decades.

DISCUSSION QUESTIONS

1. Using Barry Sternlicht and Howard Schultz as examples, briefly discuss the concept of visionary strategist for Starwood and Starbucks, respectively.
2. What makes the two leaders featured here different than leaders in the past in managing change?
3. New management calls for managers/leaders to be boundary spanners. Discuss how Sternlicht and Schultz carry out this role in their respective companies.
4. How do these two leaders practice the coalignment management process?
5. What environmental events did these leaders face, and how do you think they were able to address them in terms of the company's investments?
6. Are these two leaders characteristic of change agents?
7. Do you consider these leaders to be innovative and creative? If not, why?
8. Do you believe these leaders have consciously behaved in a contingency mindset, reflecting the changing needs of the companies they ran and the constituencies they served?

NOTES

1. H. Bond, "Lodging's New Breed of Leader," *Hotel and Motel Management* 213, no. 16 (1998): 1.
2. Ibid.
3. Ibid.
4. G. Jogaratnam and C. C.-Y. Tse, "The Entrepreneurial Approach to Hotel Operation: Evidence from the Asia-Pacific Hotel Industry," *Cornell Hotel and Restaurant Administration Quarterly* 45, no. 3 (2004): 248.
5. Anonymous, "Top CEO of the Year: Barry Sternlicht/Starwood Hotels & Resorts," *National Real Estate Investor* 41, no. 7 (1999): L16.
6. M. Warner, "First: How Barry Sternlicht Became the King of Hotels," *Fortune* 136, no. 11 (1997): 26.
7. M. Beirne, "Good Knight: Awakening an Industry," *Brandweek* 46, no. 36 (2005): M32.
8. Op. cit., no. 5.
9. Op. cit., no. 7.
10. Op. cit., no. 5.
11. Anonymous, "Lastminute.com Announces Funding from Major New Strategic Partners," *M2 Presswire*, January 13, 2000.
12. Op. cit., no. 6.
13. D. Kadlec, "Burned by the ITT Battle?" *Time*, November 17, 1997: 64.
14. Op. cit., no. 6.
15. Ibid.
16. Ibid.
17. Ibid.
18. Ibid.
19. Ibid.
20. Ibid.
21. D. Brady, "At Starwood, the CEO Is in the Details," *Business Week* no. 142 (2000).
22. Ibid.
23. R. Barker, "Is Starwood Losing Star Power?" *Business Week* no. 152 (2003).

24. Op. cit., no. 21.
25. Ibid.
26. Ibid.
27. Ibid.
28. Ibid.
29. Op. cit., no. 7.
30. D. Brady, "Sleepless at Starwood, by Spiffing Up His Hotels, CEO Sternlicht Is Betting on an Upscale Business That May Not Return Soon," *Business Week*, July 21, 2003, 56.
31. Op. cit., no. 7.
32. Anonymous, "Starbucks Interview" (2003). Retrieved from http://www.scae.de/ Starbucks-Interview-0201.htm.
33. Anonymous, "Howard Schultz: Not Your Average Joe" (n.d.). Retrieved from http://www.brandchannel.com/ careers_profile.asp?cr_id=47.
34. Op. cit., no. 32.

35. Ibid.
36. Ibid.
37. A. Yeh, "Starbucks Aims for New Tier in China Cafés," *Financial Times*, 2006, 17.
38. Ibid.
39. Op. cit., no. 32.
40. Ibid.
41. Ibid.
42. Ibid.
43. Ibid.
44. Ibid.
45. Ibid.
46. H. Schultz and D. J. Yang, *Pour Your Heart into It. How Starbucks Built a Company One Cup at a Time* (New York: Hyperion, 1997).
47. Ibid.
48. Op. cit., no. 46.
49. D. Stires, "A Darker View of Starbucks," *Fortune* 154, no. 10 (2006): 197.

ADDITIONAL REFERENCES UTILIZED AS BACKGROUND BUT NOT CITED

Galarza, P. 1996. "Natural-Born Deal Maker." *Financial World* 165, no. 11: 30.

Gibbs, M. F. 1996. "Starting from Ground Zero Starwood Builds Toward 'Greatness.' " *National Real Estate Investor* 38, no. 13: 42.

Hlotyak, E. 2003. "Profits and Passions: Barry Sternlicht." *Westchester County Business Journal* 42, no. 27: 12.

Serwer, A., and K. Bonamici. 2004. "Hot Starbucks to Go." *Fortune* 149, no. 2: 60.

Sternlicht, B. 2006. "Barry Sternlicht." *Hotels* 40, no. 8: 34B.

Vinocur, B. 1996. "The Ground Floor: Despite Concerns over Management Pay, a Hotel Company Thrives Because of Its Paired Structure." *Barron's* 76, no. 37: 39.

Watkins, E. 2001. "They Break the Mold." *Lodging Hospitality* 57, no. 11: 2.

Strategy Alignment and Implementation
Realizing Intended Strategy

Learning Objectives

Upon completion of this chapter, you will:

1. Assess the degree of alignment between competitive methods (CM) and core competencies (CCs).
2. Understand the complexities associated with implementing strategy.
3. Demonstrate how context and process variables impact the strategy implementation process.
4. Describe the process used to integrate the context and process variables to achieve effective implementation.
5. Have an appreciation for the role of leadership in achieving successful implementation.
6. Understand the implementation planning process.

Key Concepts

Assessing and achieving alignment

Strategy implementation

From Chapter 10 of *Strategic Management in the Hospitality Industry*, Third Edition, Michael D. Olsen, Joseph J. West, Eliza Ching Yick Tse. Copyright © 2008 by Pearson Education, Inc. Published by Pearson Prentice Hall. All rights reserved.

Chapter Purpose

We begin by addressing concepts related to the match between competitive methods (CMs) and CCs and then suggest ways to address the firm's need to manage and evaluate the alignment of these two constructs of the model by presenting concepts related to implementation. We are working with the firm structure construct as illustrated in Exhibit 1.

The Importance of Alignment

Our thesis is based on the firm achieving alignment among the three constructs, which in turn results in outstanding value-adding financial performance. Although the term *coalignment* has been used countless times, it has always remained an abstract and intangible idea. In the pages to follow we provide a way to actually assess alignment between CMs and CCs. As we go through this process, keep in mind that alignment is achieved when evidence from the firm strongly suggests that resources are being allocated to CMs according to their value-adding potential. It also means that processes supporting decision making and actual resource allocation follow this objective. We also attempt to measure this match to assist the manager to better assess the correlation between the match and firm performance.

Exhibit 2 presents a way of looking at the relationship between CMs and CCs that focuses attention on the importance of the alignment between the two. The intersection of the axes representing the service and product dimensions is the locus of the most important CMs and CCs for the firm. Ideally, the most value-producing CMs should fall well within the boundary of the CC circle. This would ensure that the CM will be executed properly according to the standards set forth by the firm. It can be expected that the tighter the alignment between the CMs and CCs, the greater the overall performance level of the firm. Peripheral competencies are represented by the outer circle and, as stated earlier, are needed to achieve the output desired.

For example, recent research suggests that where a firm is able to achieve this tightness of fit, firm performance is better.[1] In one instance, a study of five hotels in Jamaica indicated that when a firm is better aligned it outperformed its competition on four key operating performance variables. Similarly, an investigation into three national casual theme restaurant companies clearly illustrated that when a firm works at seeking to align internal competencies with CMs, it outperformed its competitors on a cash flow per seat basis. Although many strategy textbooks and articles suggest this to be true, these two research projects provide some validation to this hypothesis and encouragement to management in seeking to obtain as close a match as possible.

Returning our attention back to Exhibit 2, you can see that not all the CMs are within the inner circle. What this implies is that the firm may be including CMs for which it does not possess the essential competencies to deliver them at the standard sought. This is not a desirable situation, so it will be necessary for management to allocate additional resources to bring all the CMs into the inner circle. The goal should be

EXHIBIT 1 Strategic Management Model

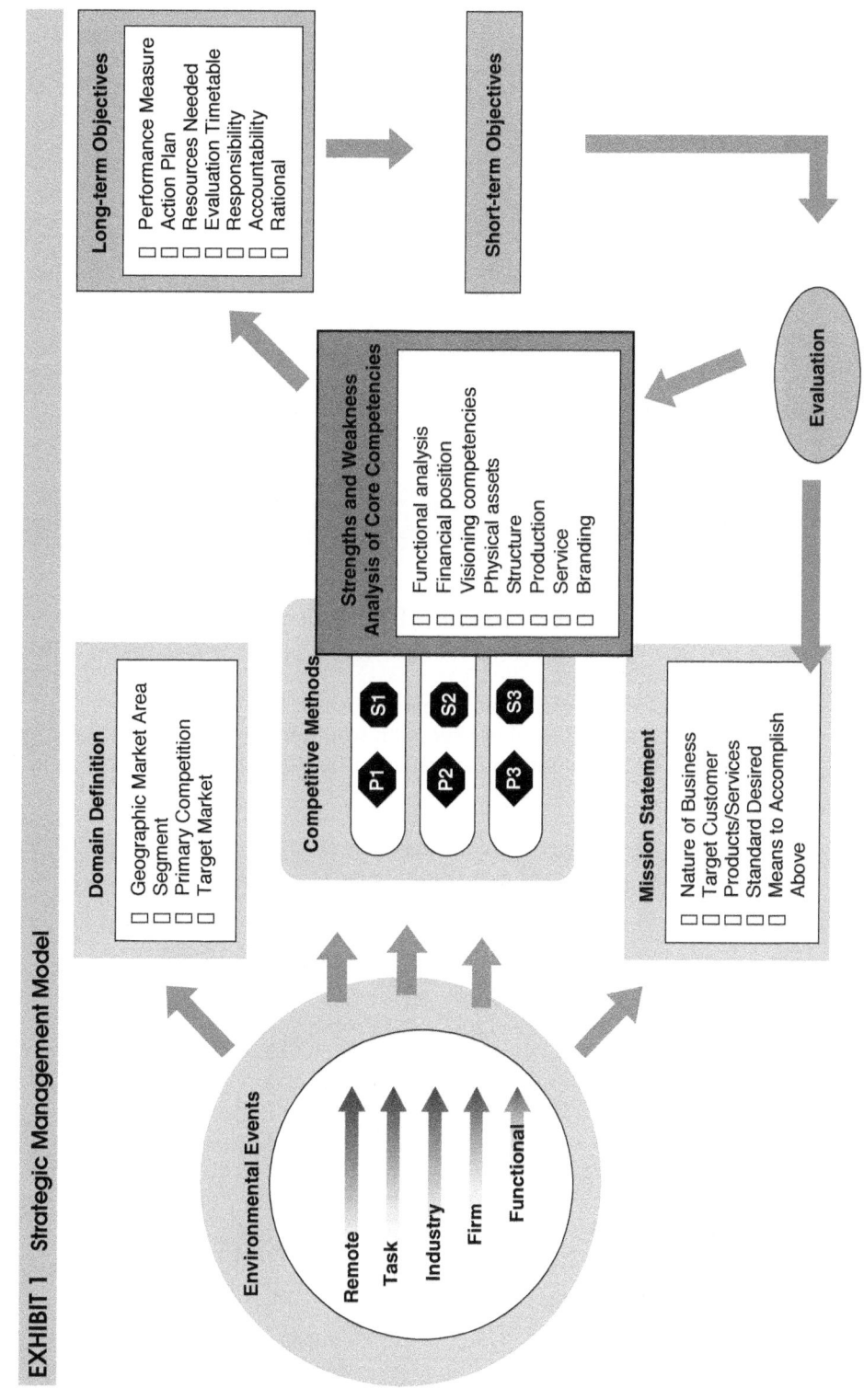

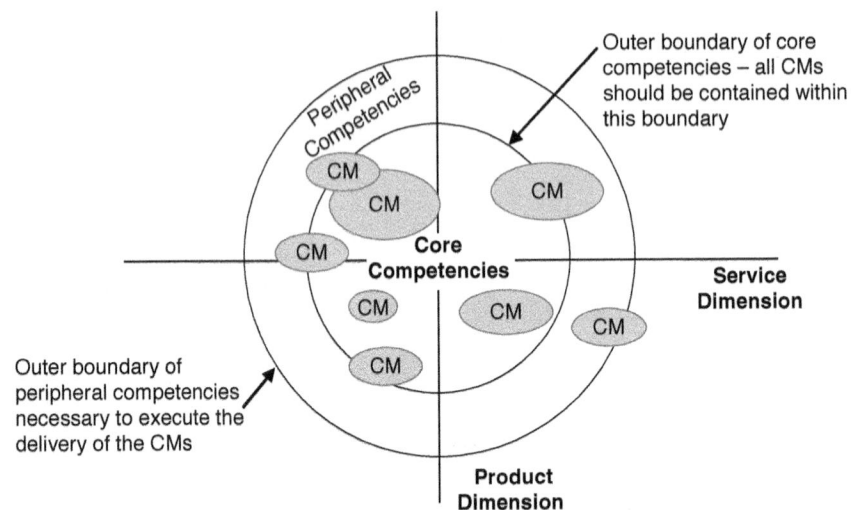

to try to be sure that the CMs offered fit as closely within the inner circle as possible. This will permit firms to enjoy the greatest synergy among their CCs while creating competitive advantage.

As you can see in Exhibit 3, this is not the case in this hypothetical illustration. Achieving the desired level of execution would be extremely difficult in this situation because the CMs are not concentrated within the CC circle. This type of situation is

EXHIBIT 3 **The Relationship Among Core Competencies, Peripheral Competencies, and Competitive Methods: Poor Alignment**

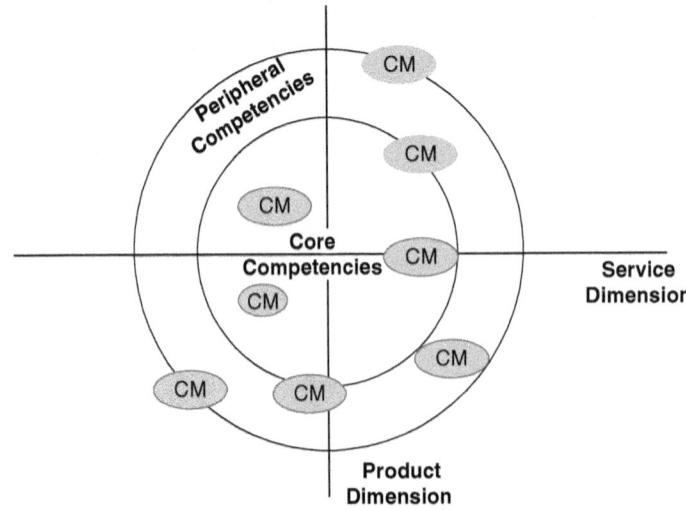

undesirable because product/service quality is likely to become very inconsistent when so many CMs fall outside the CCs of the firm. This can, and usually does, result in inconsistent quality and the subsequent variance of cash flows associated with this particular CM, thus adding risk to the owners of the firm.

The Importance of Strong Linkages

Competitive advantage can be achieved by offering the best CMs within the business environment and developing and maintaining the best CCs. However, to obtain sustainable advantage, the firm must do more. It must create a situation in which their competitors are unable to duplicate the methods on an equal scale. This is often referred to as the inability to imitate. The unique blending of the CMs and CCs with the peripheral competencies creates this inimitability, and being sure they are linked together in ways that others cannot duplicate helps achieve sustainability.

Linkages can be defined as those elements of the organization that promote the integration of the CMs and CCs with the peripheral ones. This concept is often referred to as the structure of the organization, as discussed in the previous chapter. This definition of structure contains very tangible dimensions such as communications systems, management information systems, control systems, and the definitions of jobs and tasks. Additional systems are procedural or rules and policy based. It also contains intangible dimensions such as the culture and behavioral setting of the organization along with the processes used to allocate resources. What is important to recognize here is that these dimensions are deliberate and must be thought of as any investment would be. They must be properly designed, developed, and implemented so that CMs can be executed successfully.

This relationship is illustrated in Exhibit 4. As the strength of the CMs, CCs, and the linkages among them increases, the ability of the firm to achieve sustainable competitive advantage by inimitability also increases, as can be seen by the growing thickness of the diagonal line. This growing thickness demonstrates the synergy

EXHIBIT 4 **Relationship Between Strength of CMs and CCs: Degree of Linkages and Sustainable Competitive Advantage**

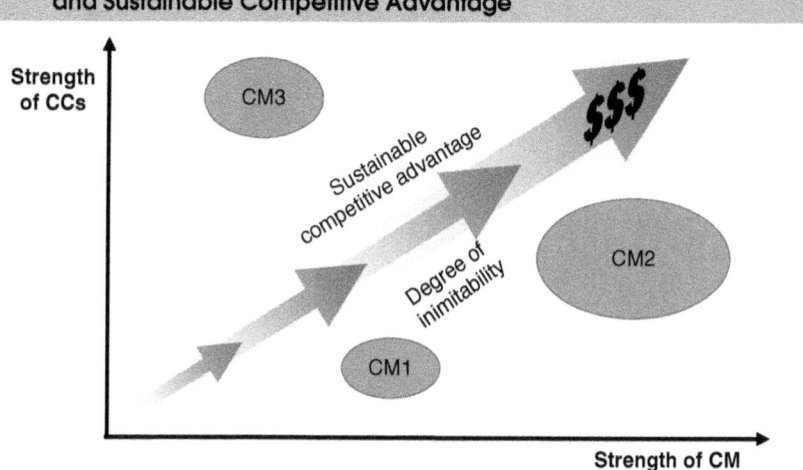

achieved when managers are able to effect close relationships among CMs and CCs and synergy generally results in greater added value to the firm.

Further analysis of Exhibit 4 suggests that greater value can be achieved from each CM when there are strong linkages between it and the CCs of the firm. CM2 in this illustration is the largest oval signifying the greatest value. The assumption here is that this value comes from the alignment with the firm's CCs, the inimitability brought about by this linkage, and the fact that the firm was in the market earlier than the competition. Also, it is difficult for competitors to fully understand the uniqueness achieved. This discussion represents the strategic thinking that managers must do and how important it is to achieve success here, especially in highly competitive environments.

As has been presented thus far, the firm must invest in and develop competencies that will allow it to achieve the value-adding potential of each of its CMs. These competencies are many and complex in service organizations. The challenge is to choose those that match the products and services that have been included into the portfolios of all the enterprise's CMs. Once this match has been achieved, it can only be maintained if the firm works hard at integrating and linking them throughout the structure of the firm. It must also continue to develop each of them if it is to achieve sustainable competitive advantage.

Analyzing the Match/Aligning CMs and CCs

We now turn back to the complete coalignment model as depicted in Exhibit 1 to determine how to assess and measure alignment. In this chapter we look at how to assess alignment to be sure we have the proper overall structure in place to implement the CMs. To do this, we then must ask ourselves what can be done to achieve the match between CMs and CCs. And is there a way to measure alignment? Exhibit 5 provides a

EXHIBIT 5 The Alignment of CMs and CCs

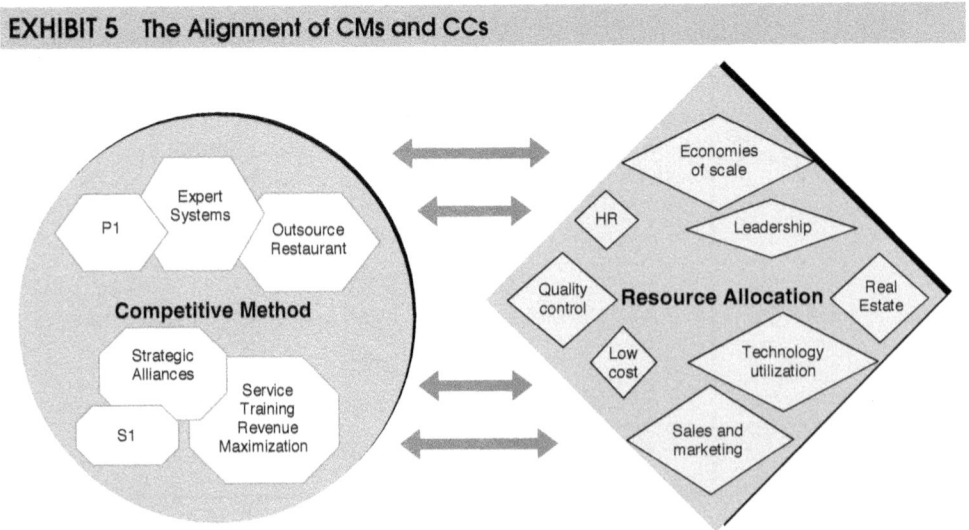

visual look at this alignment concept, suggesting the manager's need to be sure to concentrate decision making on achieving the match. To do this we have taken from Exhibit 1 the two central symbols from the model, the CMs and the diamond-shaped symbol representing the resources and capabilities of the firm.

The intent here is to show that all of the CMs must in some way be matched to the CCs. The authors' experience in studying the hospitality industry has been disappointing regarding this aspect of strategic thinking. It appears that little of this type of thinking actually exists. For example, in conducting strategic thinking activities for firms or conducting executive education programs for all types of hospitality enterprises, participants are given three simple quizzes. We call them the "one-minute manager" quizzes. These are outlined next.

The first quiz asks participants to identify within a one-minute period all the CMs that the firm employs to generate value. Surprisingly, the global average over hundreds of managers is only six. That is, within one minute they can only come up with six "top-of-the-mind" items. These items are normally representative of what one might call "industry groupthink." Such statements such as good service, nice facilities, good employees, and friendly staff are common. These are hardly CMs; they really represent critical success factors (CSFs) and CCs more than anything.

The next one-minute quiz asks managers to indicate what percentage of their budget they allocate to these CMs. As you may surmise here, the participant managers have little clue. In only a few instances have we found anyone who even comes close to answering this question. The first defense offered by most participants is that we really don't keep track of this because our accounting system is not set up to do this. Although this is no doubt true given the reliance on uniform systems of accounts, there are no rules that we are aware of prohibiting the setting up of management information systems to determine the cash flows of each CM. It is simply in our view that managers don't think this way. They have been educated and evaluated over time on operational performance-related criteria rather than strategic thinking benchmarks.

The third one-minute quiz addresses this question: If you are to sell your business today, what value would you put on that business? Here again, the results have been very poor. This is very sad considering the total value of the assets the managers are responsible for. Now this question must be raised: If a manager has a very limited understanding of what creates value and has less of an understanding of where resources should be allocated, can we expect that manager to know and understand the value of the business? The obvious answer is no. Thus a major shift in the thinking of managers must occur if they expect to gain control of the value-adding dimension of their job.

Aligning Competitive Methods with Core Competencies: The Essence of Firm Structure

Our entire purpose is to change the way managers think about strategy, and thus our objective in this chapter is to introduce a way to assist managers in achieving coalignment through improving their ability to match CMs to CCs. This is the essence of the construct of *firm structure, which is defined as how the firm is organized to permit the successful implementation of all of its CMs.* As we have stated often, the alignment process cannot really succeed, however, until the manager has become highly efficient and effective in scanning the environment and identifying opportunities that result in investments in CMs that offer sustainable value-adding advantage (the first two constructs of the coalignment model). Assuming success here, managers must then be sure the resources and capabilities of the firm (that make up its overall CCs) are consistently allocated so the firm can execute the effective and efficient implementation of all CMs.

For the alignment process to be successful, systems, processes, and procedures must be in place that permits the unencumbered flow of resources to every CM that has been identified as value positive to the firm. These are all part of the integrating systems identified earlier in this chapter. However, it is not enough to assume that systems and integrating mechanisms will achieve the proper allocation and subsequent alignment. The alignment process must be proactively managed and evaluated daily because alignment is not static, it is dynamic. *Put differently, alignment becomes the manager's primary task once the right investment opportunities (CMs) have been identified and made.* Because resources are generally limited and must be spread across all the firm's needs, the manager must make daily decisions on how they are allocated. To do this the manager needs a way to assess and measure overall alignment to ensure a consistent allocation of resources to the most value-producing CMs.

Although there are many ways to accomplish this management and assessment of alignment, we suggest a simple matrix as indicated in Exhibit 6. As illustrated, the rows consist of the primary value-driving CMs of the firm, and the columns represent the CCs that managers feel are necessary to implement the delivery of these CMs. As the coalignment model suggests, managers must first make the choices of CMs that they feel will bring about the highest level of value to the long-term future of the firm. Thus the firm must make its resource and capabilities decisions based on the CMs chosen. In other words, *the firm's structure must follow its strategy*. This should be intuitively obvious to managers, but it is often not the case. In fact, structure often limits the firm from investing in new CMs simply because the resources are not present or change in the status quo is resisted throughout the firm.

So the question becomes, "How are the cells in the matrix filled in, and how is alignment measured?" Let's take the first part of the question to begin this stage of the analysis and seek to obtain relevant information from and about the firm. Often, this information is easily obtained from company documents or observations of company actions. For example, (1) the actions of the firm's managers, (2) written documentation from company manuals and communications, (3) training and development programs, (4) franchise agreements, (5) human resource manuals including evaluation and reward systems, (6) written processes and procedures, (7) press releases, (8) customer surveys and feedback, and (9) the company website or anything else that suggests a codification of how the firm does business. Simply put, if the firm's management really believes in the value-adding potential of a CM, ample evidence clearly stating this intention must be found among the array of documents *used regularly* within the firm.

EXHIBIT 6 The Competitive Method/Core Competency Matrix

	Core Competencies				
Competitive Methods	Technological superiority in personnel and equipment	Industry leading human resource management	Most experienced and trained management	Superior site location capabilities
Reservation system	• Produces 40% of revenue from website • Innovative approach to providing inventory online	• Lowest turnover in industry in this job category	• Annual training costs $350,000	
Loyalty program	• Online query and retrieval capabilities • Cost of running program $5 million annually		• Annual training costs $200,000	
Location in key cities				• Major market presence in key global destinationcities
Revenue Management System	• Most experienced personnel in industry regarding software design and execution	• Revenue management staff voted firm the most preferred in the industry	• Most experienced revenue managers in the industry	
In room amenities	• Wireless in room computer connectivity • Touch screen concierge services			
Operating management systems	• Completely integrated systems, including reservations and revenue management		• Effective use of property management system at all levels of the hotel by all managers	
Brand Portfolio				

In this chapter our focus changes from external to internal analysis because most of the information listed in the previous paragraph is normally only available to those within the firm. No matter what perspective, the same principles apply to gathering information and drawing conclusions from what data are available.

Notice that we stressed the *regular* use of the documents in carrying out CM/CC alignment analysis. The authors are all too familiar with strategic plans, objectives statements, and other forms of declaring the firm's strategic intentions that sit on shelves never to be implemented or put into regular use. As the often quoted statement *The road to hell is paved with good intentions* suggests, many plans fail to end in positive results simply because there are no resources to make things happen. Thus, when looking through company documents, managers must be sure the evidence gathered is actually representative of actions taken and/or realized. One way we have found to assist in the analysis of this portion of the alignment process is a technique used by anthropologists called *participant observation*. That is, just watch what is happening and note where the emphasis is. Almost every employee within the firm can quickly tell you whether or not resources are going to what CMs and how. In fact, we also recommend interviewing employees to determine their feelings about the entire alignment process. Whatever method chosen, a *well-aligned* firm demonstrates ample evidence that there is significant agreement among its management, employees, and customers as to what the firm's CMs are.

As you can see so far, the alignment process is a rather subjective one. Here are some steps to take to make it less subjective (knowing that making it purely objective is next to impossible). Going back to Exhibit 6, the first step is to choose what evidence to include in each cell, what observations to make, and who to interview. What is essential is that the process is performed consistently and with reliability. Put differently, managers or other firm stakeholders should spend sufficient time to choose the documents for analysis, the observations to make, and the individuals to interview (both employees and customers). Once selected these sources must then be used regularly and consistently. In fact, we suggest a team of individuals at all levels of the company review the documents, independently and then merge their observations and conclusions.

The outcome of this process results in the information that is entered into each cell of the matrix. Let's work an example to make this clear. Suppose the fictitious firm Hospitality Services Hotel Company in Exhibit 6 has identified three CMs and three CCs (there are many more in most hotels, but we are keeping this very simple for this example). To assess the level of alignment, they have chosen the following items for analysis: (1) the operations manual, (2) the training program materials for all employees, (3) the website of the firm, (4) guidelines for employee interaction with the guest, and (5) the performance evaluation system used for all levels of the workforce. This is a good sampling of documents and activities in which ample evidence should be available to observe whether or not resources are going toward the firm's key CMs. All employees on the team should thoroughly evaluate these sources individually, seeking to identify how they relate to the firm's key CMs (interviews with customers and other stakeholders should not be forgotten at this stage).

The next step is to determine if the evidence from the selected sources is quite clear regarding how the CC relates to the CM. Examples of this evidence would include budget information linking the CM and CC, performance measures linked to each CM's performance and tied to the CC, and statements made on the firm's website that mentions the CM and how the firm's resources are linked to this relationship. Probably the best example of this may be the statement contained within the documents of the Ritz-Carlton Hotel chain where their motto states: *"We are Ladies and Gentlemen serving Ladies and Gentlemen."* The consistency of company documents relative to this motto point to a level of alignment that has helped the firm earn the prestigious Malcolm Baldrige National Award for service quality. As this example illustrates, the important criteria is that the relationship between the CM and CC is clear, precise, and strong. Subtleties are not accepted.

Thus the linkage or relationship must be clear in each of the five pieces of evidence used in the analysis. For every item of evidence that is clear, a score of 1 is placed in the cell next to that item. If it is not, the score is a zero. We have completed the first row in Exhibit 6 to illustrate. The CM is a *loyalty program* and as can be seen, the score for the cell relating to the CC, *technological superiority in personnel and equipment*, is a 3 out of a possible 5. The scores for the next two cells are 1/5 and 3/5. The total level of alignment between the loyalty program CM and the firm's identified CCs is the sum of all the cells in the row divided by the total points (7/15), or approximately 47%.

Of course, there will be different interpretations as to how solid the evidence is by different members of the team, so management must work out a system to resolve potential conflicts or disagreements, keeping in mind the need to achieve an objective assessment of alignment. In addition to different interpretations, there is always the likelihood that not all cells will be in perfect alignment as the loyalty CM suggests. In fact, this is more probably the norm. Thus the final alignment score is most likely going to be well below 100%.

The important question then becomes, "Is 47% a good score?" This brings us to our last construct in the coalignment model, which is performance. As we have stated, alignment leads to improved performance over a sustainable period. We have strongly suggested that cash flow is the primary metric for this purpose. Specifically, we concentrate on cash flow from operations because the largest share of cash flow in service businesses results from proper execution of CMs. The decision about whether 47% is adequate is determined by whether or not it results in the desired cash flows, which lead to achieving the imperatives of the investor. For example, in research cited earlier in this chapter we indicated that when alignment is present, operating performance is better.[2] In one instance, it was significantly better than nonaligned firms even when the alignment score was approximately 40%. In other words, alignment is a relative item as long as it leads to improved performance that meets investor expectations.

Let's assume that the 47% score is not satisfactory in producing the cash flow streams necessary to meet investor imperatives. Management must then seek to enhance alignment to see if this will improve the cash flows desired. This will trigger a host of actions designed to achieve this goal. Each CM and CC match must be reviewed to see if it can be improved. Questions relating to the resource allocation process must be raised along with whether or not the firm possesses all the competencies necessary to execute the CM. Individual cell scores should seek to be enhanced. Cells where no match occurs require thorough review of whether the CM is still viable and if so will more resources improve the situation. These are just a few of the questions the strategic manager must consider in seeking to achieve alignment. Naturally, a review of whether or not the environment has changed and altered the value of the

CM must also be conducted. As should be clear to you by now, the alignment activity is dynamic and complex yet essential to the long-term strategic success of the firm.

We are hopeful at this point that you are getting a sense of the dynamic and complex nature of the manager's job. Managing alignment means:

- Possessing the leadership abilities to anticipate the future, evaluate forces driving change, and assess their impact on the industry and firm.
- Making the correct investments in CMs that ensure a future stream of value-adding cash flows and reflect the forces driving change.
- Consistently allocate resources to those CMs that add the greatest value.
- Develop implementation activities and tactics to ensure consistent allocation and evaluation of success.
- Adjust and change when alignment appears to be inappropriate.

This requires of the manager a broader perspective on what this job is all about. It is not simply an operations perspective that implies the production and delivery of goods and services. It is not just locking doors and ensuring quality control. It is all of that plus the commitment to enhance the value creation of the firm. Value can only be created through the revenues and costs associated with CMs that the customer wants. It can only be created if the firm's resources and capabilities are directed properly, maintained, and developed in an ongoing process. That is the excitement and challenge of today's management position.

We have now discussed the three primary constructs of the coalignment model. It is now time to revisit the fundamentals of the model once again. It simply states that managers must engage in effective and comprehensive *environmental scanning* efforts to achieve a vision of what investments must be made that will meet the three imperatives of the investor. When done well the scanning process will yield opportunities for investments that will add value to the firm. We then explored the fundamentals of the second construct, *strategy choice*. In this overview of the investment requirements of the firm, we learned how to use the scanning process to identify opportunities that will maximize the value of the firm. The primary point here was that all CMs must meet the three imperatives of all investors. In this and the previous chapter we explored the third construct, *firm structure*, or competencies as we have referred to them. What was important here is that the firm is successful in consistently allocating resources to those CMs that created the most value. The theory is that if a successful match or alignment among the three constructs is achieved, the firm should enjoy sustainable competitive advantage and outperform firms in its strategic group. It is now essential that we address the implementation of this alignment.

Strategy Implementation Defined

The efforts that go into scanning the environment, choosing the products and services that will make up the firm's CMs, and investing in developing the right CCs reflect the firm's intentions. These intentions must now be turned into reality. In other words, they must be implemented. *Strategy implementation* can be defined as the process of allocating resources consistently to the products and services that produce the highest levels of cash flow and, most importantly, will continue to do so well into the future. This allocation process is accomplished through an analysis of the strengths and weaknesses of the firm, the establishment of the long- and short-term objectives, and the control and evaluation processes.

Many argue that it is quite easy to formulate strategy but extremely difficult to succeed in the implementation effort because there are just too many variables that cannot be easily controlled by the firm's management. They suggest that it is impossible to control the external environment and the random occurrences that take place to sidetrack strategy. They further suggest that internal processes also work against achieving ambitious objectives. Although it is no doubt true that these possibilities do exist, if every executive had this view, we would most probably have no successful firms at all. Just as we have offered ways to deal with the external uncertainties, this part of the chapter offers concepts and approaches to addressing the internal uncertainties.

The Implementation Model

Now we move from assessing the match between CM and CC to developing the business and operational plans that will fix the gaps in alignment and allow us to execute the delivery of CMs at the level necessary to meet investor imperatives. We build on the notion of the alignment between CMs and CCs by seeking to understand how we perform internally to achieve this match. Put differently, we now know what cells in the analysis need attention.

Based on this analysis and the assessment of the strengths and weaknesses identified, the next part of the implementation effort is to develop long- and short-term objectives. This includes establishing performance measures, action plans, determining resources needed to bring all weaknesses up to par, and identifying the responsibilities and accountability relative to bringing success to alignment and implementation. Lastly, the process of implementation cannot be accomplished well without a formal evaluation process in place that reflects the timing and reality of the business domain. In the sections to follow we provide an overview of this dimension of organizational structure.

Plan the Work and Work the Plan

The measure of successful implementation is when the firm is able to achieve the intentions it set out to accomplish. Although it is often the case that many firms achieve their intentions, it is not always at the 100% level. This is partly the case because intentions are often compromised by many mitigating circumstances. Emergencies, organizational politics, legal impositions, lack of discipline in continuously managing the plan, and environmental change unnoticed by the firm's leaders represent just a few of the many reasons why firms are unable to realize their intentions. To avoid these problems, management must follow this old adage: *Plan the work and then work the plan.*

What this means simply is that if the firm goes through all the effort of formulating strategy, this strategic plan should not be put on the shelf to serve as a monument to the effort. It should be a live, workable document that shapes the thinking and culture of the firm. In other words, managers must begin to develop a mindset of that of a strategic

EXHIBIT 7 A Comparison of the Meeting Agendas of Two Firms: One a Strategically Oriented Firm, and the Other One not

Typical meeting agenda	Strategically oriented agenda
1. Problems from previous week	1. New business opportunities
2. Forecasts of business this week	2. Performance of present competitive methods
3. Important communications	3. Assessment of strengths and weaknesses relevant to the most important competitive methods
4. Budget matters	
5. Status of projects	4. Appropriateness of objectives in the context of the current situation
6. Old business	
7. New business	5. Resources needed to achieve successful implementation

thinker. Thinking strategically should be the primary capability valued most in all employees if firms are to be able to compete in the contemporary business environment. In Exhibit 7 are two contrasting meeting agendas that help illustrate this point. In the first column is the weekly meeting agenda of the typical hospitality firm that is not strategically oriented; the second column represents that of a firm that is.

The contrast between these two firms is evident. The typical firm is focusing attention on past or very short-term issues. As is often the case, the people attending the meeting focus on what went wrong since the last meeting. Often, one organizational unit blames another for problems and attempts are made at trying to reconcile these situations so they don't occur again. A great deal of energy is often wasted at trying to identify who was at fault and why. Many times these sessions become finger-pointing exercises that often amount to little more than gripe sessions and opportunities for participants to get something off their chests. This type of meeting is never future oriented and focuses on problems that often pertain to CMs that are no longer of value to the firm.

This type of meeting agenda is also very short term oriented. Forecasts for the immediate future are reviewed with the idea of being sure that all resources are present to carry out this business. Although this is essential to successful implementation, the question must be asked, "If management is competent to do the job, "Why must all this time and energy be devoted to something that is a normal expectation of the position?" This may be justified at times if the necessary management talent is lacking, but it does nothing in assisting managers to learn to develop their strategic thinking skills. It only develops their problem-solving skills. Again, although this is an important skill to develop, if the problems are old problems that do not relate to the strategic implementation issues as we have defined them here, then the manager is developing the wrong types of problem-solving skills.

The agenda of the strategic thinking management firm is very different. Its number-one focus is on how new value-adding opportunities can be created for the firm. Thus it is thinking strategically and requires personnel to come to this meeting having developed the ability to scan the environment for new opportunities. It is the first item for discussion. Once new opportunities are presented, the discussion moves toward the analysis of the present CMs and how they are performing. Here problems are discussed but from a more strategic view. The focus is on the CM, not which organizational unit did or did not do its job. It is a strategic focus not a problem-oriented focus.

Here is a simple test to see if this kind of thinking is present in an organization. At the next meeting, list all of the issues brought up by each participant. Once these have been listed, ask each individual to identify to what CM these problems relate. If they are unable to do this quickly while at the same time aligning them with the greatest value-adding CMs, there is a good chance that these participants are not strategic thinkers. Successful implementation requires this kind of thinking. The remainder of this agenda is addressing this type of thinking. It is more proactive, with a strategic orientation that will ensure that all employees are thinking continuously about the coalignment model.

To help achieve this type of thinking, the two forms in Exhibits 8 and 9 help to keep managers and employees focused on achieving successful implementation. The first form (Exhibit 8) represents the preliminary thinking necessary to assist management in this process. It is designed to coordinate thinking to achieve the coalignment necessary. As can be seen, the form first asks that the environmental event be identified. Once this

---

EXHIBIT 8 Implementation Planner: The Relationship Among Environment, Domain, and Objectives

Indicate the environmental event under consideration
Technology with resulting changes in the global distribution system

Indicate what competitive method(s) you are employing to take advantage of the opportunities presented by this environmental event
Investment in Internet systems including home page creation, on line reservations with immediate confirmation to the guest.

Clearly describe how the competitive method(s) relate to your domain and mission statement
Our mission is to provide quality accommodation to our guest utilizing the highest level of technology available to communicate with that guest in every way possible.

List the product and services which make up this competitive method	**Describe the performance standard for each product and service in the context of your domain and mission statement**
1. Home page 2. Secure communications for electronic commerce transactions. 3. Electronic brochure describing the hotel 4. Customized datebase for gathering all necessary customer information in order to provide more customized service.	1. Set industry standard for home page 2. Utilize state of the art encryption and transaction systems 3. Outsource visual development to include virtual reality platform development 4. Create relational database system to more accurately customize customer information and communication

State objectives necessary to bring products and services into alignment with the performance standards required to achieve competitive advantage

1. Create new home page
2. Investigate latest advancements in electronic commerce systems and invest in those that will meet our needs over the next five years.
3. Commission media team to prepare electronic brochure and virtual reality capability.
4. Upgrade database system

is done, the CM(s) most likely to be successful in achieving competitive advantage and high cash flow per share in this context are identified. The next step in the analysis is to ensure that this matches the domain and mission of the firm. If this is not the case, this CM may not be one the firm will invest in or it will cause the firm to rethink its domain and mission statement. If a match is present, then the actual products and services are identified and the standards necessary to achieve competitive advantage are determined. Once this is done, then meaningful objectives are established.

The second form is illustrated in Exhibit 9. It is similar in many ways, but it now focuses on the resources necessary to achieve implementation. It requires the same level of attention to the forces driving change in the business environment. This requires management to always direct its attention to the environment and at the same time enforces the discipline of questioning whether or not this event is still an important force driving change. The second step in the form is to ask the manager to identify the CM relating to this environmental event. Here again, the manager is being asked to constantly evaluate the match between CM and the forces driving change in the environment. The list of objectives relates to this match and what is needed to improve the alignment score of the firm. This is taken care of by the third step, which requires managers to develop a detailed list of steps to the action plan necessary to accomplish the

---

EXHIBIT 9   Implementation Planning and Execution Form

Identify the environmental event affecting a competitive method.
Technology—the use of the internet for searching for and making room reservations in hotels.

Describe the competitive method and the products and services making it up.
Develop home page with reservations capabilities that links to revenue management and property management systems.

List the objectives to be accomplished regarding this competitive method.
To be completely operational with this objective within a four month period.

Provide a detailed list of steps necessary to accomplish objectives	Identify human, capital and material resources needed at each step	Provide measurable, time oriented measures for each step
1. Develop home page	1. Purchase software, $200, labor hours to develop home page 20 @$45.00.	1. Complete page by September 30, 200x
2. Create links to property management and revenue management systems.	2. System design and alterations, 30 hours @$45.	2. Complete linking and reading for on line booking by November 30, 200x.
3. Establish on-line payment process with appropriate security measures for guest and hotel.	3. Systems design and discussion with banks and security companies, 100 hours @$45 per hour.	3. Have on line payment capabilities reading by December 30, 200x.

Identify date which objective must be completed
January 30, 200x

Indicate person(s) responsible and accountable for completing objective
General manager, MIS manager, outsourced systems designers, department heads.

objective. The resources required to carry out each step are then listed along with the measures signifying accomplishment. The last two steps focus on the timing of the effort and who is accountable and responsible.

This form helps achieve the strategic thinking necessary to attain implementation. The form should be used not only to help formulate the overall strategic plan but should also serve to guide the day-to-day thinking of management. It becomes the guide to action for each day, always supporting a proactive view of what is necessary to achieve successful implementation. It is used at management meetings to discuss what progress is being made toward implementation and to remind managers that the coalignment model and thinking is their most important responsibility.

Implementation Requires Effective Internal Processes

Internal processes are the elements of the implementation process that ensure that all the CMs are executed to perfection. In many ways they are similar to the circulation system in the human body. They not only represent the heart pump, which is made up of the CCs, but they are also the system of veins and arteries that ensure the life blood of the firm is distributed to all components of the organization. These elements include resource allocation systems, management information systems, planning, control and evaluation systems, education, development and training programs, rewards and incentives, operating systems, strengths and weaknesses analysis, objective setting, and leadership.

Resource Allocation

Resource allocation processes must be among the first of these variables to be considered by the firm. Resource allocation can be generically defined as the *processes* designed to ensure that all necessary resources are directed at the CMs that generate the largest proportion of cash flow. Unfortunately, in many cases they have been given too narrow a definition and have been most often considered as just the budgeting process. The industry body of knowledge is rich with this narrow definition with extensive discussion of such budgets as sales, purchasing, expenses, or capital. Textbooks focusing on accounting systems that emphasize budgeting are in abundance. For over 50 years the hospitality industry has included in the body knowledge courses on cost control that also focus on budgeting. This approach does not reflect the dynamic nature of resource allocation. It seldom equates budgeting with competing. Because most firms must be accountable to boards of directors or taxing authorities such as the U.S. Internal Revenue Service, the accounting, budgeting, and control systems that have evolved throughout the centuries have reflected the legal obligations of businesses to these bodies. Although meeting the responsibilities to various oversight bodies is important, the systems of budgeting and resources allocation that have had their genesis in this thinking reinforces this narrow perspective on the strategic thinking process with respect to resource allocation.

One example may help. When one of the authors was recently involved in an executive education program for the hotel industry, the program was given in a hotel whose general manager was part of the participant group. In this case the author was using a personal computer and presentation program. The LCD projector provided by the hotel was of a very early vintage and its resolution was so poor that it was difficult to actually make out some of the words in the presentation. When the manager was asked to identify his most value-adding CM, he indicated that he thought it was that his hotel was a meetings and conventions hotel. When he was challenged as to how a hotel that indicated its most important CM was its ability to provide superior services to meetings and conventions could have such poor projection equipment, he responded by saying that his requests for better equipment went unheeded by those above him.

When asked how he requested this equipment, he responded by saying that it went on his capital budget request with all the other items that were needed. It was not ranked in any degree of importance because it was not viewed as contributing to one of the hotel's most important CMs. The point of this example should be clear. If excellent projection and media equipment are necessary for a hotel to achieve competitive advantage, and this is one of the hotel's most important value-adding methods, then investments in enhancing that method should not be left to the traditional narrow thinking of the budgeting process. This manager must develop processes that will allow him to communicate this and to demonstrate how important it is to the overall value-adding activity.

This example illustrates how important it is in the implementation process to ensure that all the resource allocation systems in the firm reflect a focus on decision making that directs the majority of resources to the most important CMs. This implies then that managers will be judged on their ability to be sure that resources are directed at the most important value-adding CMs and that the manager stays ahead of change when deciding what methods will be the most important. This means that she or he will scan the environment constantly to be sure that the each CM and CC are providing the firm with competitive advantage.

Management Information Systems

The objective of all *management information systems (MIS)* should be to achieve the most efficient and effective allocation of the firm's resources. Thus the resource allocation system should be at the heart of the management information system. As Exhibit 10 illustrates, this core is surrounded by other key processes related to implementation, and they are linked together to provide the information management needs to implement its strategy. This linking occurs both formally and informally. The formal system is illustrated by those elements enclosed within the solid line and represents the architecture that management has used to obtain the information it needs to make resource allocation decisions. The informal system is enclosed within the dotted line and created by employees of the firm as they seek to share information for their own needs. Effective implementation requires that both the informal and formal systems should be brought together where they overlap considerably. This will ensure that the goals associated with implementation are shared throughout the firm with all concerned.

Such total systems begin with an effective environmental scanning effort that provides the best information possible for the manager to decide what CMs to invest in. Once this system is in place and functioning, it is up to management to then create information that will track the value-adding performance of each CM. As suggested earlier, traditional accounting systems do not meet this goal well. Therefore, it will be incumbent on management to create information systems that will allow the performance tracking of each CM (i.e., its operational cash flows). Management information systems

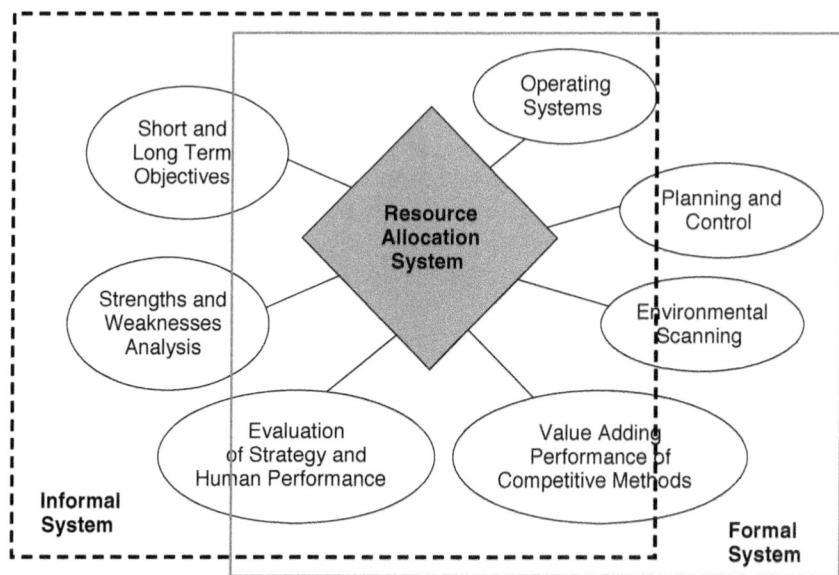

EXHIBIT 10   Management Information Systems

that follow this line of thinking become the backbone of the firm's communication network designed to ensure the maximum value-adding efforts possible. Planning and control systems, evaluation of strategy and human performance, establishing of short- and long-term objectives, operating systems, and strengths and weaknesses analysis round out the elements of the MIS.

Management information systems should be able to provide firms with evidence of progress toward the goal of achieving coalignment. They should perform in a way that allows them to serve as the primary linking mechanisms among CMs, CCs, and the implementation effort. They should reflect the communication necessary for personnel at all levels of the firm's structure to be knowledgeable about how well it is achieving its short- and long-term objectives.

One of the key ingredients in achieving sustainable competitive advantage is the ability of the firm to create linkages among and between its CCs and CMs. The relationship hypothesizes that the stronger these linkages, the greater the degree of inimitability a firm can achieve. These linkages are a function of the structure of the firm and how information is shared through a comprehensive MIS. These linkages are illustrated by the triple line surrounding the resource allocation diamond in Exhibit 10.

This triple line is meant to illustrate that communication should exist not only between the diamond and each of the elements but also among all the elements of the total system. Therefore, we have been careful to try to point out that this information exchange to and among the elements always passes through the resource allocation diamond to ensure that all decisions reflect this important focus.

Management information is becoming more important to the overall strategy of most firms. As such, firms are increasingly recognizing the need to allocate resources to systems and personnel that design and manage information systems. It is not uncommon now to see job descriptions and titles for *chief information officer* of the firm. These individuals are experiencing a growing level of influence in the overall decision-making process of many firms. In many cases, management information systems are being viewed as important CCs that can help the firm achieve its desired level of competitive advantage. The biggest challenge today for the hospitality information professional is the integration of all the dedicated systems that have emerged throughout the industry over the past two decades. This is no small task given the multitude of applications that are now being sold. Many believe that sustainable competitive advantage will accrue to those firms that are able to achieve this integration. Successful implementation will not occur without it, however.

It must be recognized that information systems are complex because they are not only internally oriented, but they also must link up with the growing number of external systems. The global distribution systems that link all members of the travel distribution channel are becoming important from the perspective of managing the firm's inventory. One of the most significant forces driving change in the industry is capacity management. That, along with the second major force, technology, support the importance of a well-developed MIS that provides a seamless integration among the distribution method, customer, and firm. This need requires considerably more emphasis on the planning of the information systems themselves. Such planning will help ensure that the firm will be able to use its information systems to its full strategic advantage.

Planning, Control, and Evaluation Systems

The strategic planning model represents the actual formulation of the strategic plan that must then be implemented. As such, it constitutes the planning system referred to here as a process. What is important in this context is the recognition that planning is a continuous process, one that cannot occur at periodic intervals. This suggests that the firm's structure, culture, resource allocation process, and information systems are all built with the idea that planning is continuous. This is necessary if firms are to be able to seek competitive advantage and sustain it. Therefore, successful implementation can only be achieved if the planning process is dynamic and all elements of the firm's structure are as dynamic as this process.

The process of controlling the firm on its course to achieve its long- and short-term objectives is a major responsibility of management. Control should be thought of in this context as keeping the firm on its desired course toward achieving its objectives. It is easier to make this statement than to actually achieve it. For example, strategy implementation can be easily disrupted by serendipitous actions of management. Or many intentions are never realized because someone, or some group, forgot that resources should be allocated to specific CMs. Although ideally, this should be a rational process, often organization power struggles, and politics, interfere with the firm achieving successful implementation. Thus control systems should ensure that resources are directed at the most important CMs, and this should only change if the CMs fail to achieve their targeted cash flow projections.

Evaluation systems are designed to encourage regular review of the firm's progress. These should be just as constant as the planning process, and the management information systems of the firm should provide the necessary information. This suggests that firms develop valid and reliable measures of performance for the firm. Operational cash flow per share has become the measure of most importance in judging whether the firm is achieving execution of its intended strategy successfully. This measure relates most directly to the operating performance of the firm. It is also the measure that should be tied most directly to the performance of managers who are given the responsibility of implementing the strategy. In other words, reward must be tied to successful implementation. This matching effort should never be taken lightly. It is essential that management understand that its performance evaluation and reward system is tied to successful implementation and/or execution of the most value-adding CMs.

Training, Development, and Education Programs

Enabling people to implement strategy is perhaps management's greatest challenge, especially in today's world where change is ever present and skilled labor is in very short supply. Although these two major problems are not new to the hospitality industry, which ranks among the world's largest employers, the problem is of greater proportion today because of the success of the free market system in creating jobs for workers in all types of industries across the world. This leaves the industry in a serious situation at a time when the customer is demanding even greater levels of service in a more customized fashion. More training cannot simply solve this problem. It will require extraordinary efforts to educate, develop, and then train individuals to achieve the highest level of perfection in the delivery of products and services.

In the hospitality industry, especially among multinational companies, a clear trend can be discerned in this area. More companies are investing in education, training, and development programs. Because the industry is becoming increasingly complex and requiring greater skills from all levels of employees, firms are trying to improve employee retention by offering opportunities for them to earn college degrees while still employed. They believe that by providing the employees with the opportunity to grow personally, they will have a more motivated individual with a higher skill level. For example, one firm, Pan Pacific Hotels & Resorts, has created the position called director of education. The individual in this position has created opportunities for employees to obtain bachelor's and master's degrees resulting from strategic alliances with hotel schools across the globe. To improve on the function of developing people, the firm has created the position titled director of people innovation. This alternative to the usual human resource function is producing exciting results as employees are given opportunities to increase their level of responsibility within the firm. Training programs serve to reinforce these two innovative efforts. This firm believes that it will only be able to achieve successful implementation if these programs work in concert with each other to raise the overall skill level of all employees.

Throughout, we have stressed the importance of allocating resources to the most important CMs and CCs of the firm. Nowhere is this alignment more important than in the human resource management function. The force referred to as *new management* contains many elements that will require firms to allocate more resources to this important process variable if they plan to achieve the level of implementation success they seek. Each of these elements requires a higher level of education, skill, and training, and there are few shortcuts to applying the necessary resources to this need.

Rewards and Incentives

The phrase "pay for performance" has never been more applicable in the business world. Just as firms are now expected to be able to add greater value, so too are individuals. As modern society moves quickly toward a knowledge-based environment, individuals will be rewarded more for what they know and how they use this knowledge than any other contribution. In other words, people and organizations will be quite willing to pay for that knowledge. As organizations continue to evolve toward the value-adding model, they will also be moving toward the development of reward systems that will compensate employees for the value they will add to the firm's CMs. This association will be measurable and assessed against the overall success of the CM.

Aligning the reward system to successful implementation of each CM is not a new concept. Employees have been rewarded for individual performance for centuries. Service personnel in restaurants have often been rewarded with excellent tips for outstanding service. Sales staffers have received incentives and bonuses for more room, convention, or banquet sales. These traditional reward systems, although important, do not always support superior execution of the firm's CMs. In some cases they may even be counterproductive, such as when a salesperson has oversold rooms or convention space to achieve a sales goal for which he or she will be rewarded for achieving. Customers, however, may not be happy when they discover the fact that there is no room for them at the time they requested. Therefore, incentives and rewards must be designed to support the successful implementation of the firm's most important value-adding CMs.

Operating Systems

Operating systems refer to those processes that transform resources into final products and services. Production, quality control, purchasing, reservations, property management, and yield management systems represent examples of operating systems. There are a great many in a hospitality firm due to the complexity associated with providing a variety of goods and services to the customer.

To achieve successful implementation, firms must work tirelessly to be sure that these systems work in concert with each other. The decision to purchase and deploy each system should be made only after considering how it can and will be integrated into the implementation scheme. As mentioned in the section on management information systems, the industry has not been particularly adept at this effort up to this point. The problem is that many systems have been developed by firms that are concentrating on ones that are dedicated to specific functions or applications. This has resulted in a proliferation of systems that often do not enhance implementation; in fact they often detract from it.

To remedy this problem, firms must design, build, or acquire systems that focus on the CMs, core processes, and peripheral processes. When taking a more holistic look at operating systems, management is more likely to be able to achieve a higher level of implementation. This is a more proactive approach as opposed to the reactive one just described.

SUMMARY

In this chapter we considered the very important notion of achieving alignment and actually measuring it to then develop implementation plans for all CMs. We closed by looking at some of the processes that must be developed, continuously reviewed, and employed to succeed in realizing the intended strategies of the firm. This completes the overview of the coalignment model, and we hope you now have a complete understanding of what is meant by coalignment.

DISCUSSION QUESTIONS

1. Discuss what is meant by alignment.
2. Provide an description of your understanding of how best to assess and measure alignment.
3. Provide a thorough discussion of the what is meant by implementation.

4. What role is a management information system in achieving implementation.
5. Explain how you believe that reward systems should be linked to alignment.

NOTES

1. P. Chathath, "Co-alignment Between Environmental Risk, Corporate Strategy, Capital Structure and Firm Performance: An Empirical Investigation of Restaurant Firms" (PhD diss., Virginia Polytechnic Institute and State University, 2002); Marcia Taylor, "A Test of the Coalignment Principle in Independent Hotels—Case Study" (PhD diss., Virginia Polytechnic Institute and State University, 2002); Jacqueline de Charbert, "Core Competencies and Competitive Advantage: A Case Study of the Casual Theme Restaurant Industry" (PhD diss., Virginia Polytechnic Institute and State University, 1998).

2. Ibid.

C A S E S T U D Y

Boutique Hotels and Service Apartments*

BOUTIQUE HOTELS ARE UNIQUE

In recent years, the success of Starwood Hotels & Resorts Worldwide W hotels and hotelier Ian Schrager's success in New York and Los Angeles has created a ripple effect throughout the hotel industry.[1] There is a boutique hotel, or as some label it a "lifestyle" hotel, fever across the industry, especially in such cities as New York and San Francisco. Boutique hotels are popular in San Francisco due to the high volume of leisure travelers visiting the city. Boutique hotels have been expanding despite setbacks caused by the economy.[2] Some industry pundits credit the origin of the boutique phenomenon to Ian Schrager. He, along with avant-garde French designer Philippe Starck, introduced a bold new style he branded "boutique hotels." However, there is the 30-room Ingleside Inn in Palm Springs, California, which owner Mel Haber has called "boutique" for three decades.

Some lodging companies see owning and managing boutique hotels as an alternative to their franchising brands from lodging chains. Today's well-traveled consumers have become more sophisticated and demanding, their tastes have changed and they seek a different lodging experience than the cookie-cutter product of the large lodging chains. Boutique hotels are noticeably different in design and feel from traditional or corporate hotels[3] which is what independent hotel operators desire in their attempt to differentiate with personalized service and comfort. The current market seems to be wide open for the development of boutique products.[4]

A boutique hotel, by definition, is unique in design and has 150 rooms or fewer.[5] As a hotel concept, boutique is a term of art.[6] Boutique hotels are considered to be leading an revolution in industry marketing. Unlike traditional hotels that differentiate themselves based on features, boutique hotels are leading the way in changing the marketing strategies from hard attributes, such as room size, to soft attributes, such as image.[7] Boutique hotels are marketed the same as many consumer goods where the experience and image are sold rather than the product.[8] These hotels create a wow effect. They strive to be associated with an atmosphere and a statement.[9]

Successful boutiques thrive on their guests desires to be associated with young, trendy, affluent, literate, or artistic fellow guests.[10] The hotels appeal to the 22 to 42 year old age groups, particularly the Generation X travelers who care about personalization and individual expression. They are quite popular with high-end female travelers who prefer the intimacy and personal attention that small boutique hotels are able to provide. These small, hip luxury hotels cater to young executives with trendy decor, rooms with themes, and

*The case is compiled based on information available up to November 2006.

rates of more than $200 a night. The target market is a small, niche market but very affluent. The choice of hotel is a reflection of whom they consider themselves to be. Accordingly, the members of Generation X ages 27 to 42 desire a relationship before, during, and after the experience.[11] They are looking for an experience based upon relationships.[12] They are comfortable with technology since they grew up with it. To target this group, customizing the marketing message is critical.[13] They are more responsive to lifestyle messages. There is a need to revise the current mass marketing/business model to focus it upon to the needs of Generations X and Y. Generation Y's are in their 20s, or Millennials, and have grown up in a totally different media world.[14]

The definition of boutiques is blurred and widely varied. Supposedly, boutiques defy conformity and standardization and lack the inherent marketing strength and cost savings built into most chain hotels.[15] Some consumers considered boutique hotels as all design and no function. It seems that the successful formula includes unique design, food-and-beverage experiences and highly personalized service. Successful boutique hotels generally achieve a 15% to 20% higher revenue-per-available room premium than traditional hotels.[16] They operate generally at above-average occupancy levels, and demand appears to be strong. Reports from Smith Travel Research indicate that boutique hotels are outpacing all segments in revenue-per-available room growth. It is predicted that the boutique phenomenon will become much more prevalent throughout the lodging industry in the near future, even in second- and third-tier markets.[17]

Design is a key component of the boutique market. The art package is a crucial element at boutique hotels, which build their reputations upon being different from every other hotel on the block.[18] Quite often, these boutique hotels base their art in culture and history.[19]

TO BRAND OR NOT TO BRAND?

One question in the lodging industry today, is whether boutique hotels can be branded. Will the uniqueness of the hotels be lost if they become simply another national chain brand?[20]

Among the properties that claim the term *boutique* proudly are the Hotel Jerome in Aspen, the Roger Smith Hotel in Manhattan, and national hotel products such as the Monaco and The W.

Marriott International discussed acquiring the Kimpton Hotel & Restaurant Group, owner of the Hotel Monaco brand.[21] Kimpton Hotel & Restaurant Group owns 34 hotels.[22] It entered into the industry by turning old buildings into charming small hotels. Marriott presently manages most of these hotels. A number of boutique hoteliers, such as Starwood Hotels & Resorts, Kimpton Hotels & Resorts, Leddy Ventures, and Ian Schrager's Morgans Hotel Group, are converting historic vacant office buildings into luxury hotels.[23] Other chains have joined the "boutique mystique." Choice Hotels launched its Clarion Collection of boutique hotels in 2004, with rooms in the $90-and-up range. Ritz-Carlton in Lake Las Vegas boasts a "boutique hotel within a hotel." There is also Hilton's London boutique hotel, the Trafalgar. It seems that boutique hotels are now an established product line. As boutique brands expand, the challenge, just as traditional hotel brands, is maintaining quality and consistency over time.

In the past, independent owners avoided franchise lodging companies because they feared standardization would cause them to lose their independence and uniqueness. Now, they can take the boutique hotel brand and establish their service and quality standards. In exchange, they then receive the reservation service and brand recognition of the franchisor.

BRANDS TO CATER TO THE GENERATION X TRAVEL MARKET

Branded lodging companies responded to the Generation X travel market by introducing new or repositioned brands beginning in 2004. Starwood Hotels & Resorts introduced Aloft in 2005, a brand similar to the W Hotel brand except that it targets a younger guests and is more suited for suburban and second-tier urban development.[24] The guest rooms have the look and feel of an urban residential loft.[25] The company has set a very aggressive goal of 500 properties by 2012.[26] Hyatt intends to convert its 140-plus AmeriSuites properties into Hyatt Place, its new lifestyle brand.[27] Hyatt Place will appeal to both business travelers and leisure guests in the Generation X demographic.[28] Choice Hotels will open its first Cambria Suites in 2006, the lifestyle brand it has been developing and nurturing for two years.[29] The select-service, all-suite Cambria has a number of innovations, both in the guest units and in the public spaces.[30] NYLO (New York+loft) may be the most radical of the new products aimed at Generation X as the design borrows from the residential loft aesthetic.[31]

Not all boutique hotels are upscale. In 2004 the InterContinental Hotel Group (IHG) launched its seventh brand, Hotel Indigo, less than six months after it acquired its sixth brand, Candlewood Suites.[32] Visioning it differently than a boutique hotel, the lifestyle Hotel Indigo brand aims at midmarket consumers who desire to trade up to a higher level of quality, with a different hotel experience, but still seek value. It is IHG's answer to the traveler who desires a lodging experience as much as the destination experience.[33] The price point is between Holiday Inn and Crowne Plaza. It is a conversion-led brand targeted to the urban and suburban markets. The properties will have about 120 to 180 guest rooms with limited meeting space.[34] IHG is also experimenting with its Holiday Inn Select brand as a vehicle to directly address the Generation X market. Although the chain's management is still working on a prototype, the new brand will focus on a few elements favored by Gen Xers, namely technology, fitness, food, and brand names.[35]

There are other new concepts focusing on this mid-market trend. Starwood is developing a lower-price version of its W brand.[36] In Europe, Accor's midscale Novotel brand is concentrating on guest room redesign with its new "Novation" room concept.[37] Their intention is a concept that is 'boutiquey' in terms of fresh and contemporary, that can be replicated.[38]

As a rule, independent small boutique properties do not have the marketing advantages of chains, it is a challenge to compete with the loyalty programs of branded hotel companies. One way they are able to compete is to associate with companies such as Mexican Boutique Hotels, which is a management company with 32 unique hotels in its operating portfolio. The company supplies marketing, reservation service, public relations, synergy development, and friendship among the members. Similarly, Design Hotels is a marketing and reservation company for over 100 design-led hotels worldwide. The hotels pride themselves in offering "distinctive architecture and interior design, balanced with functionality and impeccable service." Tecton Hospitality in Miami recently launched Desires, a new division that provides boutique hotels owners with management and marketing systems that create operating efficiencies.[39] Desires's range of services encompasses human resources, sales and marketing, and financial management.[40]

W Brand to Create Wow Factor

Starwood Hotels & Resorts Worldwide's W Hotels brand is increasing its growth internationally. Currently it has 16 properties with 4,987 rooms in the United States.[41]

The company's plan is to have 50 hotels globally while maintaining their innovative modern design, style, and service. The major focus of the development plan will be European and Asian major gateway cities, as well as continued development in the United States.[42] The company thinks that the brand has the potential to go beyond urban markets and plans to expand into new suburban markets with office, retail, and entertainment space.[43] The strategy is to have as many company-owned hotels as possible.[44] W topped Ritz-Carlton and Four Seasons in customer satisfaction in the luxury segment, according to Market Metrix Hotel Index, in 2002[45]. W hotel staff goes through extensive retraining programs to provide the service level that the corporate traveler demands. The company also applies the best practices of Sheraton and Westin into the W model.[46] Management understands that the brand must stay one step ahead of its competition.

BOUTIQUE HOTELS IN ASIA

In Tokyo, some existing hotels in attractive locations are being renovated to potentially more profitable boutique hotels. Starwood Hotels & Resorts is one of the first to realize the potential of these brands in Tokyo. The company plans to open as many as six boutique hotels in the city over the next decade.

In Hong Kong, hip boutique hotels are beginning to make a mark. These smaller stylish hotels differentiate themselves with unique architectural style, classy interior designs, or a decorative theme. They often feature trendy bars and designer rooms with the emphasis on personalized service.[47] JIA Hong Kong is the first boutique hotel and the first hotel by French designer Philippe Starck in Asia. It features 54 guest rooms. The interior focuses upon spatial clarity, comfort, and style, with ultra-modern amenities for fast-living professionals and the style-conscious

traveler. Upscale yet affordable is the trend for new boutique hotels in Asia. One example, is the Minton Hotel in Hong Kong's Kowloon neighborhood. Marketed as "stylish yet affordable," rooms start at US $115 a night. The owners intend to grow the concept in the region. The boutique hotel trend is still very new to Hong Kong. In Singapore a new value-driven boutique concept is Millennium & Copthorne's M Hotel. M's positioning is targeted to frequent business travelers who desire a product that is tasteful, comfortable, and functional.[48]

SERVICED APARTMENTS

With globalization, more companies are sending their employees overseas for "short-term assignments," which is often a business trip that lasts more than a month but does not require a full relocation. The growth of this form of business travel has spurred demand for a new lodging product—serviced apartments.[49] Serviced apartments have been around but their primary was long stay tourists. The serviced apartment term is a hybrid, part hotel and part apartment, where services are supplied, as in hotels, at varying levels.[50] It is only since the late 1980s that they have acquired a business-related emphasis.[51] There has been a significant upsurge of business assignments of between 6 and 12 months as well as a reduction in the volume of traditional expatriates—people renting for longer terms.[52] Serviced apartments usually cost somewhere between a traditional business hotel and a conventional rental unit. They offer the flexibility of time-scale and convenience. Some travelers claim that they offer greater privacy and security than a hotel, with none of the maintenance problems of a long term rental property. Some apartments offer an international level of service, with concierge, gyms, and business centers. For some executives, serviced apartments supply a more relaxing base than a hotel.[53]

Serviced apartments have become popular with business travelers who must stay in one place for an extended period of time as well as transitional housing for executives and their families moving to a new locale.[54] These apartments are preferred over hotels because they typically are more spacious and offer more than just a bed and desk. They also often include a kitchen and lounge. They are also popular with leisure travelers because they may be boutique style, individually and tastefully decorated. They provide a "home away from home" environment. Some hotel chains are now entering into the market, adding extended-stay apartments to their properties. For example, The Marriott West India Quay Hotel and Executive Apartments have 47 extended-stay apartments on four floors above the five-star hotel, with its own dedicated lounge for residents' exclusive use.

Through the years, serviced apartments have become a decentralized business, with a lack of uniform terminology to describe this type of accommodation. Americans use the term *corporate housing*; Asian real estate developers use *serviced apartments*. Brazilians prefer the term *apartment-hotels*, and the French, the similar *aparthotels*.[55]

Similar to the lodging market, the serviced-apartment industry has a luxury and middle market, and providers, such as The Ascott Group, offer different brands in each sector. The upper-middle market is likely to benefit most from the growth of companies that increasingly send their employees on short-term assignments. The concept is rare in Britain, and it is almost nonexistent in the rest of Europe.[56] The Cheval Group is a five-star provider launched in 1984. It was one of the earliest firms in the market and continues to grow steadily.[57] The construction cost of the apartments ranges about 25% less than a hotel of similar standards. Saco pioneered the serviced-apartment concept in 1997 outside London.[58] It now offers more than 3,000 apartments in 100 key cities

from Berlin and Stockholm to Sydney and Beijing.[59] To reflect the growth of this sector, the first serviced apartment's industry standards body has been created. The Association of Serviced Apartment Providers will establish a set of UK standards for serviced apartments and a code of conduct for all providers.

Oakwood is the largest serviced-apartment provider in the United States with more than 20,000 serviced apartments throughout North America, Asia, and Europe.[60] Hotels are also offering serviced apartments as incentive to longer-term guests. Shangri-La, Marriott, Hilton, Swissotel, and Holiday Inn are among the chains offering serviced flats and long-term deals in Asia.[61]

In Asia, increasing business activity is driving demand for high-quality accommodation.[62] Soft property markets have increased the availability of these units.[63] Asian cities are also home to a number of independently run serviced apartments. Foxtons Worldwide, based in London, represents owners of serviced apartments in 15 Asian cities.[64] A more specialized market has emerged for luxury-serviced apartments to meet the needs of a primarily expatriate clientele.[65]

In Hong Kong, the demand for serviced apartments, including the luxury serviced hotel sector, has seen strong growth over the past decade.[66] This is because Hong Kong remained the preferred business hub in Asia for many multinational companies either expanding their operations or setting up new offices to take advantage of proximity to China.[67] Strong economic indicators, including the rise of initial public offerings and the benefits flowing from the Closer Economic Partnership Arrangement with China, were contributing to the steady growth of the serviced accommodation market. A majority of the clients are corporate clients and business professionals.[68]

Comprehensive and high-quality service is another key factor in gaining customer approval.[69] Competition is fierce in the industry. Many upscale serviced apartments often have features such as panoramic views of Victoria Harbor or the city skyline, state-of-the-art technology, a branded kitchenette, and a unique interior design.[70] Of particular interest was the fact that the premier and boutique subsegments registered the biggest surge in rentals with the launch of major new projects, Four Seasons Place Hong Kong and Shama Mid-levels in 2005. Considered to be the first luxury serviced-suite facility, Four Seasons Place (a total of 519 suites) is located next to the Four Seasons Hotel at the International Finance Center. It features two renowned international designers, Yabu Pushelberg and Biley Llinas.[71] Shama is one of the leading boutique serviced-apartment operations, with 233 serviced-apartment units and six restaurants in the prime commercial and residential districts of Central, Soho, Mid-levels, and so on.[72]

DISCUSSION QUESTIONS

1. Provide your assessment of how alignment can be achieved in boutique and serviced-apartment hotel concepts.
2. Discuss the differences in operating systems between boutique and serviced-apartment hotels.
3. How would these hotel concepts be differently organized in terms of management structure, communications systems, and other process and contextual variables?
4. Discuss the differences between the integrating mechanisms that may be utilized in each of the hotels.
5. Design a resource allocation process for each type of hotel.
6. Discuss how the rewards and incentive systems may differ between the two types of hotel accommodations.

NOTES

1. J. Higley, "Marriott Looks for Growth Opportunities," *Hotel and Motel Management* 215, no. 20 (2000): 4.
2. P. Alisau, "Boutique Business Grows Despite Economy," *Hotel and Motel Management* 219, no. 7 (2004): 62.
3. S. Hennessey, "Can Boutique Hotels Be Branded Without Losing Uniqueness?" *Hotel and Motel Management* 215, no. 18 (2000): 10.
4. C. Blank, "Boutique Hotels Offer New Alternative to Franchising," *Hotel and Motel Management* 214, no. 9 (1999): 42.
5. Ibid.
6. Op. cit., no. 3.
7. Ibid.
8. Ibid.
9. Ibid.
10. Ibid.
11. C. Wolff, "Reaching Out to Generation X," *Lodging Hospitality* 62, no. 5 (2006): 32.
12. Ibid.
13. Ibid.
14. Ibid.
15. Anonymous, "Yes, Boutiques Can Be Profitable," *Lodging Hospitality* 61, no. 3 (2005): 18.
16. Op. cit., no. 3.
17. Ibid.
18. E. Yetzer, "Setting the Scene," *Hotel and Motel Management* 217, no. 11 (2002): 66.
19. Ibid.
20. Op. cit., no. 3.
21. Ibid.
22. Op. cit., no. 18.
23. M. Nardone, "Boutique Hoteliers Targeting Historic Office Conversions," *Real Estate Finance and Investment* (2005). Retrieved

from http://www.iirealestate.com/default.asp?page=1&SID=507532&ISS=15979.

24. E. Watkins, "Brands Take Charge," *Lodging Hospitality* 62, no. 5 (2006): 16.
25. Ibid.
26. Ibid.
27. Ibid.
28. Ibid.
29. Ibid.
30. Ibid.
31. Ibid.
32. B. Adams and J. Higley, "New Brands Join Franchising Field," *Hotel and Motel Management* 219, no. 9 (2004): 1.
33. Ibid.
34. Ibid.
35. Op. cit., no. 24.
36. K. Strauss and D. Gale, "Evolution of a Segment," *Hotels* 39, no. 4 (2005): 10–11.
37. Ibid.
38. Ibid.
39. Op. cit., no. 15.
40. Ibid.
41. J. P. Walsh, "W Brand Focuses on International Expansion," *Hotel and Motel Management* 217, no. 11 (2002): 14.
42. Ibid.
43. Ibid.
44. Ibid.
45. Ibid.
46. Ibid.
47. Anonymous, "Hip, Smaller Hotels Find Their Niche Holidaying Professionals Looking for an Authentic Hong Kong Experience Are Turning to Trendy Digs in Renovated Buildings Near the Heart of Central," *South China Morning Post,* April 26, 2006.
48. Op. cit., no. 36.
49. Anonymous, "Corporate Executives Find a Home in Serviced Apartments" (2001).

Retrieved from http://www.oakwood.com/cms/PR-2001–05–07.html.
50. Ibid.
51. L. Freedman, "Beyond Room Service" (2002). Retrieved from *FT.com*, 1.
52. Ibid.
53. Ibid.
54. S. Brady, "Home Suite Home: Checking in to Condotels," *Time Asia* (1999). Retrieved December 27, 2006, from http://www.time.com/time/asia/asia/travel_watch/9901712.html1.
55. Op. cit., no. 49.
56. Op. cit., no. 50.
57. Ibid.
58. P. Ellegard, "Serviced Apartments: Pads Are Worlds Apart from Hotel Rooms," *Travel Trade Gazette*, U.K. and Ireland November 24, 2006: 50.
59. Ibid.
60. Op. cit., no. 49.
61. Op. cit., no. 54.
62. Anonymous, "A Taste for the Suite Life Increasing Business Activity in Asia Is Driving Demand for High-Quality Apartments." *South China Morning Post* June 3, 2006.
63. Op. cit., no. 54.
64. Ibid.
65. Op. cit., no. 49.
66. Op. cit., no. 62.
67. S. Wong, "Robust Interest in Serviced Flat Sector," *The Standard* (2006). Retrieved from http://www.thestandard.com.hk/news_detail.asp?we_cat=16&art_id=27775&sid=9868559&con_type=1&d_str=20060922.
68. Op. cit., no. 62.
69. Ibid.
70. Ibid.
71. Ibid.
72. Op. cit., no. 67.

ADDITIONAL REFERENCES USED FOR RESEARCH BUT NOT CITED

Anonymous. 2005. "InterContinental's 'Mood Indigo.'" *Commercial Property News* 19, no. 11: 39.

Adams, B. 2004. "IHG Franchisees Approve of New Hotel Indigo Brand." *Hotel and Motel Management* 219, no. 9: 4.

Adams, B. 2005. "IndeCorp Now Preferred Hotel Group; Adds Boutique Brand to Its Portfolio." *Hotel and Motel Management* 220, no. 11: 38.

Fackler, M. 2003. "Why Build New Hotels? Remodel Old Ones." *Far Eastern Economic Review* 166, no. 41: 56.

Gunter, H. 2005. "Boutique Hotels: Brawn and Brain." *Hotel and Motel Management* 220, no. 12: 1.

———. 2005. "Kimpton Launches Lifestyle Branding Initiative." *Hotel and Motel Management* 220, no. 5: 3.

Higgins, S. M. 2005. "Independent Hoteliers Free to Go It Alone." *Hotel and Motel Management* 220, no. 16: 4.

Index

Page references followed by "f" indicate illustrated figures or photographs; followed by "t" indicates a table.

357

359